THE BALANCE OF
MILITARY
POWER

An illustrated assessment
comparing the weapons and capabilities of **NATO** and the **Warsaw Pact**

Authors:
Lt. Col. D.M.O. Miller ● Colonel William V. Kennedy
John Jordan ● Douglas Richardson

MILITARY POWER

An illustrated assessment
comparing the weapons and capabilities of **NATO** and the **Warsaw Pact**

Book

First published in 1981 in
the United States by
St. Martin's Press, Inc.,
175 Fifth Avenue,
New York,
N.Y. 10010,
United States of America.

© Salamander Books Ltd.,
1981

Library of Congress
Catalog Card No 81-52044

ISBN 0-312-06587-6

All correspondence
concerning the content of
this volume should be
addressed to
Salamander Books Ltd.,
Salamander House,
27 Old Gloucester Street,
London WC1N 3AF,
United Kingdom.

Credits

Editor: Ray Bonds
Designer: Philip Gorton

Filmset by
SX Composing Ltd.
Printed in Belgium by
Henri Proost et Cie.

The Authors

Lieutenant Colonel D.M.O. Miller

Lt. Col. Miller is an officer in the Royal Corps of Signals in the British Army, and is currently commanding a regiment in the United Kingdom. He has served in Singapore, Malaysia and Germany, and has filled several staff posts in Army headquarters. He has contributed numerous articles to technical defence journals on subjects ranging from guerrilla warfare to missile strategy, and is co-author of Salamander's "The Vietnam War".

Colonel William V. Kennedy, Armor, US Army Reserve

Colonel Kennedy is a military journalist who has specialized for the past 15 years in the conduct of strategic studies at the US Army War College. He is a graduate of the US Army Command and General Staff College and of the Marquette University College of Journalism, Milwaukee, Wisconsin. He has served on active duty as an enlisted man in the Regular Army and as an Intelligence Officer in the Strategic Air Command with overseas service in Japan, China and the United Kingdom. Colonel Kennedy is the author of two chapters in Salamander's "The Chinese War Machine" and his newspaper and technical magazine articles have been published extensively in the United States, Europe and Asia.

John Jordan

John Jordan has, over the past few years, contributed numerous technical articles on ships of the NATO and Soviet navies to defense journals which include "Navy International", "Warship" and "Defence". He was a consultant to the Soviet section of the 1980-81 edition of "Jane's Fighting Ships", and is at present writing a series on Soviet ASW cruisers for "Defence" magazine.

Douglas Richardson

Douglas Richardson is a defense journalist specializing in the fields of aviation, guided missiles and electronics. Formerly editor of the international technical defense journal, "Military Technology and Economics", he originally trained as an electronics engineer and worked in the fields of radar, computers and guided missiles. In 1976 he joined the staff of the respected aerospace journal "Flight International", where he served as Defense Editor. He has contributed several technical articles to defense periodicals, including analyses of Soviet guided weapons, and was Editor of "Defence Review", a Chinese language report on the British defense industry, prepared for controlled circulation in the Chinese Government, industry and armed forces.

Editor's Acknowledgments

The content of this volume is a combination of contributions from institutions and individuals from many parts of the world, all of whom have expressed an enthusiasm for this unique book and given much support. While we are unable to mention them all individually here, the publishers wish to thank all those who have encouraged and aided us with advice, information and illustrations. In particular, we express our gratitude to NATO Headquarters in Brussels, the British Ministry of Defence, the US Department of Defense, and Novosti.

Ray Bonds

Contents

The Balance of Ground Forces by Col. William V. Kennedy

The views in this section are those of the author. They are not to be considered as an expression of official opinion or policy of the US Army or the US Department of Defense.

Jacket and prelim illustrations

Jacket: A dramatic hot "mushroom" cloud develops following the test of a US nuclear device.

Endpapers: Six unarmed Minuteman III Mk 12 re-entry vehicles approaching targets near Kwajelein Atoll in the western Pacific Ocean, during an operational test of two Minuteman III ICBMs launched from Vandenberg AFB, on July 10, 1979.

Half-title: A USAF A-10A Thunderbolt II "buzzes" US Army tanks during an exercise in West Germany.

Title: US Army infantrymen unleash a salvo with their M16s during night-firing practice.

Title verso: Versatile Sikorsky UH-60A Black Hawks with slung loads on US Army exercises.

The Balance of Naval Forces 116
by John Jordan

The Balance of Aerial Forces 172
by Douglas Richardson

Photographs on these pages:
Upper left: Blast-off of a US Titan II ICBM, the biggest missile ever deployed in the West. The 54 Titan IIs can be fired from within their silos.

Upper right: Italian Navy Enrico Toti class inshore patrol submarine underway in the Mediterranean. These coastal hunter-killers are armed with four 21in (533mm) torpedo tubes.

Lower left: A Soviet exercise involving a reconnaissance patrol with a specialised NBC warfare recce vehicle, BRDM-1rkh. The yellow flag signifies that the area is dangerously contaminated, and the soldier is assessing the precise degree of contamination.

Lower right: The outstanding Tornado F.2 interceptor, armed with Skyflash missiles, gives a hint of its unequalled capabilities over its home base in Northeast England.

Foreword

FACTS are critical to any intelligent discussion. This book gives us facts, figures and details on one of the most critical topics of our time, the balance of forces between East and West, between the Warsaw Pact and NATO. The status of this East/West balance of power is a fundamental determinant of international stability. Thus, this compendium will be a very important tool for military analysts certainly, but also for diplomats and political leaders, as well as for all those who are broadly concerned with world politics.

The notion of a balance of forces or a balance of power has had a long and often colourful history. It is, and always has been, a controversial concept, often subject to criticism either because some are uncomfortable with its necessity, or because it is seen by others to have failed to maintain order. It is also to be expected that nations or leaders dissatisfied with an existing balance of power will find the concept unacceptable. Regularly, these are the nations and leaders which have sought to extend their hegemony and tilt an existing balance in their favour.

Somehow, too, the balance has been expected to be self-maintaining. When it is seen to have failed because nations sought to test it in war, the fault is often put on the idea of balance of power itself. Thus, the balance of power which, it would have to be admitted, was crucial to preserving the European peace between 1870 and the 1914-18 war, is often cited as a cause of that war. In fact, war began when the countries of Europe who thought themselves disadvantaged in the balance tried to shift it in their favour. Their unrealistic and unwarranted optimism in their own military capacity to do so led to the choice for conflict. The balance did not fail. On the contrary, the length of the First World War demonstrated just how accurate it was. What was at fault was an erroneous perception of the balance by those in charge of its constituent elements.

This example points out the vital role of accurate perceptions of prevailing force relationships. In this regard, it is necessary to distinguish two facets of a balance of power. First is the static aspect, the side more often and most easily considered. It is the description and cataloguing of all the factors involved in a balance at any one time. This book, for example, is a major effort to describe the military component as it applies to the East/West balance at the present time. A balance of power is also dynamic, involving, as it does, a process of constant reassessment with a view to taking whatever measures might be needed to maintain the balance. This book represents as well a worthwhile contribution to a better comprehension of the military dynamics that will influence the future development of the relationship between NATO and Warsaw Pact armed forces.

In as much as the balance of power concept has evolved mainly in modern times within a European context, practical analyses of that concept have tended to focus on the size and quality of forces in Europe. This calculation still remains at the core of any evaluation of the present East/West balance of power, but it is far from the whole picture. In examining the balance of forces between East and West, one must look today at the totality of those forces deployed around the world and the ability to project power to points on the globe often quite remote from the principal theatre of East/West confrontation in Europe. The advent of the nuclear age in itself has made it imperative to take this wider view. There is as well at least one other compelling reason for broadening today's concept of a balance of power. Although it is hardly novel to consider non-military aspects of the balance, these factors have become a great deal more complex and important. Some nations today, for example Japan and the oil-producing countries, exert a great deal of influence based almost exclusively on their economic capabilities and natural resources. An appreciation of the balance of power between East and West must take into account the direct and subsidiary economic and technological strengths and weaknesses of each side. It is also essential to weigh fully the less tangible factors, such as strength of commitment and political will in the respective societies of East and West.

With respect to the purely military side of the current East/West balance, one has to analyse not only the overall balance of military power, but also an aspect unique to our times, that of nuclear deterrence. After achieving strategic nuclear parity with the United States in the 1970s, the Soviet Union has continued to improve the full range of its nuclear forces at a rate with very disturbing implications for deterrence. Enormous progress has been made in submarine capabilities, in strike aircraft and in

▲ **Dr. Joseph Luns (left) in discussion with General Rogers, SACEUR.**

battlefield weapons. I would call particular attention, however, to the development of a new generation of Soviet land-based theatre nuclear weapons, largely targeted on Europe. Western publics must be made properly aware that Soviet deployment of these forces impinges upon NATO's strategy of flexible response and would, in the absence of remedial action by the Alliance, jeopardise the maintenance of deterrence across the full spectrum of the potential nuclear threat. Moreover, such remedial action is urgent and must move forward in parallel with Western efforts to limit nuclear weapons through arms control negotiations.

Another Soviet military development that causes me great concern has been Moscow's decision to devote tremendous resources over many years, and without any let-up in sight, to the acquisition of a modern, very powerful Navy. Although the Soviet Union is essentially a land power and does not depend to any great degree for its economic welfare on commerce by sea, Moscow has succeeded over the past two decades in building a large and potent offensive naval force and has increasingly deployed that force on all the oceans of the globe. In sum, Moscow seems bent on projecting its naval power worldwide, including the power afloat required to support offensive land operations far from Soviet territory. It is particularly difficult to square this massive naval development with the popular notion that the Soviet Union is designing its Navy merely to defend legitimate security interests or to enhance its international prestige.

Until recently, NATO has generally relied on qualitative superiority to balance its inferiority in sheer numbers to Warsaw Pact forces. But now, as the facts in this book demonstrate, even that margin of superiority is being challenged. The equipment and technological capability of Soviet forces have dramatically improved in recent years, thereby seriously eroding NATO's qualitative edge as a significant factor favouring the West in the overall East/West force relationship. Sad to say, the technological and scientific exchanges that have proliferated over the last decade under the banner of East/West détente have certainly contributed, quite possibly in a major way, to these important Soviet advances in the military field.

The highly unfavourable trends of recent years, to which I have just made reference, and others that could be added to the list, left the Western Alliance with little choice but to respond with decisions to improve its own force posture. By the late 1970s, there was wide agreement that urgent efforts were needed to revitalise and modernise Western defences if the NATO Alliance was to sustain its side of the balance. The Long-Term Defence Programme adopted by Allied heads of government in Washington in 1978 provided a blueprint for that effort. In 1979, Alliance Ministers took a further major decision to deploy modernised

'Until recently, NATO has generally relied on qualitative superiority to balance its inferiority in sheer numbers to Warsaw Pact forces. But now, as the facts in this book demonstrate, even that margin of superiority is being challenged.'

Long-Range Theatre Nuclear Forces, while seeking to engage the Soviet Union in negotiations to put limits on such systems. The dynamic aspect of the balance of power demands strong Western determination to follow through on such efforts, if an unacceptable further deterioration of Allied military strength is to be avoided.

Meanwhile, as I have already suggested, the military component is not the only aspect of today's balance of power between East and West that should concern us. We must consider the military calculations in light of economic strengths and, even more importantly, the political will of each side. In the East, there are the serious inefficiencies seemingly intrinsic to the Communist system which have consistently produced profound economic problems. Soviet failure in the agricultural and consumer goods sectors are notable examples. Recent speeches of Kremlin leaders give testimony to their economy's continued stagnation and its lack of internal technological innovation. By conscious policy, however, these endemic economic difficulties have not been allowed to curtail impressive growth in the military sector. Therefore, their effect on the East/West balance of power should not be over-estimated pending convincing evidence that the Kremlin is shifting its traditional priorities. To date, there have been few, if any, signs that the Soviet leadership is inclined to sacrifice military spending to improve domestic economic performance.

The West is not without considerable economic problems of its own. Many Western nations are vulnerable because of their reliance on imports of key raw materials, which could make them susceptible to political pressure and does make them dependent on the vagaries and risks of foreign sources. In many Western countries, too, economic growth has not been as fast in recent years as the public had grown to expect and double-digit inflation has emerged to compound the situation. Such strained economic circumstances have dampened the zeal in some Allied quarters to make sacrifices for defence, thus slowing efforts to correct the alarming trends in the East/West military balance.

The economic difficulties confronting both East and West heighten the importance of the political factor in maintaining the balance of power. In the absence of demonstrated political will, neither side can be sure of the sufficiency of its military forces at whatever levels. Even though the Soviet leadership has encountered little or no opposition in continuing to emphasise the military sector, it is always possible that popular tolerance for this course could be wearing thin. Events in Poland in the early 1980s should be a warning signal to the Kremlin of what could one day occur within the Soviet Union itself. Moreover, Moscow has other internal problems, among which is a certain measure of internal dissidence and increasing restiveness among fast-growing non-Slavic nationalities.

Related to national political will is the question of the cohesion of the groups of allies on each side. Within the Warsaw Pact, the voice of Moscow continues to be politically decisive. When problems have arisen concerning Eastern Bloc unity, the Soviet Union has not hesitated to resort to force if need be to enforce its authority. Can the Soviet Union rely indefinitely on such means to ensure the solidarity of the Warsaw Pact camp? It is only prudent to presume that, in fact, it can, but here too strains are beginning to appear which inspire at least some doubt over the long run.

By contrast, one finds in the West a large degree of internal stability and external unity firmly rooted in respect for and dedication to our democratic norms of government. That is not to say that the Western Alliance is immune to political frictions or that any of our societies is totally free from threats to public tranquility posed by extremist groups. Nonetheless, when compared with other regions of the world or even with their own national histories, the generally robust health of Western democracies today and their mutual cohesiveness form one of the strongest elements in their favour.

It is the very essence of democracy to provide meaningful opportunities for popular involvement in the political, economic and social questions with which governments must deal. Foreign policy and related security issues are no exception and common concern over such issues seems to be on the rise in the West. A second generation of Western voters and a first generation of their potential leaders are now coming of age who have not shared the experience of the last World War which so deeply marked their predecessors. This new electorate in Western nations and those whom they elect are more familiar instead with relative international calm, economic prosperity and generous social welfare programmes, than with the costs required to preserve those blessings and the even greater costs which would be entailed in any failure to so protect them.

The situation in the West I have just described, which in so many ways must be counted a happy one, also implies a substantial challenge to sustaining the political will required for the maintenance of nationally and collectively strong Western defencs adequate to counter an expanding Warsaw Pact military potential. The convincing exercise of that will in times of peace is absolutely vital to the Western ability to persuade the East in the future, as it has so successfully done in the past, that it would be utter folly to put Western defences to the ultimate test. Simply put, political will is the bedrock on which any balance of power will stand or fall in the end.

Thus, I would hope above all that the military facts in this volume will help to dispel any illusion that the world has become sufficiently risk-free as to enable the West to forego the effort and sacrifice, however great or unpleasant, that may be required to keep the East/West balance from veering towards a dangerous, and possibly catastrophic, disequilibrium. Those who doubt this message are encouraged to consult the history books and the Warsaw Pact order of battle as set forth in the pages that follow. Moreover, I would urge that they do so without delay.

Dr. J.M.A.H. Luns,
Secretary General,
North Atlantic
Treaty Organisation.

Dr. J. M. A. H. Luns has been Secretary General of NATO since 1971. He was formerly Foreign Minister of the Netherlands, President of the North Atlantic Council (1958-1959) and Member of the Netherlands Permanent Delegation to the United Nations, as well as holding other senior Netherlands diplomatic positions.

The Alliances

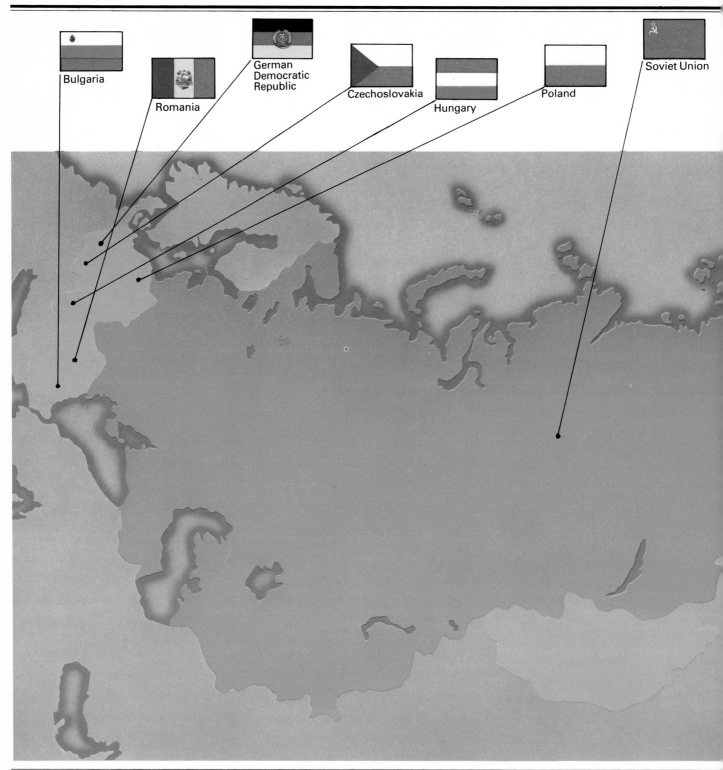

Bulgaria

Romania

German
Democratic
Republic

Czechoslovakia

Hungary

Poland

Soviet Union

THE Warsaw Pact (also known as the Warsaw Treaty Organisation (WTO) was signed by Albania, Bulgaria, Czechoslovakia, German Democratic Republic, Hungary, Poland, Romania and the Soviet Union in Warsaw on 14 May 1955. Albania has been the sole legal defector, although Romania's membership sometimes appears in question. Superficially, NATO and the Pact appear generally similar, but this is not so, the major difference being that the Atlantic Alliance is an association of independent states whereas the Pact is clearly under the domination of the USSR pursuing its own political and strategic purposes.

The military organisation of the Pact consists of a Joint High Com-

mand, charged with the "direction and coordination of the Joint Armed Forces". The Commander-in-Chief (CinC) of the Joint Armed Forces heads the Joint High Command, which also includes a joint staff and a Military Council, in line with normal Soviet practice, which meets under the chairmanship of the CinC, together with the Chief of Staff and permanent military representatives from the non-Soviet forces.

The Pact does not have its own air defence organisation, air defence being integrated into the Soviet national organisation, *Protivovozdushnoi oborony strany* (PVO-Strany). A Soviet Deputy Commander/PVO-Strany acts as the "air defence commander" for Eastern Europe and he is responsi-

ble for the six main air defence districts in the Pact area, in addition to the ten air defence districts in the USSR proper, all of which include EW systems, radars, fighter/interceptor forces and surface-to-air missiles. Local Pact air forces are responsible for the air defence of their own airspace though under general Soviet control and within the context of Soviet operational requirements.

"*Soviet representatives*" (associated with the Joint High Command) are located in each capital and are responsible for the Soviet military missions attached to the non-Soviet forces. These officers must be distinguished from the Soviet Military Attachés proper, and from the KGB and other intelligence officers assigned through-

out eastern Europe to coordinate intelligence activities and to supervise operations. There is also a Technical Committee, apparently concerned with overall coordination of arms production, the supply of equipment, joint procurement and the supervision of east European arms industries.

Pact Combat Forces

The sole nuclear power within the Pact, the Soviet Union also contributes some 60 per cent of the Pact's first line forces. Soviet forces deployed forward in Eastern Europe have never in the past 30 years fallen below 25 to 26 divisions, and currently stand at 30. Deployment comprises four "Groups of Soviet Forces" based in East Germany, Poland, Czecho-

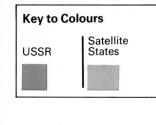

Key to Colours

USSR | Satellite States

Statistics in the Warsaw Pact

Nation	Population	Armed Forces	Annual Defence Expenditure as Percentage of GNP	Military Service*
Bulgaria	8,900,000	149,000	2.1%	Conscription 24-36 months
Czechoslovakia	15,400,000	195,000	2.8%	Conscription 24-36 months
German Democratic Republic	16,800,000	162,000	6.3%	Conscription 18 months
Hungary	10,700,000	93,000	2.1%	Conscription 24 months
Poland	35,700,000	317,500	2.4%	Conscription 24-36 months
Romania	22,200,000	184,500	1.4%	Conscription 16-24 months
USSR	265,500,000	3,658,000	11-13%	Conscription 24-36 months

Note:
*Length of service for conscripts depends upon service. In general army service tends to be the shortest, with naval and air force service somewhat longer.
Source: The Military Balance 1980-1981, IISS, London.

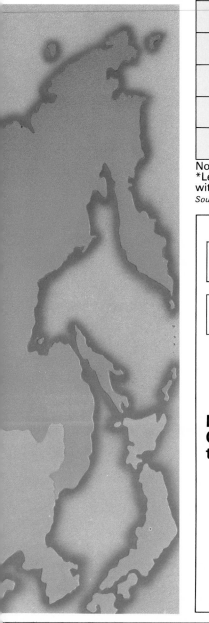

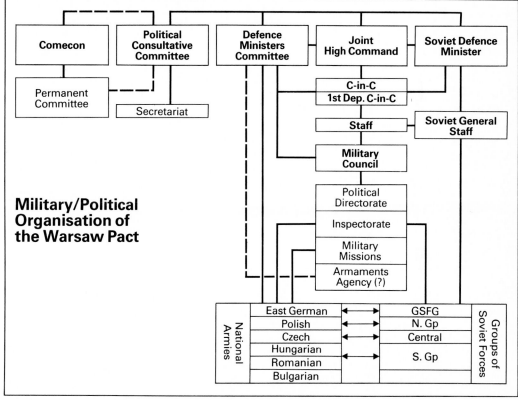

Military/Political Organisation of the Warsaw Pact

slavakia and Hungary. The non-Soviet forces are generally divided into the "Northern tier" (GDR, Poland and Czechoslovakia) and "southern tier" (Hungary, Bulgaria and Romania) which add collectively some 55 divisions.

Poland maintains the largest non-Soviet WP military establishment: over 300,000 men, 5 tank divisions, 8 motor-rifle (MR) divisions, as well as one airborne and one amphibious divisions. Overall, Poland boasts 3,800 tanks, 750 combat aircraft and a considerable navy. The recent political unrest in Poland has led to increasing pressure on the country's armed forces, with the ever-present threat of Soviet military intervention. The Polish armed forces are now inextricably involved in the political arena.

Though smaller, the East German forces rival the Poles for the position of the leading non-Soviet element: efficient, well equiped and well trained, the East German Army (NVA) can field 4 MR divisions, 2 tank divisions and many specialised troops. The air force is principally equipped with the MiG-21, while the navy contributes light forces. The East German forces are, however, unique within the Pact in being permanently and directly *subordinated* to the Soviet military command (GSFG).

Czechoslovak forces, much dispirited by the 1968 Soviet invasion, have slowly recovered their place in the Pact order-of-battle, the army currently comprising 5 tank and 5 MR divisions, 1 airborne regiment, while the air force has over 500 aircraft.

The "southern tier" presents a marked contrast in manning, training and modernisation. Hungary has an army of 72,000 organised into 6 divisions (1 tank, 5 MR), though only two-thirds of this force are anywhere near operational fitness. Bulgaria, hampered by economic problems, maintains 8 MR divisions and 5 tank brigades (the equivalent of 2 divisions). There are also some 200 aircraft, plus 2 escort vessels and 4 submarines in the navy. Bulgaria maintains particularly close links with the USSR.

Romania, however, has worked hard to loosen its ties, refusing to remove her forces from tight national control and resisting all Soviet attempts to achieve military integration. The army, in urgent need of modern weapons, comprises 2 tank divisions and 8 MR divisions, 3 mountain brigades, and an airborne brigade. The air force even has a small amount of Western equipment and is developing a joint Romanian-Yugoslav fighter. The navy is a light coastal defence force with 6 corvettes, minesweepers and FPBs.

The Warsaw Pact is not, however, a wartime command organisation, despite the existence of the "Joint High Command", but is rather an administrative and training organisation. For operational purposes the Soviet "Groups of Forces" would become "Fronts" directly subordinated to the Soviet High Command.

The Alliances

Statistics in NATO Member Countries

Nation*	Population	Armed Forces	Annual Defence Expenditure as Percentage of GNP	Military Service
Belgium	9,910,000	87,900	3.3%	Conscription 8 or 10 months
Canada	23,890,000	78,646	1.7%	Voluntary
Denmark	5,124,000	35,050	2.0%	Conscription 9 months
France	54,000,000	494,730	3.9%	Conscription 12 months
FRG	61,315,000	495,000	3.3%	Conscription 15 months
Greece	9,530,000	181,500	5.4%	Conscription 24-32 months
Italy	57,100,000	366,000	2.4%	Conscription 12-18 months
Luxembourg	364,000	660	1.0%	Voluntary
Netherland	14,000,000	114,980	3.4%	Conscription 14-17 months
Norway	4,100,000	37,000	3.1%	Conscription 12-15 months
Portugal	9,900,000	59,540	4.0%	Conscription 16-24 months
Turkey	45,500,000	567,000	5.7%	Conscription 20 months
UK	55,902,000	329,204	4.9%	Voluntary
USA	221,600,000	2,050,000	5.2%	Voluntary

*Iceland, although a NATO member, has no armed forces.
Source: The Military Balance 1980-1981, IISS, London.

NATO Military Structure

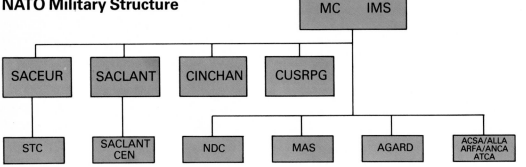

Canada

USA

Key: MC, Military Committee, and IMS, International Military Staff, (Brussels); SACEUR, Supreme Allied Commander Europe (SHAPE, Belgium); SACLANT, Supreme Allied Commander Atlantic (Norfolk, USA); CUSRPG, Canada/US Regional Planning Group (Washington, USA); STC, SHAPE Technical Centre (The Hague, Holland); SACLANTCEN, SACLANT Anti-submarine Warfare Research Centre (La Spezia, Italy); NDC, NATO Defence College (Rome); MAS, Military Agency for Standardisation (Brussels); AGARD, Advisory Group for Aerospace Research and Development (Paris); ACSA, Allied Communications Security Agency (Brussels); ALLA, Allied Long Lines Agency (Brussels); ARFA, Allied Radio Frequency Agency (Brussels); ANCA, Allied Naval Communications Agency (London); ATCA, Allied Tactical Communications Agency (Brussels).

THE North, Atlantic Treaty Organisation (NATO) was established on 4 April 1949 in response to the ever-increasing threat from the Soviet Union. The original 12 signatories were joined by Greece and Turkey in 1952 and by the Federal Republic of Germany in 1955. In 1966 the French Armed Forces withdrew from the integrated military command structure, and NATO HQs and units were obliged to leave French territory; nevertheless France remains a full political member of the Alliance. There is still considerable co-operation in the military field and few doubt that the French forces would be "there on the day". Although the French stance is inconvenient for the remainder of NATO it is the outcome of pressure of particular historical imperatives which are well understood. The only foreseeable major change to the Alliance would be the accession of Spain.

The cornerstone of NATO is that it is a free association of sovereign states; the USA may be militarily and economically the most powerful but, as it knows to its cost, it is by no means able to predominate politically. The North Atlantic Council meets twice yearly at Foreign Minister level, but is in permanent session at ambassadorial levels in Brussels. Like the Council, the Defence Planning Committee (DPC) meets regularly at ambassadorial level and twice yearly in Ministerial level. (France is a full member of the North Atlantic Council, but is not a member of the DPC.)

The most powerful political figure is the Secretary-General, currently Dr Joseph Luns, who advises the NATO Council and the various committees on political, politico-military, economic and other factors in defence planning. He is assisted by a staff drawn from the member countries.

The Commanders
The Military Committee comprises the Chiefs-of-Staff of all member countries except Iceland and France, although the latter maintains a liaison staff. The Military Committee is in permanent session of Military Representatives, and is headed by a Chairman, currently General Gundersen of Norway.

There are three Major NATO Commanders (MNC). The Supreme Allied Commander Europe (SACEUR) is an American general who is also Commander-in-Chief US Forces Europe (CINCUSEUR). The Supreme Allied Commander Atlantic (SACLANT) is an American admiral and is the only MNC located in the USA (at Norfolk, Virginia). The Commander-in-Chief Channel (CINCCHAN) is a British admiral, who combines this post with the British national command of Commander-in-Chief Fleet.

At all levels the staffs are integrated and are practising in peace the roles they would play in war. Not all forces are fully assigned in peacetime to the NATO commanders, but constant exercises ensure that such transfers of com-

NATO's Fifteen Members and the Military Commands

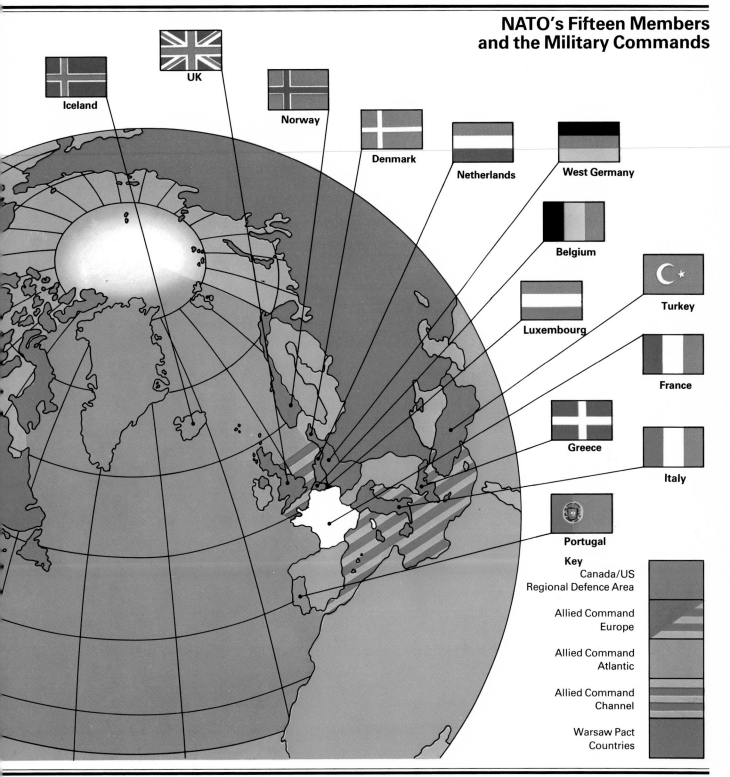

Iceland
UK
Norway
Denmark
Netherlands
West Germany
Belgium
Luxembourg
Turkey
France
Greece
Italy
Portugal

Key
Canada/US Regional Defence Area
Allied Command Europe
Allied Command Atlantic
Allied Command Channel
Warsaw Pact Countries

mand are regularly rehearsed. Unlike the Warsaw Pact where Soviet tactical doctrine and equipment predominate, there is a wide disparity in NATO, although modern circumstances are starting to apply irresistible pressure in the direction of standardisation and compatibility.

NATO Combat Forces

Allied Command Europe (ACE) is responsible for the defence of all European NATO territory, including Turkey, but excluding France, Portugal, Iceland and the UK. SACEUR has some 66 divisions assigned in war, together with over 3,000 tactical aircraft. Subordinate to SACEUR are three major commands: Allied Forces Central Europe (AFCENT); Allied Forces

Northern Europe (AFNORTH); and Allied Forces Southern Europe (AFSOUTH). The recently formed UK Air Forces (UKAIR), and the ACE Mobile Force (AMF) also report direct to SACEUR.

Allied Command Atlantic (ACLANT) is responsible for the defence of the Atlantic Ocean from the Tropic of Cancer to the North Pole. ACLANT is divided into six subordinate commands: three geographical (Western Atlantic, Eastern Atlantic, Iberian Atlantic) and three functional (Striking Fleet Atlantic, Submarine Command and Standing Naval Force Atlantic – STANAVFORLANT). The primary tasks of ACLANT in war are to establish either general or local control of the ocean in order to bring American reinforce-

ments to Europe, and to conduct conventional and nuclear operations against enemy maritime forces and bases. Nobody doubts that this would be a major battle.

Allied Command Channel (ACCHAN) is responsible for the defence of the English Channel and the North Sea. It is sub-divided into four maritime areas, and includes its own air forces and the Standing Naval Force Channel (STANAVFORCHAN).

NATO in War

The NATO command structure is designed for a defensive war and would function effectively, provided the political decisions to assign national forces were made quickly and unequivocally. One of the major difficulties arises from

the great variation in standards of training and equipment among the member countries. Further problems stem from the political reservations placed upon French military forces and the failure to allow NATO lines-of-communication to run through French territory.

Perhaps the two greatest questions, however, are whether NATO could mobilise in time to meet a surprise Warsaw Pack attack and, if so, whether the crucial US reinforcements could fight their way by air and sea across the Atlantic.

It is too easy, however, to concentrate on the difficulties which NATO has to counter. The fact is that it has existed for 32 years and looks set to continue for as long as the Soviet Union maintains its threat to Western Europe.

The Balance of STRATEGIC FORCES

I N HIS "farewell" speech to the American people, presented on television in Washington just six days before leaving office, former President Jimmy Carter issued this grave warning about the growing threat of nuclear war where ". . . more destructive power than in the entire 1939–45 war would be unleashed *every second* for the long afternoon it would take for all the bombs and missiles to fall."

To be more precise, the actual quantity of high explosive detonated in World War II was some 3,000,000 tons (3MT). Today the two Superpowers possess between them strategic nuclear weapons with an estimated total raw yield of approximately 7,368MT, *just two thousand five hundred times the*

total used in the last world war!

There are three fundamental difficulties which arise in discussing strategic nuclear warfare, of which the first is that such a war has never actually happened. The atomic bombs which were dropped on Japan in 1945 gave little insight into what a full-scale nuclear war might be like in the 1980s, and a certain amount of "inspired guesswork" is inevitable. Strategists must, however, take warning from the 1930s when the predictions of the effects of heavy bombing on cities were that the enormous damage and the *inevitable* mass panic would bring governments to surrender within a matter of days. In fact, no country has ever been defeated by conventional bombing alone.

Precise Performance Information not Revealed

The second problem is that many of the facts on strategic weapons are highly classified, while the only source of any information on both American *and* Soviet weaponry is the United States. For example, one of the most crucial factors in assessing nuclear weapon capabilities is the Circular Error Probable (CEP); the USA is, however, unwilling to reveal either *precise* performance figures on its own missiles or the accuracy of its observations of Soviet missile tests. Further, to establish the true dynamic balance between the nuclear powers requires accurate data on a whole range of subjects, many of which need intelligence reports in order for qualitative

judgements to be made, eg, serviceability rates, maintenance standards, and so on. Access would then be needed to a complex war-gaming computer.

Finally, there is a common error of comparing like with like (for example, American strategic nuclear submarines – SSBNs – versus Soviet SSBNs) as a crude measure of military power. Nothing could be more misleading, since the factor which counts is the ability of a weapon system to accomplish its mission, and the like counterpart on the other side seldom has any effect on this. Thus, nuclear submarines are countered by enemy anti-submarine warfare systems, while submarine-launched ballistic missiles (SLBMs) have to overcome early-warning systems, anti-

Only in the area of strategic forces has there been any serious attempt to achieve a balance through negotiation. Despite apparent agreement, the continuing mistrust and demonstrable circumvention have led to further competition between the Superpowers. The USSR continues to field new and more capable systems, to the point where a first-strike might, at some time in the future, seem to be feasible. The USA is struggling to restore equilibrium, but has wasted vast sums of money and effort on weapons systems which have come to nought. In this situation the nuclear forces of the UK and France have an importance out of all proportion to their numerical strength.

ballistic missiles (where they exist) and passive defences in cities; enemy SSBNs or SLBMs just do not enter into the equation.

First-Strike
It must be a fundamental assumption in a first-strike that a rational aggressor has accepted a retaliatory second-strike as a virtually certain consequence of his first-strike, and believes that he can tolerate the outcome. Herman Kahn, the American nuclear strategist, suggests a ladder of "escalation" with 44 steps, in which Step 21 is nuclear release and Step 44 the holocaust. Any rational aggressor will have made a very careful examination of his aims prior to any attack and will also have decided the maximum

price he is prepared to pay to achieve that goal. If, therefore, the aggressor were to decide to set the upper limit at Step 30, then escalation by the victim from Step 21 to Step 22 is not going to affect the aggressor significantly, since the latter has already accepted the implications not only of Step 22, but of Steps 23 to 29 as well. The victim's problem is that he is unlikely to know with any degree of certainty what upper limit the aggressor has set on the conflict.

If the aggressor were to be the USSR then she would face a further set of unpredictable factors, due to the existence of nuclear forces in the UK, France and China, which are not only outside US control (although the British force is assigned to SACEUR), but inde-

pendent of each other as well. The UK has 4 SSBNs, while France has 5 SSBNs, 18 MRBMs and a (decreasing) number of Mirage IV bombers. China has an estimated 4 ICBMs, 65 to 85 MRBMs and 50 IRBMs. It has been stated that the British force – even when only one SSBN is on patrol – has greater destructive capability than all the munitions expended in World War II. The USSR simply cannot afford to ignore these non-US nuclear forces; conversely, the US needs to consider only the USSR as a potential nuclear antagonist.

Before undertaking a first-strike using ICBMs the aggressor would have to satisfy himself on some further fundamental points. First, he would need to be sure that his own missile force would function

with the reliability and accuracy predicted from (necessarily limited) peacetime tests. Second, he would need to be sure that the victim had neither increased the hardening of his silos nor perfected some new means of neutralising attacking ICBMs.

Assessing Second-strike Capability is Difficult
From all this he would then need to be certain that the intended victim would be unable to retain sufficient nuclear retaliatory forces to impose more than the acceptable maximum damage in a second strike. Such a calculation contains so many areas of uncertainty that it would take either a very confident – or an extremely foolhardy – leadership to overcome them.

15

The Balance of Strategic Forces

Soviets Winning the Strategic Numbers Game

The figures and charts on these pages show the current balance in strategic/weapon capabilities, but simple numerical comparisons can be very misleading, and the material throughout this chapter seeks to carry out a more detailed analysis, so that balanced assessments can be made. The USSR can be seen to have a considerable lead in Raw Total Yield, but this figure is of academic significance only; in Equivalent Megatons (EMT) the US advantage disappeared in the late 1960s and there is now a degree of parity. So long as SSBNs remain undetectable, however, the West's countervalue capability (EMT) remains sufficient. But in Hard Target Kill Potential (CMP, Counter Military Potential) the balance of advantage currently rests with the USSR.

SALT II Limitations

	MIRVed ICBM launchers	MIRVed Missile launchers	MIRVed systems[1]	Aggregate ceiling	Aggregate ceiling until end 1981
	820	1,200	1,320	2,250	2,400

Current USSR/US Strategic Force Levels

	MIRVed ICBM launchers	MIRVed SLBM launchers	Non-MIRVed ICBM launchers	Non-MIRVed SLBM launchers	Heavy bombers	Total systems
USSR[2]	608	144	790	806	156	2,504
US	550	496	504	160	573[3]	2,283

1. MIRVed missile launchers + bombers with cruise missiles.
2. Breakdown reflects Soviet statement June 18, 1979.
3. Includes approximately 220 B-52s in deep storage.

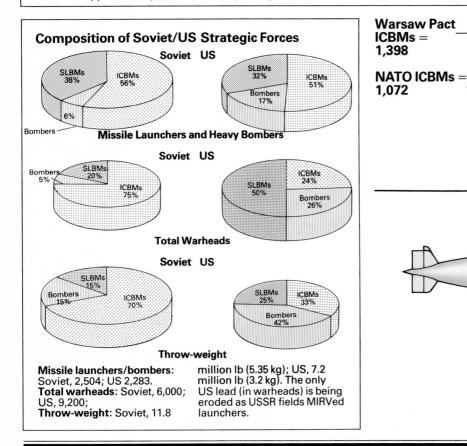

Composition of Soviet/US Strategic Forces

Missile Launchers and Heavy Bombers

Soviet: SLBMs 38%, ICBMs 56%, Bombers 6%
US: SLBMs 32%, ICBMs 51%, Bombers 17%

Missile Launchers and Heavy Bombers

Soviet: Bombers 5%, SLBMs 20%, ICBMs 75%
US: ICBMs 24%, SLBMs 50%, Bombers 26%

Total Warheads

Soviet: SLBMs 15%, Bombers 15%, ICBMs 70%
US: SLBMs 25%, ICBMs 33%, Bombers 42%

Throw-weight

Missile launchers/bombers: Soviet, 2,504; US 2,283. **Total warheads:** Soviet, 6,000; US, 9,200; **Throw-weight:** Soviet, 11.8 million lb (5.35 kg); US, 7.2 million lb (3.2 kg). The only US lead (in warheads) is being eroded as USSR fields MIRVed launchers.

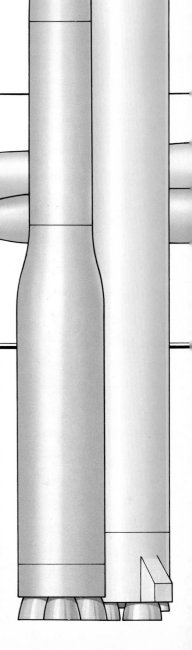

Warsaw Pact ICBMs = 1,398

NATO ICBMs = 1,072

Second-Strike

The defender's problems are manifold, too. The first is that of having a maximum of 30 minutes in which to make the gravest of all decisions. The USA is known to designate a "National Command Authority" (NCA) to make such a decision which comprises the President, the Secretary of Defense, and their duly deputised alternates or successors.[5] Clearly plans exist to ensure that at least one is available within the requisite time. It must be presumed that the USSR has a similar system, although no information on such a subject has ever been made public.

One possible scenario which causes concern is that of a Soviet first-strike on US ICBM silos, on bombers not on generated alert, and with the peacetime quota of SSBNs in port. According to former US Secretary of Defense Harold Brown, however, the USA would still "be able to launch several thousand warheads at targets in the USSR in retaliation. And we would still have the option of withholding a number of these warheads while directing still others to a variety of non-urban targets, including military targets of great value to the Soviet leadership." Brown's *caveat* to these remarks is, however, very important: "... my assessment is based upon the assumption that Soviet forces will remain within the limits set by SALT-II."

The problem of timely decision-making in this situation cannot be overestimated. The flight-time of ICBMs between the two Super-powers is some 30 minutes, but if Soviet SSBNs were to be positioned close to the US coast this warning time could be reduced to between 6 and 10 minutes.

The attacker's dilemma is that SLBMs could catch soft targets unawares (eg, bomber bases, unhardened military targets) but currently do not possess the combination of accuracy and yield necessary to destroy ICBM silos. To launch an attack employing ICBMs, on the other hand, gives greater potential against silos, but would also give the victims time to launch their bombers and also (at least in theory) ICBMs as well.

The aim of a second-strike strategy is to seek to guarantee that,

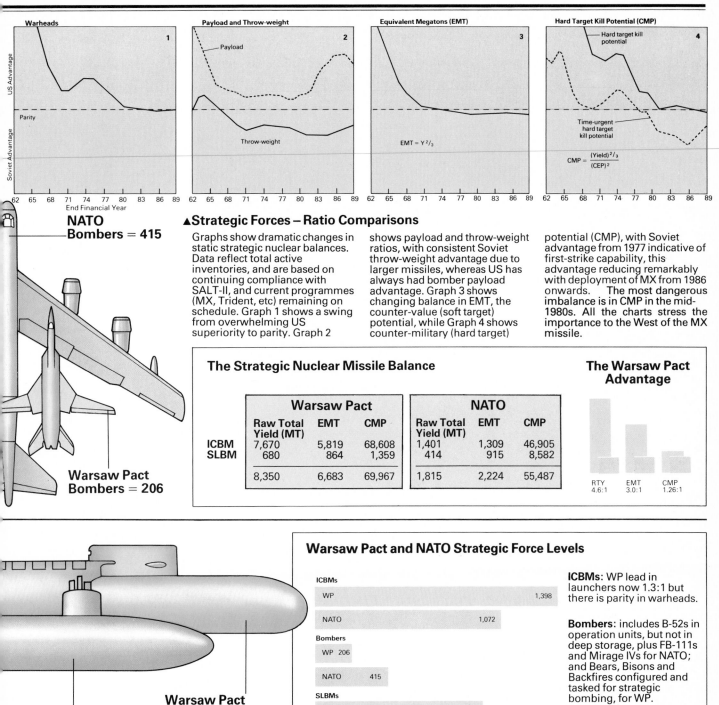

Warheads 1

Payload and Throw-weight 2
- Payload
- Throw-weight

Equivalent Megatons (EMT) 3
$$EMT = Y^{2/3}$$

Hard Target Kill Potential (CMP) 4
- Hard target kill potential
- Time-urgent hard target kill potential
$$CMP = \frac{(Yield)^{2/3}}{(CEP)^2}$$

US Advantage / Parity / Soviet Advantage

End Financial Year: 62 65 68 71 74 77 80 83 86 89

NATO Bombers = 415

Warsaw Pact Bombers = 206

▲Strategic Forces – Ratio Comparisons

Graphs show dramatic changes in static strategic nuclear balances. Data reflect total active inventories, and are based on continuing compliance with SALT-II, and current programmes (MX, Trident, etc) remaining on schedule. Graph 1 shows a swing from overwhelming US superiority to parity. Graph 2 shows payload and throw-weight ratios, with consistent Soviet throw-weight advantage due to larger missiles, whereas US has always had bomber payload advantage. Graph 3 shows changing balance in EMT, the counter-value (soft target) potential, while Graph 4 shows counter-military (hard target) potential (CMP), with Soviet advantage from 1977 indicative of first-strike capability, this advantage reducing remarkably with deployment of MX from 1986 onwards. The most dangerous imbalance is in CMP in the mid-1980s. All the charts stress the importance to the West of the MX missile.

The Strategic Nuclear Missile Balance

	Warsaw Pact			NATO		
	Raw Total Yield (MT)	EMT	CMP	Raw Total Yield (MT)	EMT	CMP
ICBM	7,670	5,819	68,608	1,401	1,309	46,905
SLBM	680	864	1,359	414	915	8,582
	8,350	6,683	69,967	1,815	2,224	55,487

The Warsaw Pact Advantage

RTY 4.6:1	EMT 3.0:1	CMP 1.26:1

Warsaw Pact SLBMs = 956

NATO SLBMs = 744

Warsaw Pact and NATO Strategic Force Levels

ICBMs
- WP 1,398
- NATO 1,072

Bombers
- WP 206
- NATO 415

SLBMs
- WP 956
- NATO 744

ICBMs: WP lead in launchers now 1.3:1 but there is parity in warheads.

Bombers: includes B-52s in operation units, but not in deep storage, plus FB-111s and Mirage IVs for NATO; and Bears, Bisons and Backfires configured and tasked for strategic bombing, for WP.

SLBMs: Assessed on basis of total launch tubes for servicing SSBNs.

if the enemy attacks first, sufficient nuclear warheads and delivery vehicles will survive to create in retaliation more than the acceptable maximum damage to the enemy. The first way to achieve such a second-strike capability is simply to have more nuclear delivery means than the enemy has warheads, the margin of excess being greater than that needed for maximum acceptable retaliatory damage. Such a course implies great expense and a constant response to the moves of any potential enemy.

Alternative Schemes to Guarantee Survival

Should this be considered impracticable, then the survival of sufficient nuclear assets must be guaranteed by different means. Strategic bombers can be on either airborne or ground alert, while the survival of SSBNs is reasonably assured since ASW is currently insufficiently developed to detect and track all SSBNs throughout their patrol, or to ensure their destruction when required.

ICBMs are, however, a different matter and two options seem feasible. The first is "launching-on-warning", which is the equivalent of bombers on alert, except that, once launched, ICBMs cannot be recalled. Alternatively, it could be decided to ride the attack out, although this presupposes a reasonable knowledge of enemy capabilities, sufficient for confidence that enough strategic assets would survive. In the light of the rapidly increasing Counter-Military Potential (CMP) of Soviet nuclear forces this would require a very fine judgement on the part of the USA's National Command Authority.

Targeting

Nuclear targeting is a complex business, the first consideration being the capability of missiles and warheads. This is not a simple matter of yield, but rather a function of yield and accuracy. Thus, the fact that the USSR has more ICBMs or greater total raw yield (megatonnage) than the USA is not strictly relevant. More important are the number of independently targetable warheads, the number of targets which can be engaged, the Effective Megatonnage (EMT) which indicates the counter-value (soft-target) capability, and the Counter-Military Potential.

Counter-value targets are cities and industrial complexes. The USA has 162 cities with a population greater than 100,000, of which 35 complexes exceed one million inhabitants. In contrast the USSR has 254 cities of over 100,000, but only 13 of these exceed one million. Western Europe has some exceptional concentrations (eight megalopoli of over 2½ million inhabitants).

For the USA and the USSR cities are the targets for SLBMs and the less effective (ie, lower CMP) ICBMs. Both sides have a credible and survivable second-strike capability, and therefore appear to deter each other in this field.

17

The Balance of Strategic Forces

The Warsaw Pact View of the NATO Strategic Threat

It is too simple in the West to concentrate on the very formidable Warsaw Pact threat, and to under-estimate the ability of the West to deter aggression. This deterrence has two main features: the first is the multiplicity of systems (graphically shown here), and the second is the triple diversity of decision-making centres—Washington, London and Paris.

This map (obtained from East German sources) shows that Western ICBM resources are concentrated in the continental USA (Minuteman, Titan II and, in the future, MX) with a second but somewhat marginal capability in the 18 S3 missiles in France. The US ICBMs have the core areas of the USSR within range, provided they could survive a first-strike.

Far more survivable are the SLBMs at sea in SSBNs and, unless there is a dramatic break-through in anti-submarine warfare techniques, these will remain to provide a guaranteed second-strike capability. Again the map shows the way in which the SSBNs can use the whole of the world's oceans as their hiding place.

The great range of Trident II will, in fact, enable US SSBNs to patrol in remote areas in the South Atlantic, Indian Ocean or the Pacific, thus making the task of detection immeasurably more difficult for the USSR.

The final elements of NATO's missile threat to the USSR would be Ground-Launched Cruise Missiles (GLCMs) and Pershing II missiles stationed in Western Europe. Both these weapon systems have sufficient range to reach into the most important areas of European USSR, which explains the extensive campaign being conducted against them.

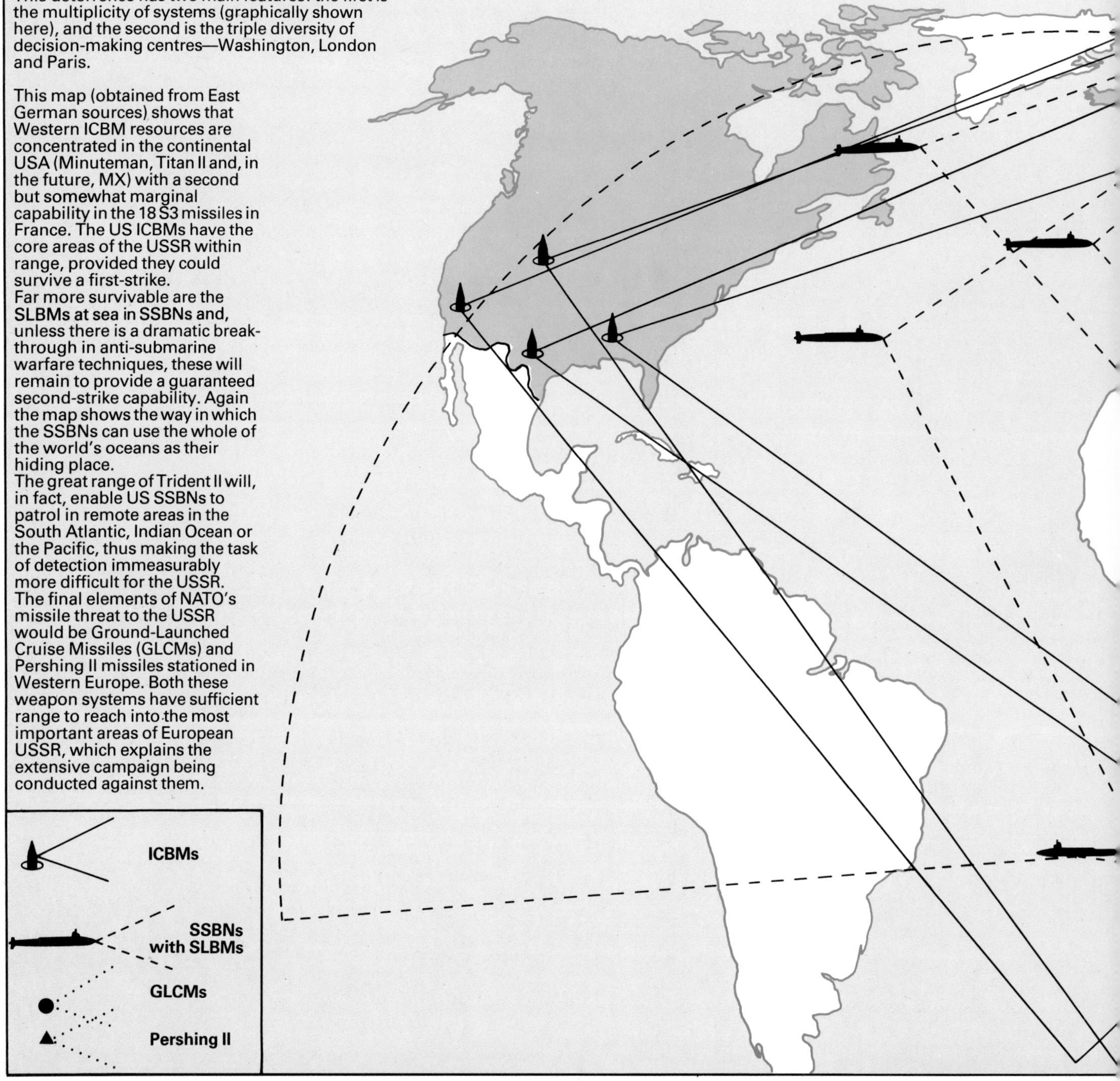

ICBMs

SSBNs with SLBMs

GLCMs

Pershing II

The situation has been stated very clearly by Admiral Sir Ian Easton, Royal Navy: "The aspect of the Polaris successor issue on which I shall concentrate is the assured independent option which it confers upon the UK to destroy numerous Soviet cities. . . . The nuclear destruction of a number – say, some dozen – of the Soviet cities with a population of over 100,000 would be a traumatic blow to the Soviet Union. Amongst these cities might be Moscow, Leningrad, Kiev, Kharkov, Ghorky and Stalingrad. The enormous loss of population and industry, the disruption of services critical to the life of the country, and the likely destruction of a proportion of the central bureaucracy of a centrally organised state, could be expected markedly to weaken the vitality of the nation and the will of its people and, perhaps, of its armies."

Hardened Counter-force Targets

Counter-force targets are the enemy's strategic nuclear forces, including political and military nuclear command and control centres, and the relevant communications systems. Virtually all of these are hardened and the ability of warheads to destroy them depends upon having a high CMP. There are, however, practical limits on hardening resulting from the nature of the construction materials, especially concrete. If the kill probability of the weapons increases to the point where de-struction of a silo is guaranteed then the only option open to the defender is to put his ICBMs on mobile launchers, otherwise his ICBMs must be a hostage to a first-strike strategy. The only known US unclassified official study esti-mates such highest value military targets to number some 1,700 in the USSR and 1,300 in the USA, most of which are extremely hard, or presumed invulnerable in the case of SSBNs at sea.

A counter-force first-strike must be targeted on all enemy ICBM silos in the knowledge that if any of those ICBMs are launched on warning, or launched under attack, then incoming warheads will be wasted on empty silos. For the defence, if they do decide to launch then they must endeavour to identify the empty silos on the aggressor's side, so that they, too, can avoid the same problem of "cracking" empty silos.

"Other Military Targets"

There is a further category of low collateral damage, high value military targets, which for convenience, and to avoid confusion with strategic nuclear forces, are referred to as *"Other Military Targets"* (OMT) and are estimated to number some 2 to 3,000 in the USSR, and 1,000 in the USA.

Both the USA and the USSR are known to devote considerable attention to detailed analyses of potential targets, with a view to discovering the one or two really critical points and, in a nuclear conflict, destroying them in order

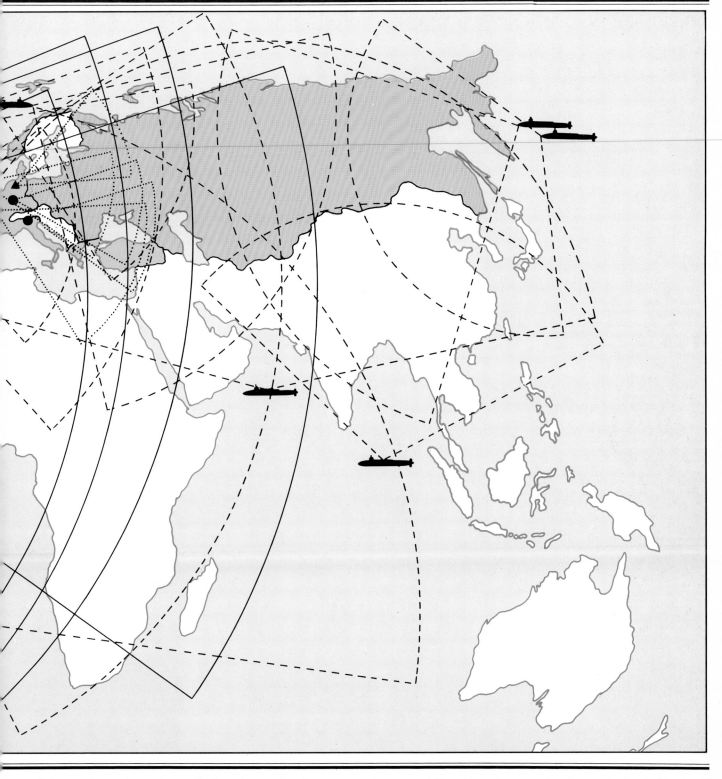

to dislocate the entire system.

The Three Primary Systems

ICBMs are currently the primary counter-force weapons, especially against time-urgent targets. Because they are not subject to the same size limitations as SLBMs they possess good range and throw-weight, but above all they are extremely accurate. The latest US RV has a CEP of 656ft (200m), while the Soviet SS-19 has one of 853ft (260m). These figures are improving all the time for MIRVs, but when MaRVs are introduced CEPs which are in the order of tens of feet should be possible.

SLBM accuracy is currently much less than that for ICBMs, mainly due to the difficulty in establishing the precise location of

the launching SSBN; their principal use must, therefore, be in a second-strike counter-value role. Current programmes aim to improve this, probably by using terminal guidance systems for the re-entry vehicles (MaRVs).

The greatest value of SLBMs is that the launch platforms – the SSBNs – are very difficult to detect and even when found are almost impossible to track throughout their patrol. SSBNs currently provide both "sides" with a second-strike capability, and a breakthrough in ASW would thus be profoundly destabilising. It should be noted, however, that while data tables always treat SSBN fleets as a whole, many fewer would actually be available in an unexpected crisis. Some 10 to 20 per cent of

SSBNs would be in long refit at any one time, and a further percentage would be in short refit or crew change. In fact the USSR is estimated to maintain only 13 SSBNs on patrol at any one time. All SSBNs in their home ports would, of course, be high value military targets and accorded priority in any nuclear strike.

Strategic Bombers

Strategic bombers come under a somewhat different category, with the US relying far more heavily on them than does the USSR. Because of the ease of detection and the relatively long flight times from base to target, they obviously could not be used against time-urgent first-strike targets.

The USA looks upon strategic

bombers as an invaluable part of their triad, with particular merit in being able to take-off under threat and then loiter pending decisions on targeting. They would then be used for precision second strikes against hard targets, using either gravity bombs or stand-off (cruise) missiles.

For the USSR the strategic bomber seems to be of much less value, although its very existence is useful (to the Warsaw Pact) in that it causes much alarm and expenditure by NATO. The existing types are old and slow, while even the notorious Backfire (formerly referred to as Tupolev Tu-26, now Tu-22M) does not affect the strategic balance of power in any practical way as far as the USA is concerned.

The Balance of Strategic Forces

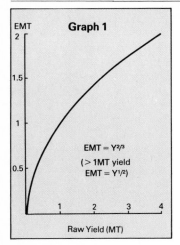
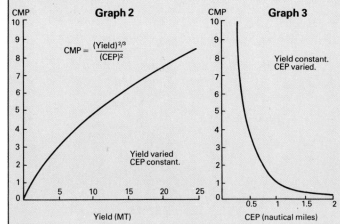

Effective Megatons (EMT)

reflects damage potential against "soft" point targets, eg, above-ground HQs, or area targets such as cities. The effect at a specific point distant from GZ (qv) is proportional to the cube-root of the yield, while the area affected is proportional to the square of the distance. From this it can be deduced that:

$$EMT = Y^{2/3}$$
(but where $Y > MT$; $EMT = Y^{1/2}$)

Graph 1 plots EMT against Y.

Counter-military Potential (CMP)

CMP reflects the ability to damage hard targets; eg, missile silos, and is influenced by accuracy and yield. Delivery accuracy is expressed as CEP (qv); hence the ability to destroy hard targets is also expressed as a probability. From this can be derived CMP which is stated mathematically as:

$$CMP = \frac{(Yield)^n}{(CEP)^2} \quad \begin{array}{l} \text{Where } Y > 200KT \quad n = 2/3 \\ \text{Where } Y > 200KT \quad n = 4/5 \end{array}$$

The effect of this is that doubling the yield increases CMP by only 1.56, whereas doubling the accuracy increases the CMP by 4. Doubling *both* increases CMP by 6.3. The effects of varying yield and CEP are shown graphically in Graphs 2 and 3.

Weapon Effect Terminology

Yield quantifies a nuclear explosion in comparison with High Explosive; ie, a 20KT explosion has the same effect as 20,000 tons of TNT.

Ground Zero is the point on the ground at which, or below or above which, the centre of a nuclear explosion occurs.

Fratricide occurs when multiple attacks on one target, or nearly simultaneous attacks on area targets lead to one weapon's explosion destroying or diverting others. The arrival of two warheads on a target can be arranged so that they reinforce each other's effect, but more than two warheads on one target is currently impracticable.

Throw-weight is the deliverable payload of a particular system, although some is devoted to the casing of the RV, bus-bars, etc.

Aggregate Probability of Damage (P_D)

is an expression of the probability of damaging silos and is expressed mathematically as:

$$P_D = 1 - 0.5 \, Exp \left(\frac{Total \ CMP \ in \ Force}{Silo \ Hardness} \right) K$$

Expressed in terms of a percentage probability, $P_D = 0.8$ means that there is an 80 per cent chance that all silos will be "killed", and, *ipso facto*, that 20 per cent will survive.

Important Caveats

A. Calculations of EMT, CMP and P_D are not precise as they are based upon assessments of values which are undoubtedly somewhat inaccurate. For example, CEP of Soviet RVs could be affected by inaccuracies in observation means, as well as by the desire of the US authorities (who are the only source of such information) to hide from the USSR its true understanding of its potential adversary's capability. Similarly, the US will wish to disguise its own capabilities. As can be seen from Graph 3 a small variation in CEP, especially below 0.5nm, can have a dramatic effect on the value of CMP.

B. There are also many dynamic factors which affect a force's war potential; eg, state of readiness, maintenance efficiency, penetration aids, ABM defences, SSBN hull noise, ASW capability and air defences against manned bombers, to name but a few.

C. Nevertheless, these calculations do have great utility in enabling static comparisons to be made, comparing like with like, and in identifying trends.

Command, Control and Communications (C³)

A vital factor in all strategic nuclear systems is C³. Any potential protagonist is, indeed, faced with yet another dilemma. On one hand, he may wish to cut his opponent's strategic communications and cause the maximum confusion and delay. Conversely, such disruption would prevent the other side from controlling its subordinates and might well lead to lower echelons acting in an illogical and unpredictable fashion, especially if communication with the political authorities is lost.

Similar arguments apply to satellites, where the destruction of one side's space-based early-warning, reconnaissance or communi-cations systems must be regarded as a major escalation, with a nuclear strike virtually the only effective and credible response.

SALT-II Agreement

The major effects of SALT-II as negotiated in Vienna in June 1979 are shown in the table on pages 18-19. It is, however, a matter of public record that US President Reagan and Secretary of State Haig are most unhappy with the Brezhnev-Carter agreement and intend to renegotiate on a tougher basis, seeking what they claim will be terms fairer to the United States. One thing is certain – some form of agreement is absolutely vital, for, as the following sections will show, a renewed strategic arms race could be disastrous, not only for the Superpowers, but for many other nations as well.

The Nature of the Balance

There are certain criteria for an aggressive nuclear power which is seeking either strategic predomin-ance or even "victory" in an actual conflict:

Possession of an effective and credible first-strike counter-force capability.
Possession of an effective and survivable retaliatory capability.
Maintenance of adequate active and passive shields over C³ assets.
Maintenance of adequate active and passive shields over the civil population.
Political determination to use these assets in an aggressive war.

On the other hand, the criteria for a defensive nuclear power, aiming only to deter aggression are rather different:

Possession of an effective, surviv-able and credible second-strike capability.
Maintenance of adequate active and passive shields over C³ assets.
Maintenance of adequate active and passive shields over the civil population.
Political determination to make timely decisions and to use the assets credibly under threat.

One point which emerges clearly is that in the Warsaw Pact the *only* strategic power is the USSR, which has total control over every single strategic nuclear asset

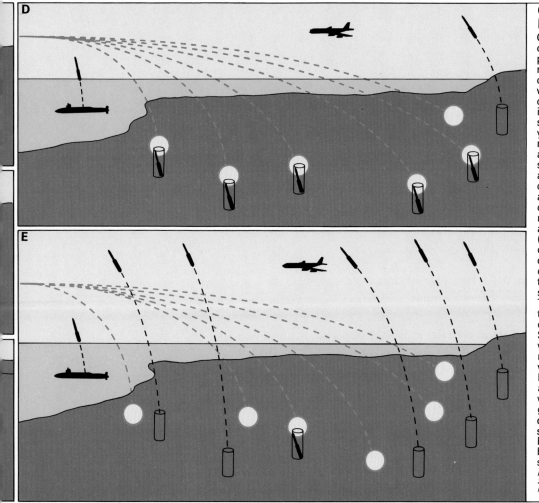

MRV

MARV

◀ *Circular Error Probable (CEP)*
This is the radius of a circle, centred on the target, within which 50 per cent of weapons aimed at that target will fall. *Re-entry Vehicles* are the protective bodies containing the warhead(s), penetration aids, etc, which return into the Earth's atmosphere.
Multiple Re-entry Vehicles (MRVs) are all aimed at the same target.
Multiple Independently Targetable Re-entry Vehicles (MIRVs) are all delivered by the same missile, but when released attack different targets.
Multiple Manoeuvrable Re-entry Vehicles (MARVs) are similar to MIRVs, but the warhead is terminally guided after re-entry on to its target.

Counter-military Potential

Counter-force capability depends on the circular error probable (CEP of the attacking missile (shown as cross-hatched circle, representing the area within which there is a 50-50 chance of a hit) and the yield of its warhead (shown as a red sphere of radius proportional to yield). Therefore the Counter-military Potential (CMP) of an attacking strategic force can be seen as a function of accuracy and yield. A hardened ICBM silo can be knocked out by a very accurate low-yield warhead (A), or by a less accurate one with a much larger yield (B). But a less accurate warhead with low yield (C) will almost certainly fail to destroy the target. An effective counter-force strike (D) would destroy many ICBM silos, but the chance (probability) of total success can never be absolute. Thus, some ICBMs will survive, together with strategic bombers on high alert and SSBNs. Should there be sufficient warning of the attack the victim may well decide to "launch-on-warning", which means that he launches his ICBMs prior to the arrival of the incoming warheads. The actual number to get away would depend on the degree of alert; the higher the status the more will be launched Bombers and SSBNs would still be able to carry out retaliatory strikes as well.

and decision. In the West, while the USA is indisputably the major military power, the existence of the independent British and French nuclear forces provides a significant complication for the USSR, a complication the Soviets just cannot ignore.

NATO's Deterrent; Warsaw Pact's Aggression

Next, there is a fundamental difference in the nature of these forces. The NATO nuclear forces are explicitly intended to deter war and a detailed examination of them shows that, should deterrence fail, they could only ever fight a defensive or retaliatory war. The nuclear forces of the USSR on the other hand are designed, organised and deployed for an aggressive,

war-fighting role concomitant with Soviet strategic doctrine.

The quantitative and qualitative evidence all points to a growing imbalance, with the USSR forging ahead in many of the critical fields. Indeed, the USSR is very near to satisfying the criteria for nuclear aggression listed above, while NATO barely meets the requirements for deterrence.

There are two absolutely fundamental points to consider about nuclear war. The first is that the use of just one nuclear device – whatever the yield – immediately creates a nuclear situation. Herman Kahn describes it thus:

"... once war has started no other line of demarcation is at once so clear, so sanctified by convention, so ratified by emotion, so low

on the scale of violence and – perhaps most important of all – so easily defined and understood as the line between using and not using nuclear weapons."

Devastation of First Strike

The second factor is that, due to their size, geographical locations and inherent military strengths, the only way that either the USA or the Soviet Union can be overcome by the other is by a devastating first strike. For each, therefore, nuclear war is the one incontrovertible threat to their national existence.

The USA explicitly, and the USSR by inference, base their global strategy on deterring each other. For such a strategy to work successfully a potential adversary must be convinced that the other

side possesses sufficient military force to ensure that should they precipitate hostilities they would be frustrated in achieving their goal, or would suffer so greatly that they would gain nothing.

Quoting estimates of fatalities caused by massive nuclear exchanges as ranging from a low of 20-25 million to a high of 155-165 million in the US and from 23-34 million up to 64-100 million in the USSR, former US Secretary of Defense Harold Brown said:

"... we must have forces, and plans for using those forces, such that in considering aggression against our interests, our adversary would recognise that no plausible outcome would represent success – on any rational definition of success."

Land-based ICBMs

▲ Early Soviet ICBM in its silo; probably an SS-7 (Sadler).

▲ SS-9 ICBM; some may still be in service.

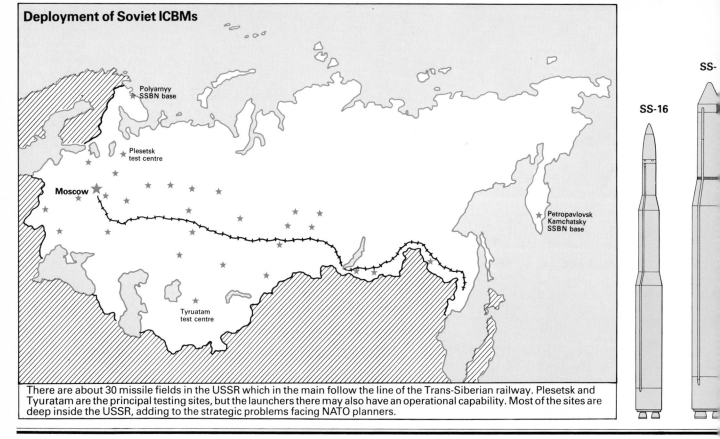

Deployment of Soviet ICBMs

There are about 30 missile fields in the USSR which in the main follow the line of the Trans-Siberian railway. Plesetsk and Tyuratam are the principal testing sites, but the launchers there may also have an operational capability. Most of the sites are deep inside the USSR, adding to the strategic problems facing NATO planners.

THE USSR currently deploys 1,398 ICBMs spread over many sites in a belt running across the centre of the country and straddling the Trans-Siberian railway. Well over 700 ICBMs are equipped with MIRVs, the remainder having very large single warheads of up to 25MT yield.

SS-9 has now been replaced but in the early 1970s SS-9 Mod 3 was tested as a Fractional Orbit Bombardment System (FOBS). As far as is known this was not deployed operationally, although 18 FOBS launchers still exist at the Tyuratam Test Centre. The threat of such a FOBS attack was sufficient to cause the USA to build a very costly radar station in Florida to cover the previously invulnerable southern entry route.

SS-11 has for many years been the most numerous Soviet ICBM, peaking in 1974 at 1,030, but these silos are now being progressively converted to take either SS-17 or SS-19. SS-11 Mod 1 has a single low-MT warhead, but Mod 3 has 3 MRVs, an interim step on the way to full MIRVs. SS-13 is still the only solid fuelled ICBM to have achieved operational status in the USSR, and 50 are deployed around Plesetsk, south of Archangelsk. For several years there were reports that the top stages of SS-13 were being deployed in a mobile role, but this has never been confirmed. Later SS-16 was also said to be a mobile ICBM, but it seems to have been a failure and has never reached operational status; in any case its production, testing and

deployment are now expressly banned by SALT-II. The principal significance of SS-16 is that its first two stages were used as the basis of the successful SS-20 which is now in service as a mobile IRBM. There is still concern in the West, however, that it would be relatively simple for the Soviets to place a third stage on an SS-20 and thus recreate an SS-16.

Re-use of Silos
SS-17 is one of two replacements for SS-11 and about 150 are now deployed. The first Soviet ICBM to be "cold-launched", the missile is ejected from its silo by a powerful gas-generator, and its first-stage motor fires only when above the ground. Such a technique virtually eliminates damage to the silos and,

as recently shown in an exercise, opens the way to re-use of the silo for a second launch. SS-17 was also the first Soviet ICBM with MIRVs, while the Mod 2 front-end is a powerful single warhead with a very high degree of accuracy.

SS-18 is the largest missile in service in the world and has two types of warhead: Mod 1, one 18 to 25MT; Mod 2, eight to ten MIRV each of 1 to 2MT. The SS-18 is cold-launched from a silo of new design and great hardness, although this is often installed in existing SS-9 launcher complexes. SS-18 has a throw-weight of 15,014lb (6,800kg), just *ten* times that of the USA's Minuteman-III and *twice* that of Titan-II.

This extremely potent weapon with its long range and great

▲ SS-11 ICBMs in containers parade through Red Square. At one time 1,030 of these missiles were deployed but only 520 remain.

SS-18

The status of SS-16 is uncertain, but it is banned under SALT-2. SS-17 (c.150 deployed) is the first cold-launch Soviet ICBM, and silo reloading has been practised. SS-18 (c.250 deployed) has a throw-weight 10 times that of the USA's Minuteman-III. SS-19 (c.300 deployed) was developed in parallel with SS-17. SS-20 is strictly an IRBM.

SS-19

SS-20

Soviet ICBMs – Performance Data

Missile		Number deployed Jan. 1981[1]	Range nm (km)	Throw-weight lb (kg)	War-heads	CEP nm (m)	Raw Total Yield[2]	EMT[3]	CMP[4]
	Mod 1	260	5940 (11000)	1500 (680)	1×0.95 MT	0.76 (1256)	247	251	435
SS-11	Mod 2	172	6480 (12000)	1500 (680)	1×1.1 MT	0.59 (975)	189	183	527
	Mod 3[5]	88	5723 (10600)	1500 (680)	3×0.35 MT (MRV)	0.59 (975)	92	90	261
SS-13		50	5076 (9400)	1200 (545)	1×0.6 MT	0.82 (1355)	30	36	53
SS-17	Mod 1	125	5400 (10000)	2205 (1000)	4×0.75 MT	0.24 (396)	375	413	7166
	Mod 2	25	5940 (11000)	2205 (1000)	1×3.6 MT	0.23 (380)	90	47	1110
	Mod 1	20	6479 (12000)	15000 (6800)	1×24 MT	0.23 (380)	480	98	3145
	Mod 2[6]	288	5940 (11000)	15000 (6800)	8-10×0.55- (MRV) 0.9	0.23 (380)	1584	1933	36547
SS-18	Mod 3	–	8639 (16000)	n.a.	1×20 MT	0.19 (314)	–	–	–
	Mod 4	–	5400 (10,000)	n.a.	10×0.5 MT (MIRV)	0.14 (231)	–0	–	–
SS-19	Mod 1	300	5157 (9550)	7000 (3175)	6×0.55 MT (MRV)	0.14 (231)	990	1208	61650
	Mod 2	–	5454 (10100)	7000 (3175)	1×4.3 MT	0.21 (347)	–	–	–
							4077	4256	110894

Notes:
1. Total numbers of each type of missiles deployed is taken from the reference document. Split into Mod 1, 2, 3, 4, etc, it has been calculated on basis of deployment dates and various statements in the technical press, and is inevitably somewhat arbitrary.
2. Raw Total Yield = Yield × Warheads × Missiles.
3. EMT = (Yield)$^{2/3}$ (but where Yield is more than 1 MT, EMT = (Yield)$^{1/2}$) × Warheads × Missiles.
4. CMP = ((Yield)$^{2/3}$ ÷ (CEP)^2) × Warheads × Missiles.
5. MRV is treated as one warhead of 1.05 MT.
6. Warheads and yields of SS-18 Mod 2 are variable. For this calculation a payload of 10×0.55 MT MIRV is assumed.
Source: "Aviation Week and Space Technology, June 16, 1980, pages 67-70.

accuracy is clearly intended for use against ICBM silos, and the Mod 1 with its large warhead and a CEP of 1,823ft (556m) has an estimated single-shot kill probability against a hard target of over 90 per cent. In fact, the CMP of the present Mod 1 is 82 (assuming a 20MT warhead) and if the Soviets could halve the CEP to 1mp (250m) the CEP would rise to a daunting 409. Fortunately, only 308 SS-18s are permitted under both SALT-I and SALT-II.

A second system, SS-19, was developed in parallel with SS-17, as a successor to SS-11, and the two missiles differ significantly. SS-19 is a two-stage missile and uses the hot-launch technique. Great accuracy is achieved in both versions with a CEP reported to be in the region of 1,519ft (463m). The

throw-weight of 7,010lb (3,175kg) is slightly less than that of Titan-II, but still five times that of Minuteman-III.

ASW ICBMs
One possible application of ICBMs by the USSR is as anti-submarine weapons against enemy SSBNs. The Soviet Minister of Defence is reported to have said in 1972 that the Strategic Rocket Forces had allocated some ICBMs to "navy groupings' at sea. The large yield of some Soviet ICBM warheads would be able to cause destruction over a large area and thus compensate for target movement during the time of flight as well as for slight inaccuracies in the initial location reports.

Deployment of SS-17, SS-18 and

SS-19 continues within the limits agreed under SALT-II and SS-11 will soon be completely replaced. A significant development in the new generation of ICBMs is that in the past the USSR kept only a small proportion of its ICBM force on quick-reaction alert, but these new launch vehicles now enable most, if not all, to be at a permanently high stage of readiness. A follow-on series of at least two new ICBMs is reportly being developed – *fifth* generation of Soviet missiles.

The current ICBM capacity available to the USSR is 1,328 launchers with 5,795 warheads.

An ominous development is the holding in 1980 of a reloading exercise during which, according to unconfirmed reports, some 40 silos were reloaded over a period of

two to five days. This certainly contravenes the spirit of SALT-II where the two nations undertook "not to supply ICBM launcher deployment areas with ICBMs in excess of a number consistent with normal deployment, maintenance, training and replacement requirements". They also undertook not to "develop, test or deploy systems for rapid reload of ICBM launchers". "Normal deployment" is defined in a clarifying document as "one missile at each ICBM launcher", while "rapid reload" is construed in the USA as anything less than 24 hours.

If the reports should be true then every single SS-18 silo would have to be targeted in a retaliatory strike to prevent a "third-strike" against CONUS.

Land-based ICBMs

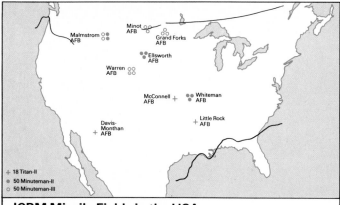

ICBM Missile Fields in the USA
US ICBM bases are in the centre of the country, apart from one Titan base in the south-west. MX basing is still undecided.

▲ Full-scale mock-up of the proposed MX ICBM (1978).

▲ Minuteman-III silo. Launch centre (right) controls 10 silos.

▲ Test launch of Ground-Launched Cruise Missile (GLCM).

THE ICBM leg of the USA's strategic triad has for some years comprised 54 Titan-II, 450 single-warhead Minuteman-II and 550 MIRVed Minuteman-III, a total of 1,054 launchers. Titan-II became operational in 1963; still by far the largest US ICBM, it carries a GE Mark 6 RV with a single 9MT thermo-nuclear warhead. This has three-target selection capability and is equipped with elaborate penetration aids. Although now elderly, Titan-II remains in service because it is the only US missile with anything like the throw-weight of the more numerous Soviet ICBMs. A recent DoD announcement that a new guidance system is under development suggests that Titan-II will remain in service for many years yet.

The main problem with Titan-II is its poor CEP which results in limited hard target kill probability. Hence it is unlikely to be consistently successful against Soviet ICBM silos.

Minuteman -I, -II, -III
The primary counter-force weapon is Minuteman. Minuteman-I became operational in 1963, but is no longer in service. Minuteman-II attained IOC in 1966 and 450 are in service with nine US Air Force squadrons. Minuteman-III has a revised third stage and a completely new front-end with three 170KT MIRVs. This GE Mark 12 warhead has a 298lb (135kg) thrust motor, and ten smaller motors for pitch-and-yaw, and roll control. A very high degree of accuracy is

attainable with a CEP of about 1,312ft (400m). The even more powerful and accurate Mark 12A warhead houses three 350KT MIRVs and has a high kill probability against very hard targets such as Soviet missile silos (1 shot, 50 per cent; 2 shots, 90 per cent). Three hundred Minuteman-IIIs are being retrofitted with Mark 12A Re-entry Vehicles.

The effect of increasing both accuracy and yield is shown very clearly by the Mark 12A RV where a decrease of 45 per cent in CEP and doubling the yield results in an increase in CMP from 6.06 to 41, a factor of 6.76.

A small number of Minuteman missiles have a special role. Their warheads have been replaced by radio equipment which can be

used as relay in the Emergency Rocket Communications System, a "last resort" system for crisis communications to strategic nuclear forces, especially SSBNs.[22]

Faced with evidence that its ICBM silos are high priority targets for Soviet ICBMs, the USA initiated development of a new system – MX – with an intended IOC of 10 missiles in July 1986. The configuration chosen for full-scale development included the maxima allowed under SALT-II.

An essential feature was that the missiles would be moved round a racetrack in a random fashion. This was at first to have been in a tunnel, but efforts were then concentrated on a loop system with a road some 14 to 20 miles (22 to 32km) long with 23 shelters on 2,296ft (700m)

▲ Launch of two Minuteman-III ICBMs.

▲ Launch of French S-3 missile; there are 18 launchers.

▲ French S-3 missile in silo.

Western ICBMs/IRBMs – Performance Data

Missile	Number Deployed 1981	Range nm (km)	Throw-weight lb (kg)	War-heads (MT)	CEP nm (m)	Total Raw Yield[1]	EMT[2]	CMP[3]
Titan-II	54	8076 (15000)	7500 (3400)	1×9	0.8 (1482)	486	162	365
Minuteman-II	450	5396 (10000)	1500 (680)	1×1	0.3 (800)	450	450	5000
Minuteman-III Mark 12 RV	250	7015 (13000)	1500 (680)	3×0.17	0.2 (556)	128	230	4543
Mark 12A RV	300	7015 (13000)	1500 (680)	3×0.35	0.11 (200)	315	447	36940
SBSN S-3 (France)	18	n.a.	n.a.	1×1.2	0.45 (834)	22	20	100
						1401	1309	46948

Notes:
1. Total Raw Yield = Yield × Warheads × Missiles.
2. EMT = Equivalent Megatonnage =(Yield)$^{2/3}$ × Warheads × Missiles.
3. CMP = Counter Military Potential = ((Yield)$^{2/3}$ + (CEP)^2) × Warheads × Missiles (but where yield is less than 0.2 MT (Yield)$^{4/5}$).
Source: "Rockets and Missiles", Bill Gunston, Salamander Books, London, 1979.

spurs. The distances and the transportation system were so designed that the MX missile could be moved from one shelter to another within the 30-odd minutes between the receipt of warning that Soviet ICBMs had been launched and the arrival of the warheads in the USA. The intention was to have had 200 missiles in service by late 1989, so that an attacker would have been faced with a permutation of 200 from 4,600 possible targets.

The "race-track" system was succeeded by another multiple shelter system, but based on linear tracks, and in December 1980 the US Department of Defense started discussions on possible sites. The arrival of the Reagan administration in January 1981 however,led

to a total reappraisal of the future requirements and a number of options are known to be under consideration.

The problem is, of course, to find an answer to the threat posed by the extreme accuracy, quick reaction time, and high reliability of the Soviet SS-18 and SS-19 ICBMs. While it is certain that an answer will be found the number of options is currently so great that speculation on the possible outcome would be dangerous. It would, however, be surprising if the MX missile was not to be deployed at all.

France's ICBMs
The only other NATO power with land-based strategic ballistic missiles is France, which currently

possesses 18 Sol-Sol Ballistique Strategique (SSBS) launch silos which will shortly complete re-equipment with S-3 missiles. S-3 delivers a 1.2MT thermonuclear warhead over a range of 1,875 miles (3,000km); the RV is equipped with penetration aids and is hardened against EMP. The first S-3 firing took place in 1976 and the missile started to enter service in 1980, replacing S-2 missiles on a one-for-one basis.[22]

President Giscard d'Estaing announced on 26 June 1980 that he had authorised development of a *lanceur strategique mobile* which could be either a strategic ballistic missile system (designated SX) or a cruise missile. The former appears the more probable, and there would be a great degree of com-

monality with the new SLBM M-4.

The West has 2,172 ICBM warheads compared to 3,550 for the USSR which gives an immediate imbalance in silo-targeting. The main dilemma facing the USA and France is the rapidly increasing accuracy (and thus CMP) of Soviet ICBMs. This means that if the launch of Soviet ICBMs is detected the two governments have the choice of either launching their own ICBMs within 20 to 30 minutes (launch-on-warning) or of seeing their missile fields demolished. The value of fixed-silo ICBMs in a retaliatory role is thus diminishing in inverse proportion to the increase in accuracy of first-strike ICBMs, and a mobile survivable system is urgently required to restore the balance.

Submarine-launched Ballistic Missiles

Side and plan elevation of Yankee class SSBN. Sixteen SS-N-6 SLBMs are carried in the raised decking abaft the fin.
▼

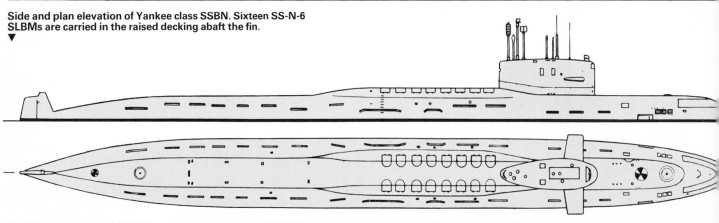

The West once hoped SS-N-8 was merely an improved SS-N-6; it is now known to outperform America's Trident C-4. ▶

▲ Hotel-II SSBN armed with 3 SS-N-5 missiles mounted in fin.

▲ SS-N-5 SLBMs of the type used in the Hotel-II shown above.

▲ Golf-II SSBN mounts 3 SS-N-5 in the fin; few are left.

▲ Delta-I SSBN armed with 12 SS-N-8 missiles.

THE FIRST true ballistic missile submarines were the Soviet Navy's diesel-engine Golf-class; all that remain are one Golf-III (3 SS-N-8), one Golf-IV (3 SS-N-6) and one Golf-V (3 SS-N-X). The first Soviet nuclear-powered submarines were the Hotel-class of which six Hotel-II and one Hotel-III survive. SLBMs in the Golf-class submarines and the Hotel-class all count towards the SALT-II missile limits, although the Golf hulls are not in launch platform totals.

The Yankee-class appeared in 1968, a total of 34 being completed by 1976. Far more formidable than the Golf and Hotel classes, the Yankees' short-comings are their rather bulky missiles which lack in range compared with Polaris. This means that Yankee-I must deploy close to the US coast to obtain good coverage of targets such as SAC bases, although a coincidental advantage is that the time of flight for such strikes would be short (6 to 10 minutes), thus effectively preventing counter-surprise "scrambles" at the bomber airfields. Yankee-I boats are being deactivated as new Delta-IIIs join the fleet to keep within SALT-II limits, and five have already been converted to SSNs. One Yankee-class has the experimental SS-N-X-17.

The Delta-class is currently the largest submarine in service in the world. Delta-I carries 12 SS-N-8 missiles, but was superseded in production by the Delta-II which carries 16 SS-N-8s, enabling the Soviet Navy to match Western boats' missile carrying capacity. Only four Delta-IIs were built, however, as the Delta-III then appeared with 16 SS-N-18 missiles, the first Soviet SLBMs with MIRVed warheads.

The first of the Typhoon-class was launched at Severodvinsk in September 1980, a monster of 30,000 tons displacement (three times the size of the Delta-IIIs and some 40 per cent larger than the US Navy's Ohio-class). This is reported to carry 20 of a new type of SLBM *forward* of the fin. Missile range is in excess of 3,507nm (6,500km) and 3 to 6 MIRVs are carried.

Vulnerability to Detection

Despite having some 70 SSBN (and three SSB) the Soviet Navy maintains only about 13 on patrol, of which a possible distribution might be three in the Pacific, five in the Barents Sea, and five in the North Atlantic. The USA mounts a very sophisticated effort to find and track these submarines (see Active Strategic Defences section). Their task is made easier by the generally poor design of the Soviet hulls which generate considerable noise, although this is slowly improving.

SS-N-18 has such a range that the Delta-III SSBNs can cover targets in CONUS from the Barents Sea and the Sea of Okhotsk, which provides them with much greater protection. The Barents Sea is currently an effective haven due to its proximity to the USSR, its distance from NATO bases and the

SS-N-6   SS-N-8

▲ 34 of these Yankee-class SSBNs were built armed with 16 SS-N-8. Five have now been converted to SSNs.

Soviet SLBMs – Performance Data

Missile		Number Deployed 1981	Range nm (km)	Throw-weight lb (kg)	Warheads (MT)	CEP nm (m)	Total Raw Yield (MT)[1]	EMT[2]
SS-N-5		18	864 (1600)	n.a.	1×0.8	2.0 (3700)	14	16
SS-N-6	Mod 2	234	1620 (3000)	1984 (900)	1×0.65	1.0 (1856)	152	176
	Mod 3	234	1620 (3000)	1984 (900)	2×3.5 (MRV)[3]	1.0 (1856)	164	184
SS-N-8		280	4860 (9000)	3968 (1800)	1×0.8	0.84 (1560)	224	241
SS-NX-17		12	2700 (5000)	16534 (7500)	1×1	0.75 (1410)	12	12
SS-N-18	Mod 1	144	8963 (16000)	n.a.	3×0.2 (MIRV)	0.76 (1000)	86	148
	Mod 2	32	4320 (8000)	n.a.	1×0.45	0.76	14	19
							666	706

Notes:
1. Raw Total Yield = Yield × Warhead × Missiles.
2. EMT = $(Yield)^{2/3}$.
3. MRV is treated as one warhead of 0.7 MT yield.
   Source: "Aviation Week and Space Technology", June 16, 1980, pages 69-70.

generally inhospitable environment. Its shallowness limits the effectiveness of long-range ASW, while the sea-ice covering large areas prevents the deployment of sonobuoys and other sensors.

Communications

Soviet sources publish little on strategic communications, but obviously the Soviet Union faces the same problems and finds generally similar solutions as do the NATO operators. A national command authority exists with buried command posts and alternatives, together with emergency national airborne command posts. The primary means of communicating with SSBNs appears to be five VLF transmitters with outputs exceeding 500kW.

The USSR has large numbers of communications satellites but none has been specifically identified as being used for communications to SSBNs. The Volna satellites launched in 1980 are very similar to US Navy communications satellites; one is over the Atlantic, the second over the Indian Ocean, and the third over the Pacific. The potential for use with SSBNs is clearly there.

As a final back-up, HF radio would doubtless be used, although the SSBNs would have to come near to the surface to receive it. Further, HF is particularly susceptible to atmospheric interference, which would be intensified in the immediate aftermath of a nuclear first strike.

Again, there is little information

available on Soviet Navy navigation methods and missile accuracy. The main navigation system is satellite based, somewhat similar to the US Navy's TRANSIT, but thought to be relatively inaccurate. There is also less redundancy than there is in the USA's system. In the absence of total precision in fixing the launch position, the Soviet Navy seems to be opting for mid-course corrections, and SS-N-18 is credited with CEP of 0.76nm (1,410m), which is much better than that of earlier Soviet SLBMs such as SS-N-6 with a CEP of 1nm (1,853m), but still much worse than that of US missiles with a CEP of 0.3nm (550m). There is no reason why the Soviets should not continue to refine their systems, eventually reaching the same degree

of accuracy as the Americans.

The Soviet Navy seems to have more problems with its SSBN fleet than do the Americans. By maintaining no more than 10 to 15 boats on patrol a sure signal would be given to the US if large numbers of SSBNs were to be seen putting to sea over a short period of time. Further, any SSBNs caught in port could be destroyed in a nuclear strike. Also, it is much less difficult for the US and its allies to keep track of 10 to 15 SSBNs on the high seas rather than (say) 30 to 40.

The major shortcoming of the Soviet SSBNs is their relatively poor navigational accuracy, leading directly to a large CEP. This must confine them to a countervalue role against cities and "soft" military and industrial targets.

Submarine-launched Ballistic Missiles

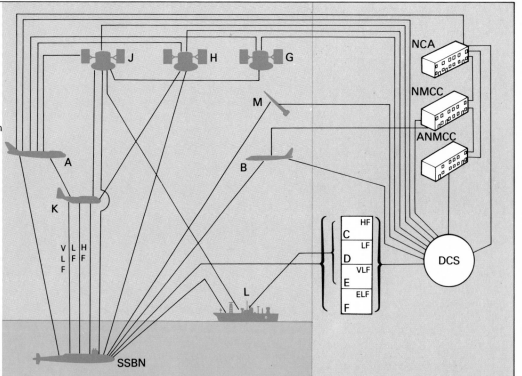

Communicating with Submarines

One of the most critical aspects of SSBN operations is to seek to guarantee communications in a nuclear war; this diagram shows some of the complicated and expensive methods available to the USA. Highest authority is the National Command Authority, which is backed up by the National Emergency Airborne Command Post (A). Orders can then be passed through the National Military Command Centre or its Alternate. CINCPAC, CINCLANT and CINCSAC also have airborne command posts (B). The Defense Communications System (DCS) has ground-based transmitters operating in the High (C), Low (D), Very Low (E) and Extremely Low (F) Frequency bands. There are also communications through the Defense (G), Air Force (H), and Fleet (J) satellite systems. Relays are also possible through the TACAMO system (K), surface ships (L), or the Emergency Rocket Communications System (M). This complex system is the price to be paid for a viable and credible second-strike nuclear deterrent.

▲ USS John Marshall (SSBN 611) of the Ethan Allen class.

▲ USS Sam Rayburn (SSBN 635) armed with 16 Poseidon SLBMs.

THE OLDEST SSBNs in service with the US Navy are the five boats of the Ethan Allen class, armed with 16 Polaris A-3 SLBMs. The short range of the missile (2,500nm, 4,630km) makes them vulnerable to Soviet countermeasures and it has been decided that the age of the hulls (all launched between 1960 and 1962) precludes conversion to take Poseidon. Two have already been dismantled and three converted to SSNs before the first of the Ohio boats even started its sea-trials.

There are 31 of the Lafayette-class currently in service. Constructed betwen 1961 and 1966, the whole class was converted to take the new Poseidon C-3 SLBM between 1969 and 1978. These will serve until 1985 at least, and the

next stage is the further conversion of 12 to take Trident C-4 missiles. The first (USS *Francis Scott Key*) was modified in 1978 to sea-test the Trident and returned to the fleet as the first operational Trident SSBN in October 1979. She will be joined by others by the end of 1982.

Purpose-built as the launch vehicle for the Trident missile, the Ohio-class of 18,700 tons displacement was thought to be large by any standard until the Soviet Navy's Typhoon-class of 30,000 tons was revealed. The USS Ohio was scheduled to be commissioned in early 1981, but this was delayed until June because of "modifications and improvements". Eight have been authorised, with long-lead funding for a further three.

These boats carry 24 Trident missiles and the hull design is much quieter than any previous SSBN, thus making acoustic detection much more difficult. The great increase in range (Trident: 3,831 nm, 7,100km; Polaris 2,500nm, 4,630km) means these submarines (and the Trident-converted Lafayettes) can operate at much greater distances from the USSR and remain in what amount to US-dominated waters. Research into future systems is continuing; one prospect is a smaller, cheaper SSBN but still capable of carrying 24 Trident missiles.

SSBN Communications

The mobility of SSBNs and their ability to hide themselves in the depths of the oceans brings two

serious problems, the first of which is command and control, ie, the ability of the national command authorities to communicate by reliable, secure and survivable links to their strategic links to their strategic forces. This is especially true of the USA where the SSBN force is specifically required to survive a Soviet first strike and then retaliate.

Implementation of the Single Integrated Operational Plan (SIOP) will originate with the National Command Authority (NCA). Executive instructions will then be issued by the National Military Command Center (NMCC) or, if that has been destroyed, by the Alternate NMCC or, in the last resort by the National Emergency Airborne Command Post (NEACP).

▲ Launch of Trident C-4 missile.

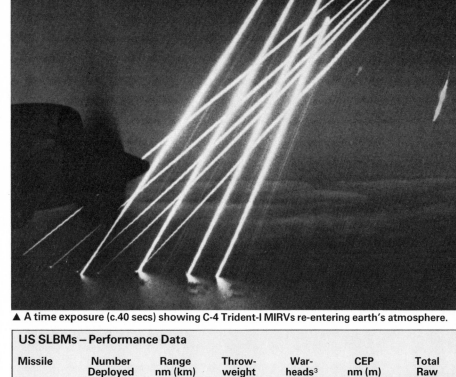

▲ A time exposure (c.40 secs) showing C-4 Trident-I MIRVs re-entering earth's atmosphere.

US SLBMs – Performance Data

Missile	Number Deployed 1981	Range nm (km)	Throw-weight lb (kg)	War-heads[3]	CEP nm (m)	Total Raw Yield (MT)[1]	Equivalent Mega-tonnage[2]
Polaris A-3	80	2498 (4630)	1400 (635)	3×0.2 (MRV)	0.5 (926)	48	57
Poseidon C-3	304	2498 (4630)	1500 (680)	10×0.04 (MIRV)	0.3 (550)	122	356
Trident C-4	96	3830 (7100)	2500 (1135)	8×0.1 (MIRV)	0.3 (550)	77	165
						247	578

Notes:
1. Total Raw Yield = Yield × Warheads × Missiles.
2. Equivalent Megatonnage = (Yield)$^{2/3}$ × Warheads × Missiles.
3. MRV is treated as one warhead of 9.6 MT.
4. Source: DoD Annual Report FY82 page 49.
Note: No US SSBN yet has an effective counterforce capability so no figures for CMP are given.

The primary survivable communications are provided by the TACAMO system, which comprises 12 C-130 Hercules aircraft, one of which is always airborne over the Atlantic and a second over the Pacific. The primary link to submerged submarines is by Very Low Frequency (VLF) transmission using a 6.2 mile (10km) trailing-wire antenna and a 100kW transmitter. When it is required to transmit, the aircraft banks in a continuous tight circle with the antenna hanging vertically below.

TACAMO is essential to the US second-strike capability and is currently regarded as survivable. The USSR must, however, treat these aircraft as prime targets and is doubtless developing satellites for detecting and tracking them;

their destruction might be quite a different matter, however.

A second major system is "Austere Extremely Low Frequency" (ELF) which lies in the 0.3–3kHz band. This will comprise some 124 miles (200km) of buried antenna to be located in Michigan state. US SSBNs are known to have received ELF at depths of about 330ft (100m).

Another major problem is precise navigation, since the accuracy of the SLBM at the target depends to a great extent upon the accuracy with which the launch point is known. Again a multiplicity of systems is used to ensure that at least one will survive. The basic system is Ship's Inertial Navigation System (SINS); unfortunately this needs periodic updating from

external sources and is also the victim of limitations of knowledge and accuracy of the precise shape of the earth.

Many other systems, eg, Omega, Loran-C and the Transit satellites are also used. One future system, Navstar, is expected to give positions to an accuracy of + 22.9ft (+ 7m) horizontally and + 32.8ft (+ 10m) vertically. Alternatively, missile accuracy can be improved by midflight corrections and terminal guidance, both under study in the USA.

Assessment

About one-third of any naval force is usallly in port at any one time for maintenance, repair, exchange of crews, or major refits. Thanks to good management the US Navy

manages to keep 55 per cent of the SSBN force at sea on average, and this will increase to 65 per cent when sufficient Trident-armed boats are available.

The Polaris/Poseidon/Trident force has up to now given the USA a reasonable assurance of a second-strike capability. There has been concern over the survivability of the communications systems but this has been overcome by multiplicity of means and a high degree of redundancy. Navigation and precise position-finding problems are being slowly mastered, to the extent where the USSR could become concerned over the possibility of the US SSBNs becoming capable of a counterforce strike against hardened targets, ie, a first-strike capability.

Submarine-launched Ballistic Missiles

▲ RN launch of Polaris A-3 SLBM.

▲ Mark 84 fire-control computer in RN SSBN.

▲ RN Polaris submarine HMS *Repuls*

▲ A Royal Navy rating at the controls of the British Polaris submarine HMS *Repulse*.

▲ Loading French M-4 SLBM.

▲ 16-Polaris Resolution.

THE UNITED Kingdom's Polaris force had its genesis in the Bermuda Agreement between President Kennedy and Prime Minister Macmillan. The four Resolution-class submarines were commissioned betwen 1967 and 1969, each armed with 16 Polaris SLBMs. The missiles themselves were purchased direct from the United States, but the warheads and re-entry vehicles have always been designed and manufactured in the United Kingdom, thus giving the British Government ultimate national control over deployment, launching and targeting, although normally the Polaris force is "assigned" to NATO. It was originally intended to build a fifth boat, but this was cancelled in 1965.

The effectiveness of the UK strategic force is being maintained by an interim programme (codename: Chevaline) which will upgrade the effectiveness of the Polaris A-3 missiles through improvements to the RVs and warheads, and advanced penetration aids will be carried. This programme has cost about £1 billion and will maintain the effectiveness of the force until the late 1990s, despite known improvements to Soviet ABM systems.

In the longer term the UK intends to purchase Trident missiles from the USA but, as with Polaris, an entirely British warhead will be installed. These missiles will be deployed in new British SSBNs; four are currently planned, but a decision on a fifth will be taken in

1982 to 83. Construction of the SSBNs will start in 1987 with an IOC in the early 1990s and a life expectancy through to 2020 at least. The four-boat programme will cost some £5,000 million, and the fifth would add a further £600 million, the total costs being spread over some 15 years.

The British government published some of its background thinking at the time of the announcement of the Trident decision. A ground-launched force in the British Isles was rejected as being unlikely to achieve the necessary degree of invulnerability to surprise attack. Air-launched missiles were also rejected because of the threat to airfields. Surface ships were ruled out mainly because of the ease with which they

can be detected and tracked. Submarine-launched cruise missiles (SLCMs) were found to be more expensive than SLBMs for an equal probability of mission success; in fact, 11 SSGs armed with 80 SLCMs had less assured deterrent capability than 5 SSBNs with 16 Trident-1s.

The French SLBM Force

France's nuclear deterrent has been developed entirely within her own national resources, a truly remarkable achievement. The first SSBN, *Le Redoutable*, was laid down in March 1964 and became operational in 1971. Her first three sister ships joined the fleet in January 1973, July 1974 and December 1976 but, unlike the British, the French then decided to

NATO SLBMs – Performance Data							
Missile	Number Deployed 1981	Range nm (km)	Throw-weight lb (kg)	War-heads (MT)	CEP nm (m)	Total Raw Yield (MT)[1]	Equivalent Mega-tonnage[2]
UK Polaris[3]/[4] A-3	64	2482 (4600)	1400 (635)	3×0.2 (MRV)	0.5 (926)	38	46
France MSBS M-20	80	1618 (3000)	n.a.	1×1	0.54 (1000)	80	80
						118	126

Notes:
1. Total Raw Yield = Yield × Warheads × Missiles.
2. Equivalent Megatonnage (EMT) = (Yield)$^{2/3}$ × Warheads × Missiles.
3. MRV is treated as one warhead of 0.6 MT yield.
4. British RV is assumed to have same performance as US Polaris A-3.

▲ French SSBN *La Redoutable* armed with 16 MSBS M-2 SLBMs. Conversion to take M-4 missiles starts soon.

build a fifth boat which became operational in May 1980. A sixth, *L'Inflexible*, a more advanced design, is now under construction and should be launched in mid-1982. French plans then envisage an entirely new class which, like the British boats, will enter service in the early 1990s and serve through until at least the 2020s.

The current French missile is the Mer-Sol Ballistique Strategique (MSBS) M-20, a two stage missile with a range of some 1,600nm (3,000km). Compared with the previous system, M-20 has a much improved RV, a 1MT thermo-nuclear warhead, counter-ABM hardening and penetration aids. The next step is M-4 which has five to seven MRVs of about 150MT each; *L'Inflexible* will be built to

take M-4, while four of the other five boats will all have been modified to take it by 1986.

Assessment

Keeping sufficient SSBNs at sea is a problem for the US Navy with 36 boats; it is much more of a critical consideration for the smaller British and French navies. The Royal Navy guarantees to have one boat at sea on patrol at all times, with a second frequently also at sea; it would also probably get a third to sea in time of crisis.[28] The French, however, have publicly stated that they must have six hulls in order to ensure that three SSBNs are continuously available, of which two are on patrol. Both navies would be very badly affected if the Soviet Union was to make

a technological breakthrough in the ASW field in view of the minimal number of boats actually on patrol simultaneously.

NATO's submarine-based strategic nuclear forces are unusual in that they are operated by three different navies, under three entirely separate national controls. SSBNs are the most survivable of the current strategic nuclear systems *when on patrol at sea*, and there is no doubt that the US Navy's force poses the major second-strike threat to the USSR.

The great benefit of the British and French SSBN fleets, however, is that they provide second and third nuclear decision making centres in Western Europe. Their value is enhanced by the fact that both countries have total control

over their warheads, unlike the position over the land-based missiles such as, for example, Lance, where, because the warheads are American, there is a dual-control arrangement. The Soviet Union must, therefore, be convinced that if she were to attack Western Europe and the USA held back, then the UK and France, individually or in concert, could inflict an unacceptably destructive blow upon Mother Russia.

The navigational accuracy of the British and French SSBNs can be expected to be nearly equal to that of the USA and probably better than that of the USSR. But, both the British and French SLBMs can currently only perform counter-value roles, especially the French with their single RV missiles.

Manned Bombers

▲ Tupolev Tu-22M (Backfire) carrying an AS-6 (Kingfish) air-to-surface missile. *(Photo: Royal Swedish Air Force.)*

▲ AS-6 (Kingfish) under left wing of Soviet Tu-16.

▲ Low-flying Tu-22 (Blinder-B) with AS-4 (Kitchen) missile.

▲ Air-to-surface AS-6 (Kingfish) missile.

THE SOVIET Union's strategic air arm – VVS-DA – comprises some 800 aircraft. The strategic bombers declared as nuclear delivery vehicles in SALT-II were some 49 Tupolev Tu-95 (Bear) and 100 Myasischev Mya-4 (Bison). More than half the Tu-95s are fitted to carry the AS-3 (Kangaroo) air-to-surface missiles, while the remaining Tu-95s and all the Mya-4s serve as nuclear-capable gravity bombers. Both these types have long since gone out of production and some Western intelligence services await the appearance of a new bomber with an intercontinental capability.

The only long-range bomber currently in production for VVS-DA (and for AV-MF) is the Tupolev Tu-22M (Backfire), and over one hundred have been deployed in various versions. According to the "understandings" reached in the Summit talks at Vienna in June 1979 the Tu-22M would be excluded from SALT-II provided that production is limited to 30 per year and the USSR does not give it an intercontinental capability.

Tu-22M is normally armed with the AS-4 (Kitchen) stand-off missile, but a new missile has recently been seen on a Soviet Naval Aviation "Backfire-B". Tu-22Ms based in the Western Soviet Union can already strike all western European countries in an unrefuelled mission, but this new missile would simply enable the aircraft to stand-off even further – maybe to the extent of not even having to leave Pact airspace.

Tu-22M is certainly a strategic aircraft as far as western Europe is concerned, but a great deal of argument has taken place over its potential as an intercontinental bomber against the continental United States. The Department of Defense states that Tu-22M could reach the USA on a one-way, high altitude, subsonic, unrefuelled mission with recovery in the Caribbean area (obviously a reference to Cuba). With Arctic staging, in-flight refuelling and certain high altitude cruise profiles, Tu-22M could "probably" execute a two-way mission from the USSR to most parts of the USA. Significantly a tanker version of the Ilyushin Il-76 (Candid) is reported to be under development.

Tu-95, Mya-4 and Tu-22M are all capable of delivering conventional gravity bombs, which obviously include nuclear warheads. In addition, however, the USSR has for many years included air-to-surface missiles in their armoury. The principal weapons in use are the AS-4 (Kitchen), AS-6 (Kingfish) and at least one completely new weapon. AS-4 was first revealed in 1961 and has slender delta wings, a cruciform tail and a liquid-propellant rocket motor. The guidance system is generally assumed to be inertial, although it may include mid-course updating by Tu-95 or other suitable aerial platform. AS-4 is assumed to be nuclear-capable; it weighs some 15,435lb (7,000kg) and has a range of about 185 miles (300km) at

▲ Egyptian Tupolev Tu-16 carrying AS-5 missiles. Of 25 launched against Israel in 1973 only 5 got through.

▲ AS-1 (Kennel) was the first Soviet ASM to enter service.

▲ AS-3 (Kangaroo) the largest ASM yet to enter service.

USSR Strategic Bombers – Performance Data

Aircraft	Number Deployed 1981	Unrefuelled Combat Radius nm (km)	Max Speed (Mach)	Estimated Weapon Load	Total Raw Yield	Equivalent Mega-tonnage
Tupolev Tu-95 (Bear)	100	3900 (7227)	0.78	1× MT (AS-3)	100	100
Myasischev Mya-4 (Bison)	49	3250 (6022)	0.87	1× MT (gravity bomb)	49	49

Mach 2. AS-6 is launched at about 36,000ft (11,000m) altitude and climbs rapidly to 59,000ft (18,000m) where it cruises at Mach 3 for some 400 miles (650km) before diving onto its target. Warhead yield is an estimated 200KT,

Recent US reports identify two new Soviet manned bombers. One, designated Bomber-X, is a 250,047lb (113,400kg) Mach 2.3 variable-geometry penetrator; the second, Bomber-H, is a subsonic, large (390,064lb, 176,900kg) missile-launching platform. A prototype intercontinental bomber is known to have been tested unsuccessfully in the mid-1970s, and another (and completely different) machine has been undergoing flight testing since 1976. Tenta-

tively designated Tupolev Tu-160 by some Western sources, this may be Bomber-X.

Assessment
The intended use of the present range of manned bombers and ASMs of the Soviet nuclear forces must be a matter for conjecture. Precision attacks in a conventional phase would be practicable using stand-off weapons, but without elaborate deception measures it seems unlikely that Tu-95 and Mya-4 would be able to get through. Even ASMs would not be guaranteed success in the face of determined and capable air defences. In a nuclear war the most likely task of the VVS-DA would seem to be to overfly target countries after the strike to assess

success and then fill in any gaps in the bomb plot where considered necessary.

The Backfire (Tu-22M) seems less of a threat to CONUS than the USA's own forward-based tactical nuclear strike aircraft are to the USSR. Tu-22M is nevertheless a most serious threat to Western Europe, where the US forward-based nuclear strike aircraft tend to redress the imbalance in theatre terms.

A most tantalising question is whether the USSR has, either in the course of its own researches or as a result of espionage, paralleled the reported American breakthrough in "stealth" technology. If this is so then the aircraft would presumably be similar to those types in the USA which, according

to an official spokesman "are virtually invisible to air defence radars, infrared and other electronic detection systems, and even acoustic detectors".

The present "air-breathing leg" of the Soviet triad can be seen to be largely irrelevant to the USA, but the threat is much more significant to European members of NATO, especially from the Tu-22M. Should any of the current development programmes (Bomber-H, Bomber-X) result in production aircraft, however, the implications for CONUS could be very serious, since the US air defences have been virtually dismantled over the past 10 to 15 years, while civil protection is for all practical purposes non-existent (see Passive Strategic Defences – NATO).

Manned Bombers

NATO Strategic Bombers – Performance Data

Aircraft	Number Deployed 1981[1]	Unrefuelled Combat Radius nm (km)[2]	Max Speed (Mach)	Estimated Weapon Load[3]	Total Raw Yield[4]	Equivalent Mega-tonnage[5/6]
B-52D		3100 (5744)	0.95			
B-52F		3385 (6272)	0.95	1.6×1 MT gravity bomb	555	555
B-52G	347	3385 (6272)	0.95	3.84×0.2 MT SRAM	266	456
B-52H		4060 (7523)	0.95			
FB-111	65	1550 (2872)	2.5	2×0.5 MT gravity bombs	26	44
				2×0.2 MT SRAM	65	82
Mirage IVA (France)	33	770 (1426)	2.2	1×0.6 MT gravity bomb	20	23
					906	1160

Notes:
1. Figures used here for the B-52 fleet are those for aircraft on operational units, ie, those that would be immediately available in a crisis.
2. Combat radius depends on many variables, eg, bomb and fuel loads, mission profile, etc.
3. Gravity bomb and SRAM loadings depend on the mission, range, etc. Weapon loads used here represent an *average across the whole bomber fleet,* and are derived from "American and Soviet Military Trends Since the Cuban Missile Crisis" by John M. Collins, Center for Strategic and International Studies, Washington, DC, 1978, page 106.
4. Total Raw Yield = Yield × Warheads × Bombers.
5. Equivalent Megatonnage (EMT) = $(Yield)^{2/3}$ × Warheads × Bombers.
6. Strategic bombers must of necessity take some hours to reach their targets and are thus second-strike weapons. No CMP figure is therefore given although they could be used in a precision role against any remaining hard targets.
Source: "Air Forces of the World", Salamander Books, London.

▲ Proposed FB-111H.

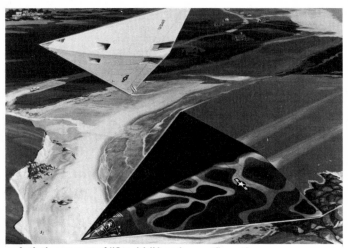

▲ Artist's concept of "Stealth" bomber configuration.

▲ AGM-86A ALCM launched from a B-52G trials aircraft.

LONG-RANGE bombers remain an integral part of the USA's strategic triad, the Pentagon describing them inelegantly as "the air-breathing leg". Their mission would be to carry out a second-strike, penetrating Soviet defences at low level, following flight profiles which avoid known or suspected radars and SAM sites. They would use the full spectrum of electronic aids to confuse the enemy and delay identification. Attacks would be carried out using stand-off missiles of various types, but the large number of aircraft (347 B-52s, 65 FB-111s) should ensure that a good proportion would penetrate.

In addition to the US aircraft the French Air Force maintains a force of 33 Mirage IVA bombers. These 400-odd aircraft would have to penetrate the most comprehensive air defence system in the world.

Long-serving B-52

The mainstay of the US bomber fleet is the Boeing B-52. When the production lines closed in June 1962 a total of 744 had been built, and the remaining aircraft are expected to serve until the year 2,000.

The models remaining in service are approximately 80 B-52D, 22 B-52F (training),172 B-52G and 90 B-52H, although there are a further 219 in "deep storage". B-52Ds are capable of delivering only gravity bombs (a maximum of four thermonucler devices per aircraft) and are currently being fitted with a Digital Bombing-Navigation System (DNBS). B-52Gs and -Hs were all modified in the 1970s to carry a maximum of 16 Short-Range Attck Missiles (SRAM), an effective weapon armed with a nuclear warhead.

A lengthy development programme for an Air-Launched Cruise Missile (ALCM) has led to a production order for some 2,300 Boeing AGM-86B. The B-52Gs are scheduled to be ALCM launch-platforms, with an IOC of December 1982, although the full operational capability will not be attained until 1990. It was announced recently that in addition to the B-52Gs all B-52Hs are to be fitted with the new Offensive Avionics System (OAS) which gives the USA the option of converting the -Hs to the ALCM role.

Two wings of FB-111As will remain in the inventory for the foreseeable future. They can be armed with up to six SRAM, but a more likely load is two SRAM and four gravity bombs. The FB-111A is a very sophisticated and highly effective aircraft and with air-refuelling has a very good penetration probability.

Two attempts have been made to develop a successor to the venerable B-52. The first was the Boeing B-70 Valkyrie, a fixed-wing aircraft which was cancelled in the 1960s. Next came the Rockwell B-1, a swing-wing aircraft which first flew in December 1974, but this was cancelled in its turn by President Carter in June 1977. The USAF requirement was for 241 aircraft, but all that remains are four test-programme prototypes.

▲ B-1 may now be procured to replace ageing B-52s.

Strategic Aircraft Bases in the USA
USAF SAC bases are scattered throughout the USA, but overseas bases can also be used in time of tension. All can be considered prime targets for Soviet ICBMs and SLBMs.

- • 18 B-52
- ◎ 15 EC/RC-135
- + 30 SR-71/U-2
- ▲ 30 FB-111

▲ The ASALM concept.

▲ FB-111A with SRAM.

▲ Mirage IVA of the French Air Force taking off using ATO rockets to shorten its run. Payload is one 60KT atomic bomb.

Even the Carter Administration became concerned about the state of the B-52 fleet, however, and in 1980 initiated long-range planning for a possible follow-on manned bomber. This will presumably make use of the "stealth" technology which, according to former US Defense Secretary Harold Brown, "enables the US to build manned and unmanned aircraft that cannot be successfully intercepted by existing air defense systems" (but early service use cannot be expected).

In another field the USAF has recently completed system definition for a Cruise Missile Carrier (CMC), a subsonic aircraft capable of rapid production should the B-52 become ineffective as an ALCM launch vehicle either through old age or some unexpected advance in Soviet air defences. One of the leading proposals is for a converted Boeing 747 airliner carrying no fewer than 72 ALCMs.

ASALM Project
Another project under active consideration is the Advanced Strategic Air-Launched Missile (ASALM). One role for this weapon would be to replace SRAM as a stand-off bomb, but a further capability being planned is the destruction of Soviet AWACS during a penetration mission; whether these two disparate roles could be performed by one missile system remains to be seen.

The only other NATO country with a strategic bomber capability is France, with a total of 33 Mirage IVs in two wings. These aircraft are armed with AN-22 gravity bombs with a 60 to 70KT nuclear warhead. Tasked with low-altitude penetration the prospect of mission success for these aircraft is diminishing and their nuclear role is scheduled to disappear in 1985, leaving 12 Mirage IVAs in a strategic reconnaissance role only. There is, however, growing pressure in some circles in France for the new Mirage 4000 to be developed as a successor to Mirage IVA in the strategic bomber role.

Assessment
NATO's strategic bomber force suffers from several inherent problems. The first is that of pre-launch survivability against SLBM attack, which can be alleviated by improved warning times, faster getaway and nuclear hardening. Once in the air the bomber has a considerable transit in which it must endeavour to escape detection. Following that it must fight its way through an electronic jungle over Soviet territory, a battle in which failure will result in direct physical attack. The fact is, however, that provided enough bombers start the mission at least some aircraft and missiles will get through; clearly the USSR believe this to be a credible threat as their massive air defence system shows. Indeed, it might be that the primary achievement of the bomber fleet is to cause the USSR to divert massive resources into air defences.

Military Space Programmes

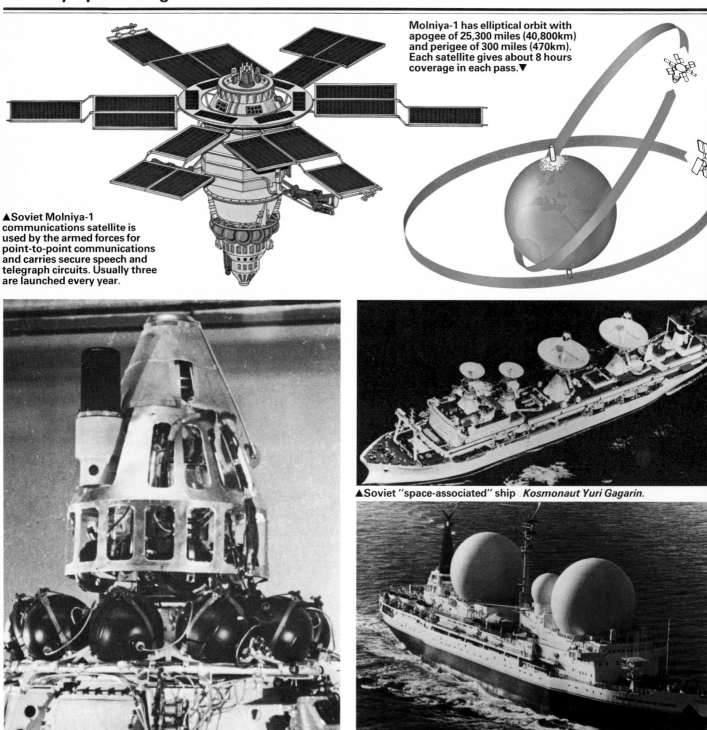

Molniya-1 has elliptical orbit with apogee of 25,300 miles (40,800km) and perigee of 300 miles (470km). Each satellite gives about 8 hours coverage in each pass.▼

▲Soviet Molniya-1 communications satellite is used by the armed forces for point-to-point communications and carries secure speech and telegraph circuits. Usually three are launched every year.

▲Correcting drive unit of Molniya-1 satellite.

▲Soviet "space-associated" ship *Kosmonaut Yuri Gagarin.*

▲A second "space-associated" ship, the *Kosmonaut Komarov.*

SOVIET MILITARY comsats fall into three groups. For point-to-point communications Molniya-1 satellites are used, placed in highly elliptical orbits which allow about 8 hours coverage during each pass. About three are launched each year, interspersed with the later Molniya-2 and -3 series. All are equipped to carry television, radio, telephone and telegraph channels.

The Soviet military also use a series of storage/dump satellites. Placed in orbit eight at a time, they pass information when real-time transmission is impossible. Launches are made about two or three times a year and some 30 are operating at any one time. The third type of comsat is also believed to be a storage/dump type, used to record data from clandestine sensor equipment and agents and then replay it to receiving stations in the USSR.

Early Warning and Surveillance
Soviet EW satellites are placed in elliptical 12-hour orbits. The first is believed to have been Cosmos 159, launched in 1967; launchings were then carried out at a rate of one per year until 1977 when three were launched, indicating a move to operational status. Cosmos 775, launched in October 1975, is in a geosynchronous orbit, and this may indicate a new generation of Soviet EW satellites.

Ferret satellites are launched about four times per year. As with the USA, larger ferrets are used for a detailed examination of the sources, and these are launched at a rate of about one a year.

In ocean surveillance the Soviets appear at first sight to have a clear lead. The fact is, however, that they lack overseas bases from which to fly long-range patrol aircraft, and those that are available (eg, Cuba) provide limited logistical support. Satellites therefore offer the ideal solution to the problems of ocean surveillance.

Cosmos 198 (December 1967) was the first test mission for a system which became operational in 1974. Two of these satellites are launched within a few days of each other; each carries a powerful radar for locating ships in any weather and a radio-isotope thermal generator to provide the power. The Soviets also use a smaller, non-nuclear ferret-type ocean surveillance; the first was launched in December 1974 and one has been flown each year since, interspersed with the nuclear-powered satellites.

US Ships Targetted?
In the wake of the Cosmos-954 disaster, however, the ocean surveillance programme underwent a reorientation. None was launched in 1978 and then in April 1979 two of the non-nuclear type were launched which were described by US Defense Secretary Brown as being fully capable of targeting US naval ships at sea.

The Soviet photographic reconnaissance programme began with Cosmos-4 in 1962 and the number

Laser Beams in Space

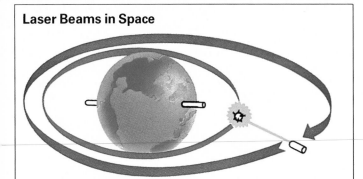

Laser beams directed from satellites might be used to knock out enemy satellites, either by destroying them outright or by damaging sensitive equipment. The diagram shows laser equipment pursuing an elliptical orbit 4,300 × 6,000 miles (6,92 × 9,650km) above the Earth to counter low-to-medium altitude satellites on reconnaissance or other military duties, such as strategic communications.

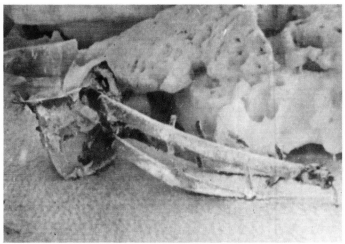

▲Wreckage of Cosmos-954 which crashed in Canada in 1978.

"Death Ray" ABM system

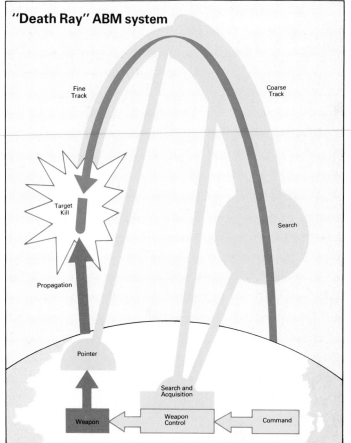

Could a death ray be devised to destroy ballistic missiles in flight? The diagram shows a hypothetical weapon system which first identifies and tracks the incoming warhead. After a period of coarse tracking the beam projector locks on and the weapon discharges to achieve a "kill". Nearer operation are high-energy lasers but the atmosphere can cause the beam to bloom or defocus, reducing its target lethality.

USSR Military Satellites

Name	Length ft (m)	Diam ft (m)	Weight lb (kg)	Launch Vehicle	Orbit miles (km)	Purpose
Vostok-based recon satellite	16.4 (5)	6.56 (2)	8820 (4000)	A-2	105×186 (170×300)	Orbital reconnaissance satellites carry high resolution camera plus manoeuvre engine. Normal lifetime is 12 to 14 days. Numerous sub-varieties
Ferret (large)	16.4 (5)	4.9 (1.5)	5512 (2500)	A-1	391×404 (630×650)×81.2°	Detailed survey of operational characteristics of military radar and radio stations
Ferret (small)	6.56 (2)	3.28 (1)	?	C-1	311×342 (500×550)×74°	General survey of military radar and radio stations
Nuclear-powered ocean surveillance satellite	45.9 (14)	6.56 (2)	?	F-1-m	161.5×174 (260×280)×65.1° (after separation) 590 (950) circular orbit	Locate shipping by use of radar. A pair of satellites are launched within a few days of one another. Uses nuclear reactor to power equipment. After completion of 60-70 day mission reactor unit is fired into higher orbit

of launches increased through the 1960s, finally stabilising at about 30 annually. Both the high-resolution and the search-and-find satellites eject capsules for recovery, while should the retrorocket fail the satellites can be destroyed, thus preventing them from falling into unfriendly hands. An improved version appeared in 1968 with a lifetime of 12 days.

Since 1976 an advanced reconnaissance satellite has been under development which is believed to be a modified Soyuz spacecraft; the first was Cosmos 758. Initially there were about two launched per year, and the satellite's lifetime is approximately 30 days. The most advanced recconnaissance satellite is a modification of the Salyut space station, which gives the

USSR capabilities equal to the USA's Big Bird or KH-11. With resupply by Progress spacecraft, or a Soviet shuttle, they could conduct year-long missions.

Weather and Navigation Systems

In contrast to the USA, the USSR was slow to fly weather satellites but since 1967 the Meteor series has been operational. Soviet navigation satellites use exactly the same procedures and frequency bands as the US Transits. The Soviet system was first flown in November 1967 (Cosmos 192) and reached operational status in 1971. About five a year are launched.

The Soviets appear to lead the US in ASAT capability. In October

1967 the USSR began testing an ASAT system. In the early tests between 1967 and 1971 seven successful interceptions were achieved. Tests were resumed in 1976 when Cosmos 804 intercepted Cosmos 803. The next test in April 1976 used a new technique; the whole mission occupied less than one orbit, reducing the warning time during which the target could take evasive action. Also, unlike previous profiles there was no extensive manoeuvring before interception. These tests which continued through May 1978 indicated that the USSR could destroy low-altitude reconnaissance, ferret and navigation satellites. A further series of tests was started in April 1980, culminating in a very obvious attack on a Soviet target

satellite positioned over eastern Europe. Also alarming are reports of Soviet charged particle beam weapons carrying out successful attacks on targets returning from space.

Even more threatening that ASATs is the possible establishment of nuclear weapons in orbit. In late 1967 it was revealed that the USSR had been carrying out test flights of a FOBS, which, as it does not describe a high ballistic arc through space, would seriously shorten warning time, and could approach the USA from any direction. 18 FOBS launchers still exist at Tyuratam, but are now considered obsolescent. The USSR has indicated its intention to dismantle them when SALT-II is ratified by the US Congress.

Active Strategic Defences

The Strategic Environment

A basic tenet of Soviet military thinking is that the defence of the USSR is best achieved by offensive actions outside the national borders. Nevertheless, the USSR, in addition to being the Homeland, is also the national military and economic base and must therefore be defended by conventional means. The first problem facing Soviet planners is that of sheer size: the USSR stretches for 5,250 miles (8,000km) from its border with Poland to its Pacific coastline with a total area of 8,599,300sq. miles (22,271,327km²). The second major problem is that, as viewed from Moscow, the USSR is totally surrounded by potential enemies, but with three predominant threats: by land from Europe in the West and from China in the East, and by air (ICBMs SLBMs, cruise missiles and manned aircraft) from almost any direction, but particularly from the USA. In such a strategic environment the active strategic defences of the USSR, while being numerically strong are, in fact, faced with a major task.

The Airborne Warning Competition

Below and below right: With their ground and air forces in the European theatre fully manned in peace and at a high state of readiness for war, the major concern for both sides is that the other might catch them by surprise. Increasingly important in preventing such surprise are the AWACS and SUAWACS systems whose coverage is shown below (solid arcs represent radar coverage of low-flying attackers; dotted arcs, coverage of high-flying attackers). On constant patrol they confer greater confidence that the other side will not be able to "steal a march".

Soviet Air Defences

★ Air Force Div/Reg HQs   ▨ PVO Concentrations   ● Space/Missile Complexes

Above: This map shows the major concentrations of the USSR's air defences and illustrates very clearly the scale of their problem. Obviously, they see the most immediate air threat as coming from Western Europe, while the most vital economic and population concentrations are in the western USSR. This must lead to a concentration of air defence effort in that area. There is still, however, a vast area to be covered, a situation exacerbated by the advent of ALCMs and GLCMs which can threaten the USSR from any direction. Remaining air defences are either thin or non-existent.

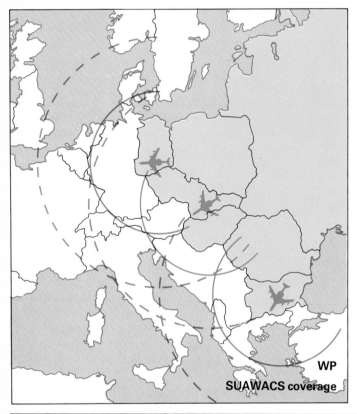

WP
SUAWACS coverage

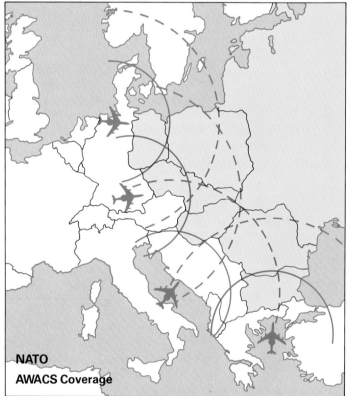

NATO
AWACS Coverage

THE RUSSIAN people have been obsessed with the security and defence of their homeland since Napoleon's invasion of 1812 and the subsequent attacks in 1904, 1915–17, 1917-1919 and 1941–44. Therefore, it is hardly surprising that strenuous efforts should be made to provide the people with the most effective defences, especially against air attack.

The Soviet early-warning system starts, like the USA's, with satellites, great numbers of which have been launched annually; in 1979, for example, the USSR launched 83 military space vehicles compared to 9 by the USA.

Ballistic missile acquisition and initial tracking is the responsibil-

ity of the huge 20 × 984ft (20 × 300m) Hen House radars, which are believed to be capable of detecting targets at ranges of 3,200nm (6,000km). These delegate to a Dog House radar which is capable of identifying and discriminating between warheads and decoys at ranges up to 1,500nm (2,800km). Finally, if warheads were aimed at the capital city, Moscow, one of the Try Add sites would acquire the targets and launch Anti-Ballistic Missiles (ABM).

Patchy ABM Forces

The USSR still retains this unique Galosh system; there were four sites around Moscow with a total of 64 launchers, but the Soviets announced in 1980 that they have

dismantled 32 of these. A total of 100 launchers is permitted under the 1972 ABM Treaty. There are persistent reports of continuing R and D into ABMs, which is also allowed, and that a mobile system may be ready for production, which is not. The Moscow system could easily be saturated by incoming warheads, and there is at present no ABM protection at all for any other part of the Soviet Union, which is not, in any case, permitted.

A new phased-array radar, said to be four times the size of the USA's PAVE PAWS is reported to be nearing completion near Moscow. This might well be able to combine acquisition and engagement functions, handling a large number of simultaneous targets,

and able to sort out warheads from decoys.

Aircraft and attack missile intruders are acquired in the first instance by the large radars (Hen Egg, Hen Roost) scattered around the periphery of the USSR and targets are then handed over to the thousands of smaller radars further inland. There are some 2,700 interceptor aircraft and 12,000 SAMs in the National Air Defence Command (PVO-Strany). There are also ten Tupolev Tu-126 AWACS aircraft, augmented by a growing number of the new Ilyushin Il-86 SUAWACS.

Improving Anti-aircraft Missile Forces

SAM defences were first deployed around Moscow in 1956 and the

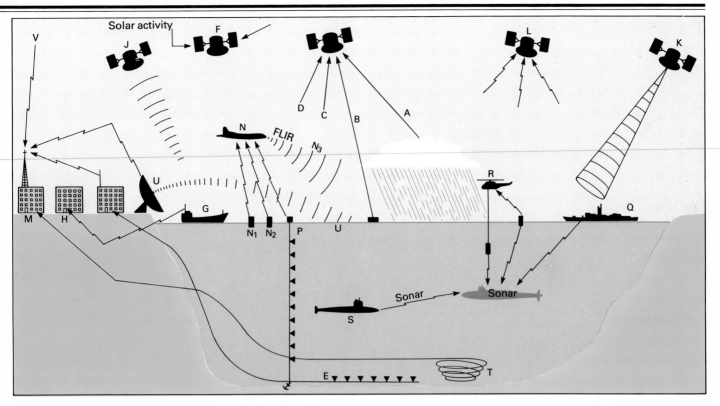

The Detection of Ballistic Missile Submarines

Great efforts are devoted by the major navies to improving their ASW capability, especially against SSBNs. The diagram shows the major systems involved and can be assumed to apply equally to the USA and USSR.

Because water is a complex propagation and conduction medium it is first necessary to establish what the existing conditions are. Satellites monitor weather (A), sea-state (B), oceanographic data (C) and thermal variations (D), while one of the functions of seabed surveillance systems (E) is to locate and identify all unwanted noise sources (eg, fish). Another satellite relates solar activity to natural variations in the earth's magnetic field (F). It is also important to identify and eliminate merchant vessels (G), either by voluntary reporting (H) or by satellite tracking of their radar emissions (J).

Separating-out Submarine Emissions

The first step in tracking SSBNs is by satellite photography (K) as they leave port. Thereafter the first line of surveillance is electronic monitoring with surveillance from satellites (L) and land-based stations (M).

Active seekers include aircraft, surface ships and hunter/killer submarines. ASW aircraft (N) use a combination of detectors including: magnetic anomaly detection (MAD), sonar (using expendable sonobuoys (N_1), temperature measurements (N_2)

and forward-looking infra-red (FLIR) (N_3). A new US system (Rapidly Deployed Surveillance System) (P) uses a torpedo-sized sonobuoy which is delivered by aircraft or submarine and then lowers a string of hydrophones, and anchors itself. Switched on and off by remote commands, RDSS transmits data to aircraft or satellites. Surface ships (Q) depend primarily upon sonar, the sensors usually being hull-mounted. Increased use is now being made of Variable Depth Sonar (VDS) by the Soviet Navy, whilst western navies seem more interested in towed arrays. Ship-based helicopters (R) use sonar (either sonobuoys or dunking) and many are also equipped with a MAD magnetometer. Hunter-killer submarines (S) depend upon sonar, either hull-mounted or on a towed array.

The most important passive devices are sea-bed arrays, such as the USA's Sound Surveillance System (SOSUS) (E). Large coil arrays (T) are also laid on the seabed to monitor variations in the electric field of the oceans. Finally, traces of an SSBN's passage through the water can be detected at considerable distances by Over-the-Horizon-Backscatter (OTH-B) (U), aircraft-mounted Forward Looking Infra-Red (FLIR) (N_3) and satellite.

All these sensors produce such a vast volume of raw data that it must be fed into a computer for analysis (V). The Americans, for example, use a computer called Illiac-4 for real-time collation and analysis of array-gathered information; this uses 64 normal computers in parallel, with a 10^9 (one billion)-bit memory.

---

missile used – SA-1 – is still in use today. The current mainstay of the surface-to-air system is SA-2 (Guideline), widely deployed throughout the USSR as part of the extensive system estimated at some 12,000 launchers on 1,650 sites. There are six SA-2 launchers surrounding a central fire-control unit; missile guidance is by automatic radio-command with radar target-tracking.

SA-3 (Goa) is a low altitude missile with a slant-range of 15 miles (24km) and is widely used throughout the Warsaw Pact. It complements SA-2 and is radio-command guided with radar terminal homing. SA-5 (Gammon) is deployed in the Moscow-Leningrad complex for long range, high altitude interception, and may

have an ABM capability. Its guidance system is radar homing.

SA-4 (Ganef) and SA-6 (Gainful) are battlefield SAMs, but also protect the westernmost Military Districts in the USSR as well as the Eastern European countries. Like all radio/radar directed systems these Soviet SAMs are all vulnerable to jamming, and an ECM counter to SA-6 has been developed in the USA, based on examination of a system captured in the Yom Kippur war.

SA-10, which covers 984 to 13,123ft (300 to 4,000m) is now being fielded; this has active radar terminal guidance and a speed of Mach 6. Trials of SA-10 radar being used in the ABM mode have been detected and are causing concern in the USA. A new ABM capable of

intercepting incoming ICBM and SLBM warheads in the atmosphere has also reached the trials stage.

Fighter Aviation

Defences against manned aircraft have made enormous progress since the Tallinn Line was set up along the western boundary of the USSR in the mid-1950s. Today the air defence system has been improved in quantity and quality of radars and interceptors deployed along the entire western border from Murmansk in the north to the Turkish frontier; depth has also been added with particular emphasis on the Moscow-Leningrad area and Baku.

More than 2,700 interceptors are deployed by the IA-PVO, many of which have an all-weather capa-

bility. The most important type is the Sukhoi Su-15 (Flagon) which is steadily replacing earlier types such as MiG-21 (Fishbed), Su-9/11 (Fishpot), and the trans-sonic Yak-28P (Firebar). A specialised long-range interception function is performed by the big Tu-28P (Fiddler). MiG-25 (Foxbat-A) interceptors are being joined in service by the much improved MiG-25M (Foxbat-E).

To this must be added aircraft of the Warsaw Pact countries, especially those of the Polish, Czech and East German air forces, which together have more than 1,000 interceptors.

It must be concluded that, despite the vast expenditure, the WP air defence system is not likely to be foolproof in the near future.

Space Systems

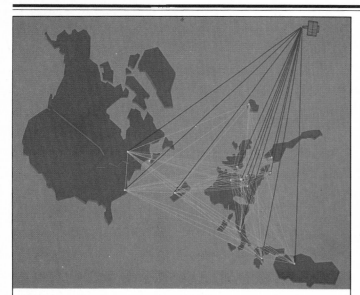

NATO Communications Satellite

The NATO satellite communications system uses three satellites to provide reliable and efficient communications between 12 earth stations. Such strategic comsats are very cost-effective but are totally vulnerable to any anti-sattellite (ASAT) interceptor.

▲ US missile satellite monitoring ship—USNS *Vandenburg.*

USA Military Satellites

Name	Length ft (m)	Diam ft (m)	Weight lb (kg)	Launch Vehicle	Orbit miles (km)	Purpose
KH-11 also Project 1010	64 (19.5)?	6.56 (2)?	30000 (13605)?	Titan IIID	155×329 (250×530)×96.95°	Orbinal reconnaissance. Possibly both high resolution and search-and-find cameras. Live "real time" television transmissions of photos. Lifetime in excess of one year.
Titan IIIB-Agena D reconnaissance satellite	26.2 (8)	5 (1.5)	6615 (3000)	Titan IIIB-Agena D	84×205 (135×330)×96.4°	Orbital reconnaissance. Believed to be a search-and-find type which seeks out new targets for Big Bird and KH-IIs. Lifetime in excess of 50 days.
Big Bird also Project 467	50 (15.2)	10 (3.05)	30000 (13608)	Titan IIID	99×168 (160×270)×97°	Orbital reconnaissance. Carries large high resolution camera, having resolution better than 1 ft (0.3m). Film returned by six capsules. Also carries search-and-find camera equipment. Lifetime approximately 180 days.
TACSAT 1	25 (7.6)	9 (2.7)	1600 (726)	Titan IIIC	Geostationary	Tactical communications between US forces in the field using small transmitters
FLTSATCOM	16 (4.9)	8 (2.4)	2176 (987)	Atlas-Centaur	Geostationary	Communications between US Navy vessels
NATO 2	5.25 (1.6)	4.5 (1.37)	285 (129)	Thrust-Augmented Delta	Geostationary	NATO Comsat, links US and NATO countries
Defense Meteorological Satellite (Block 5D)	17 (5.18)	6 (1.8)	1043 (473)	Thor-Burner 2	500 (804.5)×98.7°	Provides weather information for US forces, available for civilian use
DSCS 2	13 (3.96)	9 (2.74)	1100 (499)	Titan IIIC	Geostationary	Real-time communications between the US forces
Vela *Data refer to Vela 11 and 12 throughout*	4.17 (1.27)	4.17 (1.27)	571 (259(	Titan IIIC	Vela 11: 69106×69796 (111210×112160)×32.4°	Detection of nuclear detonations on Earth's surface, within the atmosphere and out to 100 million miles (161 million km); solar flares and other space radiation. Instruments: X-ray, gamma ray, neutron, optical, electromagnetic pulse and energetic-particle detectors

THE USA WAS the first nation to fly a military comsat system – Defense Satellite Communications System (DSCS 1), which reached full operational status in June 1968. Next came DSCS 2, employing a much more advanced satellite with multiple channel access and utilising smaller ground stations. Now four such satellites plus three spares are flying. The DSCS 3 series were launched in the Spring of 1981.

For communicating between ships the US Navy has developed the Fleet Satellite Communications System (FLTSATCOM). Four satellites plus one spare make up the operational system, each having 30 speech and 12 telegraph channels. A more mysterious craft is the Satellite Data System, which is launched into a highly elliptical orbit similar to that used by the Soviet Molniya comsats; this is believed to be used to communicate with US nuclear forces in the polar regions.

Early Warning Systems

On 5 May 1971 the first successful Integrated Missile Early Warning System (IMEWS) was launched. Further launches have been carried out at a rate of about one per year. These satellites carry large infra-red telescopes and television cameras to transmit the pictures of detected ICBMs. This technique has been adopted to overcome the failings of earlier systems such as MIDAS, which was affected by sunlight reflected off high-altitude clouds. They can detect an ICBM within seconds of ignition, and warnings are transmitted to ground stations in Australia and Guam from where they are relayed to North American Air Defense Command (NORAD).

Replacing them is a new system codenamed Rhyolite. These satellites are placed in geo-synchronous orbit; the first of a total of four was launched in March 1973. A follow-on system, codenamed Aquacade, is under development.

A very important role of military satellites is the verification of agreed limitations of strategic arms and the monitoring of new developments. By 1961 Discoverer satellites were returning high quality pictures which were instrumental in ending US fears of a massive ICBM build-up.

The other part of the US orbital reconnaissance effort is the "search-and-find" satellite – principally an effort to locate and identify new weapon developments and deployments in the USSR. The fourth generation recce satellites were a departure in that they combined the functions of earlier types: "Big Bird" made its debut in June 1971. It is equipped with a large camera, possessing a resolution better than 1ft (0.3m) from an altitude of 100 miles (161km). An average of one or two Big Birds are launched per year, and their time in orbit is now 90 to 180 days. A CIA satellite, Key Hole 11 (KH-11) was launched in 1976; similar in size to Big Bird it flies in a higher orbit and uses digital transmission systems. Tragically, a

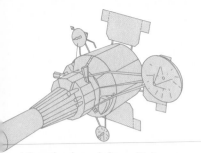

▲Carrying large infra-red telescopes and television Cameras, the Integrated Missile Early Warning Satellite (IMEWS) of the USAF can detect an ICBM within seconds of ignition and can transmit the warning to ground stations in Australia and Guam, with relays to NORAD HQ near Colorado Springs. It has complex safeguards to prevent false alarms.

▲ American NKC-135 aircraft is being used to test laser weapons in the anti-satellite role.

Artist's concept of USAF's Big Bird recce satellite. Films are ejected in capsules recovered by aircraft in mid-air "snatches". Big Bird plays a key role in tracking down and identifying new Soviet aircraft and missiles.▼

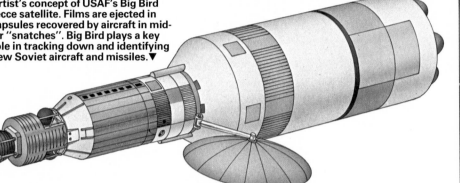

▲ Courier 1, an early US Army Comsat.

▲ The Belgian terminal station on the NATO Comsat system.

ASAT Attack

How an air-launched anti-satellite system based on the Boeing SRAM missile/Thiokol Altair 3 would work. The missile is launched in a zoom-climb by an F-15 using target data supplied by NORAD. The satellite is destroyed by an infra-red homing device which separates from the Altair stage. The head incorporates cryogenically cooled IR telescopes capable of identifying a satellite by its thermal signature against the space background. This is one of two American concepts being considered. The other, mounted on a missile or satellite, would destroy its target with impacting fragmentation warheads.

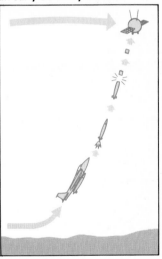

former CIA employee sold the KH-11 manual to a Soviet agent in March 1978 – for a meagre $3,000.

The US Space Shuttle has considerable military potential and could be used to deploy the next generation of reconnaissance satellites. The very large payload could be used to allow comprehensive tests of various systems, as well as the construction of large structures such as radar antennas in space.

The US also flies a series of "ferrets" – highly classified electromagnetic monitors, as well as devices for detecting and analysing nuclear tests.[38]

One of the benefits of the space programme is the provision of accurate weather information, giving both long-range military forecasts and key support to the reconnaissance satellites, preventing valueless pictures being taken of clouds. The latest USAF weather satellite is RCA's Block 5D, which provides infra-red and visual imagery, temperature/moisture soundings, auroral detection and upper atmosphere soundings. Two are operational at a time.

The US Navy Transit system was designed to provide fixes for SSBNs, accurate to 0.1nm (160m). Transit's successor is the Navstar Global Positioning System which is accurate to 33ft (10m). It had been hope that the final 24-satellite network, in three orbital planes would be completed in 1984, but budget cuts envisage a reduced system of 18 with a decrease in accuracy of 19.7ft (6m).

Anti-Satellite Systems

In times of crisis satellites would make tempting targets and the USA first studied ASATS in 1959, which led to a limited operational system in the mid-1960s. In late 1976 the USAF began a new series of ASATS studies, and a research contract was awarded for two separate concepts. One is a direct-ascent system launched from a high-flying aircraft, and the other a fast-approach killer satellite.

Recent US studies indicate that laser satellites might be able to blunt a mass ICBM attack, laboratory tests indicating that an ICBM would explode within one second of being hit. An ASAT application would, however, be easier since beams of moderate strength could damage highly sensitive electronic equipment. Much research is now being devoted to the problem of protecting satellites from such beam weapons. Efforts are also being made to produce optically and radar "invisible" satellites akin to the "stealth" aircraft identified by President Carter.

An alternative is the charged-particle beam, but this requires enormous power, and massive and expensive installations. Directional control must be exact, and the earth's magnetic field bends the beam. If the beams could be directed at their targets from space, however, they could well be effective weapons.

Since both systems are still in the experimental stage there may well be still further limitations not yet identified or understood.

Active Strategic Defences

▲SR-71 strategic reconnaissance aircraft of the USAF.

▲USAF U-2 electronic surveillance and research aircraft.

▲NATO Air Defence Ground Environment (NADGE) station.

▲The first Boeing E-3A AWACS for NATO in its new livery.

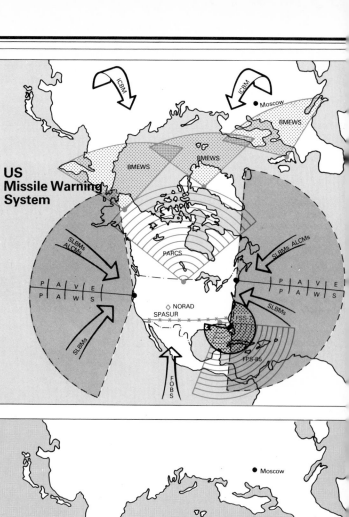

THE USA's attack-warning and assessment facilities are, at first glance, impressive. First warning of any attack should come from satellites, and would be confirmed by ground-based radars. Covering the northern approaches are three BMEWS radars, backed up by PARCS (a converted radar originally built as part of the abortive Safeguard ABM system). BMEWS and the PARCS stations are currently being upgraded to provide quicker detection and earlier impact predictions for a greater number of incoming RVs.

The USAF contribution to the Space Detection and Tracking System (SPADATS) comprises two radars in the USA and two overseas, complemented by an optical system using Baker-Nunn cameras at four sites, around the world. The USN operates the Space Surveillance system (SPASUR) which detects and tracks objects in space passing through an electronic "fence"; there are three transmitting and six receiving stations in the USA. Coordination and analysis are provided by the Space Defense Center at the NORAD Combat Operations Headquarters.

Detecting SLBMs

Surveillance radars, based on the ground around the seaboards confirm SLBM attacks. Two new PAVE PAWS radars became operational in 1980 replacing six of the seven FSS-7 stations; the seventh FSS-7 and the single FPS-85 — both situated in Florida — continue to cover the south-east approaches, especially the very sensitive Caribbean area. FPS-85 also guards against the possibility of a FOBS attack from the south.

These systems are designed with one aim in mind: to present to the NCA accurate and timely information of a Soviet missile attack to enable quick decisions to be made on the appropriate response. There is, no other "defence" than to launch the USA's retaliatory strike as there are now no ABM systems.

Detecting manned bombers and ALCMs is a different matter, especially at low-level. The elderly Distant Early Warning (DEW) line is still operational, but plans are under consideration to replace the 31 remaining stations with more modern equipment (Enhanced DEW). To improve further detec-

tion of Soviet intruders the USA is considering two Over-the-Horizon Backscatter (OTH-B) radars, one on the east coast, the other on the west. Northern cover is not feasible due to problems with electrical interference from the aurora borealis; Enhanced DEW will fill the gap. One OTH-B station is under test in Maine; system validation should be completed in 1981/2 when a decision will be made on the second.

These systems are completed by seven AWACS aircraft, whose prime function is to provide "lookdown" cover against attempts at under-the-radar penetration. Once thousands of SAMs were deployed; there are now only eight batteries of Nike Hercules: three in Alaska, four in Florida and one at

US Ballistic Missile Warning System

NORAD satellites over the Indian Ocean would sense Soviet ICBM launches within 90 seconds of blastoff and instantly warn ground stations at Guam and near Alice Springs, Australia. But they would lose sight of missiles before penetration aids separated, so BMEWS would take over to track and identify missiles coming from the north. PARCS could determine the number of RVs and warn of impact sites. Satellites and PAVE PAWS phased array radar systems would warn of SLBM and ALBM attack and there is improved coverage of threat from the Caribbean and FOBS attack from the south. The US Naval Space Surveillance System (SPASUR) is stretched across the southern US; this is one of the satellite detection and tracking nets reporting on earth-orbiting space objects to NORAD's Space Defense Center inside Cheyenne Mountain. There are blind spots though, especially with Soviet SS-N-6 and -8 SLBMs.

US Detection of Manned Bombers and ALCMs

Because, currently, Soviet bombers flying at low altitudes could probably penetrate undetected through radar coverage gaps in Canada and the ocean approaches, the US DoD is experimenting with Over-the-Horizon Backscatter radars (as shown in the diagram below left). Funding has been planned through 1982-86 with IOCs in FY 1984 and FY 1986. The gaps are in the Pine Tree Line long range radar coverage; moreover it is felt the ageing DEW Line stations in the north could also be bypassed. Options being considered for improvement here are an enhanced Distant Early Warning (EDEW) Line and a north-looking OTH-B. As a long-term goal the US is pursuing the capability to detect and track bombers from space. Further, AWACS flying surveillance and management stations add their capabilities for maintaining perfect watch on every kind of aerial vehicle, friendly and otherwise, over a radius exceeding 200 miles (322km).

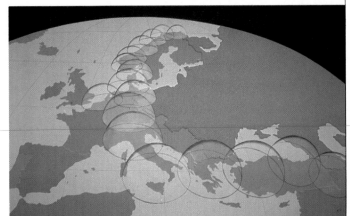

NATO's NADGE System

The NATO Air Defence Ground Environment (above) provides the air defence system for the whole of NATO Europe and involves a large number of locating sites consisting primarily of radars, computers and electronic data transmission facilities.

Underwater Detection

The map below shows: Known and presumed location of US and allied sea-bottom sonar arrays. Probable maximum area for this system. Additional area under surveillance by USN P-3 ASW aircraft.

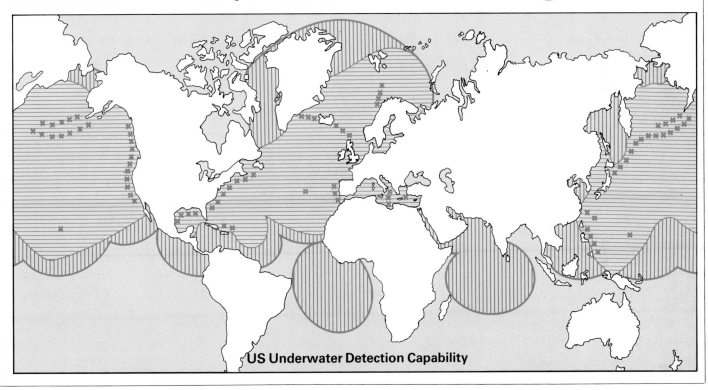

US Underwater Detection Capability

Fort Sill. The only other AD forces deployed to defend North America are 386 elderly interceptors of the USAF and RCAF.

Western Europe

In western Europe early warning and active air defence is characterised by:

A recent reassessment of the air threat from the Warsaw Pact;

A fair degree of commonality between nations except – and for different reasons – the UK and France;

A much greater commitment to active AD than in CONUS.

Typical of the change of heart is the UK where for some 20 years defensive measures were allowed to run down, whereas recently there has been a marked upgrading in the British air defences.

Radar cover has been extended to give all-round protection against aircraft such as Tu-22M, and interceptor aircraft are being improved, especially with the advent of Tornado ADV. Archaic Shackleton AEW aircraft will shortly be replaced by Nimrods giving a quantum leap in effectiveness. SAM defences are still thin, but long-established Bloodhounds have recently been suplemented by Rapiers to give point defence at selected key RAF airfields, while the USAF has ordered Rapier SAMs for the defence of its airfields in East Anglia.

For European countries a major element is the USA's sophisticated inputs, especially for intelligence derived from strategic surveillance means such as satellites. Tactical information comes from the chain of radar stations of the NATO Air Defence Ground Environment (NADGE), into which is linked the UK system (UKADGE). France has its own ground-based system (STRIDA) which is linked to both NADGE and to the autonomous Spanish system (Combat Grande). All this will be reinforced by the NATO AWACS force (18 Boeing E-3A) and the UK's contribution (11 Nimrod AEW).

Active AD is, with the exception of France, under command of SACEUR. His AD assets include 565 interceptors in peace, to be augmented in tension and war by reinforcements from CONUS as well as with other fighter aircraft in their secondary role. French interceptors (134 aircraft) would also work in cooperation with SACEUR, although remaining under French command. A great improvement has taken place with the arrival of the USAF F-15 and yet further enhancement will follow as F-16, Tornado ADV and Mirage 2000 enter service with various NATO air forces.

Over 1,000 SAMs are in service, most of them rather elderly (eg, Nike Hercules) and their ability to deal with low-flying aircraft and cruise missiles is suspect. Though they may have seemed adequate to face a bomber force comprised of lumbering Tu-95s and Mya-4s, the air defences of NATO are now sadly inadequate, considering current Soviet long-range bomber and ALCM development.

Passive Defences

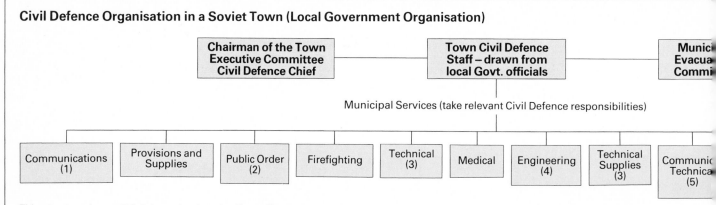

Civil Defence Organisation in a Soviet Town (Local Government Organisation)

```
┌─────────────────────────┐   ┌─────────────────────┐   ┌──────────┐
│ Chairman of the Town    │   │ Town Civil Defence  │   │ Munic    │
│ Executive Committee     │───│ Staff – drawn from  │───│ Evacua   │
│ Civil Defence Chief     │   │ local Govt. officials│  │ Commi    │
└─────────────────────────┘   └─────────────────────┘   └──────────┘
```

Municipal Services (take relevant Civil Defence responsibilities)

Communications (1)	Provisions and Supplies	Public Order (2)	Firefighting	Technical (3)	Medical	Engineering (4)	Technical Supplies (3)	Communic Technica (5)

This structure is parallelled in regional and "oblast" (district) level local Government organisation, and a similar, although more basic, system operates in a large industrial or on a State Farm.

Key to diagram
1. Local Post Office Staff. 2. The local Militia and their volunteer "People's Squad". 3. Drawn from municipal maintenance, planning and supply departments responsible for the supply and maintenance of all equipment, and establishing water supplies. 4. Drawn from local building and construction agencies. Tasks are shelter construction, repair, route and rubble clearance and rescue. 5. Involves local laundry, shower baths and street cleansing departments, responsible for decontamination. 6. Local veterinary and agricultural services, responsible for decontamination of plants and animals and checking basic food stocks for contamination.

▲ Soviet Civil Defence troops on an exercise. Such troops constitute a separate arm of the Soviet Ground Forces.

CIVIL Defence in the USSR is being pursued in a continuing programme directed by General Altunin, involving some 100,000 full-time staff in military CD units, communications elements and civilian CD appointments. Costs are probably a little under 1 per cent of defence spending, compared with 0.1 per cent in the USA, and perhaps less in other NATO countries. Hardened command posts have been constructed near Moscow and other major cities to accommodate some 100,000 people in the "leadership" category, but those shelters so far detected would be vulnerable to direct attack, according to the former US Secretary of Defense, Harold Brown. (DoD Report, FY81, p. 78.)

The Role of the CPSU

The Communist Party of the Soviet Union (CPSU) plays a crucial role in CD planning, because the Party provides the leadership, direction and discipline that the Russian nature needs, and it controls every social activity in the USSR, even in peacetime. The means of control it uses in peacetime will be those upon which it will rely for post-strike recovery: the armed forces, police and MVD forces, and the KGB. The CPSU also controls the central and local government system, with its centralised direction of finance, communications, food production and distribution, production facilities, and the labour force. Further, the mass media and the education system are both entirely in government,

and therefore in Party, hands.

The chief function of the CD organisation is to coordinate, under Party control, the relevant CD functions of all these agencies. It attempts to achieve this by providing an organizational and personnel structure to enable the masses to be educated in, and mobilised for, effective CD work. It also prepares plans, and organises exercises.

Structure of CD Network

The central HQ of the Soviet CD apparatus is an integral part of the Ministry of Defence. This HQ directs national and local civilian and military CD programmes, and commands military CD personnel. Officers and conscripts (estimated at between 20 and 50,000) of the

Army's CD Troops are trained in basic soldiering as well as CD skills: operating machinery, firefighting, traffic control, first-aid, etc. In addition, Construction Troops, Railway and Road Construction Troops, and the Transport Organization Service (VOSO) are called upon to fulfil CD tasks, especially building shelters.

There are also full-time civilian CD personnel, occupying posts in central and local government, and in industrial enterprises. They are subordinate to the local Councils of Ministers in each of the 15 Republics of the USSR, receiving their orders from the Deputy Minister of Defence in charge of the CD network via local government channels. The full-time civilian CD officials are respons-

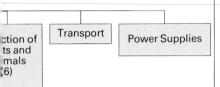

▲ Military Construction Troops on a project. This arm is over a quarter of a million strong.

▲ Civilian firemen are a key element in the Soviet Civil Defence organisation.

▲ Civil/military team on NBC recce.

▲ All Soviet students must undertake a Civil Defence course while at school.

ible for preparing plans for their respective organizations (eg, town, factory, school) and for recruiting and training the large number of part-time CD personnel upon whom any such system must depend.

Each town or large factory has full-time and part-time CD staff, but the directors of the various municipal services also have official responsibility, as *de facto* CD officers, for the CD preparations of their own branch or organization. All people in municipal departments are expected to have done a 20-hour basic course in CD knowledge, and managers are expected to be fully conversant with the CD functions of their department. Courses are run at training centres and staff colleges.

Protection of the People

In addition to the 100,000 in the "leadership" shelters, hardened accommodation exists for between 6 and 12 per cent of the total workforce at key industrial installations. There are also some 20,000 civilian shelters; with an occupancy factor of 5.38sqft (0.5m²) per person they could protect some 13 million, or roughly 10 per cent of the population of cities with over 25,000 inhabitants. At the present rate of building the number of people that could be sheltered will double by 1988, but this will be more than offset by the rate of growth of urban populations in the USSR, so the size of the problem will remain unaltered.

For the rest of the urban population the only protection would be

by evacuation, but US estimates suggest that, on average, some two to three days would be needed to clear most cities, but as many as seven days for large urban complexes like Moscow and Leningrad. A particular factor in such evacuations is the weather, and the prospect for millions of city dwellers on arrival in the countryside in the depths of the Russian winter is daunting, to say the least.

Stockpiles of food and fuel reserves exist, together with stocks of protective masks and clothing, but there is no evidence of exercises in distribution. A comprehensive CD handbook has been published, and over the past few years there has been a growing number of exercises in specific areas.

It is certainly true that the USSR

has inherent advantages in its enormous geographical size and in its natural population dispersal. Many of the more enthusiastic claims made for the Soviet CD system, particularly in the West, cannot be substantiated, however.

There is little evidence that the USSR's CD apparatus could succeed in its primary aim, ie, to guarantee the survival of the political structure of the CPSU, at any rate in the foreseeable future. Nevertheless, much progress has been made since 1971 and work in many areas is continuing. Thus it cannot be taken for granted that at some time in the future the Soviet Union's Civil Defence effort could not be sufficiently effective to become of any great strategic significance.

Passive Strategic Defences

▲Photos 1 to 7 show nuclear weapon effects on timber house. Pictures 3 and 4 show thermal effects up to 1.75 seconds after explosion.

▲The blast wave completes destruction. Basement shelter remained intact.

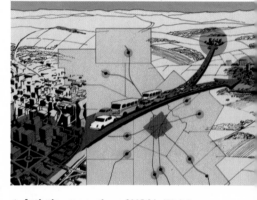

▲ Artist's conception of USA's "Crisis Relocation Plan" (CRP) in which domestic vehicles would evacuate non-essential people from risk areas, ie cities.

▲Civil and military officials man a Civil Defense control centre in the USA.

▲US "Fallout" monitoring class.

CIVIL Defence is the third element in strategic defence and the USA's efforts in this field have passed through several phases, most of them characterised by low funding and a general lack of enthusiasm.

In 1980, however, President Carter revealed Presidential Directive 41, which set US CD authorities the task of enhancing "deterrence and stability in conjunction with our strategic offensive and other strategic defence forces". The President had issued Executive Order 12148 in July 1979 which transferred responsibility for the US CD programme from the Secretary of Defense to the Federal Emergency Management Agency (FEMA), and in 1980 was seeking $2 billion for a 5-year programme to improve CD preparations. As the cost of a comprehensive national network of blast-proof shelters would be in the region of $60 to 80 billion, something well short of total protection is intended. Attention is being concentrated instead on evacuation of the most threatened sections of the population – "crisis relocation".

High-risk Targets

FEMA planning is based on the assumption that the primary Soviet missions in a first strike will be against "counter-force targets", ie, ICBM launch silos, SSBN home ports, SAC bomber and recce bases, communications centres, and key command and control sites. FEMA has identified 51 such possible targets across the USA, with a high-risk population in their vicinity of some 40 million people. It is apparently intended to build a number of shelters in these areas, although capacity would certainly fall well short of 40 million.

The new crisis relocation plans are based on the high degree of mobility inherent in America, with an extensive highway system and large-scale motorcar ownership. Any move of such large numbers, even if not all from the same areas, presupposes adequate warning, detailed planning, at least some degree of rehearsal, and housing, food and other life-support necessities in the reception areas. The critical factors in achieving this are, however, more likely to be warning time and timely decisions rather than money or the allocation of resources.

Warning the Population

Two crucial tasks of any CD organisation are the pre-strike warning of nuclear attack and post-strike warning of fallout, and a good example of this is the United Kingdom Warning and Monitoring Organisation (UKWMO). UKWMO has a small number of full-time officials, but depends for the bulk of its manpower on 10,000 part-time volunteers of the Royal Observer Corps. There are 25 Group Controls, each located in a protected building, and five of these are colocated with a Sector Operations Centre (SOC), each of which directs a number of groups.

4
5

last wave arrives caving in the front wall.

▲Danish civil defence workers on a training exercise.

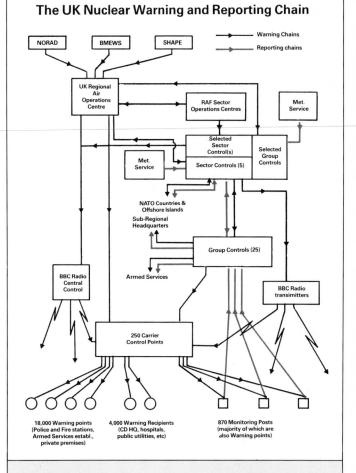

The UK Nuclear Warning and Reporting Chain

→ Warning Chains
→ Reporting chains

NORAD — BMEWS — SHAPE

UK Regional Air Operations Centre

RAF Sector Operations Centres — Met. Service

Selected Sector Control(s)
Sector Controls (5) — Selected Group Controls

Met. Service

NATO Countries & Offshore Islands
Sub-Regional Headquarters

Group Controls (25)

BBC Radio Central Control

Armed Services

BBC Radio transimitters

250 Carrier Control Points

18,000 Warning points (Police and Fire stations, Armed Services establ., private premises)

4,000 Warning Recipients (CD HQ, hospitals, public utilities, etc)

870 Monitoring Posts (majority of which are also Warning points)

UKWMO is a good example of a pre-strike warning and post-strike monitoring organisation. Warning of an impending attack could come from a number of sources, but the most likely is from the Ballistic Missile Early Warning System (BMEWS) site at Fylingdales in Yorkshire. National warnings would be initiated from the Home Office cell at the UK Regional Air Operations Centre (UKRAOC) where one key would activate special equipments scattered around the country in 250 major police stations (Carrier Control Points). The CCPs would in their turn activate sirens in urban areas, as well as some 11,000 more warning points in rural areas. The latter are then tasked with operating hand-sirens. Simultaneous broadcasts would be made on TV and radio. By these means a very large proportion of the population should receive adequate warning of an impending attack.

For the post-strike role there are some 873 monitoring posts in a grid covering the entire national territory. These report to 25 Group Controls, who, in turn, come under 5 Section HQs. Sectors and even Groups can operate autonomously if necessary.

This organisation exists in peace and is manned by a very small number of officials and by a large number of well-trained volunteers of the Royal Observer Corps. Regular exercises are held, not only on a national scale, but also in conjunction with similar organisations in other NATO countries. It is a most cost-effective system.

Groups and SOCs are linked by telephone and radio; there is considerable redundancy built into the system, but most authorities believe that little cognisance has so far been taken of EMP effects.

Nuclear attack warnings would originate from such installations as the BMEWS station at Fylingdales in northern England, from where they would be passed to the UK Regional Operations Centre (UKRAOC). This centre would activate 250 Carrier Control Points (CCPs) located throughout the UK in selected police stations. CCPs would then activate powered sirens (7,000 throughout the country), and also relay the warnings to a further 11,000 lower level warning points in selected industrial premises, smaller police

stations, fire stations and UKWMO monitoring posts. All these are equipped with a Carrier Warning Receiver which would superimpose distinctive audio signals on a normal telephone circuit. A number of these warning points would sound hand-sirens to fill in the gaps between the powered machines, thus completing the nationwide warning coverage.

UKWMO's second task is to monitor fallout in the post-attack period and to give warning when the safe level is about to be exceeded. The bomb-plot and the fallout picture would be completed by UKWMO from reports provided by 870 monitoring posts – three-man protected shelters, each fully equipped with a variety of survey and recording devices.

Reports would be collated and interpreted at group controls from where they would be passed to SOCs, regional government HQs and local military units. The population would be informed by siren, radio broadcasts and maroons. There are also arrangements for an interchange of information with the warning and monitoring organisations in other NATO countries.

CD in the NATO European countries varies widely in scope and effectiveness. All have some form of warning system similar to that described above, which is tied into the military surveillance network. Countries with a policy for providing shelters are Norway, Denmark and West Germany, while others pay lip service only.

The Conventional Threat
A new factor has emerged recently as it has become apparent that nuclear weapons are not the only strategic threat to Western Europe, and that there is an increasing possibility of non-nuclear strategic bombing from manned aircraft delivering precision-guided missiles, free-fall gravity bombs, and air-launched cruise missiles.

The conventional threat posed to the West by Tu-22M (Backfire) and Su-24 (Fencer) is very serious and CD organisations are being reviewed with reference to them; currently the peacetime emergency services would be quickly overwhelmed. The problem facing all governments is the very high cost of any realistic CD programme.

The Balance of CONVENTIO FORCES

THE balance between the conventional forces of the Warsaw Pact and the North Atlantic Treaty Organization is but one aspect of a much larger struggle for control over the Eurasian Continent. The Soviet Union controls a much larger part of Eurasia and its periphery than is indicated by its own political boundaries and those of the countries it controls in one way or another. This derives from the fact that the ability of the Soviet Union to control the air space along its borders is contested by major permanently deployed forces only in the NATO area.

Air space control is a product of two factors. First and foremost is control of the electromagnetic spectrum, that is, the ability to gain

early warning of hostile forces, to obtain and maintain accurate location of targets and to vector defending air defence forces to the targets in time to destroy them before they enter the defended home territory. Secondly, airspace control is the product of airborne fighter-interceptor and ground-based surface-to-air missile forces in numbers and quality sufficient to destroy the hostile forces.

The ability to control airspace for defensive purposes imparts a major offensive capability as well, in that land, sea and supporting air forces can strike with relative impunity against targets within the protective air defence canopy.

The maps and tables in these pages, giving data on capabilities and ranges of Warsaw Pact inter-

ceptor aircraft and other air defence systems, show that the extent of air space under Soviet control is considerable indeed.

Three Vital Regions

When considered in regard to the military (ie, air defence) boundaries of Soviet power, therefore, rather than simply the political boundaries, the military balance confronting NATO takes on quite a different meaning, especially if viewed in the light of strategic concepts evolved by an American, Homer Lea, in the early years of this century.

Writing of the British Empire as it then existed (in "The Day of the Saxon," Harper, 1942) Lea warned that if it were to be defeated in any one of three areas of vital interest

the Empire would be defeated worldwide. These three areas were Western Europe, the Persian Gulf and Northeast Asia. Citing, the advantage of interior lines of movement, Lea concluded that the continental opponents of the British Empire, ie, Imperial Germany and Russia, could be defeated only in one place – at the seat of their power.

NATO and Japan today occupy the exterior strategic arc of which Lea wrote. The Soviet Union now holds a clear military advantage in at least two of the three regions that Lea considered essential to survival of the "circumscribing" as opposed to the "interior" power.

In the Middle East, Soviet occupation of Afghanistan has extended its permanently deployed

Military control of the Eurasian continent will depend first and foremost on the ability to control the electromagnetic spectrum and, secondly, on the ability to gain control of the air. Control of the land and the surrounding oceans can only be a subfunction of the outcome of the electronic and air battles. Both alliances are clearly capable of wielding influence and control far beyond their own borders, but the USSR could be faced with war on two quite separate fronts — the Far East and Europe. Without yet having sufficient conventional forces she could not risk being involved in such a war. It would certainly bode ill for NATO and world peace were that situation to be reversed.

air defence system virtually to the shores of the Persian Gulf. In terms of air forces in being and their supporting bases, the Soviet Union has the ability to destroy the indigenous air forces of the Persian Gulf region in a matter of hours, to occupy with airborne and air-landed ground forces all of the major airfields in Iran and to render all other air bases in the region inoperable. The effect would be to threaten NATO and Japan with the cut-off of Persian Gulf oil supplies and thereby precipitate a world-wide economic and political crisis.

Aircraft Carriers and the Flanks
The United States has sought to counter this inherent Soviet advantage in the Middle East and Southwest Asia by deploying air-craft carrier battle groups into the Indian Ocean and the Arabian Sea. While this was a dramatic initial stop-gap measure, it served to expose long-term weaknesses deriving from the increased vulnerability of aircraft carriers, the strains imposed on the US Navy by the decision to abandon conscription in favour of a volunteer military manpower procurement system, and the decline in size of the US Fleet during the past decade.

Whatever its increased vulnerability, the fact remains that there is no substitute for the aircraft carrier in maintaining sea control, in all the dimensions of that term – surface, subsurface and air. If, however, the carriers are to be the primary support for indigenous air forces the requirement to operate relatively close to shore will increase their vulnerability to Soviet land-based air power, notably the Backfire bomber, and deny them the sea space and manoeuvrability needed to counter and defeat the submarine and ship-to-ship missile threats.

Of direct concern to NATO is the impact on NATO's northern flank (Norway, in particular the North Cape) of the drawing off of sea power to the Indian Ocean. The battle for control of the North Cape region is primarily an air and sea affair, since NATO has not been willing to station enough land forces and land-based air forces permanently in Northern Norway to counter the relatively large Soviet ground and land-based air threat there.

Somewhat the same apprehension might be expressed about the diversion of sea power from the Eastern Mediterranean. There, however, land-based air power can replace the carriers more easily. Apart from Indian Ocean requirements, there is good reason to doubt the wisdom of risking carriers in the Mediterranean when they could perform more effectively and at less risk elsewhere.

Can NATO and Japan Fill the Gap?
It seems imperative, therefore, that NATO and Japan find some alternative means to establish in the Persian Gulf region a sizeable (10

The Balance of Conventional Weapons

Comparison of WP/NATO   Non-strategic Force Strengths

The graphics and tables seek to provide comparisons between current Warsaw Pact and NATO forces, globally on the left and related to Europe on the right.
Far left: Total divisions available. This is a measure of the fighting ability of armies, but some divisions on both side are committed to other tasks; eg, Soviet divisions in the Far East facing China, and US divisions in the Pacific.
Left: Total combat ships available. While there is a global advantage in numbers to the Pact navies, the actual availability of ships in a crisis might be different; eg, the USSR has problems of access to oceans.
Right: In Europe the imbalances in the Pact's favour are very clear. The figures exclude US dual-based aircraft (about 100), US Navy and USMC carrier-borne aircraft and Air National Guard mobilisation; French squadrons (about 400 fighter aircraft) and Soviet medium bombers are also excluded.
Below right: the figures show NATO ground forces available without mobilisation. Only French forces in Germany are included (although even these are not under NATO command); forces in West Berlin are also not under NATO command and are excluded.

WP/NATO Total Operational Combat Vessels

Note: Different reference sources include or exclude training, obsolescent and other vessels not in front-line service, and this leads to confusion. Further, various reference works differ in vessel classification methods, as do navies.
Such obsolescent vessels as the Whisky class submarines, Skory destroyers, Kola and Riga class frigates and all but the two command versions of the Sverdlov cruisers have been specifically omitted from these figures.

Vessel Type	Soviet Union	Bulgaria	GDR	Poland	Romania
Cruise missile subs.	61				
Attack subs.	133	4		4	
Battle cruisers	1				
A/C carriers	2				
Helo carriers	2				
Cruisers	27				
Destroyers	60			1	
Frigates*	150	2	2		
Minesweepers**	303	18	52	15	14
Patrol craft	460	29	75	44	72
Amphib. warfare ships	83		14	23	

*Includes corvettes.   **Includes ocean and coastal.

Vessel Type	USA	Belgium	Canada	Denmark	France	FGR	Greece	Italy	N'lands	Norway	Portugal	Turkey	UK
Attack subs.	73		3	6	21	24	11	11	6	15	3	15	27
A/C carriers	13				2								
Helo carriers					1			1					2
Cruisers	37				1			2					1
Destroyers	70		16		18	7	12	6	5			12	12
Frigates*	83	4		2	23	6		14	9	5	17	2	42
Minesweepers**	3	29		8	32	57	14	42	34	10	4	7	37
Patrol craft	3		6	40	20	46	28	17	11		54	18	73	26	8
Amphib. warfare ships	61				10			11	2			5	8

to 15 squadrons) air defence force operating from bases protected by revetments and surface-to-air missiles and supported by a hardened land-based aircraft control and warning system. One means of accomplishing this is to begin with the development of regional air defence capabilities among the states of the Arabian Peninsula, with the Western powers and Japan providing high technology equipment, training and advisers. Added to this, if desired by the local states, could be rotation of NATO units for air defence exercises.

The possibility of an adequate NATO response has been strengthened by the strong position Turkey has taken toward further Soviet moves in the Persian Gulf, offering to send its forces to defend threatened states. Assistance to Turkey in modernizing its forces becomes, therefore, an urgent NATO requirement. Further, the possibility of British forces being used to assist American defence of Middle East oilfields was referred to early in 1981.

The Third Vital Region
The dispatch of US aircraft carriers from the Western Pacific to the Indian Ocean has greatly weakened the Allied position in Northern Japan. There are now no Japanese or American fighter-interceptors north of Chitose in the southern part of Hokkaido, and no SAM positions to challenge Soviet air control of the Soya Strait, a principal exit route for the major surface units of the Soviet Pacific Fleet into the Pacific Ocean.

Ironically, these major strategic advantages have been handed over to the Soviets in the one area of the world in which they do not have freedom of movement on interior lines. This is due to the fact that Eastern Siberia is virtually a trackless wilderness with enormous obstacles of terrain and climate to overland movement. US and Japanese sea power, on the other hand, enjoys unlimited freedom of movement supported by what could be a chain of airfields all the way across the North Pacific in the US-owned Aleutian Islands.

It is of more than passing interest that, in training for contingencies in Northern Norway, the US Navy and Marine Corps are gaining the experience and possibly the technology needed if they were to be used to exploit Soviet vulnerabilities in Eastern Siberia.

It has been suggested by some in the West that if the Western nations and Japan find themselves in some grave difficulty with the Soviet Union they need only say the word and the Chinese will leap at the Russian flank. Of all the fairy tales the West has spun for itself about China down through the ages this is surely the most bizarre. The Chinese cannot defend their own borderlands against the Soviet forces already in place. To suggest that they would risk an attack likely to bring down on themselves the full arsenal of Soviet weaponry, nuclear as well as conventional, is to suppose that

WP/NATO Forces Deployed in Europe

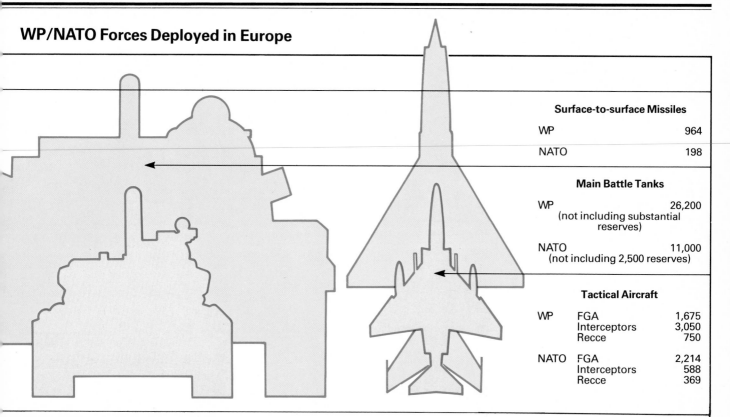

Surface-to-surface Missiles

WP	964
NATO	198

Main Battle Tanks

WP	26,200 (not including substantial reserves)
NATO	11,000 (not including 2,500 reserves)

Tactical Aircraft

WP	FGA	1,675
	Interceptors	3,050
	Recce	750
NATO	FGA	2,214
	Interceptors	588
	Recce	369

WP/NATO Total Ground Forces

	Soviet Union								Non-Soviet Warsaw Pact					
	Foreign deployments				Home deployments									
Divisions*	GDR	Poland	Hungary	Czech.	European USSR	S. USSR	Cen. USSR	Sino/Sov. border	Bulg.	Czech.	GDR	Hungary	Poland	Romania
Airborne					6	2			1/3	1/3			1	1/3
Motor Rifle	10		2	3	38	21	6	40	8	5	4	5	8	8
Tank	9	2	2	2	23	1		6	1 2/3	5	2	1	5	2
Amphib.					2½									1

*No differentiation has been made between the three categories of war readiness of Soviet and other WP divisions.

	United States: Foreign . . . Home								Other NATO Armies											
Divisions	FGR	Berlin	S. Korea	Japan	Panama	CONUS	Alaska	Hawaii	Belgium	Canada	Denmark	France	FGR	Greece	Italy	Neth.	Norway	Portugal	Turkey	UK
Airmobile						1				1/3		1 1/3		1/3						
Airborne						1			1/3	1		1								
Infantry			1/3	2/3		2 1/3	1/3	2/3				2/3		8	1 2/3		1/3	1/3	16 1/3	2 2/3
Mech/Inf	2 1/3				1/3	4			1	1	1 2/3	4	4	3	3 1/3	1 1/3		5	3 1/3	
Mountain												1	1		1 2/3	1/3			1/3	
Marine	1 2/3			1		1 2/3		1/3						1/3		1	2/3	1/3	1/3	1/3
Tank	1 2/3					2 2/3			1/3			8	6	1	1	2/3		1/3	3	4

the Chinese lack the most ordinary common sense.

New Strategy Needed

The successive crises in the Middle East and Afghanistan, in particular during the past two years, have unsettled all of the comfortable old strategic myths. It is now at least beginning to be recognized in Western Europe and Japan that the Middle East cannot be considered an "American" problem. Indeed, the United States has less at stake in that area than any of its major allies. The possibility that Western Europe may not be the prime military target area of the Soviet Union at least for the time being is implicit in the foreign policy of Chancellor Helmut Schmidt of West Germany. The

forbearance of the Soviets in dealing with the Polish labour movement suggests that the Soviets do, indeed, have other priorities.

How NATO resolves the question of upgrading its theatre nuclear forces will have an important and probably decisive bearing on whether or not the military balance in Europe can be stabilized. Central to this issue is the military fact, however unpleasant, that there is no such thing as a "ladder" of escalation to nuclear warfare.

It has been established since the mid-1960s (Joint US Strike Command Exercise *Desert Strike*) that the moment a theatre commander can prove the need to use tactical nuclear weapons any delay

in using them, even of a few hours, will be almost certain to result in collapse of the defence.

Enhanced radiation (ER) warheads (so-called "neutron bombs") offer NATO the most effective anti-armour weapon yet devised. Perhaps even more important, ER technology with its powerful electromagnetic pulse offers a means hitherto beyond NATO's grasp to wreck the elaborate Warsaw Pact command and control arrangements in the crucial early hours of an attack.

In short, the best hope of establishing deterrence in Europe during the decade of the 1980s almost certainly rests on a decision to deploy modernized delivery systems armed with ER warheads.

In the succeeding pages of this

section on conventional forces and in the sections dealing with the other aspects of the overall strategic equation the reader has available the principal military elements that the statesmen of the West and Japan must consider as they seek to sort all of this out. Can tanks for Europe be "traded off" against aircraft carriers for the Pacific or fighter squadrons for the Middle East? How long can the United States, Britain and Japan rely on volunteers alone for their forces? In attempting to arrive at judgements concerning these matters the individual citizen should keep in mind the words of US Gen. William E. Depuy in an address to the US Army Armor Association, "There are no more secrets."

The Balance of

GROUND FORCES

IF SIZE were the arbiter of war the disparity of numbers shown on the map on page 55 would surely lead to despair. However, from sergeants to generals among the NATO soldiers who must confront this disparity there is confidence that, properly supported, the NATO armies could stop an initial Warsaw Pact onslaught and gain a fighting chance to disrupt the second echelon necessary to sustain the attack. If it is assumed that the Warsaw Pact would consider it to be to its advantage to attack with conventional arms only there is solid reason to accept the "guarded optimism" of this view.

The tediousness of democratic procedure and parliamentary debate tends to obscure the fact that far more progress has been made in the building of a modern, efficient NATO military establishment than is generally recognized.

"Interoperability"

Although much has been made of disparity among the military establishments of the 15 NATO nations, an amazing degree of commonality ("interoperability" in bureaucratic parlance) has been achieved. This is true not only of the "software" of orders and procedures, but of "hardware" as well.

The British L7 105mm gun has been the primary tank weapon of the NATO forces for over a decade. A basic 7.62mm small arms calibre was achieved early in NATO's history and still is widely employed. During this same period the US M-113 Armoured Personnel Carrier has been accepted to one degree or another by all of the NATO armies. More recently, the German Leopard tank series has won wider acceptance than anyone would have guessed 10 years ago.

Prospects of continuing and improving such commonality are good. Although a change is occurring to a larger calibre tank cannon and to a smaller calibre rifle, the retention and expansion of a common base of ammunition seems reasonably assured.

In the process a compromise has been worked out that retains for NATO a powerful psychological benefit that its opponents in the Warsaw Pact armies conspicuously lack. In short, when the NATO soldier looks around him he sees uniforms, equipment and ways of doing things that are distinctly those of his own nation. Of the foreign items in his army's inventory, he knows that they were acquired by the free decision of his own people and government.

The Warsaw Pact soldier, on the other hand, lives in a military environment that is distinctly Russian and he knows full well that commonality was imposed.

Mobilization

From the standpoint of mobilization, the NATO soldier lives within 24 hours, in most cases, of the place where his unit is to fight. Time is needed to report, draw equipment, form motor convoys and deploy but this is done over

For different reasons, logistics is the great worry of combat commanders on both sides of the Iron Curtain. The Soviets worry about an East European population held in place only by walls, barbed wire and minefields. NATO commanders worry about a lifeline that runs parallel, and close, to the front line. They worry, too, about the reliability of supply and maintenance facilities manned by civilians who may not be there if war breaks out. But the greatest NATO weakness of all may be the strategic concept whereby though the NATO nations are at risk their war plan, unlike that of the Warsaw Pact, would be totally defensive, without threat to the Communist governments.

one of the finest road and rail networks in the world.

The farther East one goes in Europe the thinner and more unreliable that road and rail network becomes. This makes the task of moving up the large number of divisions that must come from the Soviet and East European rear areas a difficult and time-consuming task. Once deployed, those divisions place a heavy strain on a distribution system that does not work too well even in peace.

From the experience of tests and partial mobilizations, NATO commanders believe that their soldiers can be in place and ready to fight before the Warsaw Pact can complete organization of its assault formations, assuming that

NATO has the political will to act when the time comes to act.

France the Central Reserve
Much has been made in the Western academic press in recent years of the lack of a NATO central reserve in Europe. That ignores the existence of large and increasingly well-armed French forces. The fact that her forces continue to be deployed as shown in the accompanying map provides ample evidence that France intends to meet the enemy beyond her frontiers. As discussed in more detail in later sections, there is emerging in the French forces a high-speed counterattack capability the power of which is only just beginning to be understood.

There has been a steady

improvement in recent years of European NATO territorial forces capable not only of protecting rear areas but of serving as front-line units. This has compensated to a considerable degree for the sharp decline in readiness of US reserve units subsequent to the end of conscription. Adequate manpower for all US units, active and reserve, remains a serious problem and one that will not be resolved until a decision is made to return to conscription.

The Warsaw Pact forces must deal with a somewhat different manpower problem. Their vast arsenal of weapons is thinly manned. Even when brought to full wartime strength, there are scarcely enough people in the fighting formations to operate the

equipment assigned. What would be relatively minor losses in US divisions, for example, would lead very quickly to failure of entire weapons systems in the Warsaw Pact divisions. This arises from the fact that the Warsaw Pact forces are structured for a large-unit rather than individual or small-unit replacement system.

WP Allies Reliable?
The questionable loyalty of the East European members of the Warsaw Pact is a weakness of unknown and, for the time being, unknowable proportions. A political convulsion in Poland would jeopardize Soviet lines of communications and engender hope among a population in East Germany that is held in place only

The Balance of Ground Forces

The Imbalance in Europe

Although the Warsaw Pact/NATO manpower under arms in Europe appear to be approximately equal, the Warsaw Pact capacity for very rapid mobilisation would give its forces a three-to-one majority in fighting troops after three weeks of mobilisation. NATO could only close that gap after a further month had elapsed. To what extent the Soviet Union's Warsaw Pact allies could be relied on would depend, of course, on the political situation in which conflict occurred. However, the startling improvement in the quality and quantity of equipment which the Soviet Union has supplied to non-Soviet Pact countries since 1970 seems to indicate that these countries are increasingly being considered by the USSR as quite reliable allies. The East German and Bulgarian armies have particularly benefited from this trend. The Poles, Czechs and Hungarians also use good quality domestically produced equipment. Only the Romanian Army has failed to show a marked improvement since 1970. Presumably due to Romania being the least controllable regime and having the least important position strategically, her army is accorded the lowest priority of resupply by the USSR.

Neutral countries

Warsaw Pact

NATO

--- NATO lines of communication

━ ━ Soviet lines of communication

Moscow

Likely Areas of Warsaw Pact Ground Attack▶

A Soviet/WP ground attack on European NATO could be expected to come via the North Cape, the North German Plain, the Fulda Gap and into E. Turkey, stretching their lines of communication (LOC). NATO's LOC run parallel and close to that probable "front line".

United Kingdom

Be

Franc

NATO

Strengths
Voluntary NATO membership
Shared values
Intense national pride
Concern for preservation of each member state
Efficient logistics based on sound economies
Superior training with advanced equipment

Weaknesses
Defensive strategic concept requiring war to be fought only on NATO homelands
Dependence of major partners (US, Britain) on voluntary recruitment
Diverse military doctrines, organisation and sources of logistic support

◀ When these NATO soldiers look around them they at least know their allies share the same values.

WARSAW PACT

Strengths
Universal conscription
Interior lines
Strong central control
Common doctrine
Common military organisation
Common logistic system and sources
Commonality of equipment

Weaknesses
E. European resentment of Soviet Control
Poor management of economies and logistics
Strong central control tends to reduce initiative and imagination at operational level
Reliability of Soviet soldier questionable

◀ This Russian soldier knows he has to control his "allies" as well as overcome his foes.

---

by walls, barbed wire and mine-fields. Even assuming the full loyalty of the Soviet forces, unrest or the threat of unrest in Eastern Europe could absorb upwards of 20 Soviet divisions to maintain the security of their most vital logistic systems.

Poor Soviet Management: Military and Economic

European officers who have first-hand knowledge of Soviet operations in World War II doubt that the Soviets have the ability to manage key aspects of a future continental-scale war, in particular the air battle that must be won if there is to be any hope of victory on the ground. In the opinion of one of these officers, "On the only occasion when the Soviets had to

manage a complex air and land battle on their own – in 1941–42 – they lost. They were not able to launch a decisive counteroffensive on the ground until the Americans and British had already won the air war in the final phase."

The chronic mismanagement of the Soviet economy in all of the years since the October Revolution adds additional weight to that argument. There are other "straws in the wind". For example, Czechs who have defected since the Soviet reoccupation in 1968 recount instances of Soviet soldiers begging for bread at farmhouse doors because their rations were not reaching them.

The worry of NATO commanders is not defeat of the front-line forces, but the weaknesses in-

herent in a logistics system that runs parallel to the front rather than perpendicular to it, and the excessive civilianization ("host nation support" in US budgetary "Pentagonese") of the support echelons. The reconstitution of a more rational NATO logistics system through France rather than, as at present, through the Netherlands, Belgium and Northern Germany is unquestionably the primary political task facing NATO today.

Better use of reserve forces in all of the NATO countries, including the United States, seems to offer the best means of rebuilding a military logistics system that can function at minimal cost in peace but assure reliable support in time of war.

NATO's Fatal Strategy

It is a tribute to the loyalty of military leadership to civilian authority in all of the NATO countries that there has been no challenge to date to what the military leadership knows in its heart is a fatal strategic concept. This is the implied NATO intention to fight only to restore the *status quo ante* if attacked and not to threaten a counteroffensive that will bring into question the security of the Communist governments at least in Eastern Europe.

There is a consensus among Western military leadership that the eventual defeat of South Vietnam is traceable to a decision to guarantee the security of the North Vietnamese Communist

Introduction

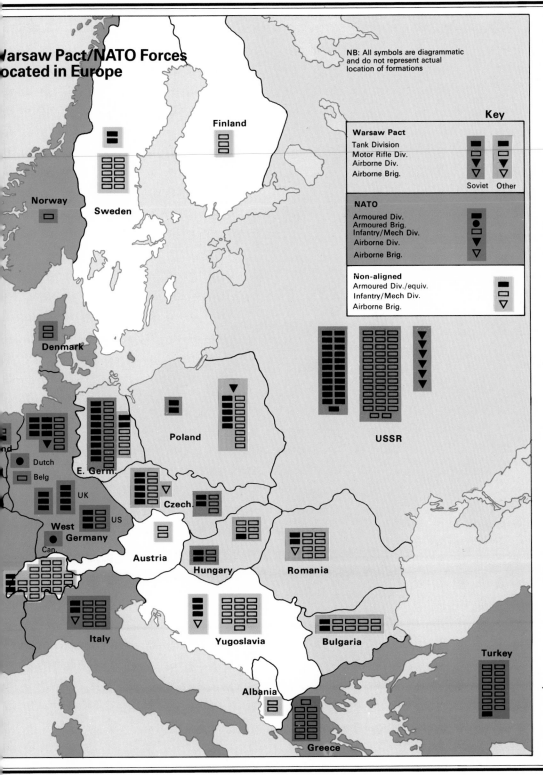

Warsaw Pact/NATO Forces located in Europe

NB: All symbols are diagrammatic and do not represent actual location of formations

Key

Warsaw Pact
Tank Division
Motor Rifle Div.
Airborne Div.
Airborne Brig.
Soviet   Other

NATO
Armoured Div.
Armoured Brig.
Infantry/Mech Div.
Airborne Div.
Airborne Brig.

Non-aligned
Armoured Div./equiv.
Infantry/Mech Div.
Airborne Brig.

Finland

Norway

Sweden

Denmark

Dutch

Belg

E. Germ.

UK

US

West Germany

Can

Poland

USSR

Czech.

Austria

Hungary

Romania

Italy

Yugoslavia

Bulgaria

Turkey

Albania

Greece

Who would face whom?

In a general war situation, Warsaw Pact forces committed against NATO might be allocated as follows:

Against Norway—Soviet forces in the Leningrad Military District.

Against Denmark, the northern coast of West Germany and Holland—Soviet ground, naval and air forces from the Baltic Military District, plus Polish and E. German airborne and amphibious forces.

Against North Germany (Hanover and the Ruhr)—Soviet ground and air forces from the Group of Soviet Forces in Germany (GSFG) and the Soviet Northern Group of Forces (NGG) in Poland, and from the Moscow and Belorussian Military Districts, plus ground force elements from the E. German and Polish armies.

Against Central Germany (Frankfurt)—these same forces together with Czech army units and elements of the Soviet Central Group of forces in Czechoslovakia (CGF) and Soviet troops from the Kiev Military District.

Against Southern Germany (Stuttgart-Munich), Austria and Italy—Soviet forces from GSFG, CGF and SGF (Soviet Southern Group of Forces in Hungary), plus elements of the E. German Czech and Hungarian armies, and troops of the Kiev and Carpathian Military Districts.

Against Southern Europe and Turkey—Soviet troops of the Odessa and Caucasian Military Districts and elements of the Hungarian, Romanian and Bulgarian armies.

This would give a comparison of strengths as follows:

Divisions: WP 140-150, NATO 45.
Tanks: WP 27,000, NATO 10-11,000.
Artillery pieces: WP 8-9,000, NATO 6,000
Men (under arms now): WP 1,240,000, NATO 1,200,000.

NB: Any analysis of Soviet military power based on peacetime man-power levels is a gross under-estimation. Within a week the effective strength of Soviet Army could be doubled or even trebled with "reservists".

◀The map shows approximate WP/NATO force strengths in Europe, including reserves immediately available. NATO forces are depicted in equivalent divisions equated to Warsaw Pact divisions.

---

government by refraining from any ground assault against Hanoi. Defence may indeed be the strongest form of war, as Clausewitz described it, but he meant that only in the context of gaining strength for a counteroffensive. In Europe today, as in Vietnam in the 1960s, the real or potential aggressor could assume from public discussion in the West that if his initial attack fails, he will be permitted to withdraw into a sanctuary, reorganize and prepare to try again. For one thing, that tells the people of Eastern Europe that any attempt on their part to threaten the Warsaw Pact rear areas will gain them only bloody repression on the model of Hungary in 1956 with no hope of rescue by NATO forces.

It must be recognized, of course, that the German Army is more and more the central factor in any successful defence of Western Europe on the ground. This accelerating trend derives from severe constrictions imposed on the British Army of the Rhine by economics and dependence on volunteer recruiting, from France's decision to form its defence behind a German glacis and on the need for the United States to regain freedom of action in dealing with a worldwide rather than a localized European threat only. That being the case, any NATO counteroffensive beyond the present borders of East Germany can succeed only if the Poles are willing to accept German soldiers as liberators, and only if it is plain

to the Russian Army and the Russian people that this is not to be another assault on "Mother Russia".

NATO's Empty Threat?

Ironically, however, in the minds of American and European officers a threat to Russia itself is a moot question in that NATO does not have the forces in being or in reserve to conduct a counteroffensive on the scale of World War II operations in the East. A plain indication to the Soviets, however, that a Warsaw Pact attack on Western Europe will put at risk Soviet domination of at least the region West of the Vistula River (Polish Wisla) would free NATO from a self-imposed strategic and psychological liability.

If the Warsaw Pact forces were to attack with the full chemical warfare capability at their disposal the basis for the growing optimism in the NATO forces would disappear. For the reasons set forth in the NBC Warfare portions of this section, NATO has neither the offensive nor the defensive means to deter such an attack or to defeat it short of resort to nuclear weapons. Failure to make full use of the nuclear technology available, with notably enhanced radiation weapons, could force NATO to make even this choice at a higher level of escalation than might be needed.

If there is to be a true stabilization of the military situation in Europe then this "hole in the dyke" must be plugged, quickly.

▲ T-55 still serves in great numbers in the Warsaw Pact.

▲ T-10 heavy tank; some still in service and reserve.

▲ T-55s of the Soviet Army with new laser rangetaker.

FROM the total tank inventories shown on these pages, it would be easy to imagine a nightmare wherein the sky from the Baltic to the Alps erupts with a simultaneous burst from the blast of artillery and tank cannon while the ground trembles under thousands of tanks lunging forward as a single echelon. Something very much like that did occur, in the opposite direction, when Hitler's Germany launched "Operation Barbarossa" in June 1941.

Some observers, often for the purpose of controlling Western defence budgets, have gone to an opposite extreme. Anxious to establish that the Soviets are not "ten feet tall", they foresee Russian tanks bursting into flames because of exposed auxiliary fuel tanks, or because Soviet armour alloyed with magnesium is thought to be ignitable. The magnesium myth is just that. The fuel tanks can be jettisoned; they contain diesel fuel which is difficult to ignite, especially below 80°F, and they save space and weight in tank design by reducing the cube of internal fuel tanks and the armour necessary to protect them.

Soviet Vulnerabilities

The real vulnerabilities of Soviet armour lie elsewhere. Rugged, often crude construction has been a feature of Soviet tanks since World War II. The famous T-34/85 and its successors were relatively easy to operate and maintain. As tanks became more complicated and as the long-term mass armies of World War II were replaced by relatively short-term conscripts a different problem emerged. Two years – the standard term of service – is barely long enough to train a proficient tank crew, let alone proficient tank automotive and turret mechanics. Without the large, experienced corps of non-commissioned officers and technicians common to the NATO armies, the Warsaw Pact forces will have difficulty obtaining the full design performance from their newer, more sophisticated tanks.

The low silhouette common to Soviet tanks has been obtained at the expense of crew comfort, and that would exert a severe fatigue penalty in sustained operations. Perhaps most important of all, the vaunted "teeth-to-tail" ratio of Soviet combat units has been gained by sacrifice of maintenance and other logistics units.

That combination of partially trained crews and mechanics operating and maintaining increasingly sophisticated vehicles with inadequate maintenance and support and scant crew replacements in the forward echelons could see the failure of large numbers of Warsaw Pact tanks after the first few days of operations. That is a significant factor in the assessment by NATO commanders that they could defeat the initial Warsaw Pact onslaught.

The Soviets have not sought large technological advances in any one model. Their development policy has been one of incremental change, and it has served them

▲ T-72 with schnorkel tube stowed on turret side.

▲ Soviet T-72 MBT has a 125mm gun with an automatic loader and crew of 3. Hull is of "special" armour and side plates are designed to defeat hollow-charge warheads.

▲ Dozer blade fittings can be seen under bow plate.

▲ T-55 using flamethrower.

The Warsaw Pact Tanks

Type	Crew	Weight (tonnes)	Height ft(m)	Road Speed mph(kph)	Calibre	Main Gun Effective Range yards (metres)	Main Gun Rounds	Cruising Range miles(km)	Stabil- ization
T-72	3	41t	7.54 (2.30)	50 (80)	125mm	2,186 (2,000)	40	279 (450)	Yes
T-64	3	38t	7.54 (2.30)	50 (80)	125mm	2,186 (2,000)	40	279 (450)	Yes
T-62	4	37.5t	7.86 (2.40)	31 (50)	115mm	1,748 (1,600)	40	279 (450)	Yes
T-10	4	50t	7.70 (2.35)	30 (48)	122mm	1,640 (1,500)	30	155 (250)	No
T54/55	4	36t	7.86 (2.40)	31 (50)	100mm	1,640 (1,500)	34	248–310 (400–500)	Yes

T-80 will be fielded soon; it is expected to have a 125mm gun, laser rangefinder, laminate armour, and a hydro-pneumatic suspension system.
NATO is thought to be facing more than 10,000 T-72s and T-64s. There are an estimated 4,000 T-72s and T-64s in the Group of Soviet Forces in Germany, and an estimated total of 26,000 T-54/55 and later models in E. Europe. Estimated annual production of T-72s is 2,500, plus 1,000 earlier models.

Sources: *Warsaw Pact Ground Forces Equipment Identification Guide: Armored Fighting Vehicles*, US Defense Intelligence Agency, August 1980; estimates of tank strength and production: US DoD document, "Soviet Military Power", September 1981.

well. Especially as concerns main tank armament, a major strategic decision by the Soviets in the early 1960s has enabled them to keep up with and in some areas stay ahead of what should have been superior Western technology. In short, a premature belief in the West (in particular in the United States) that the missile was about to replace the big gun led to diversion of scarce research, development and procurement funds into what proved to be a blind alley, notably in the US M60A2 programme. The Soviets saw, correctly as it turned out, that the big gun still had development potential.

Fortunately, German and British development of big gun technology generally kept pace with Soviet developments. The result is

that NATO and Warsaw Pact tanks confront each other with what amounts to a revolutionary array of tank ammunition. Most spectacular of the new ammunition is the Armour Piercing Fin-Stabilized Discarding Sabot (APFSDS) round projecting a subcalibre penetrator at 5,902 feet per second (1,800m/ sec) in the NATO versions.

Greater Accuracy

Because most tank engagements in European terrain will probably occur at ranges less than about 1,640 yards (1,500m), the extreme velocity, and hence greater accuracy, of the new guns and ammunition have led the Soviets to place less emphasis on sophisticated fire control systems. On the other hand, NATO emphasis on

just such items tends to compensate for the advantage in Soviet ammunition velocity.

The newer Soviet tanks (T-72, T-80) are thought to have advanced armour protection comparable to NATO Chobham armour and its equivalents. However, the older models (T-54/55, T-62, T-64) will continue to make up the greater part of the Warsaw Pact tank inventory through the early 1980s. While the newer models would probably be used in the assault echelons, large numbers of the older models would be required to sustain a major attack on Western Europe. Defeat of the initial attack, therefore, would help to equalize the balance as NATO reserves with older models are brought into action.

A much more severe limitation on the number of Soviet tanks that can be employed in the initial assault is imposed by the factors necessary to create surprise. Even in 1941, the marshalling of a vast German offensive force on the Soviet border could not be accomplished without detection. It would be much more difficult today to organize such an offensive undetected.

It is likely, therefore, that a surprise attack on NATO would find the Warsaw Pact tanks attacking from line of march rather than from assault positions that would enable them to employ maximum strength. NATO ability to disrupt following echelons, therefore, would play a crucial part in the final outcome.

Main Battle Tanks

▲ An outstanding tank – the German Army Leopard 1.

▲ AMX-30 of the French Army; some 1,220 are in service.

▲ Leopard C1. Canada has bought 114 of these tanks for use in Germany.

▲ FV 4030/3, experimental British tank.

▲ Italian Army Leopard 1. Oto Melara built 920 after M-60 proved unsatisfactory.

▲ Inside a British Chieftain.

THE German Army is rapidly emerging as the increasingly predominant element in the ground defence of NATO Central Europe. Nowhere is this more apparent than in the development of the Leopard series tanks during the past 20 years. Seen from the start as not only a German, but a European tank, Leopard 1 has achieved a remarkable degree of acceptance not only in Europe but in Canada and Australia as well. It has many (though subdued) supporters in the US Army, albeit with some reservations about cramped crew spaces particularly as concerns the gunner's position. To date, in Europe, Leopard 1 is in service in the armies of West Germany, Belgium, Denmark, Italy, Netherlands and Norway.

Continuing severe economic restrictions on British tank development and production and the growing likelihood of some substantial redeployment of US land forces from Europe make it seem likely that the latter 1980s will see the Leopard series as even more the principal NATO main battle tank in the forward areas than is the case today.

Britain's Key Contributions
Despite the severe economic restrictions on British tank development, and bad luck with the original engine designed for the Chieftain, all of the NATO nations, including the United States, have benefited from the British 105mm L7 gun, which has kept NATO main battle tanks up

with or ahead of Soviet tank gunnery for most of the past two decades. The British-developed "Chobham" armour and a 120mm rifled gun hold forth the promise of major improvements for future NATO main battle tanks. It is now generally recognized that only tanks equipped with Chobham armour, derivatives such as that of the US XM1 or the spaced armour of the German Leopard 2 (also Leopard 1 turret) will be able to close with Warsaw Pact tanks and anti-tank guided missile positions.

France's Role
Echeloned behind the first-line NATO forces (and expected to assume full NATO partnership responsibilities) are French armoured forces equipped with the

AMX-30, a tank developed independently by France after French-German efforts to develop a "Standard" tank broke down. The AMX-30 is well armed, agile, but too light to engage Soviet tanks in the sort of toe-to-toe battles that characterized the 1973 war in the Middle East.

There are plans now to reequip the French forces with an AMX-30B2 featuring an improved transmission, fire control system and fin-stabilized ammunition, pending development of a new main battle tank for the 1990s. Once again, an attempt is being made to develop a future tank acceptable to both the French and German armies, as well as to all other armies already using German tanks.

▲ British Army Chieftain negotiating rough ground.

▲ Leopard 2 has good mobility, firepower and protection.

▲ German Army Leopard 1A3 at speed.

Type	Crew	Weight[2] (tonnes)	Height ft(m)	Road Speed mph(kph)	Calibre	Main Gun—Effective Range yards (metres)	Stabil-ization[3]	Number Available	Main Gun Rounds	Cruising Range miles(km)
Leopard 2	4	55.15t	9.05 (2.76)	44.7 (72)	120mm	3,280+ (3000+)	Yes	100	42	342 (550)
Chieftain	4	55.8t	9.34 (2.85)	29.8 (48)	120mm	3,280+ (3,000+)	Yes	960	64	308 (496)
Leopard 1	4	42.4t	8.59 (2.62)	40.36 (65)	105mm	2,186 (2,000)	Yes	4,296[4]	60	348 (560)
AMX 30	4	36t	9.34 (2.85)	40.36 (65)	105mm	2,186 (2,000)	No	1,220	50	404 (650)
Centurion	4	51.8t	9.83 (3.00)	21.7 (35)	105mm	2,186 (2,000)	Yes	540[5]	66	118 (190)

The European NATO Tanks[1]

1. Sources: Interpolation of data from Spielberger, Walter J., *From Half-Track to Leopard 2*, Bernard & Graefe, Munich, 1979; "Comparative Characteristics of Main Battle Tanks," US Army Armor School; *Jane's World Armoured Fighting Vehicles*; *The Military Balance*, International Institute for Strategic Studies, 1980-81.
2. Combat loaded.
3. Ability to fire on the move by gyrostabilization of the main gun on an even plane.
4. Includes Belgium, Canada, Denmark, Italy, Netherlands and Norway as well as the German Bundeswehr.
5. Includes Denmark (200) and Netherlands (340). Netherlands' Centurions are to be replaced by 445 Leopard 2s between 1982 and 86.

Two Classes of NATO Tanks

The 1980s, then, will see two distinct classes of main battle tanks in NATO – those capable of confronting the full range of current Warsaw Pact weapons and those which must place greater reliance on deception, cover and conceal-ment if they are not only to survive but gain the degree of combat superiority necessary to defeat larger numbers.

The question of how the NATO tanks are to be used extends beyond the capabilities of the tanks themselves. The NATO "forward defence" concept requires that the front-line NATO armies be able to absorb and contain the initial Warsaw Pact onslaught long enough for reinforcements to be mobilized and long enough for

NATO air power and long-range missiles to disorganize and defeat the follow-on WP echelons.

The Tank in the Combined Arms Team

Tank-to-tank combat is only one aspect of this great task. The tanks on both sides must be evaluated in reference to high-performance aircraft, the attack helicopter and the anti-tank guided missile as well as opposing tanks. And by no means least, they must be examined in terms of how they are organized and would be employed.

The capabilities of ground-launched anti-tank guided weapons have been greatly exag-gerated in recent years, largely because the effect on legislative appropriations committees of a

misapprehension by journalists covering the 1973 Middle East War. In fact, examination of tank casualties on the battlefield showed that by far the larger number on both the Israeli and Egyptian sides had been caused by tank-fired kinetic energy rounds. What had occurred was essentially what a former Commandant of the U.S. Army War College recalled of the attempt to defend Germany in 1945 with a last-ditch militia armed with the shoulder-fired *Panzerfaust*: "*Volksstrommers* A and B scored quite a success with the initial surprise engagement, but when *Volksstrommers* C and D saw what the follow-on tanks did to *Volksstrommers* A and B they tended to lose interest."

Although there is a considerable

variation as to how the brigades are to be formed, the present NATO organizational approach is to use tanks as the core of combined arms brigades capable of "rolling with the punch" of the first onslaught, of maintaining their combat inte-grity and thereby disorganizing and confusing the attacking forces. Considering the terrain and weather of Central Europe, it is a concept that permits even the less capable NATO tanks to operate with good effect. The historical evidence of what occurs in a Russian army once confusion sets in provides probably the best assurance that the concept is sound. But it is difficult to foresee what NATO can or will do if its forward combat echelons succeed in this first battle.

Main Battle Tanks

▲ US National Guard M48A5 with 105mm gun.

▲ M1 tank on the range firing its 105mm main gun.

▲ M60A1 of US Marine Corps on a NATO exercise.

▲ First 3,000 M1s will have 105mm gun; later 120mm will be fitted.

▲ There are no more US M60A2s in Germany. 526 were built.

THE United States has an uneven history of armour development. Building on British and French experience and technology in World War I, the US Army successfully organized and fought tank formations. Yet the United States entered World War II with but a relative handful of obsolescent tanks and never quite caught up in terms of armour protection or firepower. Its great strength was the enormous capacity of its industrial plant.

Technological "Edge" Proving Elusive

The US Army has been striving ever since for the technological leap that would put it ahead of the competition. A large research and development investment in the Main Battle Tank 70 program came to nought when Congress refused to finance what was made out in the press at least to be a tank that was too expensive to be risked on the battlefield. A parallel attempt to gain the desired technological lead by abandoning the gun in favour of a gun/missile system, on the M60A2, also proved to be a disappointment. A combination of low missile velocity as opposed to the increasing velocities of opposing tank cannon, electronic countermeasures and difficulties with the conventional round to be fired as an alternative to the M6OA2's "Shillelagh" missile brought about abandonment of the effort.

The tribulations of the MBT-70 and M6OA2 programmes led many US Armour officers to look with envy on the successful evolutionary development of the German Leopard series. The development of a new American tank, the M1, with many features carried over from the MBT-70 does not seem to have diminished the pro-Leopard constituency, although there is a uniform chorus of praise for the M1 from the staff of the US Army Armor Center at Fort Knox, Ky.

In general, it appears that the M1 is on about a par with the Soviet T-72, with advantages over the T-72 in terms of survivability and crew habitability. From what has been published in the open press to date, it appears that the long effort to gain a leading edge in armament still has not succeeded. The first 3,000 models of the M1 are to be equipped with the 105mm M68 (British L7) gun thought by some unofficial observers to be of lesser capability than the 125mm gun on the T-72 which can fire ammunition at 5,900fps (1,800mps).

According to a US-West German agreement signed in February 1979, M1s produced after the first 3,000 (probably in 1985) will be fitted with the Rheinmetall smoothbore 120mm gun identical to that of the Leopard 2. The first 3,000 M1s will then be retrofitted with the same 120mm gun. Depending on Britain's choice of a future tank cannon, it appears, therefore, that a substantial standardization of NATO tank main armament will occur in the latter 1980s promising to maintain the simplification of ammunition

▲ M1 tank is now in service with US Army, but not until fitted with a 120mm gun will it equal the Soviet T-72.

The US Tanks – Specifications [1]

Type	Crew	Weight[2] (tonnes)	Height ft(m)	Road Speed mph(kph)	Main Gun Calibre	Main Gun Effective Range yards (metres)	Stabil- ization[3]	Number Available	Main Gun Rounds	Cruising Range miles(km)
M1	4	52.2	7.86 (2.4)	45 (72)	105mm	3,280+ (3,000+)	Yes	(3,000 by 1985?)	55	299 (482)
M60A3[4]	4	47.7	10.62 (3.24)	30 (48)	105mm	2,186 (2,000)	Yes	615	63	308 (496)
M60A1	4	47.7	10.62 (3.24)	30 (48)	105mm	1,748 (1,600)	No	6,495[6]	63	308 (496)
M60	4	47.7	10.49 (3.2)	30 (48)	105mm	1,748 (1,600)	No	1,555	63	308 (496)
M48A5[5]	4	46.8	10.03 (3.06)	30 (48)	105mm	1,748 (1,600)	No	2,064	62	308 (496)

Note:
Modifications within the M60 series were in survivability, night vision, rate of fire and automotive reliability, except that there was a major upgrading of firepower between the M60A1 and M60A3 through installation of a laser rangefinder and improved ammunition. The M48A5 was retrofitted with M60-series gun, power pack and fire control system.

1. Sources: Interpolation of data from "Comparative Characteristics of Main Battle Tanks," US Army Armor School; *Armor* Magazine; *International Defense Review*; *Jane's World Armoured Fighting Vehicles*; *The Military Balance*, International Institute for Strategic Studies, 1980-81.
2. Combat loaded.
3. Ability to fire on the move by gyrostabilization of the main gun on an even plane.
4. Teledyne of Muskegan, Michigan, has developed a "Super M60" offering improvements that the manufacturer believes may upgrade M60-series tanks almost to the level of the new M1 and Leopard 2. Improvements include an upgraded engine, improved armour and a lower-silhouette cupola.
5. The M48A5 is used by US National Guard and Reserve units. A similarly upgraded M48 is in use by German Reserve forces. Only the German M48s would be immediately available in Europe.
6. Includes 300 Italian.

resupply, achieved during the era of the 105mm L7.

The total curent US Army main battle tank requirement is reported to be 14,000 vehicles. Current planned M1 production is for 7,000 vehicles. This means that a large number of the earlier M60 series tanks are likely to remain in US units through the 1980s. As a tank whose basic design dates from the 1950s, the M60 series is acknowledged to be clearly inferior to the Soviet T-72 but, in its later modifications at least, an even match for earlier model Soviet tanks, many of which are still to be found in Warsaw Pact formations.

Large numbers of M60-series tanks were used by Israel in the 1973 Middle East War. Asked to compare them with Soviet T-62s

and earlier models, an Israeli Armour Division commander commented, 'The difference is too close to call. The difference in performance I observed was entirely a matter of crew capability."

Why after all these years, has Why, then, after all these years, has the US Army been unable to gain the wide technological superiority in main battle tanks that American industrial genius would seem to assure? The problem lies in the long period of development. Twenty-one years elapsed between the introduction of the M60 series and the M1. The United States had an edge in the laboratory and in technology available from the civilian market, but it seems to have given up that advantage by looking up one avenue and down

another. In the same period that it took the United States to get from the first M60 to the M1, the Soviet fielded the T-62, the T-64 and the T-72, and they are reportedly soon to display the T-80. The Soviets follow a policy of incremental development, and it works. However, from what is known to date of the T-80, it appears that the M1 is at least equal in performance and in key areas, such as fire control, superior.

The Margin of Superiority
It has been assumed for years in the US and Western press generally that NATO could accept numerical inferiority to Soviet tanks because of what came to be regarded as an inherent technological superiority. If some margin of overall

technological superiority exists, it is best defined in a letter published in *International Defense Review* (issue 5/1979, p. 848) by Sgt. Christopher F. Schneider of B Troop, 3rd Squadron, 12th U.S. Cavalry: "A five-tank (US) platoon can destroy a threat tank company in 4 to 6 seconds."

Great battles are won or lost by men such as Sergeant Schneider and his comrades at the company and platoon level. His statement is one of confidence in equipment, crew training and, above all, in himself. It is an accumulation of such opinions that has led the NATO military leadership to believe that the NATO armies, if properly supported, can defeat a Warsaw Pact onslaught despite the great disparity in numbers.

Light Armoured Fighting Vehicles

▲ BMD is an exceptional vehicle designed for airborne operations.

▲ BMD advancing across dropping-zone.

▲ The basic recce version of BRDM-2 is armed with 14.5mm KPV and 7.62mm PKT machines guns. It is fully amphibious.

THERE is a pattern of Soviet offensive action apparent in the incursions into Czechoslovakia in 1968 and Afghanistan in 1979 that bodes ill for NATO in Europe, or wherever the Soviets choose to move next. Occupation of airfields by airborne and airlanded troops well ahead of the forces moving overland or by sea has been an established aspect of warfare for decades. It takes on a new meaning in Soviet hands because of two high-quality light armoured vehicles in service in the eight Soviet Airborne divisions.

The BMD and ASU-85 Pose a Major Threat

These are the BMD Airborne Combat Vehicle and the ASU-85 Airborne Self-Propelled Tank De-

stroyer, both of them full-tracked.

The BMD first appeared in 1973. At eight metric tonnes, it is air transportable, providing the Soviet Airborne divisions with a potent armour-protected firepower "package" in the airhead. It is equipped with a 73mm gun, backed by an auxiliary AT-3 Sagger anti-tank guided missile. These provide a respectable anti-tank capability to a range of about 9,840ft (3,000m) in the case of the Sagger and 2,624ft (800m) for the high explosive anti-tank (HEAT-FS) 73mm ammunition. There are no less than three 7.62mm machineguns, one coaxial and two in the bow. In addition to a crew of three, the BMD can carry a half squad of infantry.

With 40 73mm rounds, four Sag-

ger rounds and more than 2,000 rounds of 7.62 ammunition on board, a maximum road speed of 50mph (80km/hr) and fuel for a range of 198 miles (320km) the BMD arrives at the airhead as an offensive as well as a defensive threat.

"Imagine a platoon of rear area soldiers assembled from support units to defend a bridge," a US Army intelligence officer comments. "Suddenly, bursting out of a wood 1640ft (500m) away are 10 BMDs, moving at 50mph (80km/hr) and firing 30 machineguns at the bridge guards. To believe that a defending platoon armed with only a few light anti-tank weapons (LAWS) will stay at the bridge expects a lot."

In addition to a crew of three, the

BMD can carry a half squad of infantry. There are 110 squads mounted in BMDs in each of the Soviet airborne divisions.

The ASU-85 dates from 1962. It is slower (27mph, 44km/hr) and with less range than the BMD. Its high velocity armour piercing ammunition will penetrate 5in (130mm) of armour at 3,280ft (1,000m). There is a battalion of 18 such weapons in each Soviet airborne division.

Reinforced by two companies of BMDs, it is now possible to envision a Soviet airborne attack marshalling against one defending company a total of 18 85mm guns, 20 73mm guns, 20 AT-3/Sagger ATGMs and 78 7.62mm machineguns. When support by attack helicopters is included, this

▲ ASU-85 is standard equipment in airborne divisions. It featured in the first-wave of operations in Prague and Kabul.

▲ PT-76, being replaced in Soviet service by BMP-recce.

▲ Soviet airborne division ASU-85s.

potential changes the entire context of airborne operations.

New Role for the Airborne Forces

Traditionally airborne units drop to an overload speed of dismounted infantry (2.5mph, 4km/hr) once they establish themselves at an airhead. The Soviets have now overcome this limitation by mounting one entire regiment of each Airborne division in BMDs and by assigning a company of 10 BMDs to each of the remaining two regiments.

Thus, the Soviets have reduced the inherent vulnerability of airborne units to armour counterattack. More important, they have given them the capability to move out from the airhead and to per-form the rear area exploitation mission once associated only with a breakthrough force.

For protection of their own rear areas, the Warsaw Pact forces have an extensive collection of lightly armoured, wheeled combat vehicles. Principal among these is the Soviet BRDM-2 series. First produced in the early 1960s, the basic BRDM is a fast (62mph, 100km/hr), light (6.9 tons, 7 tonnes) and versatile vehicle. It is amphibious, with a road range of 466 miles (750km) and four powered auxiliary wheels that can be lowered to improve cross-country performance. In the basic configuration the BRDM-2 is armed with a turret-mounted 14.5mm (KPVT) machinegun and a coaxial 7.62mm machinegun. Four infantrymen can be carried in addi-tion to the normal two-man crew.

The BRDM is adaptable to a wide variety of uses. Principal among these is conversion to an anti-tank mode by removal of the turret and installation of launch rails for the Sagger, Swatter or Spandrel. From 8 to 14 missiles can be carried on the vehicle depending on type. Four-tube launchers have been observed on BRDMs converted to anti-aircraft missile use. Eight SA-9/Gaskin SAMs can be carried.

Hungary produces a wheeled amphibious scout car (FUG-70) which must also be classed as a rear area security vehicle due to its light armament and limited cross-country capability. This vehicle is used by East Germany as well as Hungary. Variations of an earlier design (FUG-63) are in use by Hungary and Czechoslovakia as ambulances, radiological-chemical reconnaissance vehicles and armoured personnel carriers.

A Double-edge Sword?

Some 5,350 of these BRDM and FUG vehicles are reported in the East European armies, suggesting that they may be directed as much, or more, to an internal security role as to a combat reconnaissance role. There is a double edge to that. In a situation where elements of the East European armies made known a desire to turn against their Soviet masters, NATO Special Forces units might be able to turn these fleets of fast armoured vehicles to the same purpose intended for the BMD in the Soviet airborne divisions.

Light Armoured Fighting Vehicles

▲ Striker anti-tank vehicle armed with Swingfire missiles.

▲ M551 Sheridan of US Army with 152mm gun/launcher.

▲ British Fox armoured car armed with 30mm Rarden cannon.

▲ British and Belgian armies use Scimitar recce vehicle.

▲ Fox scout car has exceptional cross-country performance.

PROTECTION of NATO rear areas and the ability to slow down and harass deep-penetrating Warsaw Pact armoured columns are critical defensive missions for the NATO nations. The Warsaw Pact poses not only a threat of massive breakthroughs overland but, also, an extensive airborne capability greatly expanded by addition of the BMD Airborne Combat Vehicle to the Soviet Airborne divisions.

Considering the disparity in numbers between NATO and Warsaw Pact main battle tanks, it is apparent that NATO's first-line tank fleet will be fully engaged from the moment an attack begins. A second belt of defensive positions must be formed behind the front-line NATO forces as quickly

among them are the French AMX-10RC and a new French product, the Panhard ERC 90 S *Sagie*.

The AMX-10RC has a road speed of 53mph (85km/hr) and a range over roads of 497 miles (800km). It is armed with a 105mm gun and anti-tank ammunition capable of penetrating 5.8in (150mm) of sloped armour at an indicated range of 4,000ft (1,225m). A total of 190 of these vehicles are in service in the French Army or on order.

The ERC 90 S is armed with a smooth bore 90mm gun firing a fin-stabilized round capable of penetrating 4.7in (120mm) of sloped armour at ranges assumed to be in the neighbourhood of 4,900ft (1,500m). It has a maximum road speed of 68mph (110km/hr) and a range on roads of 590 miles

as regular formations not immediately engaged can be brought forward and reserve units mobilized. It would be reasonable to expect that NATO's entire inventory of older, less capable tanks (M-48s, Centurions, etc.) would be used in this manner.

Containing the Deep Penetrations

Anti-tank helicopter formations offer an ideal means to break up and destroy deep armoured penetrations without drawing NATO main battle tanks away from the forward battle areas, *if* those penetrations can be contained and slowed. There are a variety of well armed, wheeled NATO light armoured vehicles capable of performing this vital role. Chief

(950km). Both vehicles are amphibious.

Advantages of the Wheeled Fighting Vehicle

As wheeled vehicles, the AMX-10RC and the ERC 90 S offer the advantage of long-distance, high-speed travel over the excellent West European road networks without the loss of time and the inevitable breakdowns involved in using full-track vehicles. Supported by logistic vehicles carrying ammunition resupply, they could perform a valuable role in moving rapidly to the flanks of a major armoured penetration, slowing or pinning down enemy tanks until attack helicopters could finish them off. Produced in quantity, the AMX-10RC and the ERC 90

▲ French ERC-90 firing its 90mm main gun.

▲ Sheridan's gun/launcher can fire shells or missiles.

▲ Some 700 AML armoured cars serve with the French Army; they are armed with a 90mm gun.

S would seem to offer a means to create a quick-reaction armoured reserve at a fraction of the cost of full-track vehicles.

Available in both the new and an older (AML) Panhard series, are wheeled vehicles of similar automotive performance configured to anti-tank and anti-aircraft roles. Although older and less capable than the AMX-10RC, France has in service 485 Panhard EBR-75 heavy armoured cars equipped with a 90mm gun and firing a fin-stabilized round. The heavy-gun French armoured cars would be more than a match in most situations for the Soviet airborne BMD's 73mm gun, the older EBR-75s proving a most useful NATO reserve in this role.

Both the British and German armies have a substantial number of more lightly armed wheeled armoured vehicles in service. Although developed as combat reconnaissance vehicles, both the German Spahpanzer 2 and the British Fox can perform effectively in the rear area security role.

Like the EBR-75, the Spahpanzer 2 has a driver at each end of the vehicle, providing these relatively thin-skinned vehicles with their best defence when encountering a heavily armed opponent. The 8x8 Spahpanzer 2 mounts a 20mm cannon and a 7.62 machinegun fired from the tank commander's position. There are 408 of these vehicles in service with the Bundeswehr.

The principal limitation of the Spahpanzer is its relatively high profile. That problem, however,

can be overcome by judicious use of terrain. An especially quiet engine coupled with its "fore and aft" driving controls more than make up for the problems imposed by profile.

The British Fox is the fastest 64.5mph (104km/hr) of the light armoured vehicles considered here. With a 30mm cannon and 7.62 coaxial machinegun it would perform effective service in patrolling lines of communication, as well as in its primary reconnaissance mission

Resurgence of Old Idea

From this overview, it appears that France's faith in heavily armed, fast, wheeled fighting vehicles offers an economy-of-force measure which has been too lightly

regarded up to now by the other NATO nations.

In theory, the deployment of home-guard, anti-tank missile teams at crossroads and behind barnyard walls might wear down an attacking armoured force before it could reach its strategic objectives. In practice, the lonely, immobile ATGM team is prone to demoralization and defeat before it has a chance to take its toll (see page 115). An armoured, high-speed and heavily gunned force capable of effective fire and rapid displacement is another matter. It could be the long-sought means by which a properly trained reserve force could be brought into action quickly and effectively enough to make a decisive contribution.

Battlefield Rockets and Missiles

▲ RPU-14 140mm rocket launcher used by airborne forces.

▲ Czech Army RM-70 40 round RL has automatic reload.

▲ Soviet BM-21 launcher firing a single 122mm rocket.

▲ Frog-7 battery of the East German Army about to fire.

▲ The Soviet 240mm BM-24 rocket launcher (RL) is a spin-stabilised weapon with a maximum range of 12,029yds (11,000m). The BM-24 is now in second-line use only.

BECAUSE they are on the borderline between nuclear and conventional warfare, and because of their large numbers and extensive deployment, the Warsaw Pact arsenal of "battlefield support" missiles is perhaps the most worrisome single category of weapons to be considered in this analysis of "conventional" ground force weapons. Assuming a stand-off air battle during at least the first few days in which most tactical aircraft on both sides would be engaged primarily in some form of air-to-air warfare, the long range missiles of the ground forces could play a decisive role.

Political Influence of SS-20
Although with a range of approximately 1,863 miles (3,700km) it is more properly described as a theatre rather than a battlefield support weapon, the Soviet SS-20 has exerted a powerful influence not only on the military situation in Europe but on the political situation in the entire North Atlantic Alliance. Launched from the Western USSR, where most of the estimated 100 initial production models are thought to be deployed, the SS-20 could cover tactical as well as strategic targets in all of Europe.

While it would be an expensive means of delivering a high-explosive warhead, use of the SS-20 in such a role against air bases critical to deployment of reinforcements from the United States and Britain could not be ruled out.

Used in the conventional mode, the SS-20 would greatly complicate the worldwide strategic situation if initial hostilities were confined to the immediate land battle area. If conventional warheads only were being fired from Soviet soil how would NATO respond? Cruise missiles with conventional warheads would seem to be the most rational response, yet the SS-20 is already deployed and the cruise missiles that could counter it are still the subject of debate in NATO political councils. While this is being worked out, the improved NATO Pershing II is capable of functioning as an interim conventional counter to at least some of the SS-20 forward positions.

Next in order of size and importance is the SS-12 (Scaleboard).

Also considered to be deployed only in the Soviet Union, Scaleboard is thought to be limited to a nuclear role, with a warhead possibly in the order of one megaton. Only if deployed into Eastern Europe, or if the land battle were to spread into Poland, would Scaleboard's estimated 310 miles (500km) range permit it to become a threat. The appearance of these weapons in Eastern Euorpe would be one of the key indicators of a Soviet buildup for attack.

Scud and Frog
Even though the problems posed by the SS-20 and, more remotely, by Scaleboard are large, the most immediate threat to NATO land forces are the weapons known to NATO as Scud A, Scud B and Frog

▲ Scud-B in the firing position.

▲ Frog-7 missile battery on the move. Missile has a range of about 37 miles (60km).

▲ Soviet soldiers reload BM-21 122mm RL.

(Free Rocket Over Ground) and their prospective early 1980s replacements, respectively the SS-22 (for the Scud weapons) and SS-21 (for Frog).

Chemical Warheads the Chief Threat?

What may be the chief threat posed by these three missile types falls midway between the nuclear and conventional (high-explosive, HE) modes. In short, from their present positions in East Germany and Czechoslovakia these weapons could deliver chemical munitions on every major logistics complex in the NATO Corps rear areas. Given the present state of NATO defences against chemical warfare, such attacks could threaten the logistics lifeblood of the fighting forces even if supplies, transportation and all the rest remained substantially intact. The civilianization of much of the NATO rear area support, of course, greatly increases this risk since even the threat of such an attack might be sufficient to disperse the civilian work force, except where these civilians are organized as immediately mobilizable reserve units **with chemical warfare training and the relevant equipment.**

Scud A is a single-stage, liquid-fuel missile with a maximum range of 93 miles (150km). It can be armed with nuclear, high-explosive or, presumably, chemical warheads. It is an unguided weapon, except that its range can be controlled by radio cutoff of the **engine when it nears the target.**

Scud B is an improved weapon with an estimated range of 105.5 miles (170km). Like Scud A, it is supersonic but with an inertial guidance system and, therefore, an assumed considerable improvement in accuracy.

These older Scud missiles are deployed in brigade-size units in Bulgaria, Czechoslovakia, Hungary, Poland and Romania in addition to the Soviet Union

As in the case of the SS-20, Scaleboard with its one-megaton warhead is more of a theatre than a battlefield support weapon. The Scud systems and their follow-ons are Front and Army (NATO Corps equivalent) support weapons. Frog is a division-level system generally comparable to the NATO Honest John system being phased out.

Seven models of Frog have been identified, six of them mounted on self-propelled, full track vehicles adapted from tanks of the JS-III and PT-76 series. What appears to be the latest in the series, Frog 7, is mounted on a truck chassis.

Depending on the model, Frog is considered to have a range of from 22 to 45 miles (35km to 72km). The heavier Scud missiles and Scaleboard are carried on wheeled transporter-erectors.

Because of the SS-20 the future role of battlefield missiles and rockets is now a microcosm of the worldwide Strategic Arms Limitation Talks (SALT), with the Soviets in the strong position in any "trade-off".

Battlefield Rockets and Missiles

▲ Lance missile lifts off from launcher/erector vehicle.

▲ Over 100 Pershing IIs are expected to be deployed by 1983.

▲ Pluton is in service with the French Army. Entirely French, it has 15KT or 25KT warheads.

ON the balance side of this most dangerous single category of land force weapons, NATO has at its fingertips what its military leadership regard as the most effective single anti-tank weapon yet devised—the Enhanced Radiation (ER) warhead.

Misreported initially as a "neutron bomb" that "kills people but saves property", the enhanced radiation warhead was intended from the start as an anti-armour weapon that would reduce the "collateral" damage associated with mass destruction weapons. More important, and potentially decisive in the NATO-Warsaw Pact land battle, is the powerful electromagnetic pulse (EMP) projected by ER weapons. Indeed, fear of the effect of EMP on their rigid system

of command and control by disruption of battlefield communications may well be the real reason for the thus-far successful Soviet opposition to ER deployment.

Pershing, Lance and Pluton

Although still the subject of intense political debate, ER warheads if and when deployed would be particularly adaptable to NATO's three principal battlefield rockets—the US Pershing and Lance and the French Hades (under development).

The original Pershing (Pershing I) has a maximum range of 397 to 453 miles (640 to 730km). It is a two-stage, solid-propellant missile first deployed in 1964. About 100 are now operated in West Germany by German and US units. The

United States retains control of all nuclear warheads.

It is expected that Pershing II will begin to replace Pershing I in 1983. It will have a more accurate terminal guidance system by which on-board radars and computers will compare targets with prestored data and images. Explosive power of the nuclear warhead is expected to be 60 to 400 kilotons. Conventional warheads designed to penetrate earth and concrete to a depth of nine storeys are reported under development. A total of 108 Pershing IIs are expected to be deployed in West Germany, the United Kingdom and Italy.

France is the only NATO member other than the United States to deploy a nuclear-capable battlefield support missile—

Pluton. This is a two-stage, solid-fuel weapon with a range of 99 miles (160km) and a choice of warheads ranging from 15 to 25 kilotons. A total of 75 are known to be in service. Pluton and the follow-on Hades seem to indicate that in the event of conflict in Europe France would engage a Warsaw Pact attack beyond the French border.

Other than Pershings, Lance is the only battlefield support missile now in the US active Army arsenal suited to attack beyond the range of cannon artillery. Its warheads are intended for quick conversion to ER technology once the decision is made to deploy such weapons.

Six Lance battalions with a total of 36 launchers are deployed in

▲ Launcher for Multiple Launch Rocket System (MLRS).

▲ MLRS can be reloaded quickly and moved to new positions.

▲ West German Army detachment about to launch Lance missile.

▲ Pershing I serves with US Army and German Luftwaffe.

Europe. Each missile is controlled by a "simplified" inertial guidance system. Mid-course corrections are made by a distance-measuring ground station which monitors the flight path and relays commands by radio data link.

Lance replaced both the older US Sergeant and the division-level US rocket, Honest John. The Honest John is still to be found in US National Guard divisions and in other NATO armies. It has a maximum range of 20 miles (32km) and a minimum range of 10 miles (16km), in both the nuclear and conventional modes. The original Honest Johns were true ballistic missiles, their range determined by elevation of the launcher. There has been testing, however, of a laser guidance kit to enable the rocket to home on laser energy reflected from the target.

Two US developments promise an important new dimension in battlefield support weapons in the 1980s. The Multiple Launch Rocket System (MLRS) will consist of 12 9in (230mm) rocket launchers mounted in two six-round pods on a full-tracked chassis adapted from the M2 Infantry Fighting Vehicle. The rockets can be fired singly or in ripple sequence with the ability to dispatch all 12 in less than a minute. Range is understood to be in excess of 18.6 miles (30,000 metres). Teamed with new radars, MLRS's primary mission is to be counterbattery fire.

Also under development is an "Assault Breaker Antiarmour Missile System" consisting of a Lance warhead and submunitions to be capable of destroying a company-size armour unit for each carrier missile fired.

European Battlefield Rocket Systems

In July 1979, Britain, France and West Germany signed an initial agreement with the United States to acquire 200 MLRS and 250,000 rockets through licensed manufacture in Europe. Italy has also entered the field with its FIROS 25. This is a 122mm system capable of firing 40 rockets from two truck-mounted pods to a range of 11 to 16.7 miles (18–27km).

A major limitation of all long-range rocket and missile systems used in the battlefield role, whether in the NATO or Warsaw Pact arsenals, is the ability to acquire and retain targets. If there is to be a fluid, wide-ranging battle flowing back and forth through a band 31 to 62 miles (50 to 100km) wide along the present frontier it may be very difficult for any of these weapons, in the conventional or nuclear role, to be effective. It is because this problem would be compounded by a major breakthrough that many military authorities believe authority to fire nuclear weapons must be delegated to the battlefield commander.

The most important exception to the target acquisition limitations is the ER warhead, in that its use to disrupt Warsaw Pact communications by means of its EMP effects would not require precise engagement of ground targets.

Artillery Systems

▲ 85mm SD-44 serves with airborne anti-tank companies.

▲ M-30 122mm howitzers in typical in-line firing position.

▲ SAU-122 M-1974 122mm self-propelled guns of Guards unit.

▲ SAU-122 has good cross-country performance.

THE Warsaw Pact has available over 24,000 artillery pieces of 100mm or larger calibres. Supplementing these are some 3,600 multiple rocket launchers and 11,500 anti-tank and assault guns of 85mm or larger. Further, the Warsaw Pact armies field large-calibre mortars for which there is no NATO counterpart. There are known to be about 10,000 of these weapons.

As is the case with tanks, it is easy to be psychologically overwhelmed by these huge numbers—and that, of course, is part of the purpose in producing them in such quantity. When the question of how these vast numbers are to be employed is addressed it becomes somewhat easier to cope with them psychologically and militarily.

First of all, this mass of conventional firepower could be employed at or near full potential only if the Warsaw Pact were to deploy its formations in battle array across the entire NATO-Warsaw Pact frontier, an action that would precipitate a world crisis and raise the question of immediate use of NATO theatre nuclear weapons. In short, given such complete Warsaw Pact preparations, it would be virtually impossible for NATO to defend with conventional means alone.

Considered in its much more likely form, that is, a surprise attack from march columns, the ability of the Warsaw Pact to employ artillery is drastically restricted in that masses of artillery would still be in assembly areas, and out of range, when the forward Tank and Motorized Rifle divisions crossed the frontier.

The Primary Threat

In this context then, the artillery weapons listed are those which would constitute the primary threat to NATO forces during the first crucial hours and days of an attack. Whether the mass of follow-on, largely towed artillery ever would come into play would depend, first and foremost on the outcome of the air battle and, of equal or perhaps even greater importance, on the outcome of the battle for control of the electromagnetic spectrum.

No aspect of modern land warfare is so dependent on reliable communications as the artillery.

Especially in the sort of fast-moving operations contemplated in Warsaw Pact assault doctrine, accurate target information must be transmitted instantly, plotted and transmitted to the gun crews before the target disappears. More often than not the fires of several batteries or battalions must be co-ordinated over a considerable distance. In a fast-moving attack, almost all of that must be done by some form of radio communications susceptible to jamming by the enemy, interference from the sheer volume of friendly and enemy sets on the air and, in nuclear operations, the still largely unknown factor of electromagnetic pulse.

Nor is any element of the land combat arms quite so sensitive to

▲ 152mm D-20 field howitzer; range is 19,685yds (18km).

▲ 122mm D-30 towed howitzers being brought into action.

▲ Soviet SAU-152mm M-1973 self-propelled howitzer.

▲ SAU-152 can fire nuclear, chemical, HE and AT rounds.

Principal Attack (Front) Warsaw Pact Artillery					
Type	Size	Motive Power	Range yards (m)	Rate of Fire	Employment
M1974[1]	122mm	Self-propelled	23,936 (21,900)[2]	5rds/min (max)	Attack echelons, Division direct support
M1973[1]	152mm	Self-propelled	19,674 (18,000)	Unknown	Division direct support
S-23	180mm	Towed	47,873 (43,800)	1 rd/min	Front and Army general support
M-46	130mm	Towed	29,674 (27,150)	6 to 7 rds/min	Army general support
D-30	122mm	Towed	23,936 (21,900)[2]	6 to 7 rds/min	Division direct support

1. Automatic loaders.
2. Rocket-assisted projectiles.

weaknesses of doctrine as is the artillery. And in this sensitive category the Soviets are known to have serious problems.

Soviet Advanced Planning

The Soviets have devised an intricately detailed system by which coordinated artillery barrages are to be shifted along successive lines as the tank and infantry attack progresses. This tells the artillery commander that when the attack is being conducted at a speed of 6.2mph (10km/hr), for example, he has one minute and 20 seconds in which to fire a barrage if he is to keep the barrage at least 218 yards (200 metres) ahead of the attacking tank-infantry formation. Nowhere else is there so vivid an example of the Soviet attempt, evident in all

Warsaw Pact doctrine, to plan out everything in advance.

The application of such intricate doctrine is not an easy matter. From current Soviet military publications it is apparent that difficulty is being encountered in application during training, on familiar ground and presumably with no real threat to communications. Application under battle conditions on unfamiliar ground and subject to major failures of communications suggests that substantial numbers of Warsaw Pact artillery units will be unable to engage at full potential because of troop safety factors, lack of adequate firing data and the inevitable confusion about what to do when the rigid planning scenario goes awry.

Self-propelled Guns
The Immediate Threat

In essence, this seems to indicate that the M1974 122mm self-propelled gun will be the most immediate threat faced by NATO forces in the early phase of an attack. Well forward in the attacking columns and capable of direct as well as indirect fires, these weapons are the most likely to have available reliable data both as to targets and the location and scheme of manoeuvre of friendly forces.

If, as the NATO military commanders believe, the initial Warsaw Pact offensive can be stopped and the following echelons disrupted by air power and long-range missiles it will be possible for NATO reserves to launch a counteroffensive that

could make it impossible to bring the full weight of Warsaw Pact artillery to bear. If NATO is unable or unwilling to go over to the offensive, then, of course, it will be possible to organize the full potential of the Warsaw Pact guns.

Positional warfare in which Warsaw Pact multiple rocket launchers and the large-calibre mortars as well as tube artillery could be brought to bear would virtually solve the difficult command and control problems inherent in the rigid Soviet doctrine. For all of the lip service the Soviets pay to fast-moving operations, it is the Western armies that have developed such operations to their highest forms to date and there is reason to believe that it is they who still can employ it best.

▲ The British Army's Abbot is an amphibious 105mm SP gun.

▲ West German LARS mounts 36 110mm rockets on a truck.

▲ M110 8in (203mm) nuclear-capable SP howitzer is in service with many NATO armies: range, 18,372yds (16,800m).

NEW AND in many ways revolutionary developments in artillery ammunition now reaching production and deployment are responsible to a large degree for the increasing optimism NATO commanders are expressing about the chances of stopping and disrupting a Warsaw Pact offensive. At the same time, large-scale modernisation and re-equipment is underway in most NATO artillery arms, which even at last includes marked improvements in standardisation and interoperability among what have been up to now very disparate systems.

Among the most spectacular of the new developments is the US Army's "Copperhead" precision-guided missile (PGM), a totally new concept in artillery projectiles. This is a remarkable "marriage" between traditional tube artillery and the guided missile. Fired quite conventionally from a 155mm cannon, wing and tail control surfaces deploy from the round after it has left the muzzle. At its apogee a homing device activates, which is sensitive to laser energy spotted on the target by "laser target designators" mounted in aircraft or on the ground. So long as the laser beam continues to illuminate the target the Copperhead projectile can manoeuvre to seek out a moving target within a circle 3,280 yards (3,000 meters) in diameter. Stationary targets are, of course, much easier game. One of the many advantages of Copperhead is that the gun crews need only minimal extra training to handle this new system.

Poor-weather Usability

Laser designation of the target can be broken by the destruction or abandonment of the observation post from which the beam is transmitted. Smoke, fog, rain, snow and vegetation, also, can interfere. According to Testimony to Congress by a US Deputy Under-Secretary of Defense, Copperhead should be usable 50 per cent of the time during the winter months in Central Europe around midday. Planned improvements in both the missile and the ground-based laser designator are expected to increase efficiency. Even with these limitations in mind, however, Copperhead and other new artillery systems offer a new and dramatic means to reduce the Warsaw Pact's current 3:1 superiority in total artillery pieces. Equally important, if less immediately dramatic, is the question of logistics, as the Copperhead round and other US ammunition is interoperable with the new Anglo-German-Italian FH-70 155mm howitzers now being deployed. In fact, Copperhead is now in production by a European consortium and will be procured by most, if not all, NATO countries. There is, at the moment, no known Soviet counterpart to Copperhead and so it would appear that, at long last, some of the qualitative superiority of Soviet artillery has been dissipated by this unique and potentially devastating system.

Until the introduction into ser-

▲ French 105mm Mark 61 SP gun is mounted on the AMX-13 tank chassis.

▲ M107 175mm SP gun of the West German Bundesheer.

▲ French 155mm GCT SP gun has a burst fire rate of 8 rounds per minute.

▲ M107 175mm of the US Army.

Principal NATO Artillery

Type	Size	Motive Power	Range yards(m)	Rate of Fire	Employment
M109	155mm	Self-propelled	17,500 to 26,232 (16 to 24,000)[4]	45 rds/hr[5]	Division direct support
GCT/AMX-30[2]	155mm	Self-propelled	26,232 (24,000)	6 rds/45 sec	Division direct support
FH-70	155mm	Towed	27,325 to 32,790 (25 to 30,000)[1]	6 rds/min	Division direct support
M110	(8″) 203mm	Self-propelled	31,806 (29,100)	1 rd/2 min	Div/Corps general support
M107	175mm	Self-propelled	35,741 (32,700)		Corps general support
M198[3]	155mm	Towed	32,790 (30,000)[1]	4 rds/min	Div/Corps general support

1. Rocket-assisted projectile. 2. Automatic loader. 3. To be deployed with reinforcements from the United States. 4. Copperhead limited to 17,488 yards (16,000m). 5. Sustained fire.

vice of the FH-70, the French 155mm GCT/AMX-30 self-propelled howitzer and the improved US M109 series self-propelled howitzers, NATO was consistently outranged by Soviet artillery. Now, with such modifications as lengthened barrels and new rocket-assisted ammunition, NATO is extending the range of its weapons.

A group of NATO "cluster munitions is expected in the late 1980s, which will be capable of showering Warsaw Pact BMPs and other light armoured vehicles with hollow-charge (HEAT) projectiles released from 155mm and larger casings. This could help to defeat a major current advantage of the light armoured vehicle, which is designed to protect troops from conventional shell fragments. Mines, also, are to be delivered by this means, offering a way to close off enemy avenues of approach when a surprise attack precludes the use of the more effective but very much slower traditional minelaying techniques.

Among the newer weapons only the French 155 GCT, the British Abbott and the US M109 series howitzers provide their crews with overhead armoured cover. The US 8-inch (203mm) howitzer, the principal NATO corps artillery weapon for the foreseeable future, lacks such protection as, at least for the moment, do its Soviet counterparts. A self-propelled, armoured version of the FH-70 is to be deployed in the mid-to-latter 1980s.

But protected or unprotected, counterbattery fire from the larger Warsaw Pact artillery force is of crucial concern to the NATO gunners. Hope for major progress in this area is offered by the long-range Multiple Rocket Launcher System (MLRS) (see NATO Battlefield Missiles and Rockets) and by several forthcoming surveillance systems expected to be deployed in the 1980s.

RPVs Replace or Supplement Ground Observers

The US Aquila miniature remotely piloted vehicle (RPV) may provide the means both to reduce the vulnerability of human ground designator teams in support of anti-armour fire by Copperhead, and to enhance the lethality of that system in counter-battery missions against enemy artillery. Equipped with both a laser designator and an on-board television sensor, Aquila is being designed for real-time relay of the television image to a ground station which can then operate the laser designator by remote control. Night surveillance can be provided by the addition of forward looking infra-red (FLIR) or more advanced sensor systems.

Less exotic developments of existing systems are the AN/TPQ-37 artillery locating radar and the AN/TPQ-36 mortar-locating radar, both improved over earlier models and both now in production.

One of the most important developments in fire support over recent years has been the rapid increase in the use of computerised control systems. The basic prob-

Artillery Systems

▲Anglo-German-Italian 155mm SP-70 self-propelled gun.

▲Over 3,000 M109 155mm SP howitzers have been built.

▲ British 105mm Light Gun; range 18,600yds (17,000m).

▲ M109 155mm SP in winter camouflage in Norway.

lem for NATO gunners is quite simply that the number of targets in the forward area will greatly exceed the fire support means available. It is, therefore, vital to make the most effective use of the limited resources available, including rapid reaction to requests for fire support as well as quick switching from one target to another.

Early systems included the US Army's Tacfire and the British FACE (Field Artillery Computing Equipment). The latter, for example, will be succeeded in the next two years by BATES – the Battlefield Artillery Target Engagement System. BATES' principal use will be to coordinate artillery fire within 1st (British) Corps in Germany, but this can be extended to include other sources

of fire support such as infantry mortars and close air support. It will also be used in nuclear fire planning. BATES will make use of Clansman radio nets and the Ptarmigan trunk communications system for data exchange between elements of the system, as well as with the Wavell general staff command and control system at the major headquarters.

Other developments are also being made, again with the purpose of increasing accuracy in order to make the very best use of the limited resources available. One such development for the British Army is the Artillery Meteorological System (AMETS), a self-contained, mobile, computer-based equipment for automatically obtaining and proces-

sing information on atmospheric conditions.

Artillery Logistics Becoming a Problem

Greater demands on the gunners to engage more targets with more fire, and to switch more rapidly from one target to another has also led to further complications. Increased rates of fire mean obviously that more ammunition will be required at the gun lines, which is placing increasing strain on supply systems. One of the solutions being pursued in the USA is the M109 Ammunition Delivery System (ADS) in which a converted M109 SP gun chassis is used to carry projectiles (118 155mm), propellant charges (120) and fuzes (192). The ADS can transfer rounds to an

M109 SP gun at a maximum rate of 8 rounds per minute. Whether even this will cope with the tremendous demands which will be placed on the artillery in the opening stages of any future war is, however, by no means certain. A further consideration is that in order to save money many armies now reduce their war maintenance reserves of ammunition. There will be little time in a future war to increase production, so armies will have to fight with what they have.

Most NATO Armies Have Nuclear-capable Artillery

The two gun systems capable of firing nuclear shells are the US M109 155mm and M110 8in (203mm) SP howitzers. Belgium, Denmark, FRG, Greece, Italy,

74

▲ M101A1 105mm towed howitzer of the US Marine Corps. Widely used in NATO, this weapon is now overdue for replacement.

▲ M107 175mm gun of the Royal Artillery. This gun has excellent range: 35,800yds (32,700m).

Netherlands, Turkey, the UK and the USA all hold M-110s and M-109s, whilst Canada and Norway only possess the latter. How many of these armies refuse to fire nuclear shells is not known with certainty, although Denmark and Norway both state that no nuclear weapons are held on their territory. In all cases the nuclear warheads are held in US custody and are only released with Presidential approval and immediately prior to use. Yields are in the low KT range.

President Reagan's announcement in August 1981 that the US intended to proceed with production of ER ("neutron") warheads, which could be built into 8in (203mm) shells, was greeted with understandable villification from the Soviets, with threats to pro-

duce similar weapons themselves.

One of the more noticeable changes in artillery weapons has been the swing to self-propelled gun carriages. Virtually all divisional and corps artillery in Western Europe is now SP, while the earlier open-topped versions, eg, M109, are being replaced by vehicles with traversible turrets. These SPs can move over terrain unsuitable for wheeled gun tractors and can get into and out of action more quickly. They also provide NBC and shell splinter protection for their crews, as well as carrying more ammunition and radios.

Towed artillery still has its place, however, for use on airborne, amphibious and mountain operations where the weight, size or complexity of self-propelled

guns would make them unsuitable.

As is obvious, all of the new surveillance systems, Copperhead and related lasers and computers, together with the command and control communications, depend to one degree or another upon the ability to use some part of the electromagnetic spectrum. Electronic warfare, therefore, becomes more and more a crucial part of the land battle.

Tube Artillery at Limit of Development?

There are other limitations accompanying the new technology. Increased muzzle blast from the new guns and their improved munitions are already known to be a hazard to the crews. Tube wear is increased by improved propel-

lants. Although the increased ranges are more than welcomed by NATO gunners there is no doubt that there is lessened accuracy at the extreme ranges, and a necessarily reduced explosive "payload". All these appear to suggest that, as some people claim to be the case with the tank, tube artillery of the 1980s may be at the limit of its development. The counter-argument is that artillery will continue to combine a degree of accuracy, economy, flexibility and effectiveness which cannot be equalled by any other system of fire support (such as missiles or aircraft).

Indeed, the major concern about NATO's artillery is that it is so outnumbered by the Warsaw Pact and many informed observers would like to see many more guns.

Helicopters

▲ Mil Mi-24 (Hind-D) being prepared for a mission. Note six stores pylons.

▲Airborne, Mil Mi-24 (Hind-A).

▲ Mil Mi-4 (Hound) is still in service with many Pact armies.

▲ Mi-6 (Hook). Max. slung payload: 9 tonnes.

▲ Mil Mi-8 (Hip) is the main Soviet transport helicopter.

▲ Hind-D with Swatters and UB-32 rocket pods.

THE Soviets have taken a Western idea, and the gift of a well-meaning former American President and formed them into a threat of large proportions—a threat against whom is not yet quite certain.

From a Sikorsky VH-3 passenger helicopter given by President Dwight D. Eisenhower to Soviet Premier Nikita Khrushchev the Soviets have developed and produced an estimated 750 copies of the Mil Mi-24 Hind assault helicopter, versions of which are considered to be the most advanced attack helicopter (AH) currently deployed.

Festooned with weapons suspended from its stubby wings and mounting a redesigned "chin" turret, Hind D presents a formidable appearance. Its size alone is impressive—4,530lb (10,000kg) compared to 2,050lb (4,525kg) of the US AH-IS. The chin turret mounts a 12.7mm Gatling gun. Four AT-2 Swatter anti-tank missiles are hung from the outer pylons and four pods of 32 57mm rockets each from the inner pylons. It is estimated to have a cruising speed of 121mph (195km/hr) and a combat radius, fully loaded, of 62 miles (100km). Range of its AT missiles and rockets is estimated to be 3,825 yards (3,500m).

Hind D is organized into regiments estimated at anywhere from 44 to 52 aircraft each. The basic attack element appears to be a flight of four. These are believed trained to approach their targets at low altitude (between about 5 and 10 yards), "pop up" to an altitude of 22 to 109 yards (20 to 100m) and fire at ranges of 2,186 to 3,279 yards (2 to 3,000m). Soviet officers appear to believe these tactics are adequate to keep the Hind out of reach of NATO air defence weapons. A late-model version has been observed with launcher rails, suggesting employment of air-to-air missiles and more advanced AT missiles.

Unique among attack helicopters, Hind retains the capability of carrying 8 to 10 fully equipped troops in addition to its full weapons load.

There is speculation in NATO circles that Hind, teamed with high-performance fighters and other troop-carrying helicopters could pose a threat to airfields and other key NATO rear-area objectives, greatly expanding the threat posed by the Soviet Airborne divisions.

Testing the Soviet Theories

There are several reasons, however, to question the validity of these theories. First, the helicopter in its present stage of development is not an attractive weapon for direct offensive operations where it is likely to encounter a high density of anti-aircraft weapons. American losses in Vietnam, even against a relatively "thin" air defence threat, attest to that. Nor would a breakthrough by Warsaw Pact land forces into NATO rear areas assure helicopters a significantly reduced degree of risk so

▲ Hind-D firing an anti-tank missile. It also has an anti-helicopter capability.

▲ Mil Mi-26 (Halo) shown for the first time at Paris 1981.

▲ Ground suppression rocket pods fitted on Mi-8 (Hip).

long as NATO could contest control of the air.

Although early studies showed that helicopters flown at low altitudes ("nap-of-the-earth") were poor targets for high-performance fighters, further development of the look-down, shoot-down NATO capability (AWACS and associated systems) seems likely to change that situation.

Second, the most efficient use of the gunship to date has been in wide-area counterinsurgency operations. Soviet forces are engaged in one such, in Afghanistan. Faced with unrest in Eastern Europe, Hind and its supporting aircraft would offer an economy-of-force substitute for divisions needed at the front. In a strategic sense, they could become the

"machinegun-at-the-back" that has been used before in Soviet history to assure the advance of its own troops and "allies".

Gains outside Europe

Third, the most promising areas for major strategic gains from the new airmobile technology lie not in Europe, but in the Persian Gulf region and on the Sino-Soviet border where there are vast undefended areas open to airmobile exploitation at minimum risk. Using the advantage of their interior lines, the Soviets could mass their attack helicopter formations anywhere on the arc from Central Europe to Khabarovsk much faster than their opponents could redeploy their forces.

Less advanced, but even more

heavily armed than the Hind D and E is the Mil Mi-8 Hip E. Originally produced in the early 1960s, Hip E carries 192 57mm rockets, a nose-mounted 12.7mm machinegun and four anti-tank missiles. Some 1,600 Hip Es are reported in the Soviet inventory with perhaps 200 more in other Pact Fleets

Both Hind and Hip are capable of night flying but the extent of their night and all-weather attack capability is questionable. In general, Soviet technology in those areas is considered to be less capable than that available to NATO, leading to further questions about the ability of the Soviet AH fleet to perform in its supposed role of providing fire support to Soviet European operations that could be expected to continue day and night.

Climate and Terrain versus Soviet Tactics

Climate and terrain, as well as likely enemy opposition, raise doubts about the indicated Soviet tactics. Whether in mountainous terrain on the northern and southern flanks, the rolling forested terrain of Southern Germany or the urbanized North German Plain, the ability of Warsaw Pact helicopters to maintain the low altitudes suggested and to gain firing positions at or near the extreme ranges of the on-board munitions without encountering disruptive, if not fatal, ground fire is open to question. Diversionary attacks by NATO scout helicopters, now present in all NATO large units, add a further hazard.

Helicopters

▲ RAF Chinook HC.1 carrying underslung US Army load.

▲ Westland Lynx of British Army demonstrates its agility.

▲ Hughes 500MD Defender of the US Army.

▲ Agusta A 129 is Europe's first day/night AT helicopter.

SEVEN NATO nations—Belgium, Britain, France, Germany, Italy, Netherlands and the United States—deploy or plan to deploy attack helicopters (AHs), that is, helicopters with a primary mission of anti-tank and general combat. The scout and troop or cargo-carrying helicopter has been present in all NATO armies for some time and their roles are well defined. As is the case with the Warsaw Pact nations, the role of the attack helicopter is only beginning to be thought out since there is no base of experience in large-scale European operations. The primary function of the NATO attack helicopter will be defeat of enemy penetrations.

Principal aircraft available in the NATO inventory during the early

1980s to carry out this important mission are the British Lynx, the French Puma, the German PAH-1, the Italian Mangusta and the American Cobra series.

Cobra (AH-1S) is the only type developed solely as a gunship. Its primary weapon is the TOW anti-tank guided missile. In addition, it carries a six-barrel 20mm automatic cannon. Speed of the AH-1S in the TOW configuration is 196mph (315km/hr). Maximum range is 315 miles (507km).

Lynx and Puma are products of a combined Franco–British development program. They can be configured to a variety of missions. In the gunship configuration the Lynx AH.Mk1 carries 6 to 8 anti-tank missiles (TOW, HOT, AS.11) depending on type, a 20mm

cannon or 7.62mm minigun, or two rocket pods launching 68mm or 2.75in rockets. Maximum cruising speed for the basic design is 175mph (282km/hr), with a maximum range of 335 miles (540km). Puma can mount a similar variety of armament, with similar performance.

An All-weather Capability Emerges

Italy's A.129 Mongoose (Mangusta) is the first West European AH designed for day and night all-weather combat operations (as is the US AH-1S). It carries eight TOWs and a 7.62mm Minitat machinegun. An earlier version (the A 109) carries four TOW launchers or, alternatively, 19 2.75in rockets. Maximum speed of

the A.129 will be 193mph (311km/hr) with endurance in the anti-tank role of 2 hours 30 minutes with a 20-minute reserve. The A.129 is expected to begin entering unit service in 1984.

The German PAH-1 is a derivative of the MBB B0105, a transport helicopter capable of carrying up to 10 soldiers in its basic configuration. In the PAH-1 configuration it can carry up to six anti-tank missiles. Belgium and the Netherlands are planning to acquire gunships in the early 1980s.

In all, NATO had approximately 600 AHs available in Europe in 1981. This total is expected to reach the 1,000 mark by the mid-1980s and could go higher if older models are retained.

How the new attack helicopter

▲ Still widely used by the US Army is the Bell AH-1 HueyCobra.

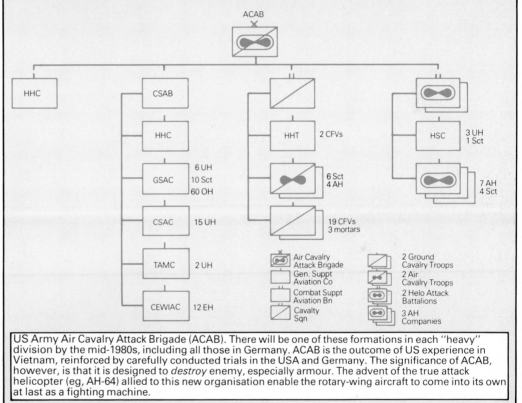

US Army Air Cavalry Attack Brigade (ACAB). There will be one of these formations in each "heavy" division by the mid-1980s, including all those in Germany. ACAB is the outcome of US experience in Vietnam, reinforced by carefully conducted trials in the USA and Germany. The significance of ACAB, however, is that it is designed to *destroy* enemy, especially armour. The advent of the true attack helicopter (eg, AH-64) allied to this new organisation enable the rotary-wing aircraft to come into its own at last as a fighting machine.

(AH) capability is organized and employed is at least as important as the quality of the weapons systems themselves. The United States, in consequence of its extensive combat experience in Vietnam, has the most highly developed organization to date in the form of its Air Cavalry Attack Brigade (ACAB). By the mid-1980s there will be one of these in each US division, structured as shown in the diagram above.

The ACAB is the outgrowth of a series of US Army studies (1978–80) focusing on a heavy and a light division, a heavy and a light corps and echelons above the corps. It was determined that significantly increased firepower and tactical mobility had to be introduced into both the light and

heavy divisions if either was to perform its mission in the latter 1980s and the 1990s. Only the helicopter offered the means to achieve such advantage in a single "package".

Emphasis on Destruction
The US 9th Infantry Division at Fort Lewis, Washington, was the first US unit to acquire an ACAB, in April 1980. Approval of the heavy division application came in August 1980 and transition is now in progress. (All US divisions in Europe are in the heavy category.)

A major change of emphasis from the US Cavalry units as they existed in the 1970s has occurred, in that the missions of these earlier units were primarily concerned with location and tracking of the

enemy. Now the emphasis is on destruction. As a result, the two Air Cavalry troops now in the ACAB are much smaller than their predecessors.

The attack helicopter unit is now central to the effectiveness of the ACAB. Its strength is felt to lie in situations in which rapid response time is important, when there are inadequate friendly ground forces in the area of contact, or when friendly ground forces are restricted by terrain. The AH units are to be integrated into the tactical plan of the ground commander to exploit their mobility advantage, flexibility and heavy long-range firepower.

Experience with individual aviation from World War II to the 1970s led the US Army planners to

provide unity of command for all divisional aviation assets while internally separating command, control and communications (C³) between the "fighters and supporters".

Dramatic Exchange Ratios
Although there had been many reservations about the ability of a unit such as the ACAB to function in the highly developed European combat environment, an instrumented test at Ansbach, West Germany, in 1973 provided the most dependable data so far on the utility of the scout/attack helicopter combination. For most engagement situations, average helicopter–versus–tank loss exchange ratios were 18:1 in favour of the helicopter. But in the break-

▲ Sikorsky CH-53 serves with US forces and West German Army.

▲ Scout helicopter of British Army fires SS-11 ATGW.

▲ BO 105 launches HOT missile.

▲ UH-60A tactical transport serves with US Army.

▲ BO 105P operating in PAH-1 interim anti-armour role.

through situation averages ran as high as 30:1.

The final influence in pushing the Army toward a fully integrated ACAB was the finding by aviation battalion commanders participating in 1979 NATO exercises that their units were too large for effective control.

The Combat Support Aviation Battalion (CSAB) shown on the chart supports both the ACAB itself and the division as a whole. For the division, it conducts airmobile operations, supply and artillery lifts and provides aircraft for command and control. Artillery forward observer aircraft support all elements.

The principal manoeuvre elements of the ACAB are, of course, the two Attack Helicopter Battalions (AHB). Their mission is to "find, fix, and destroy enemy armour and mechanized forces as an integral member of the combined arms team".

The Tactical Plan

The basic combat element of the AHB is the attack helicopter company, consisting of four scout helicopters and seven AHs. The mission of the scouts is to locate targets and then protect the AHs as they make their attack. There are three such companies in each of the two AH battalions.

The reconnaissance function, though reduced in emphasis, continues in the Cavalry Squadron.

Although centrally administered, it is not envisaged that the ACAB will normally be employed as a single unit. Rather, normal employment is considered to be the parcelling out of the attack helicopter battalions, one to each of the two divisional ground brigades likely to be employed at any one time (US doctrine calls for the third ground brigade to be held in reserve). The Cavalry Squadron will work independently under direct division control.

Mixes of attack and scout helicopters are determined by the ACAB attack battalion commander. He may employ all companies forward for maximum short-term impact or rotate them to maintain continuous pressure.

The British concept of helicopter employment is generally similar to that of the US. There will be five anti-tank helicopter squadrons in the British Army of the Rhine, each of them with 12 TOW-equipped Lynx aircraft replacing the Westland Scout AH-1 which has been armed with SS-11s.

On-site Recce of Breakthrough Areas

British Army units have completed a close reconnaissance of all of the divisional areas of responsibility where an enemy breakthrough might occur. Plans have been made to coordinate the AH counterattack with artillery fires, while scout helicopters carry out a continuous screening and target-acquisition task.

The French Pumas are organised into five helicopter combat regiments with a mix of aircraft similar to the US ACAB. Considered in

▲ AH-64 has 30mm chain-gun, 76 rockets and 16 TOW ATGW launchers and is in production for the US Army.

▲ France's AS 332 is similar but superior to Puma.

relation to the AMX-1ORC (see Light Armoured Vehicles – NATO) and supporting vehicles, it is this high-speed, highly mobile combination that seems to offer NATO a strategic reserve whose power is not yet fully appreciated.

Future Development of the AH

The mid-to-latter 1980s will see deployment of a far more powerful American gunship – the AH-64 equipped to fire the Hellfire anti-tank missile of much improved performance over the TOW.

France and Germany have been working on a combined development program to produce an improved PAH-2. Difficulties have been encountered in that the French Army prefers a light air-craft with French-made night and all-weather sensors, while the German Army seems to prefer a heavier, more survivable aircraft with US night vision equipment. These differences could lead to a separate procurement program in which the German Army would choose the US AH-1S.

The Hughes AH-64 has emerged with a weapons array consisting of the Hellfire anti-tank missile (representing a major upgrading over the present TOW), a 30mm cannon and 2.75in rockets. On-board capacities are 16 Hellfires, 1200 rounds of 30mm and 76 rockets, in varying mixes.

In terms of its own survivability, the AH-64 is the best-protected helicopter yet developed. Able to continue flying on one of its two engines, the airframe has proved invulnerable to 12.7mm fire and resistant to 23mm damage. Redundant flight control systems, self-sealing fuel cells, armour plating of critical components, blast shields for the crew and a high degree of manoeuvrability promise a vast improvement over the Vietnam-era AH.

Deployability and Turnaround

If the primary thrust of US Army tactical development were to be placed on the attack helicopter rather than the tank, major gains in strategic deployability would be achieved. The present known capability of the AH-64 in this regard is in excess of 800 nautical miles (1,482km) unrefueled. This has been achieved over the Newfoundland - Greenland - Iceland - Prestwick, Scotland route. Inflight refueling is being considered. The prospect this holds of a readily deployable US strategic reserve centered on the attack helicopter is a far more hopeful one than the present situation in which huge amounts of prepositioned equipment are largely useless for training purposes, and other heavy equipment, in the United States, must be loaded onto ships.

Once in theatre, the AH-64 can be completely rearmed and refueled within 10 minutes. In all, the AH-64 promises not only a transformation of battlefield tactics, but a means to revise an increasingly burdensome and outdated worldwide US strategy.

Armoured Personnel Carriers

▲ Czech-made OT-64 8×8 wheeled APCs.

▲ BMP armoured personnel carriers of the Soviet Army.

▲ From l to r: Column 1 – T-72 tanks; Columns 2-4 – BMP; Column 5 – BRDM-2; BRDM-2U and trucks; Columns 6-7 – ACRV-2 and SAU-152.

▲ BTR-50PK was the first tracked APC in the Soviet Army and is still in service with some Category II tank divisions.

THE practice of mounting infantry in armoured vehicles so that the infantry could keep up with the support tank formations dates at least from World War II. From their practice then of simply having infantry ride on tanks and by way of a long series of wheeled armoured personnel carriers the Soviets have moved to a vehicle that has revolutionized the concept of modern ground warfare.

The BMP-1 Mechanized Infantry Combat Vehicle clearly went well beyond the traditional concept of an armoured truck or "battlefield taxi" that served merely to move infantry to within walking distance of an objective. The BMP was to be capable not only of bringing up infantry under armoured cover,

but of engaging in the battle itself with organic fire support weapons and a capability to engage other light armoured vehicles and even tanks.

Main armament of the BMP is a 73mm smoothbore gun with a launch rail for the Sagger ATGM mounted over the gun. There is a coaxial 7.62mm machinegun supplemented by the individual weapons of an 8-man infantry squad. Firing ports along the sides of the vehicle enable the squad to fire while mounted.

The BMP has a three-man crew consisting of commander, driver and gunner. This, also, is a considerable departure from the past in that only the driver remained with the vehicle in most earlier APC models after the infantry had

dismounted. Basic ammunition load of the BMP is 30 rounds of 73mm, five Sagger missiles and 1,000 rounds of 7.62mm.

A Questionable Doctrine

Neither the Soviets nor anyone else is yet quite sure how the new form of mechanized infantry would be used in battle. Current Soviet doctrine calls for the BMPs to follow the tanks in an assault. The infantry squads would dismount some 328 yards (300m) from the enemy's defences. They would then accompany the tanks onto the objective behind an artillery barrage with BMPs supporting by fire.

There are a number of questions about such a doctrine. Why the large investment in the elaborately armed BMP if it is still to be used as

a "battlefield taxi"? Also, if it is to support by fire it is difficult to see how it will gain suitable positions to avoid being masked by the tanks and infantry.

Unless fully integrated into the tank formation, the assemblage of BMPs to the rear would tempt a defender to make a flanking counterattack with tanks to destroy the BMPs and their infantry short of the dismount point and while Soviet tanks are engaged with the NATO defensive position.

This and related problems have set off a debate in the Soviet military press. Supposedly this was settled by a set of rules handed down by Col. Gen. Merimskiy, Deputy Chief of Combat Training, Ground Forces. Other published discussions indicated that difficult

▲ BTR-60P APC of Soviet Naval Infantry has open top and SGMT MG on flexible mounting. Hydrojet gives speed of 10km/h.

▲ MT-LB is used as an APC and as an artillery tractor.

▲ BTR-60PB. New 8×8 wheeled APC has recently been identified.

problems of troop control and the general level of training in the Soviet ground combat arms raise some doubts about the ability of the Soviets to apply the announced doctrine without serious complications. These doubts, apparently in the minds of the Soviets themselves, parallel the assessment of NATO front-line commanders that the NATO forces can disrupt and bring to a halt at least the initial Soviet assault.

The "mix" of Soviet APCs

The BMP is not the universal armoured personnel carrier of the Warsaw Pact armies. The standard mix in the Soviet Motorized Rifle Division is one regiment mounted in BMPs and two in the older BTR-60. The latter is an 8×8 wheel vehicle carrying 8 to 12 infantrymen, depending on the model. The more recent models mount a turreted 14.5mm (KPVT) machinegun and a coaxial 7.62mm machinegun.

There is a difference in speed between the BMP and the BTR-60, although not as much as might be expectyed. The BMP is rated by the US Defense Intelligence Agency at a maximum of 43mph (70km/hr) on the road, and the BTR-60 at 50mph (80km/hr). Both the BMP and BTR-60 are considered to have a road range of 310 miles (500km). As a track vehicle, of course, the BMP is almost certain to be less reliable over long distances.

Generally, it appears that the BMP relates much more directly to chemical and nuclear operations followed by deep, high-speed exploitation than it does to the sort of conventional operations discussed in the "debate" in the Soviet military press.

NBC Protection

If the Soviets had made up their minds that an attack on Western Europe would begin with a nuclear bombardment it would make good sense to have available a large fleet of well armed APCs that could cross contaminated areas quickly, deal with any remaining opposition without dismounting the infantry and accompany the tanks in the exploitation. This is exactly what the Soviets have got. The care taken to provide the BMP with the means to seal out chemical and radiological contaminants and to provide individual protection for the crew and infantry squad fits in quite well with this pattern.

The Soviets appear to have transferred some 6,430 BMPs to the East European armies, principally to Poland (5,500 vehicles). There are estimated to be some 5,500 BTR-60s and earlier-model wheeled and tracked APCs in the non-Soviet Warsaw Pact forces. Of the earlier tracked APCs the most common is the BTR-50 series. Although limited to one 7.62mm vehicle-mounted machinegun, the BTR-50 can carry up to 20 infantrymen, the largest troop capacity of any Warsaw Pact APC.

Poland and Czechoslovakia produce an OT64 wheeled APC in place of the BTR-60. The Czechs also produce a variant (OT62) of the Soviet BTR-50.

Armoured Personnel Carriers

▲ M113 is the most widely used APC in NATO armies.

▲ USMC LVTP-7 emerges on to Turkish beach on exercise.

▲ FV423 APC of the British 3rd Armoured Division.

▲ US Army M113 modified for use as a command post.

▲ British FV432s fitted with a turret-mounted MG.

THE single most successful NATO armoured personnel carrier of the past two decades, in terms of worldwide usage, has been the US M113 and its derivatives. Some 20,000 are still in the US inventory, with at least equal that number spread around the world, some 12,000 of them in other NATO armies.

The amphibious, all-aluminum M113 replaced earlier more heavily armoured M59s and M75s, some of which are still in service in the Belgian, Greek and Turkish armies. Although the switch to aluminum proved itself in terms of trafficability, air transportability and fordability it is notable that US infantry in Vietnam rode on top of the vehicle rather than inside because of the often catastrophic

effects of mine damage. This tended to validate the original tactical concept under which the M113 was developed, ie, that it would follow tanks and not be used alone as an assault vehicle.

Extensive development of the armoured personnel carrier took place in Britain, France and West Germany parallel with development and deployment of the M113.

Britain's FV432 series of full-tracked carriers is generally similar in development and concept to the M113, except that the British vehicles are of steel construction, and weigh about a third more than the M113. Like the M113, the FV432s have proved adaptable to a wide range of missions, including command, medical, cargo, maintenance and re-

covery and anti-tank missile launchers.

French APC development was along the same lines as the American and British APCs, leading to the full-tracked AMX-10P of all-welded alloy construction with a nine-man troop capacity in addition to the driver and commander.

The German Experience

The first West German officers to attend the US Army Armor School in 1956 had firmly fixed in mind, from World War II experience, that future armoured personnel carriers must give infantry the choice to fight mounted through side firing ports. This concept was incorporated into the German Marder Mechanized Infantry Vehicle of

which there are now 2,136 in Bundeswehr formations. This is the heaviest by far of the current NATO APCs (28.2t, 28.6 tonnes, as compared to 13.5t, 13.7 tonnes, for the US M113A1, combat-loaded). Although it lacks the amphibious capability of the M113 series, the heavier armour of the Marder provides protection against projectiles up to 20mm and a greater margin of safety against mine damage.

The Marder and the AMX-10P are the most heavily armed of the standard NATO APCs, both being equipped with turret-mounted 20mm cannon. In addition to a 7.62mm machinegun coaxial with the 20mm gun, the Marder has a well-protected, remote-controlled 7.62mm machinegun at the rear of the vehicle. All of these weapons

▲ Rear view of voluminous LVTP-7.

▲ French AMX-10P amphibious MICV mounting 20mm cannon and co-axial 7.62mm MG.

▲ Dutch AIFV developed from M113.

▲ Most modern NATO APCs are tracked; an exception is the British AT105.

▲ An air defence version of the Marder APC launches a Roland missile.

are capable of a high angle of fire to engage aerial targets, a further product of experience hard-earned from dealing with the World War II air threat.

All of the current and generally successful generation of NATO APCs are now in the process of replacement to include, in France, a significant revision of concept.

The United States and France have started production of a new series of infantry fighting vehicles. The US M2 IFV incorporates the long-held German and recent Russian concept of infantry fighting mounted from sealed firing ports. It is the first NATO tracked APC to match or exceed the firepower of the Soviet BMD, at least in terms of missiles. Twin TOW ATGM missile launchers are

mounted on the M2's turret. They can be reloaded from protected positions within the fighting compartment. Seven missiles are carried as basic load, including two on the launchers. The 25mm cannon fires a tungsten penetrator deemed capable of penetrating light armour at ranges over 1,090 yards (1,000m). A Belgian MAG-58 7.62mm machinegun completes the firepower array.

For the first time in US history, one third of the mechanized infantry squad will be integral crew members of the vehicle, the gunner and the driver remaining with the vehicle if the commander dismounts with the six remaining squad members. The M2 retains the expensive amphibious feature built into earlier vehicles.

Britain, having for some time considered purchasing the US M2, has decided to adopt its own advanced MICV still under development. Belgium and the Netherlands have chosen the FMC-designed Armoured Infantry Fighting Vehicle similar to the M2, but with a larger troop capacity.

French Tracks and Wheels
France will retain the full-tracked AMX-10P for infantry organized to accompany main battle tanks. Other mechanized infantry units, however, are in the process of being reequipped with the Renault VAB 6x6 wheeled armoured personnel carrier capable of carrying 12 soldiers, including the driver, and armed at optimum choice to date with a 20mm cannon.

The choice of the wheeled VAB enhances the possibility discussed earlier (see NATO Light Armoured Vehicles) of a high-speed armoured reserve capable of teaming with the attack helicopter to engage and defeat Warsaw Pact penetrations beyond the forward belt of NATO units equipped with main battle tanks.

At the very moment when the APC has developed into something of a roving fortress there have begun to emerge such misgivings. The growing dependence on such vehicles by the Infantry squad is a major limitation. Now there is growing concern that "too many eggs have been placed in one basket". Future development may be in the direction of simpler vehicles.

Infantry Weapons

▲ Soviet infantry patrol with AK-74 5.4mm rifle.

▲ Soviet paratroops carrying new folding-stock 5.45mm rifles.

▲ Soviet soldier using an LPO-50 flame-thrower.

▲ Infantry sections with 7.62mm AKMs.

▲ A novel weapon developed by the Soviet Army is this AGS-17 automatic grenade launcher. The magazine contains 30 grenades.

THE space available inside the armoured personnel carrier is determining the size of the infantry squad. Further, the steadily increased firepower of the APC is becoming the determinant of tactics, at least in the mechanized – or as the Soviets call it – "motorized" infantry.

There are some who say this is a case of the tail wagging the dog. Whatever the logic, it is the established trend on both sides of the Iron Curtain.

Because they have accepted more readily the notion of nuclear and chemical operations as the norm in future warfare, the rapid conversion of virtually the entire Warsaw Pact infantry – less the airborne divisions – to an armour-protected configuration is per-

fectly reasonable. That, however, creates a dilemma. The Soviet BMP (see Armoured Personnel Carriers – Warsaw Pact) is well designed for a mounted attack with or just behind assaulting tanks over an objective contaminated by radiological or chemical weapons and where only a residual, disorganized defending force has to be overcome by weapons fired from within the vehicle.

Different Problems with Conventional Warfare

If the Warsaw Pact limits itself to conventional warfare, an entirely different problem emerges. Developments discussed in the pages on NATO engineering equipment and mine warfare make it apparent that with as little as 48 hours

warning, NATO is likely to be able to create a respectable series of defensive positions. Except where a gap can be exploited, it will not be possible to employ Warsaw Pact APCs in the assault role. Nor is it likely that the tanks will be able to make a direct assault against a defence of integrated minefields, tanks and anti-tank weapons. It will be necessary, therefore, for the attacking infantry to dismount before the APCs are exposed to destructive fire. With tanks and APCs supporting by fire, it then will be necessary for the infantry to assault in the traditional dismounted mode.

In urban areas, the supporting APCs may be able to stay close behind the infantry, using buildings or rubble as protection against

direct-fire weapons. That would mean that the infantry squad would have available all of the weapons and equipment that the vehicle can carry but which are not practical for the rifle squad to carry dismounted. In more open country, a gap of about 330 yards (300m) to as much as 1,000 yards (over 900m) or more could open up between the last cover available to the supporting armoured vehicles and the enemy defensive positions.

The Dismounted Assault Weapons

The principal individual weapon in the hands of the dismounted Warsaw Pact infantryman through at least the early 1980s is likely to be the 7.62mm AKM assault rifle, an improved version of the AK-47

▲ M-1953 160mm mortar has range of 8,792yds (8000m).

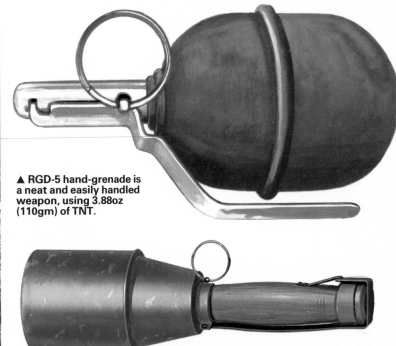

▲ RGD-5 hand-grenade is a neat and easily handled weapon, using 3.88oz (110gm) of TNT.

▲ RKG-3M stick-grenade, standard anti-tank weapon; it has HEAT warhead.

▲ M-1952 240mm mortar. An SP version now exists.

▲ There are 6 M-1943 120mm mortars in each motor rifle battalion.

of the Vietnam era. Later on in the decade it seems possible the AKM will be replaced by the new 5.45mm AKS-74, which appears now to be in full-scale production. Although ideally designed for use at close quarters in either the single-shot or automatic mode, neither weapon is fully effective beyond 440 yards (over 400m).

The most easily carried long-range support weapon for the infantry squad is the 7.62mm RPK light machinegun with a range of 880 yards (over 800m). This weapon weighs 11lb (5kg). Each 40-round magazine weighs 2.49lb (1.13kg).

Support is available, also, from the PK general purpose machine gun fired either dismounted, on a bipod mount, or from armoured

vehicles. The PK is also a 7.62mm weapon, with a range of almost 1,100 yards (almost 1,000m). It weighs 19.8lb (9kg) and is belt fed with a choice of 50, 100, 200 and 250 rounds.

Indirect Fire Support

At some point, probably when the infantry is about 220 yards (200m) from the objective, Warsaw Pact artillery will shift its fires beyond the enemy defensive positions to avoid hitting their own troops. Indirect fire support for the assault units will then depend upon infantry mortars. These are generally in the 82mm class, with a range of about 2,730 yards (about 2,500m). They could be fired from armoured vehicles or dismounted, from positions to the rear of the

tanks and APCs supporting the infantry attack.

Because of their inherent dispersion, the mortars, also, must shift fire beyond the enemy position to avoid excessive danger to their own troops. At that point the infantry alone must work its way through mines and other obstacles not destroyed by the artillery barrage and overcome the defenders who survive the preparatory fires.

A new Soviet multiple grenade launcher called Plamya (Flame) provides a means of disrupting defensive fires until the infantrymen can break into the last defensive positions with AKMs and hand grenades. The Plamya is estimated to be 30mm, with a magazine for 30 rounds. Range is estimated to be 765 to 875 yards

(700 to 800km). Anti-tank rocket launchers such as the RPG-7V and the RPG-16 can assist in this role by engaging tanks and automatic weapons.

Coordination is the Key to Success

No one doubts that the Warsaw Pact forces have the numbers of men and weapons needed to press a major offensive of the sort described against the NATO armies. Whether the Warsaw Pact can perform the intricate task of coordination necessary to make it work is another matter, particularly where it concerns artillery support. There is, also, the question of political cohesion between the non-Soviet, possibly less determined armies.

Infantry Weapons

▲ Soldier of West German Bundesheer with an MG3 LMG, derived from World War II MG42.

▲ British 4.85mm LMG, now being rebarrelled to 5.56mm.

▲ US soldier prepares to throw a smoke grenade.

▲ US M29 81mm mortar is due to be replaced soon.

▲ Italian Bersaglieri armed with US M14 7.62mm rifles.

NATO had scarcely adopted a standard 7.62mm cartridge for its infantry weapons when the US forces shifted to a 5.56mm rifle (M16A1). The trend thus established has led to a widening choice of the lighter weapon and it appears that a 5.56mm round is to be NATO-standardized, at least for the rifle. As seen in the previous section, there is an indication that the Soviet forces may have begun to move in the same direction. Here again the matching of infantry to the armoured personnel carrier may be at least one factor in this trend, the smaller and lighter rifle being more adaptable to the confined interior space of the APC.

Whatever the advantages of the 5.56mm weapons and ammunition

in terms of light weight and adaptability to confined spaces, the question of the role of dismounted infantry in NATO and its weapons remains open to debate.

Is NATO Surrendering an Advantage?

On the Northern and Southern flanks of NATO there is much mountainous terrain unsuitable to mechanized operations and where accurate, long-distance marksmanship could still have a major influence. Until now, at least, the 5.56mm round has not had the long-range reliability and hitting power necessary for such a role. If all of the NATO infantry, including US Marine and National Guard divisions, is to be mechanized and continue with 5.56mm rifles and

eventually a 5.56mm light machinegun, NATO may be surrendering an important advantage over an all-mechanized and increasingly roadbound Warsaw Pact infantry. Some re-reading of the 1940 Winter War in Finland may be in order.

For the time being, the basic infantry weapon of the NATO armies other than those of the United States and France is a 7.62mm rifle. This is either the Belgian FN FAL, or variants, effective to a range of almost 550 yards (500m), or the German G3 with an effective range of almost 440 yards (400m). Both weigh 9.48lb (4.3kg) compared to 6.39lb (2.9kg) for the US M16. The M16 is credited with an effective range of 400 metres, but not with the stability and

striking power of the 7.62mm ammunition. France has been using the 7.5mm rifle (M49/56) but is shifting to a 5.56mm weapon (FA MAS).

The Machineguns

Three classes of machineguns are in use, generally speaking, in the NATO armies. Both Britain and Germany use light machineguns of proven quality in World War II. These are, respectively, the L4A1 Bren Gun (7.62mm) and the MG42 (7.92mm) now modified as the 7.62mm MG3. The Bren Gun has an effective range of 656 yards (600m). The MG3 is credited with 874 yards (800m) when fired in the light machinegun role from a bipod mount.

Although it has no light

▲ The Belgian 7.62mm L1A1 SLR currently used by British Army.

▲ Turkish marines with 7.62mm Hecker & Koch G3 rifles.

▲ British paratrooper with 9mm L2A3 Sterling SMG.

▲ NATO exercise in Norway; weapon is a Browning LMG.

▲ Uzi SMG used by Luxembourg.

▲ Men of 82nd (US) Airborne Division firing Colt Browning Model 1911A1 0.45in pistols.

machinegun at present, the US Army has a Squad Automatic Weapon (SAW) program underway intended to produce what will be, in effect, a 5.56mm light machinegun.

In the standard machinegun class, Belgium has been specially successful with its FN MAG (7.62mm) in use in several NATO armies. US infantry is equipped with the 7.62mm M60. Both the Belgian and the US weapons include features of the World War II German MG42. The standard French machinegun is the AA, originally a 7.5mm weapon converted to 7.62mm.

All of the NATO standard machineguns are effective to a range of over 1,300 yards (over 1,200m) and the German MG3

when placed on a tripod mount and converted to the standard machinegun role has a range of 2,400 yards (2,200m).

Infantry's Arsenal now Includes Light Artillery

The development of the armoured personnel carrier into an Infantry Fighting Vehicle (IFV) has led to the incorporation of what must be considered light artillery into the infantry arsenal. Both France and Germany use 20mm weapons mounted on APCs. The French version is the Heavy Machinegun M621. The German and Norwegian armies use the Rheinmettal Mk20. Both weapons are effective to 2,186 yards (2,000m).

Although the United States still makes extensive use of the

Browning M2HB .50 calibre on infantry support vehicles, the M2 Infantry Fighting Vehicle coming into use in the early 1980s will be armed with the M242 25mm Chain Gun. Effective range of the Browning M2 is 1,530 yards (1,400m). Range of the M242 has not been disclosed but is assumed to be beyond 2,186 yards (2,000m).

The NATO Mortars

The United States and Britain are in the process of re-equipping with the new British light mortar ML 81mm L16. This has a maximum range of 5,465 yards (5,000m) and a rate of fire of 15 rounds-per-minute. The range is equal to that of the 4.2 inch (106.6mm) mortar formerly used in US armoured vehicle mountings, but with major

savings in weight of ammunition. Canada and Norway, also, have adopted the L16.

The German Army has adopted a large (120mm) mortar on the Soviet model by way, strangely enough, of Finland and Israel. This "Tampella" model has a maximum range of 6,940 yards (6,350m).

A 60mm mortar is in use in several NATO armies for dismounted infantry operations. France uses both the traditional trench mortar version with an effective range of 2,186 yards (2,000m) and a unique Hotchkiss gun mortar with a range of 3,280 yards (3,000m) in the indirect fire mode and a flat-trajectory capability to 437 yards (400m). The gun mortar is mounted on light armoured vehicles.

Engineering Equipment

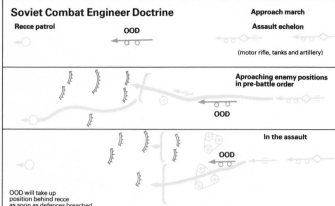

Soviet Combat Engineer Doctrine

Recce patrol   OOD

Approach march

Assault echelon

(motor rifle, tanks and artillery)

Aproaching enemy positions
in pre-battle order

OOD

In the assault

OOD

OOD will take up
position behind recce
as soon as defences breached

Top: OOD (Otyrad Obespecheniya Dvizheniya—Divisional Combat Engineer Movement Support Detachment) behind armoured recce patrol in the approach. Centre: it stands to one side to let assault echelon move into position. Bottom: It supports exploitation when defenses are breached then moves back behind lead combat elements.

▲GSP heavy ferry; note vehicle cabs between pontoons.

▲ PMP floating bridge held in place by BMK-150 boats.

▲ Czech-made MT-55 bridgelayer serves most Pact armies.

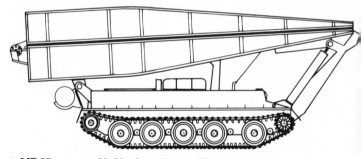

▲ MT-55 armoured bridgelayer in travelling position.

THE above illustration (based on Soviet published information) showing the typical position of a company-strength divisional combat engineer movement support detachment indicates the importance of combat engineers in modern armoured warfare.

On the march, they are just to the rear of the forward reconnaissance patrols, ready to remove road-blocks, breach minefields, repair roads, bulldoze obstacles out of the path, repair bridges, or prepare fords and emplacements for military bridging.

In the assault, the engineers must be prepared to emplace minefields and other obstacles to protect the flanks of the attacking unit, or to remove such obstacles

barring the way of friendly units' manoeuvre. In defence, the engineers assist front-line units in clearing fields of fire, building obstacles and construction of fortifications.

Engineering Equipment Throughout Formations

There are engineering capabilities throughout the Warsaw Pact troop structure. Each tank battalion, for example, at least in the Soviet Army, is authorized a tank 'dozer blade and its own mine clearance equipment. There is an Engineer Company in each Tank and Motorized Rifle regiment equipped with mine detectors, construction materials and demolitions. A bridge platoon has folding bridges (MTU) mounted on tank chassis

and just under 44 yards (40m) of truck-carried bridging (TMM) capable of carrying a 59 ton (60 tonne) load.

Depending on type, the MTUs can supply quick bridging over gaps 12 to 19.6 yards (11 to 18m) wide. These are used only when units cannot fill such gaps by pushing in earth with organic 'dozer blades.

Each Tank and Motorized Rifle division has an Engineer Battalion. The Reconnaissance Platoon is responsible for identifying the tasks the Engineers are likely to be called upon to perform, with special attention to NBC warfare requirements. It is outfitted generally with the same light armoured vehicles as other reconnaissance units, its specialization

being mainly in the skills of its soldiers. The Sapper Company is the principal construction force, with a wide range of heavy equipment for obstacle construction or removal, roadbuilding, mine-laying and removal, and camouflage.

A Camouflage Platoon in the Sapper Company is equipped not only with the standard nets and related equipment, but with reflectors and other active and passive electronic countermeasures devices designed to block or confuse radar surveillance and infra-red homing.

The heavy emphasis on river crossing capability apparent in the Division Engineer organization expresses an emphasis on high-speed offensive operations hardly

▲ KrAZ-214 truck lowers TMM 59 ton bridge into position.

▲ MAZ-537 (8×8) tank transporters carrying T-55 tanks.

▲ MDK-2 ditching machine.　　　　▲ 25 tonne BAT tractor/dozer.　　　　▲ BTM digging/trenching machine.

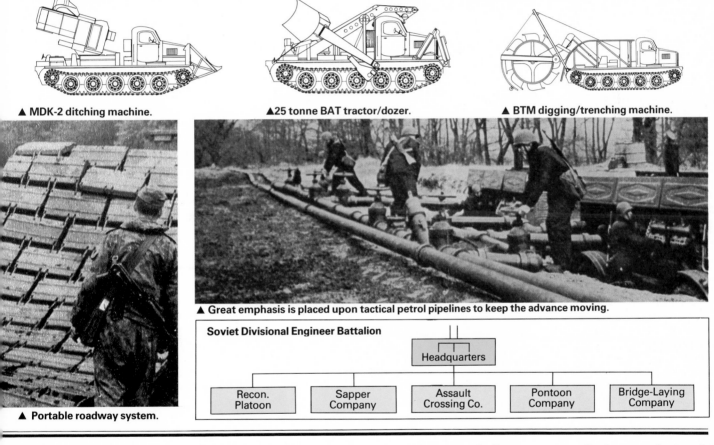

▲ Great emphasis is placed upon tactical petrol pipelines to keep the advance moving.

▲ Portable roadway system.

Soviet Divisional Engineer Battalion

Headquarters

| Recon. Platoon | Sapper Company | Assault Crossing Co. | Pontoon Company | Bridge-Laying Company |

consistent with Soviet claims that they are merely preparing to defend against a NATO attack.

The Assault Crossing Company is designed literally to hit a water obstacle on the run, with or ahead of forward combat elements. Engineers in assault boats would move toward the far bank while Combat Engineer (IMR) armoured tractors and tanks with 'dozer blades begin preparation of the near bank for launching ferries made from sections of PMP Class 60 pontoon bridging from the Pontoon Company. Later, as the far bank is secured and a suitable exit is graded, connected pontoon bridges and fixed (KMX) bridges would be installed.

All of this might be taking place under fire as part of a more in-volved combat assault crossing, or it could be conducted as described without extensive participation by the other combat arms if there is little opposition.

Snorkel and Amphibious Capabilities

Where fords only can be established, Soviet tanks are elaborately equipped to ford in depths over their turrets by use of "snorkel" arrangements. Many of the lighter Warsaw Pact vehicles are amphibious and in an opposed crossing would lead the attack.

To the rear of the divisions, at Army and Front, there are large reserves of engineer units to support or replace the regimental and division engineers to assure driving forward the attack with maxi-mum momentum and efficiency.

Mine clearing could be an even more difficult and dangerous task than coping with the many water obstacles to be overcome in a dash across Western Europe. The deployment of rapid mine-emplacing techniques and equipment now taking place in the NATO armies will mean that the 48 hours warning NATO hopes to obtain may be sufficient to emplace more extensive mine barriers than once was thought possible.

Basic Soviet techniques for clearing mines range from the crude to the highly sophisticated. In keeping with the extreme emphasis on speed, forward units are supposed to move forward at maximum speed until someone is blown up – a tactic that must eventually dampen enthusiasm in the reconnaissance units. Once minefields are identified they will be marked and by-passed, if possible, or breached by a combination of ploughs, explosive charges pushed or shot forward by rockets in rigid or flexible "snake" form and by tanks with field-installed heavy rollers.

The Soviets are equipped to perform more deliberate clearance using a variety of vehicles and hand-held detectors as time and circumstances require. The fastest of these is the DIM system mounted on a GAZ/UAZ 69 light wheeled vehicle. This system sweeps for metallic mines to a depth of almost 1ft (30cm) over the width of the vehicle, automatically stopping when metal is detected.

Engineering Equipment

▲ M88 ARV serves with US, German and Norwegian armies.

▲ US Special Forces combat engineer about to blow a bridge.

▲ Bringing ashore Lance missiles over a floating bridge.

▲ Many types of bulldozers serve in the NATO armies.

▲ US Army 25-ton truck-mounted hydraulic crane under test.

FOR all the emphasis the Warsaw Pact forces put on speed, it is the NATO engineers for whom time is the most critical. Limited in what they can do in peacetime in a free, market society, the NATO engineers must use whatever warning may be available of a Warsaw Pact attack to build a system of barriers.

Tasks of the NATO Engineers

Once an attack begins, the NATO engineers must keep open lines of communication and the counter-attack routes for NATO manoeuvre units in what one of the senior NATO engineers describes as a "swirling violent affair requiring execution of highly complex meeting engagements, delays, ambushes, reinforcements and counterattacks to parry the enemy's lightning thrusts and blunt his main attack". The engineer functions associated with such a situation are mine and obstacle emplacement and clearance, demolitions, gap crossings, the digging of fortifications and the maintenance of roads and trails.

Anti-tank ditches and craters will be the principal obstacles required. Rapid digging of individual foxholes, weapons emplacements and command posts and the provision of overhead cover requires both mechanical assistance and prefabricated protective materials.

If 48 hours is about all the pre-attack alert NATO can expect, it is easy to see that the engineers will be very busy indeed.

Capabilities – Early 1980s

The beginning of the 1980s found the NATO engineers generally in poor condition to accomplish these demanding tasks. All of those tasks fall first and foremost on the combat engineer squad. That basic team of eight or so men must be able to work under fire and defend itself, sometimes to the extent of taking responsibility for holding key positions.

Many of the NATO engineer squads entered the 1980s with 1950s technology. Some indeed were still mounted in dump trucks. At best, they were mounted in 1960s style armoured personnel carriers designed for infantry, not engineer work. There is simply not enough room in the standard APC to carry men, weapons, basic supplies *and* the tools, demolitions, mines and mine detectors necessary for engineer tasks.

As a result, the Engineers are found towing 1½-ton trailers behind the APCs for extra cargo capacity. That limits the mobility of the engineer vehicles and often exposes their crews to unnecessary hazards. For example, the rear ramp of the US M113 APC cannot be dropped when the trailer is attached, forcing the squad to dismount through more exposed hatches.

One of the few specialized engineer vehicles available dates from the 1960s. This is the US M728 based on the M60 tank

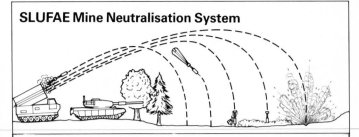

SLUFAE Mine Neutralisation System

Surface Launched Unit, Fuel Air Explosive (SLUFAE) is a multiple rocket system to deal with buried pressure mines. Rockets are ripple fired to land in the minefield at about 10m intervals. The fuel-air mixture is dispersed and then exploded to clear the mines by blast.

▲ Leopard Bergepanzer (ARV) recovering a Leopard 1 MBT.

▲ British Army Centurion Armoured Vehicle Royal Engineers (AVRE) with trailer.

▲ French AMX-13 VCG engineer vehicle.

▲ M578 light ARV of the US Army. Many such specialised vehicles exist throughout the NATO armies.

chassis. Armed with a 165mm gun in place of the standard 105 of the M60, the M728 was designed to blast and bulldoze its way through roadblocks and other obstacles. There are 235 of these vehicles in use by American units. They are being retained and upgraded by addition of a range-finder to avoid reliance on supporting tanks for ranging with the 165mm gun.

The greater part of the task of moving large quantities of earth – vital to rapid obstacle emplacement – is still largely entrusted to 'dozers lacking protection from artillery and small arms fire. Demolitions available to NATO engineers in the early 1980s were often poorly packaged and difficult to assemble under adverse light and weather conditions. Hand-

held mine detectors are slow, require an excessive number of troops to operate, and expose the users to enemy fire. The same can be said of continued reliance on manual methods of mine emplacement.

Fortunately, all current combat engineer problems were under intensive study during the last decade. The beginnings of improvement were evident as the new decade began. Adequately funded, these projects promise a dramatic increase in capabilities by the middle of the decade.

Prospects for improvement of NATO mine warfare capabilities are discussed in the NATO Mine Warfare section. The most immediate concern in that area is with defensive mine warfare.

Looking beyond to the possibility of a NATO counteroffensive there is a development in the offing that could bring about a radical change in the prospects for such action. This is the Surface Launched Fuel Air Explosive Mine Neutralization System (SLUFAE).

SLUFAE consists of a 30-tube rocket launcher mounted on the US M548 six-ton tracked cargo vehicle. Rockets are fired individually and are slowed by parachute to come down vertically over the targeted minefield. Upon detonation, the rocket generates overpressures of 500 pounds per square inch (35kg/cm²). This has proven adequate to explode or displace all surface mines and most buried mines in an area 26ft (8m) in diameter. Sequen-

tial firing from ranges of from 983 to 3,279ft (300 to 1,000m) gives SLUFAE the capability of clearing a 26ft (8m) breach through a minefield 983ft (300m) in depth at a median range of 2,623ft (800m).

SLUFAE was listed as "Standard A" (ready for deployment) by the US Army in 1980. Funding was requested in the 1982 budget.

US Ribbon Bridge Outmatches Soviet PMP

In terms of both offensive and defensive NATO ground mobility, what is probably the single most important development now underway is the deployment of a US Ribbon Bridge. This is a design prompted to some degree by the advanced Soviet PMP pontoon bridge, but exceeding that model

▲ On left is an M2 Bailey bridge, and on right a Mobile Assault Bridge of the US Army.

▲ US Army M60 Armoured Vehicle Launched Bridge (AVLB). It can span a gap of 60ft (18.3m).

▲ Medium Girder Bridge.

▲ M113 APCs are transported across a German river on a Mobile Assault Bridge (MAB).

▲ Turkish Army tank repairs.

by quite a considerable margin.

The basic unit of the Ribbon Bridge is a 6.3ft (5.8m) interior bay which folds to the dimensions of a 5-ton truck bed. To launch the bay, fastenings are undone, the truck backs into the water and the bay rolls off, unfolding to its full length as it hits the water. Two bays can be connected in about one minute to form a raft capable of carrying a main battle tank. An entire 695ft (212m) bridge (representing the capability of a Divisional Bridge Company) can be emplaced at the rate of 9.8ft (3m) per minute, five times the speed of emplacement for the older, heavier US M4T6 bridging.

A three-man crew can emplace and retrieve the bridge bays with the assistance of a 27-foot (8.2m)

bridge erection boat, also carried and launched by a 5-ton transporter.

By use of aluminium, the designers of the Ribbon Bridge made it a third lighter than its Soviet PMP counterpart, which is made of steel. Although the Soviet bridging will take harder wear, it takes considerably longer to install and retrieve. The Ribbon Bridge can be dismantled about as quickly as it is emplaced, the carrier vehicles retrieving each bay by an A frame and winch carried on the truck bed.

US units have been receiving the Ribbon Bridge since 1977 and German units since 1978. The new bridging represents a saving of over 50 per cent in the time required to emplace the older

German float bridge, or to assemble the older equipment into rafts. A considerable saving in manpower is also achieved.

Supplementing older Mobile Assault Bridging (MAB) in several NATO armies, the new Ribbon Bridge greatly improves the ability of NATO tactical and strategic land forces to manoeuvre and to counterattack.

MAB is an individually motorized bridge unit capable of working independently as a raft or being linked with other units to form a float bridge. Although extremely expensive, this type of bridging is worth its cost where enemy fire is too intense to risk more conventional bridging.

Britain, the United States and Germany are working toward a

further refinement in assault tactical bridging for deployment in the latter 1980s. This development seems to be headed toward a scissors-type bridge unit that can be flipped into the water from a full-tracked vehicle.

Line of Communications Bridging

The ability to replace damaged bridges in the NATO rear area is essential to resupply and to a successful delaying action. To the venerable World War II Bailey Bridge has now been added another British development, the Fairey Medium Girder Bridge (MGB). This is a hand-erectable deck bridge adjustable to varying length and loads. The basic 115ft (35m) set can be installed in 45

▲ Chieftain AVLB of the British Army can span a gap of 75ft (22.9m).

▲ Soldiers of the German Bundesheer hurry across an infantry pontoon bridge.

AMX-30D Armoured Recovery Vehicle (ARV) of the French Army. The crane can lift a maximum load of 14.8 tons (15,000kg). ▼

minutes by 25 men without mechanical assistance. A reinforcement set is available to extend the length to 161ft (49m).

Each US Bridge Company equipped with MGB is authorised four bridges. Each set is carried on seven 5-ton dump trucks and six 4-ton trailers.

The US Army has acquired or ordered a total of 48 MGB sets and expects to use the MGB throughout the 1980s for gaps greater than 59ft (18m). The standard Armour Vehicle Launched (scissors) Bridge (AVLB) mounted on an M60 tank chassis will continue to be used for the shorter gaps.

Since they will likely still be engaged in their preparatory tasks when an attack begins, it is essential that the NATO engineers be able to continue to work under fire. A major improvement in this forward area capability is occurring with the deployment of the British Combat Engineer Tractor, a 17-ton armoured, full-tracked vehicle with a road speed of 31mph (50km/hr) and capable of the full range of battlefield engineer tasks, in most cases without the need for crewmen to leave the vehicle.

The US M9 Combat Engineer Vehicle is in the same class. This is a high-speed, full-tracked bulldozer and scraper providing its crew full armoured and NBC warfare protection. Its primary use will be to dig fighting positions for tank and other weapons systems, and anti-tank ditches. In addition, the M9 can carry a substantial load of road and barrier materials or troops. It has a limited amphibious capability (3.1mph), 5km/hr). A total of 351 are programmed for procurement through 1986, with initial operational capability scheduled for September 1984. The Belgian and Netherlands armies are interested in acquiring the M9.

France, also, is planning to modernize its Combat Engineers with a new, NBC-protected armoured combat tractor on an AMX-30B2 tank chassis. Deployment should be in the latter 1980s.

Entrenching Devices
NATO has been working hard on means to create barriers to enemy forces and to dig in its own forces more rapidly than could be done by entrenching tools and tank 'dozer blades.

Various vehicular and explosive systems for rapid cratering or entrenchment are under development or being deployed. One, the US M180 cratering kit can be operated in less than 30 minutes. Its suspended projectile-shaped charge can dig a crater in damp soil 6.5ft (2m) deep by about 26 to 29ft (8 to 9m) across.

The M180 system may be supplemented shortly by the XM268 blasting agent consisting of two inert components which, when mixed, can produce 1.5 times the excavating energy of TNT. Individual and collective prefabricated protective devices are in the offing, providing a quick means to convert craters into the needed fortifications.

Mine Warfare Systems

▲ Soviet anti-personnel mine used in Afghanistan (130×50×25mm).

▲ Automatic flare-dispenser marking cleared lane in minefield.

▲ Soldier in NBC suit using metallic mine detector.

▲ Manual clearing using detector and prodder: sure but slow.

▲ Soviet soldiers with a TM-46 anti-tank mine.

BECAUSE of the nature of the "Great Patriotic War", 1941-45, the Soviets were forced to develop a high degree of skill and improvisation in defensive mine warfare. They were on the defensive through at least half of that period and even during the latter years of the war found it necessary to secure extensive areas against counter-attack. The Soviet mine inventory today still reflects the World War II conditions.

The Soviet TMD-B wooden anti-vehicular mine was developed in the latter phase of World War II. It contains a charge of from 11 to 15lb (5 to 7kg) and is designed to explode under a weight of 441lb (200kg). Like the other wooden mines it has the advantage both of lessening the chances of detection from mine clearance equipment attuned to metal, and conservation of manufacturing materials and labour.

An anti-personnel counterpart is the PMD-6, simple enough to be made up in the field. It responds to the minimal pressures necessary to force together its two sections. A smaller PMD-7 series, is also cased in wood.

The most powerful of the wooden anti-tank mines is the YaM-10, packing 22lb (10kg) of high explosive. This is matched by the MZD general purpose mine, used with varying charges to destroy such targets as railroads, buildings and roads. It is activated by a particularly deadly vibration fuze, or triggered remotely by explosion of the smaller DM general purpose mine in which the same type vibration fuze can be employed.

Principal disadvantage of the wooden mines is that they are not suitable for emplacement by mechanical means, or by helicopter.

The Metallic Mines

The great monument to the failure of the Soviet political system is, of course, the belt of barbed wire and minefields that defines the Iron Curtain. Designed primarily to imprison the East European and, ultimately, the Soviet population, this system makes heavy use of anti-personnel mines. Fairly typical of these is the Soviet POMZ-2 series emplaced on wooden stakes in clusters above ground and with a lethal radius of 65ft (20m) when exploded by trip wire. A likely supplement is the ground-emplaced OZM3 which is propelled into the air upon activation by trip wire and discharges its fragments throughout a wide arc.

A NATO counter-offensive, or local counter-attack could require crossing of this barrier. Both to prevent defections by vehicle and to provide a suitable military barrier, it can be assumed that the mine barrier contains extensive anti-tank emplacements. The largest of the metallic mines available for such use is the TM46 containing a charge of 12.5lb (5.7kg) of TNT.

Mines are apt to be the enemy rather than the helper of the sort of high-speed, wide-ranging offen-

▲ Soviet soldiers setting out to lay an anti-tank minefield on exercise.

▲ Mine-clearance is time consuming.

▲ Booby-trapped TM-46 anti-tank mines.

▲ OZM-4 "bouncing" anti-personnel mine.

sive the Warsaw Pact has in mind for Western Europe. Provided with a timed self-destruct capability, however, mines could be useful to protect the shoulders and flanks of penetrations and to obstruct likely routes of NATO counter-attacks.

The Soviet Mi-8 (Hip) helicopter has been observed with a mine-laying chute estimated to be capable of laying mines at 6 to 10ft (2 to 3m) intervals: The disadvantage of this method of delivery is that the minefield is visible and can be cleared with relative ease.

The Soviets have a number of towed and tracked, self-propelled minelayers. With PMR-3 and PMZ-4 trailers, a four or five man crew can emplace up to 200 anti-tank mines, depending on the carrying capacity of the towing vehicle, in less than 20 minutes. The GMZ tracked minelayer with a four-man crew can lay 150 to 200 mines either on the surface or buried in about the same period.

Although the mines themselves are more difficult to locate and remove when emplaced by these means, the trace of the vehicle and its entrenching means remains as visible evidence that a minefield has been established. And as soon as they are emplaced they become as much a hazard to Soviet as to NATO manoeuvre.

Minelaying by helicopter, therefore, along likely routes of NATO reinforcement and counter-attack seems the more likely use of offensive mine warfare by the Warsaw Pact than extensive emplacement of mine barriers within the imme-

diate area of the battle zone.

The use of small, air-delivered anti-personnel mines for harassment and to induce panic and confusion in the NATO rear area should not be ruled out and certainly would be easier to accomplish than the methodical laying of anti-tank mine barriers.

One such Soviet mine is known to be in use in Afghanistan. It is being scattered from canisters by helicopters and measures 4.9in long, 1.9in wide and 0.9in thick (127×51×25mm), containing a small explosive charge in a plastic casing.

The Mine Clearance Task

By far the most immediate Warsaw Pact mine warfare problem is not minelaying but clearance of NATO

mines, assuming NATO had time.

The hasty nature of likely Warsaw Pact offensive mining suggests a reexamination of German experience in dealing with such Soviet minefields in World War II. Among the methods reported to US Army interrogators by German officers were these: small mounds or depressions, dry grass and differences in the colour of the ground frequently gave away mine locations even in prepared fields; German infantry sometimes crossed narrow minefields after engineers laid down beside the mines as human markers; mines were marked by small flags when there was not time to clear them immediately; captured minefields were used as training in recognition and clearance.

Mine Warfare Systems

▲ British Centurion towing Giant Viper mine clearance equipment.

▲ US Army Claymore mine.

▲ British barmine layer.

▲ Barmine layer (right) and Ranger vehicle (left) operate together to produce a minefield.

A S indicated earlier (Engineering Equipment – NATO) the pressure of a short warning period falls most heavily on the engineers whose task it is to guard the gaps between NATO combat units and the flanks with obstacles that can gain time and inflict losses. Defensive mine warfare is the most critical of the means available to accomplish this mission.

Rapid Mine Emplacement

The United States has developed a "Family of Scatterable Mines" (FASCAM) designed to meet the challenge of rapid emplacement in the face of impending attack. Britain, Germany and other NATO nations have been working in the same direction. As a result there is

promise that from the early 1980s onward, NATO will be able to deploy a fleet of mine-laying helicopters immediately upon alert to emplace the first barrier while land forces are moving into position.

As the engineers move up, these first hasty barriers will be reinforced in the US sectors by a Ground Emplaced Mine Scattering System (GEMSS), the first 30 vehicles for which were to be bought in 1981. GEMSS consists of a trailer anti-tank mine dispenser carrying up to 800 4lb (1.8kg) mines and capable of sowing a 2,732 yard (2500m) minefield in three hours.

The basic mine of the GEMSS is activated by magnetic influence. Tripwire-initiated anti-personnel mines can be mixed in to hinder

clearance. The mines can be timed for inactivation.

Where smaller minefields are required, a Modular Pack Mine System (MOP-MS) has been developed, using the same mine as the GEMSS. MOP-SS requires no more than a truck and a two-man crew. A suit-case-size module is emplaced which then launches activated mines by remote control using a coded radio signal. Deployment is expected by 1982.

The British Barmine System

Typical of the British and German equivalents of GEMSS is the British Barmine System, consisting of an entrenching and mine-dispensing trailer towed behind an armoured personnel carrier, and

operated by a three-man crew. Mines are armed automatically as they pass through the layer and are then automatically buried. An elongated pressure-type mine is used which increases the density of the field beyond what could be achieved by the World War II circular mine. This is the L9A1 (Bar) anti-tank mine encased in non-metallic, waterproof material and carrying a charge of 18.5lb (8.4kg).

In general, the NATO mines are more sophisticated and more effective than the Warsaw Pact mines so far publicly revealed.

The German DM 31 anti-personnel mine, for example, has a lethal range of 328ft (100m) compared to the much smaller effective radius of Warsaw Pact equivalents. It is of

▲ All armies are equipped for this sort of manual mine clearing but it is of necessity very slow and painstaking.

▲ US Army engineer team clearing mines on a track during an exercise in West Germany.

the "bouncing" type in that it is activated either by pressure or tripwire and propelled to a height of one metre before the main charge explodes discharging machined metal fragments.

French influence is reflected in the US M24 anti-tank mine which fires a rocket actuated by a pressure switch sensitive only to wide-tracked vehicles.

Most sophisticated of all mine systems known to be in development to date is the US Astrolite liquid mine system consisting of a spray which can then be exploded by a detonator. Successful achievement of this system could change the tactical situation in NATO's favour almost on a scale with deployment of enhanced radiation battlefield nuclear weapons.

Cluster anti-tank munitions under development for NATO artillery would effect a similar improvement as concerns ability to disrupt and defeat the second and following echelons of a Warsaw Pact attack. These would enable NATO guns to deliver mines across approach routes to a depth of 21,860 yards (20,000m).

The Mine Clearance Systems

Although less critical to the initial stage of NATO operations than mine-barrier emplacement, mine clearance is essential both to keeping open lines of communications and maintaining the freedom of manoeuvre essential for execution of a mobile defence. Should there be an opportunity for a mechanized

counter-attack across the East German border with its deep mine belt, the means for rapid breaching are at hand.

The British Giant Viper is a 750ft (229m) hose filled with plastic explosives, projected by a cluster of eight rocket motors and arrested and straightened in descent by three parachutes. The rocket motors are activated from within the carrying armoured vehicle and the explosive is set off upon landing.

Immediately behind this initial breaching might come tanks equipped with a roller and chain system currently being issued to US units in Europe. The system can be installed in the field by a tank crew in less than 15 minutes. It is considered to be 90 per cent

effective against pressure-type mines buried up to 3.9in (10cm). A weighted chain between the rollers clears anti-personnel and tilt-rod-actuated anti-tank mines that survive the Giant Viper treatment. The roller can be released in less than 30 seconds once through the minefield.

While the tedious manual emplacement, detection and clearance of mines combines to occupy an important place in modern land force tactics, it seems obvious that the rapid emplacement and clearance techniques are changing the face of mine warfare. Indeed, it is conceivable that the engineers, the least spectacular of all the combat arms but expected to be busiest in the first 48 hours, could tip the balance in NATO's favour.

Anti-tank Weapons

73mm SPG-9 recoilless anti-tank gun. Soldier in foreground is holding the rocket-assisted round.

▲ RPG-7 rocket launcher has a dummy missile; inside is a rifle used to economise in training costs.

THE Soviets are under no illusions about the ability of anti-tank guided weapons (ATGW) by themselves to halt a mass attack by fully organized and trained combined arms formations. Although their military publications and anti-tank training show a healthy respect for the ATGW, the superior firepower, mobility and armour protection of the tank is usually still given the advantage in offence or defence.

NATO tankers, therefore, can expect to find Soviet ATGWs interspersed with tanks wherever Warsaw Pact defensive positions are established. This would be primarily on the flanks and shoulders of a penetration, or along the original line of departure of the attacking forces.

Because the firing platform has mobility far superior to the tank, the most dangerous of all Warsaw Pact anti-tank weapons are those launched from attack helicopters, such as Hind D (see Helicopters – Warsaw Pact). In the 1980s, the AT-6 Spiral (NATO terminology) seems likely to be the primary weapon with whch NATO must be concerned in this class, largely because of its range, thought to be about 5,465 yards (5,000m). That, in the Soviet view, would enable Warsaw Pact AHs to engage NATO tanks beyond or at least at the extreme range of NATO army air defence systems.

To accomplish that, the Soviet helicopter would have to reach an altitude that provides a clear shot, and then hover for the estimated 17

to 20 seconds it would take for the missile to travel to its target. All the while, the gunner must keep the missile in view if the radio command or laser link were to be preserved. Smoke, dust, rain, snow and fog or darkness would be present a high percentage of the time, requiring high-quality electromagnetic sensors and night vision devices—all of which are subject to accidental or intentional interference.

Air-air Threat to Helicopters

NATO's expanding fleet of scout helicopters and the increasing trend to think of these in terms of air-to-air combat are the first of several considerations that may distract the heli-borne AT-6

gunner. For what must seem a painful period of time he must hang in full view of surface-to-air missiles and other ground-based air defence weapons, making it somewhat difficult for him to maintain concentration!

From this and other considerations, it seems likely that the helicopter-borne AT-6 will be fired from much less than its extreme range, under less than optimum firing conditions and subject to the full range of NATO air defence weapons from rifles to Roland missiles since it will difficult or impossible to assure safe routes of approach.

More likely extreme range of ATGW engagement seems to be that of the AT-2 Swatter, the original AT missile for the Soviet

▲ AT-5 Spandrel missile vehicles.

▲ Latest Soviet AT weapon – AT-4 Spigot – closely resembles Milan.

▲ Close-up view of AT-5 Spandrel vehicle.

▲ All BMPs have AT-3 Sagger over 73mm gun.

▲ AT-3 Sagger gave Israeli tanks problems in the Yom Kippur War.

attack helicopters. This is estimated to be 3,825 yards (3,500m). Swatter is guided by radio command and may have an infra red homing system. Alternate frequencies are provided for the radio command link as a measure of defence against any electronic interference.

Swatter is also the most immediate AT missile NATO tankers are likely to encounter from ground mounts. The missile is mounted in a variety of numbers and configurations on reconnaissance and other light armoured vehicles. Once they fire and thereby reveal their position such vehicles must be prepared to move quickly to alternative, protected firing positions. Even so, with a time of flight of 23 seconds to extreme range,

Swatter can be engaged and destroyed by high-velocity, large-calibre tank cannon before the missile can reach its target.

Flight-time Improvements

The AT-5 Spandrel wire-guided missile is also expected to be present on Warsaw Pact light armoured vehicles in the 1980s. Although its range is currently estimated to be less than that of Swatter its performance in terms of time of flight to the target is expected to be superior (11 seconds to a range of 1.5 miles (2.5km).

An older but still widely deployed weapon is the AT-3 Sagger with a range of 3,280 yards (3,000m). Sagger is wire-guided with infra red homing and appears on BMP, BMD and BRDM.

Sagger carries over into the man-portable category since its small size permits it to be fired from a ground mount. It has a remote firing capability enabling the gunner to be about 16 yards (15m) from the weapon. In the vehicle mode, this separation can be as much as 87 yards (80m).

The AT-4 Spigot (former NATO designation Fagot), also, is to be found on a tripod mount. It is thought to be a replacement for Sagger, again offering an improved time-of-flight (20 seconds to 2,186 yards (2,000m), for Sagger; possibly as little as 8 seconds for Spigot).

The standard man-portable ATGW of the Warsaw Pact armies at least during the early 1980s is expected to be the RPG-7V. This is

the latest Soviet version of the World War II German Panzerfaust. It has an effective range of 546 yards (500m) and self-destructs at about 984 yards (900m).

The Soviets have traditionally interspersed anti-tank assault guns among their attacking tank formations to enable the tanks to deal with the most powerful and dangerous targets. The SP-74 howitzer continues in this role with a high-explosive-anti-tank round. Still to be found in the same role is the SU-100, a self-propelled 100mm assault gun dating from World War II.

All of the towed Soviet field guns possess some armour-defeating capability, usually to a maximum effective range of about 1,093 yards (1,000m).

Anti-tank Weapons

▲ Euromissile Milan is now used by many armies in NATO.

▲ West German Mamba ATGW has a range of 2,000m (2,187yds).

▲ US Army Dragon ATGW, propelled by 30 pairs of miniature thrusters arranged around missile. Range is 1,000m (1,093yds).

▲ French SS-11 still serves in large numbers in many NATO armies. Here are quad installations on AMX-13 light tanks.

ONE of the major irritants within the North Atlantic Alliance is what some of their European military comrades regard as an excessive American "can do-ism". This is expressed sometimes as proposals for NATO to "defend in depth" or "trade space for time" by shifting to a "territorial defence" organized around anti-tank guided weapons (ATGW). These proposals, sometimes offered by Europeans as well, are usually linked to the publicity since the 1973 Middle East War suggesting near-omnipotence for "precision guided missiles".

In one recent case "American military planners and politicians" are urged to convince West Germany to adopt a "territorial home defence . . . that would add tre-

mendous relational depth to the modest manoeuvre area in West Germany". The endorser of this proposal says, "Admitted, this would require considerable moral courage and resolve on the part of US leaders."

What might be required of the Europeans who are supposed to carry out this brave new concept is left unsaid.

ATGWs—a Convenient Israeli Excuse?

Misreporting of the effectiveness of the ATGW in the 1973 war derived, in part, from the fact that both participants barred the foreign press from the battle areas and, in part, from the embarassment of the Israelis over a strategic and tactical surprise. In short, the

large numbers of Soviet ATGWs in the hands of the Egyptians gave the Israelis an excuse for losses that resulted, in fact, from failure to carry out the timely mobilization of artillery and infantry. As a result, Israeli tank units on active duty in the forward area were forced to counterattack without the combined arms organization their commanders knew full well was essential. The losses that occurred were expected but unavoidable, the alternative being to do nothing until the infantry and artillery arrived. Once those arms were available in sufficient strength, opposing ATGW operators were overwhelmed in short order, as they had been during World War II whenever they attempted to confront armour in open terrain, or

without combined arms support.

Proof that this is what occurred in the Sinai lies in the count of opposing tanks destroyed. By far the greater number of losses were due to tank gunnery.

What ATGWs Can and Cannot do

What *can* be accomplished by the new anti-tank weaponry? Defence of a fortified area is greatly enhanced by such new weapons as the US TOW and Dragon, the British Blowpipe and the Euromissile HOT and Milan. That, however, depends on the degree of fortification. For the man- or light-vehicle-portable infantry weapons, there must be both overhead cover against artillery fire and substantial protection against

▲ British Swingfire ATGW fired from Belgian Striker CVR(T).

▲ SADARM (Sense and Destroy Armour) in successful test.

▲ Cannon-launched Copperhead.

▲ Laser guidance is precise.

NATO Anti-tank weapons

Type	Range (km)	Guidance	Seconds to Target[1]	Ground motive means
TOW	2.32 (3.75)	Command/wire[2]	15	Tripod/vehicle/aircraft (AH)
HOT	2.48 (4)	Command/wire[2]	17	Tripod/vehicle/aircraft (AH)
Swingfire[3]	2.48 (4)	Command/wire[2]	15	Pallet/vehicle
Milan	1.24 (2)	Command/wire[2]	10	Vehicle/man-portable
Cobra	1.24 (2)	Command/wire[2]	7	Vehicle/man-portable
SS-11	1.86 (3)	Command/wire[2]	17	Vehicle/aircraft (AH)
Dragon	0.62 (1)	Command/wire[2]	2	Tripod/vehicle/man-portable
Folgore	0.62 (1)	Recoilless[4]	2	Tripod/man-portable
Carl Gustav	0.43 (0.7)	Recoilless[4]	2	Man-portable
M72 (LAW)	0.62 (1)	Free flight[6]	7	Man-portable
SARPAC	0.93 to 1.24 (1.5 to 2)	Free flight[6]	12	Man-portable
Hellfire[5]	3.76 (6)	Laser/infra red Homing	?	AH (US AH-64)

1. At maximum range.
2. Wire connected to launcher throughout; gunner must keep aiming cross on target or guide by manual control.
3. Operator can be at remote location up to 109.3 yards (100m) from launcher.
4. No control after launch.
5. Under development.
6. Light anti-tank weapon fire from disposable launcher.

large-calibre tank cannon. The stone walls of German villages did not suffice, of themselves, in World War II and they offer even less protection now. The elaborate construction (and diversion of valuable land) necessary for such a task has not occurred and is not likely to occur in peacetime. Nor is the Warsaw Pact likely to grant the necessary long period of alert.

To some degree, armoured vehicles can be substituted for prepared fortifications. Even these, however, must be dug in, with alternate positions prepared if they are to survive long enough to create a viable defence.

Not least of the ATGW limitations is the development in recent years of advanced armour plate and design which has diminished the effectiveness of the shaped-charge warhead on which the ATGW depends. To achieve its desired effect, the shaped-charge missile round must strike at an angle necessary to assure penetration, and the resulting stream of particles must not be diffused by an intervening barrier. By sloping armour plate, by providing intermediate armour barriers or by improved armour, tank designers have reduced ATGW penetration to the point that there is now public acknowledgement that early US TOWs must be redesigned. This improved "TOW 2" should arrive in the early 1980s.

Smoke emission accompanying the firing of all current ATGWs and the relatively slow velocity of the ATGW round increase the likelihood of detection and successful engagement by opposing tanks and artillery.

The greater the number of ATGW positions, of course, the greater the likelihood that some proportion of the rounds fired will reach a target—if smoke, rain, snow, darkness, fear or fatigue do not disturb the operator's aim.

Protecting Flanks and Rear

If it is recognized that they are not a panacea, ATGWs can perform valuable service for the NATO armies in a variety of roles. In the field army, they can protect the flanks and rear of tank formations carrying the main brunt of the battle. In terrain where tanks are restricted ATGWs can be used in conjunction with hastily laid minefields to establish ambush positions, inflicting losses and gaining time for the tanks and attack helicopters to manoeuvre into position for a counterattack.

Where they are not worked into a combined arms air and ground team, it seems likely that the ATGW can perform no more than a harassing function with a rather dismal future for the isolated, relatively immobile teams destined to employ them.

But, used in conjunction with a high-speed strategic armour reserve built around the French AMX-10RC or similar wheeled armour vehicles, ATGWs mounted on similar vehicles could perform the same sort of security and ambush roles described for ATGWs in the forward battle area.

Air Defence Weapons

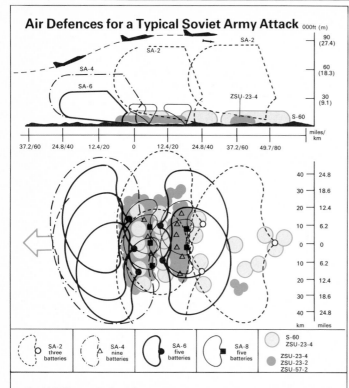

Air Defences for a Typical Soviet Army Attack

No NATO attack aircraft can deliver weapons from almost 90,000ft, shown to be necessary to defeat even current Soviet air defences, but would have to fly low with ECM to confuse SAM guidance systems.

▲ Provisional drawing of latest Soviet SAM – the SA-11.

▲ SA-9 SAMs mounted on BRDM. Note operator's windows.

▲ SA-6 SAMs had early successes in Yom Kippur war in 1973.

▲ 12.7mm DShKM adds to the low-level air defence cover.

AIRSPACE control—of which air defence is only one aspect—is the most difficult management problem facing the Warsaw Pact. No one, NATO included, has resolved the complexities of a situation in which high-performance aircraft and fleets of helicopters, friendly and enemy, would be competing for the airspace available and for the electromagnetic spectrum on which they all depend for coordination, navigation, identification of friend or foe (IFF) and target acquisition and engagement.

So crucial is the resolution of this problem that the outcome of any major land and air battle resulting from a Warsaw Pact attack on NATO could turn on this more than on any other single factor.

Peacetime Aspects

Indeed, the problem is just barely manageable in peacetime when there are only friendly aircraft to contend with, when there is no comprehensive attempt to jam communications or radars, when aircraft can be routed around ranges where high-angle artillery fire is being conducted and, above all, when air crews and ground controllers alike can concentrate on their work without the distractions of enemy fire.

The Soviet Union has collected, and distributed to its Warsaw Pact partners, a huge array of air defence radars, fighter-interceptors surface-to-air missiles (SAMs) and automatic weapons. Those related to high-altitude, high-speed penetrators are discussed in the aircraft

analysis pages of this section.

The diagram above depicts a cross section of the air space above the Warsaw Pact field armies *once they are deployed*. It shows virtually at a glance how difficult it will be for the overlapping weapons systems to sort out and engage targets without destroying friendly air vehicles in the process. Not shown in the diagram are the masses of artillery projectiles that will be passing back and forth through the lower altitudes and which will complicate the problem enormously.

Electronic Recce of Crucial Importance

To a considerable extent, success or failure of any given air defence system on either side will depend

on the efficiency of the reconnaissance being conducted daily, in peacetime, by both sides. This is aimed at identifying frequencies on which the various control systems operate, the "signature" of each type of system in the form of a pattern of radiation peculiar to that system and the use of such intelligence to devise electronic countermeasures and anti-radiation weapons to seek out specific frequencies and signatures.

The Warsaw Pact enjoys a great advantage in this regard since the open NATO societies provide almost all of the information needed to anyone with the means to gather it. The Pact forces have capitalized on this advantage by organizing and equipping electronic warfare units down to the

▲ Battery of effective ZSU-23-4 exercises in Siberia.

▲ Artillery sergeant with well-worn SA-7 Grail launcher.

▲ SA-8 Gecko; 25 in every Soviet MR and Tank Division.

▲ Polish missilemen work on elderly SA-2 Guideline SAM.

"Breakthrough" Warsaw Pact Air Defence Weapons[1]

Type	Range/miles (km)	Guidance	Ground motive power	Degree of dependence on electromagnetic spectrum	Altitude
ZSU-23-4	1.55 (2.5)	Radar or optical	Self-propelled, tracked	Marginal[2]	Low
SA-7 Grail	2.17 (3.5)	Infrared homing	Man-portable	50%[3]	Low
SA-9 Gaskin	4.96 (8)	Infrared	Self-propelled, armoured wheel vehicle	50%[3]	Low
SA-8 Gecko	4.96 to 9.93 (8 to 16)	Command	Self-propelled armoured wheel vehicle	100%	Medium
SA-4 Ganef	43.47 (70)	Command/semi-active radar homing	Self-propelled, tracked	100%	High
SA-6 Gainful	21.73 (35)	Semi-active radar homing	Self-propelled, tracked	100%	Medium

1. Weapons likely to be found within columns breaking through forward NATO defences.
2. Kinetic energy ammunition and optical tracking independent of radar.
3. Optical sighting.

regimental and battalion level with the mission, in part, of disrupting NATO airspace surveillance and communications.

US Air Force operations against what was, in effect, a Soviet air defence system in North Vietnam showed that NATO technology can penetrate at least the older versions of the Warsaw Pact system and successfully attack targets, but at a considerable cost in aircraft and trained crews. This experience and similar experience during the Korean War against massed automatic weapons have led many observers to believe that the cost of operating manned aircraft of any type against targets within the zone of large, fully deployed mechanized ground units and within the zone of a homeland air

defence system is no longer worth the cost. Priority of attack, in this view, should be against second-echelon forces not yet fully deployed and, of first priority, against forces penetrating the NATO front.

Air Defence of Second Echelon Units

If this is the case, NATO air operations against second-echelon units on the march would be primarily a battle to penetrate the same "homeland" fixed air defences that protect the rest of East Germany, Czechoslovakia and the USSR itself. Once through those defences, NATO fighter-bombers would accomplish a significant part of their mission simply by forcing ground units to deploy into a formation that would enable

them to use the full potential of their organic weapons. That, in turn, would slow the Warsaw Pact forces sufficiently to open a gap affecting the progress of the front-line units and expose the reinforcing units to attack by NATO battlefield missiles and rockets.

The Warsaw Pact air defence weapons of most immediate concern to NATO ground force commanders, therefore, are those upon which breakthrough Warsaw Pact units must depend to maintain their advance.

These are the weapons listed in the table above. Most reliable of them all, because it can operate at a high degree of efficiency regardless of electronic interference, is the ZSU-23-4. Normally assigned on the basis of four per Motorized

Rifle Regiment and Tank Regiment, it would seem reasonable to expect that these allocations would be doubled or tripled for the exploitation.

Assuming that NATO maintains the lead in countermeasures that was evidenced in Vietnam, the most reliable, indeed the indispensable high-altitude air defence cover for the breakthrough column is most likely to be the tactical fighter.

The principal function of the mobile and man-portable SAMs, then, would be to force NATO attack helicopters to fly at extremely low altitudes where their fields of fire would be limited, and of forcing A-10 type aircraft to altitudes where they would be prey to high-performance fighters.

Air Defence Weapons

▲ British Rapier SAM is being widely deployed in UK.

▲ British man-portable Blowpipe weighs 47lb (21.3kg).

▲ US Patriot, designed to replace Hawk and Nike-Hercules, is now in full production.

THE fact, touched on in the previous section (Air Defence Weapons—Warsaw Pact), that amid the wonders of the electronic age the most reliable air defence weapon of the ground forces continues to be the visually sighted kinetic energy system is difficult to accept but nonetheless true on the NATO side as well as in the Warsaw Pact armies.

No Assured IFF

Assured electronic identification of friend or foe (IFF) simply does not exist. For one thing, the pilot must remember to turn it on. NATO has an effort underway to develop a NATO Identification System that will correct these problems, looking to a replacement for the current Mark 10 and

12 IFF systems by the mid 1980s.

In the meantime, reliance is on positive (visual) identification in the case of air defence weapons in the hands of troops and physical separation of friendly air elements as in the wartime "no go" areas for friendly aircraft established by Britain's Royal Air Force off the East coast of the United Kingdom. These necessary control measures reduce the theoretical capability of NATO surface-to-air missiles, as well as of those of their Warsaw Pact counterparts.

There is, however, a significant advantage for NATO, deriving from the fact that it is defending rather than attacking. Warsaw Pact forces would be moving out from under their fixed "homeland" air defence system while the NATO

forces would remain under theirs.

Acquisition of Improved Hawk missile by Belgium in 1980 filled the last major medium-altitude gap in the NATO air defence system. As modernization of the NATO medium and high-altitude system progresses through the 1980s, with deployment of Patriot, the "homeland" advantage of the NATO land forces will be greatly increased.

For the low-level battle against helicopters and fixed-wing close support aircraft, NATO has fielded a variety of high-quality gun systems. France's Panhard M3 VDA light armoured vehicle offers radar-directed 20mm air defence fire support for the sort of high-speed counter-penetration capability described in earlier NATO sections (Light Armoured Vehi-

cles; Helicopters). For support of tank formations, the French twin 30mm system on an AMX 30 chassis provides visual or radar-directed fire to 3,825 yards (3,500m).

Germany has reequipped its 11 divisional anti-aircraft battalions with 432 armoured, full-track twin 35mm Gepards, also with on-vehicle search and tracking radars, as well as optical equipment. Belgium and the Netherlands operate an additional 150 Gepards.

The US Army in Europe gave up its last twin 40mm tracked vehicles in the early 1960s and now has thought better of it. A competition is underway for selection of a Division Air Defense System (DIVADS) to consist either of a Bofors twin 40mm (Ford/Westing-

▲ US Army Gatling exists in both towed and SP versions.

▲ USA, France and West Germany will use Roland SAM.

▲ The 35mm German Gepard Flakpanzer.

▲ Hawk in service with the Dutch Army.

house) gun carriage, or a General Dynamics/Oerlikon 35mm vehicle, both with on-carriage acquisition and fire-direction radars.

All of the NATO armies except the United States and Britain field a variety of towed 40mm and 20mm weapons. Properly deployed, these weapons will provide a valuable air defence capability for rear area installations far into the future.

A Major Upgrading with Roland II

A major upgrading of the NATO field army air defence system is taking place with deployment of the Roland missile system in several national configurations. Developed as a Franco–German program, Roland was originally an optically-aimed, infra red homing system (Roland I) and now has been further developed as an all-weather system with addition of a target-tracking radar (Roland II).

The Roland missile is a two-stage, solid-propellent round with a minimum range of 546 yards (500m) and a maximum of 6,560 (6,000m), making somewhat doubtful the published Soviet view that the Hind D attack helicopter will be able to engage NATO tanks beyond the range of organic land force air defence systems. The French version is mounted on an AMX 30 chassis and the German on an SPZ Marder chassis.

The United States is producing Roland II under licence and will deploy it mounted on a full-tracked chassis. The core elements of Roland also can be deployed on truck or trailer bodies for defence of fixed installations. Roland II is expected to be deployed by Belgium and Norway soon.

Chaparral to Continue?

Pending availability of funds for full Roland and DIVADS production, the US Army will continue to deploy the Chaparral version of the air-to-air Sidewinder, mounted on an M113 APC chassis, and the six-barrel 20mm Vulcan mounted on an M113 chassis or in a towed configuration.

In addition to Roland, France fields the short-range Crotale system (maximum range 5.3 miles, 8.5km) on both wheeled and tracked mounts.

The Man-portable Systems

There are a variety of man-portable air defence missiles in the NATO armies, feared perhaps as much by NATO aviators as by the potential enemy! In the absence of an error-proof IFF system, the man-portable weapons rely on the skill of the operator in sorting out enemy aircraft from the "friendlies" in a very confused environment.

British and Canadian units are equipped with Blowpipe, a radio command and optical tracking weapon. US units employ Stinger, an infra-red homing system replacing the older Redeye. Danish, German and Greek units use the American equipment. Average range of the manportable weapons is considered to be in the vicinity of 3,280 yards (3,000m).

NBC Warfare Equipment

▲ Soldier decontaminating RPG-7 rocket launchers.

▲ Polish Army team marking chemically contaminated areas.

▲ Special washdown for an NBC-contaminated BTR-60 APC.

▲ TMS-65 has turbojet to wash down contaminated vehicles.

THAT the Soviet Union has the world's most formidable chemical warfare capability is now generally recognized. As in the case of some other major weapons systems (see Helicopters —Warsaw Pact) about all that remains in doubt is where the Soviets might be most likely to use this capability.

As is shown in the succeeding section, NATO lacks the means to defend against the sort of massive chemical assault of which the Warsaw Pact is capable. The effect conceivably could be to force NATO either to accept defeat or to employ nuclear weapons.

Used elsewhere, the Soviet chemical warfare capability could produce dramatic strategic gains with little or no risk of retaliation, chemical or nuclear. First among these areas is China, where chemical weapons could clear the border provinces of defending forces, and block any effective counterattack, at little cost to the USSR. Chemical weapons would be particularly effective against the sort of guerrilla operations envisaged in a Chinese "people's war". Indeed, there have been repeated reports through United Nations and refugee channels of Soviet use of lethal agents against just such opposition, directly in Afghanistan and by proxy in Yemen and Laos.

The Soviets could use chemical weapons more selectively against NATO, attacking only a few key targets such as the depots holding prepositioned equipment for US reinforcements. It would be more difficult for NATO to resort to nuclear weapons if only such a limited use were made of chemical weapons. Any delay in the NATO decision to escalate would act to the advantage of the Warsaw Pact in two ways—the attack would disarm the US reinforcements but impose no commensurate penalty on the Warsaw Pact forces.

The CW systems

The offensive weapons available to the Warsaw Pact for chemical attack begin with the long-range aircraft, missile and rocket systems discussed in other sections. Of most immediate concern to ground commanders are the Frog 7 and Scud systems, and the follow-on SS-21 and SS-23. It is estimated that one-third of the warheads produced for these missiles are chemical warfare rounds.

The principal agents likely to be carried by these delivery systems are Soman (Agent GD), a nerve gas, or less lethal blood and blister agents. Two to 10 milligrams of GD on unprotected skin can cause death in a few minutes from disruption of the nervous system.

The chief value of the blister agents (the "mustard gas" of World War I) is persistency. They can remain effective for several days or weeks. Some nerve weapons known as "V" agents, also, are persistent.

Although the risk of a NATO nuclear response would be greater, chemical attacks limited to a few breakthrough points and carefully

▲ Soldiers in old pattern ShM respirator and ZFK-58 suit.

Typical WP/NATO CW Offensive Capability

Key

WP
1. Mortar
2. Multi-round rocket launcher
3. Artillery
4. Missiles and rockets
5. Tactical aircraft

NATO
1. 4.2in mortar
2. 105mm howitzer
3. M109 155mm howitzer
4. 8in howitzer*
5. M109A1 155mm howitzer*
6. Tactical aircraft

*NATO's M110A2 and M109A1 both capable of 28km range with rocket-assisted projectiles.

Above 800km 5

Above 800km 5

4

Up to 800km

6

Above 600km 5

3

2

1

2

4

1

2

3

km
30
25
20
15
10
5

Warsaw Pact doctrine emphasises employment of chemical weapons in coordination with conventional and nuclear weapons to capitalise on the attributes of each; NATO has a stated plan to use them in retaliation to convey the message of high resolve to win, and to persuade the enemy to terminate chemical warfare.

▲ Soviet NBC warfare training is thorough and frequent.

▲ Marking of contaminated areas is thorough and effective.

---

controlled in time and area might succeed without appearing to justify NATO escalation to nuclear warfare.

Tube artillery, heavy mortars and multiple rocket lunchers could deliver such attacks on key terrain objectives ahead of the initial Warsaw Pact ground thrusts. In some areas there might be no NATO casualties at all, military or civilian, but ground on which NATO forces were depending to set up defensive positions could be denied them. The possibility of conducting such limited chemical attacks is enhanced by Soviet progress in converting its weapons from "gas" to liquid (usually in droplet form). Being less susceptible to dispersion, these liquid agents can be con-centrated in an area a few thousand yards square.

NBC Protection Thorough and Effective

The Soviets are well equipped to exploit such opportunities. All of their late-model tanks and ar-moured personnel carriers can be sealed against chemical and radio-logical contamination. Positive overpressure systems exclude con-taminants, and assist in fording. Air filters provide additional pro-tection. Individual masks and pro-tective clothing permit troops to operate outside the vehicles if necessary. For protection against radiation resulting from a nuclear burst, the T-62 and later model tanks are reported to have an automatic system for closing hull openings (except personnel hatches) and warning crews upon detection of the first pulse of a nuclear explosion.

Rapid exploitation by these NBC-protected vehicles and troops through contaminated areas could be decisive in achieving break-throughs if NATO forces are un-able to reach or to maintain their defensive positions because of in-adequate equipment and training. Once through the breakthrough areas the first echelon units could stand aside for passage of second echelon units through uncontami-nated, or decontaminated areas. The original assault units could then be decontaminated quickly enough to follow on in the exploitation.

Specialized chemical troops estimated to total somewhere be-tween 50,000 and 100,000 are available to assist in the decon-tamination process. One means of quick, partial decontamination of vehicles is to pass them between modified turbojet aircraft engines mounted on trucks or trailers tow-ing tanks of decontaminant solu-tion, operating somewhat as an automatic car wash.

It might be possible to repeat this each time major resistance is en-countered. The power of such attacks would be magnified by the panic induced in an unprotected and untrained NATO civilian population. Thus the wisdom of NATO fighting the defensive battle at the frontier and then of carrying the war into Pact territory becomes even more compelling.

NBC Warfare Equipment

▲ RAF Regiment team at NBC alert on a Rapier position.

▲ Soldiers rush to don NBC gear; time is of the essence.

▲ NBC warfare requires complete protection.

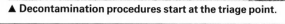

▲ Decontamination procedures start at the triage point.

AT best, the NATO defence capability against chemical and radiological warfare must be described as "spotty".

If the ability to retaliate is considered as one form of defence, through deterrence, NATO is in a very poor stance for two reasons. First, virtually all of the NATO offensive chemical arsenal is in the hands of the United States, with about half of it locked up in Western US depots beset by groups of environmentalists and pacifists. The bombs, artillery, projectiles and mortar shells that make up most of this capability are old and overdue for replacement.

Second, NATO chemical retaliation against attacking Warsaw Pact columns would be a difficult proposition from the tactical standpoint. Since, initially at least, NATO must accept battle on its own soil, chemical attacks on the forward enemy units would be likely to inflict further casualties on the NATO civilian population and cause little damage to an army that, as the previous pages have shown, is the best trained and equipped in the world to handle this sort of warfare. There is a further problem of finding and fixing targets in a fluid, fast-developing battle.

Binary Weapons may Soon be in Production

There is some hope that the deficiencies of the NATO retaliatory arsenal will be rectified, at least in part, by construction of a US plant for production of binary chemical munitions. These are projectiles in which the components of the lethal agents are separated, and harmless, until the projectile is dispatched toward its target. Since chances of Congressional approval for production now seem stronger, there is an increasing likelihood of modernization of NATO chemical munitions in the early 1980s. At least until that time, therefore, NATO will not have the means to respond, measure for measure, against large-scale use of Warsaw Pact chemical munitions.

Considering the large-scale preparations of the Warsaw Pact forces and the vulnerability of the NATO civilian population, the utility of expanding the use of chemical weapons on NATO soil merely for the sake of retaliation raises more questions than it answers. In short, it is very doubtful that the long Soviet technological lead and the attitudes of the Western societies will ever permit the development of a NATO offensive chemical capability sufficient to end the present large Soviet advantage.

Something more potent than chemical weapons will be necessary to discourage the Warsaw Pact from their use. That "something" is ready at hand in the form of NATO enhanced radiation nuclear technology. The Soviets fear, and rightly so, a nuclear attack that would disrupt their rigid ground force command and control system. ER weapons offer an unparalleled means to achieve that purpose, as well as to attack

▲ British soldiers in full NBC protective clothing during an exercise on Salisbury Plain.

▲ US soldiers in NBC gear.

▲ Individual decontamination.

US Chemical Warfare Delivery Systems Common to Other NATO Nations US Delivery System	Belgium	Canada	Denmark	France	Greece	Iceland	Italy	Luxembourg	Netherlands	Norway	Portugal	Turkey	United Kingdom	West Germany
4.2-inch mortar	X	X	X						X	X	X	X		
105mm howitzer	X	X	X	X	X		X		X	X	X	X	X	X
155mm howitzer	X	X	X	X	X				X	X			X	X	X
8-inch howitzer	X		X	X			X					X	X	X

Characteristics of Typical Chemical Agents

Category	Symbol	Normal Physical State when Disseminated	Persistency in Target Area	Tactical Use	Time to Incapacitation
Nerve Agent	GB	Vapor or Aerosol	A few minutes	Lethal effect on unmasked troops	Very short, death may occur in few minutes if agent is inhaled
Nerve Agent	VX	Liquid	A few hours to a week	Lethal effect on troops, contamination of terrain and equipment	A few hours (delayed casualties)
Blister Agent	HD	Liquid	Usually a few days, possibly a few weeks	Incapacitation of troops, contamination of terrain and equipment	A few hours (delayed casualties)

This chart shows typical US agents and their effects. Threat forces use similar agents with similar effects.

massed armoured formations. Used against second echelon forces and the command system on the Eastern side of the Iron Curtain, these weapons would achieve maximum military effect yet limit, to the extent that limitation is at all possible in modern warfare, civilian casualties among potentially friendly populations.

If the Soviets are to be deterred from use of chemical, or any weapons, against NATO it seems necessary, first, to provide the means to deliver ER weapons on a large scale and, second, to make it plain to the Soviets that use of chemical weapons would produce an immediate theatre nuclear response limited to targets in immediate support of the attacking formations.

Biological warfare is supposedly outlawed, although a recent outbreak of anthrax near what are thought to be biological warfare laboratories in Sverdlovsk, USSR, suggests tests continue.

Since it is difficult or impossible to control once unleashed, and since ordinary public health measures are the best possible defence, the utility of biological weapons in Europe is doubtful. The level of immunity in populations that have enjoyed a lifetime of good medical care is likely to be high. Also, any resulting epidemics almost certainly would spread to Eastern Europe and the USSR itself. If the Soviets are developing biological weapons they are most probably intended for use against China.

Radiological warfare can be waged by spreading the waste products of nuclear plants without the direct explosion of a nuclear weapon. The fine distinctions of that process, however, are apt to be lost on the victims. The "threshold" to direct use of nuclear weapons would most certainly have been crossed and from that point radiological contamination must be considered as an aspect of nuclear warfare as a whole.

NATO's Protective Measures Insufficient

Although on a far more modest scale than the counter threat suggested, NATO defensive preparations against NBC warfare are also an essential aspect of deterrence. Britain has NATO's most highly

developed protective clothing technology. Some 200,000 UK Mk 3 overgarments and boots have been acquired for US forces in Europe pending large-scale production of US protective clothing and the British boot. Added to the masks on hand in the NATO forces this provides some elementary measure of defence.

All of the newer NATO combat vehicles and aircraft have internal NBC protective systems equal to or superior to Soviet technology. Very little has been done, however, to protect the NATO logistic system. Protection of the NATO logistic facilities will be useless unless the surrounding civilian population is also trained and protected. Political leaders should look at this problem urgently.

Reconnaissance and Surveillance Equipment

▲ Soviet reconnaissance section of BRDM-2U and BTR-60PU.

Soviet Battlefield Electronic Surveillance: Normal Maximum Ranges (km)

No limit

HF Sky wave

HF Ground wave 80

VHF 40

Radar 25

Sound 14

FEBA

Sound ranging | Artillery ground radar | VHF radar intercept | HF radio intercept

Electronic surveillance is just as important to the Soviet Army as air or ground reconnaissance, and the ground forces have an extensive intercept capability for both radio and radar. Special intercept units are moved up as close to the forward troops as possible and have the capability to intercept all enemy transmissions at the distances shown on the diagram. All the ranges would of course be greatly extended when airborne intercept equipment is used.

▲ OT-64 APCs of Czech Army on a reconnaissance mission.

▲ Recce patrols comb divisional frontages and flanks.

THE Warsaw Pact forces have the benefit of what is probably the most complete picture of enemy dispositions, capabilities and even personalities ever possessed by a potential aggressor in the history of warfare. This is a product of the open societies of the NATO nations and the ability of the Soviet intelligence services to operate in those societies with almost complete freedom.

Ironically, it is not what little knowledge NATO has denied to the Soviets that has kept the peace thus far, but what the Soviets *do* know about overall NATO defence capabilities, nuclear and conventional. This relatively clear Warsaw Pact picture would grow cloudy very quickly after an attack began as units became intermingled, communications were garbled or jammed and the general "fog of war" was generated by conflicting reports. Warsaw Pact ability to regain the knowledge needed to make continuing tactical decisions depends on a variety of means.

Radio Monitoring

Assuming an air battle in which neither side could gain supremacy at least for the first few days, the rapid shift of friendly and enemy units that would be likely to be taking place and the increasing quantity and lethality of air defense weapons in the NATO ground units, it would be unlikely that low-flying aircraft could gain a comprehensive tactical picture, or even be able to survive for long.

In this situation, radio monitoring would very quickly become the principal means for the gathering of tactical intelligence. The Soviets have a major advantage in this area in that there is a radio and radar reconnaissance company in the Reconnaissance Battalion of each division and a radar reconnaissance section in the Reconnaissance Company of each regiment. Comparable US units are at Division level, but are not found at all in most other NATO divisions.

To process efficiently what is learned from signal intelligence (SIGINT) and electronic intelligence (ELINT) and to get the results back to ground commanders in time for it to be of use is another matter. In short, for the Soviet and East European ground forces, reliable reconnaissance and surveillance in the battle area would rest primarily with the same sort of troops described in the section that follows, on NATO Reconnaissance and Surveillance.

Radars on Flanks

Sophisticated devices such as surveillance radars would be set up to guard the flanks of a Warsaw Pact penetration once a breakthrough was made, but for the assaulting Soviet formations in the first crucial hours of an attack on Western Europe they would be virtually useless.

How good, then, are the Warsaw Pact ground reconnaissance units? For it is upon them primarily that the attacking battalion, regimental

▲ Soviet frogmen recce the bottom of the River Elbe in East Germany.

▲ PT-76 recce tank is now being replaced by the recce version of the BMP APC.

and division commanders must depend to fight the land battle.

Of special value is the Long Range Reconnaissance Company in the Reconnaissance Battalion of each Motorized Rifle and Tank Division. These can be deployed in small teams to a considerable depth by helicopter in the enemy rear area. When all else fails they are the one sure means of verifying intelligence from other sources and for gaining first-hand knowledge of enemy strong points, obstacles and terrain features.

Either moving to the border ahead of Warsaw Pact columns, or more likely operating to cover the shoulders and flanks of the column once it crosses the border, would be Division and Regimental ground reconnaissance elements

seeking to put as much distance as possible between themselves and the main body in order to keep direct fire off the main body, warn the main column of flank attacks and defeat or at least delay such attacks.

The Recce Vehicles

For much of the past 20 years this was the task of units built around the PT-76 light amphibious tank and the BTR-50 light armoured personnel carrier in the Soviet Army and various combinations of wheeled armoured cars in less privileged Pact forces.

The BMP mechanized infantry vehicle is now replacing the older track vehicles in this role. As in the infantry units, the BMP is matched in the reconnaissance elements by

a BRDM-2 or other wheeled equivalent company.

In the words of a US Army study of Soviet Army operations, "divisional-level reconnaissance groups drawn from the division reconnaissance battalion and operating at platoon-company strength . . . will provide mobile, wide-ranging reconnaissance patrols to cover each division route and axis of advance. Using one main and several subordinate reconnaissance patrols (one to three vehicles each), divisional reconnaissance groups will attempt to determine the strength, composition and deployment of the defense."

All that is easy to say, but most difficult to execute. Are Soviet units built around relatively short-term conscripts equal to the task?

Nowhere else is the skill and initiative of the individual soldier so critical. Yet experience in the Western armies indicates that such skills are chiefly to be found in long-term non-commissioned officers who have made the cavalry a career. The odds in this critical mission area would seem to fall with the American, British and German scout leaders who have been constantly patrolling the sectors in which they would fight, often on repetitive tours of duty over a period of 20 years or more.

The Soviets have had unlimited opportunity to acquaint themselves with the border region. The East German and Czech frontier guards who patrol those borders on a more routine basis could be a valuable asset—but would they?

Reconnaissance and Surveillance Equipment

▲ West German 8×8 recce vehicle.

▲ Luxembourg jeep recce vehicle.

▲ M113CR recce vehicle with TOW launcher observing from a ridge line.

▲ OV-10 Bronco is used for recce and FAC missions.

▲ OV-1D Mohawk with APS-94 sideways-looking radar in pod.

DURING the only full-dimension manoeuvre that has been conducted of a NATO-Warsaw Pact war (Joint US Strike Command Exercise *Desert Strike* in the United States, May-June 1964) the Exercise Director, US Gen. Paul D. Adams told his assembled commanders, "Everywhere I go I find people staring into radar scopes, examining aerial photographs and listening to radios. Yet this is the country where the Indians stood on a hilltop and saw the US Cavalry coming 25 miles away. If you people don't start doing the same thing someone is going to run over you."

Nearly 20 years after General Adams issued that warning the situation is, in the eyes of a number of observers, worse. The marvels of aerial and satellite photography have bred a dangerous assumption that they reveal virtually everything that a nation needs to know about the military capabilities of a potential enemy.

Misleading Picture of the Enemy

The increasing dependence on the vehicles described in earlier pages of this section breeds a similar danger. That is, almost all of these modern vehicles are equipped with an increasingly elaborate array of night and bad-weather vision devices dependent on one or several aspects of the light and electromagnetic spectrum rather than on direct observation and examination. That means they are subject to deception by an enemy who "paints" a misleading picture by creating false signals.

US Army Lt. Col. Henry G. Gole, a veteran of extensive ground combat service in Korea and Vietnam, believes that his own army is afflicted with a "fascination with gadgets". He cites as the worst symptom the fact that "the combat intelligence and target acquisition capability inherent in Long Range Reconnaissance Patrols (LRRP) has been almost totally erased since our Vietnam experience. Our allies in Europe are fully aware of the need for LRRP. The Bundeswehr assigns an airborne-qualified LRRP company to each of the three German corps deployed . . . Belgian LRRPs, also airborne-qualified, consist of small cells of highly skilled soldiers who remain in four-man teams for years . . . The British Special Air Services (SAS) troops are among the best in the world and prepare for the LRRP mission as do the French. . . ."

These highly trained patrols would become of increasing importance as a Warsaw Pact attack on NATO developed. Gaps between friendly units would tend to grow wider and a vast area for first-hand intelligence gathering would open up behind enemy lines.

But the immediate burden for army tactical human intelligence (HUMINT), will fall upon on the NATO cavalry units deployed along the Iron Curtain day by day. It is they who must sense and report the first specific intelligence on which the major NATO unit

NATO

▲ Scorpion and Scimitar are airportable in C-130 Hercules.

▲ French AML-90 armoured cars at range practice.

▲ A recce patrol of Royal Marines skijoring in Norway.

▲ US Army M2. The M3 cavalry/scout vehicle is similar.

▲Ski patrol recce on NATO's northern flank in Norway.

commanders rely for planning their deployments.

In part, this mission is performed by the Scout helicopter, but for continuous, day and night, good and foul weather surveillance there is as yet no substitute for the ground reconnaissance unit.

Two approaches to this mission are apparent in NATO. The US Army has "heavied up" its armoured cavalry regiments deployed on the border and the armoured cavalry squadrons organic to each of the US divisions in Germany. In the main this was done to increase firepower. Some claim has been made of late, however, that the presence of heavy fighting vehicles in the forward cavalry areas tends to deceive the

enemy about the location of the main body.

The Scorpion Family of Light Vehicles
All the other NATO allies with units on the border have opted for more traditional cavalry vehicles. The most comprehensive group of these is the full-track British Scorpion family consisting of a 76mm light tank (Scorpion), an ATGM vehicle (Striker), an armoured personnel carrier (Spartan) and command, recovery and ambulance variants. All are built on the same basic chassis with the great advantage of simplifying spare parts supply. All are amphibious and have a top road speed of 54mph (87km/hr).

In addition to the British Army,

Belgium operates 552 Scorpion family vehicles, some of which were co-produced in Belgium.

The German Army has gone lighter still, depending on the 8×8 wheeled Spahpanzer 2 Luchs armed with a turret-mounted 20mm cannon and a 7.62mm machinegun at the vehicle commander's hatch. With drivers front and rear it is probably the best single reconnaissance vehicle on the border in terms of ability to observe undetected and to displace before becoming engaged and thereby identified.

Despite the somewhat lame arguments about the value of heavy vehicles in the covering force area, US armoured cavalrymen have long sought lighter vehicles. Several long and dis-

appointing development programs have been conducted. Now, a Cavalry Fighting Vehicle has gone into production as the M3 variant of the M2 Infantry Fighting Vehicle (described further under Armoured Personnel Carriers – NATO). The M3 is different from the M2 only in respect to its internal arrangements. The M3 has only three scouts in place of the six infantry men carried in the M2. The space gained has been used for stowage of additional TOW missiles, and an AN/PPS-15 battlefield surveillance radar.

In the meantime, there is a fairly continuous call among US cavalrymen for a family of light armoured reconnaissance vehicles almost identical in description to the British Scorpion family.

The Balance of NAVAL FORCES

THE United States is a naval power with an army; the Soviet Union is a land power with a navy. The United States counts among its allies a number of other powers with strong naval traditions – the United Kingdom, France, the Netherlands, Portugal – whereas not one of the Soviet Union's Warsaw Pact allies has ever had either the ability or inclination to do more than defend its own coastline.

This fundamental difference in outlook is crucial to an understanding of the nature of sea power as it is seen through Soviet and Western eyes. For in spite of the formidable build-up in Soviet naval forces since World War II those forces remain committed to tasks which are very different to

those ascribed to the NATO forces opposing them. Nowhere is the "numbers game" less relevant than in the naval theatre. And nowhere can one see a greater difference in the basic force structures and in the design philosophy of the individual units than in the opposing naval forces. A Russian tank and a German tank look much the same to the uninitiated observer, but the difference between *Kiev* and the average American carrier is self-evident. The difference is not one of architecture, but of purpose.

Geography
The difference in outlook is rooted in geography. The traditional maritime countries are all characterised by good access to the sea, and also by the need to use the sea

for political and mercantile purposes.

The older European powers built up large overseas empires, and even now when those empires have crumbled away they still rely heavily on imports of raw materials from their former colonies to feed their industries. Sea power for these nations is therefore the means by which their merchant fleets can be defended.

The United States, whose maritime forces were built up for political rather than mercantile reasons, needs to use the sea in order to wield its influence on world affairs and to support its NATO allies. No home-based US soldier can fight anywhere unless he – or at least his heavy equipment – can be transported by sea. Sea power for the

United States is therefore the means by which its political and military power can be projected.

The Soviet Union is surrounded on three sides by land and on the fourth by ice. Its maritime position is characterised by poor access to the high seas. There were no great Russian navigators, nor was there any attempt to build up sea-borne commerce links, nor an overseas empire. Russian "imperialism" has never looked further than its own borders, and has been concerned only with creating defensive "buffers" against land-borne invasion. Even now, at a time when the Soviet Union has assumed the position of a world power and has extended its political influence throughout the underdeveloped regions of the world, there is

The most publicised increase in Warsaw Pact capabilities has been the Soviet Navy, which has developed into a well-balanced force capable of projecting Soviet military power into the most distant corners of the globe. Its one shortcoming, lack of air power, is being rectified with the development of aircraft carriers. The US Navy is intent on vast increases in shipbuilding through the 1980s – toward the 600-ship fleet. More typical within NATO is the British Royal Navy's planned cuts, since for the West the major problem is the ever-increasing cost of sophisticated warships, which is limiting naval inventories and reducing strategic options.

hardly a base outside the Warsaw Pact area where Soviet warships could be repaired or replenished in the event of hostilities.

Traditionally the major Soviet fleets were based in the Baltic and Black Seas, and the main ship-building and ship repair yards of the USSR are located there to this day. As the world has grown smaller, so these two land-locked seas have diminished in their importance for naval operations. The need to extend the defence of the Soviet Union around the periphery to ward off NATO's sea-borne strike forces, and the need to threaten the vital life-line which links the United States to its European allies has compelled the Soviets to invest heavily in base and maintenance facilities in the

Arctic in order to ensure free access to the North Atlantic and Norwegian Sea. The prevailing weather conditions make both maintenance and operations diffi-cult, and ice is also a problem in the Baltic and in the Far East, where some ports are only ice-free for six months per year.

Fleets Isolated
Worse still, in the event of a con-frontation between the Warsaw Pact and NATO, the four Soviet fleets – Baltic, Black Sea, Northern and Pacific – would immediately be isolated from one another. The Baltic Fleet could easily be penned in by mining the Danish straits combined with skilful use of land-based air and missile-armed FPBs. The large missile cruisers of the

Northern Fleet would then be cut off from the Baltic shipyards which have built and refitted them. The powerful Black Sea Fleet could be bottled up by the simple expedient of closing the Dardanelles, and the 50-strong Mediterranean Squad-ron would then find itself between the hammer of the US 6th Fleet and the anvil of the Greek, Turkish and Italian airfields, with no plausible means of escape. And in the Far East the Pacific Fleet based on Vladivostok, already encircled by the Japanese Islands, would be very vulnerable to a blockade of the Tsushima Straits by US naval forces of the 7th Fleet.

The only significant factor which favours the Soviet Union is that, although its geographical situation makes it difficult to exer-

cise sea control, there is no com-pelling reason why the Soviets need to control anything other than the waters adjacent to their own coastline. The entire Soviet Army can be transferred overland to the West German border. The large merchant fleet which has been built up over the past 20 years carries other people's goods, as the Soviet Union possesses all the natural resources required by its own industries and those of its Warsaw Pact allies. The Soviet Navy therefore finds itself with the classic "sea denial" mission, while the security of the NATO allies demands that they exercise control over vast expanses of ocean.

The composition of the oppos-ing naval forces and the design philosophy of the individual units

The Balance of Naval Forces

Warsaw Pact and NATO Naval Force Strengths

The table below gives the numbers of major warships available to NATO and the Warsaw Pact. Such figures, however, need to be regarded with a degree of circumspection, since sheer numbers can never be a precise measure of the comparative effectiveness of any military force. There are always several ships in every navy in long or short refit, while others can be unavailable through breakdown or damage. Ships can also be in reserve and their availability in a crisis will depend upon the speed with which they can be returned to operational status. Further, there are vast areas of oceans to be covered and thus the skill and strategic judgement of the admirals will affect the stationing of the units of their fleets. In a short war the position of ships at the outset could be critical, and the advantage will lie with the aggressor, who will be able to choose the time and place for the opening of hostilities.

The static balances given below do nevertheless reveal some interesting information. First, the non-Soviet Warsaw Pact nations contribute only in a small way to the Pact's naval forces; much less than the non-US navies do to NATO. Secondly, in terms of absolute numbers the advantage appears to lie with NATO, but this ignores the modernity of the Soviet fleet and its much greater building rate. The remainder of this section sets out to put flesh on these bare statistics.

	AIRCRAFT CARRIERS			CRUISERS			DESTROYERS			FRIGATES	
WARSAW PACT	Soviet Union	ASW	4	Soviet Union	Large	1	Soviet Union		60	Soviet Union	
					SSM	8	Poland	AAW	1	Bulgaria	
					ASW	17				GDR	
					Command	2					
NATO	US	Attack	13	US	AAW	37	US	AAW	27	US	
	UK	ASW	2	France	AAW	1		ASW	43		
	France	Attack	2	Italy	ASW	2	UK	AAW	13	UK	
	Italy	ASW	1				France	AAW	6	W. Germany	
								ASW	12	Netherlands	
							W. Germany	AAW	3	Portugal	
								SSM	4	Belgium	
							Netherlands		5	Norway	
							Italy	AAW	4	Denmark	
								ASW	2		
							Greece	ASW	12		
							Canada	ASW	16		
							Turkey	ASW	12		

reflect these differing requirements.

The positive side of the "sea control" stance adopted by NATO can be seen in the wide-ranging carrier task forces, with their ability to strike anywhere they are needed, totally independent of ground support. It can also be seen in the large ocean-going amphibious fleet which enables the United States to project land power to any point on the globe.

The reverse side of the coin is NATO's need for large defensive forces to defend the long and vulnerable sea lanes against threats from above and below the water. A major part of this mission in the North Atlantic is performed by Canada and the European allies, with the Royal Navy particularly preeminent. It is a mission which makes considerable demands on Western resources in ships and manpower, as hostile attacking forces would be able to choose when and where to strike and could concentrate their strength. Few people believe that in a long-drawn-out war of attrition NATO would be able to provide adequate protection to its merchant shipping in every region of the globe.

The "sea denial" stance enforced on the Soviet Navy has resulted in a totally different force structure, but one which mirrors the two sides of the "sea control" coin.

Area Defence Zones
First and foremost the Soviet Navy must defend Soviet territory against marauding carrier task forces. Area defence zones have therefore been created in all four fleet areas using land-based strike aircraft and concentric rings of cruisers and patrol craft armed with anti-ship missiles, supplemented by submarines. As the Soviet Navy has grown in numbers and sophistication these area defence zones have been moved progressively outwards in order to encompass large expanses of sea in the Arctic and N.W. Pacific in which to conceal their latest SSBNs, whose missiles can target large areas of the United States from within their own fleet areas.

The second part of the "sea denial" mission involves contesting control over the open seas essential to the NATO allies. The now traditional weapon of the nation which is unable to exercise control over the surface is the submarine, and of these the Soviet Navy has over 200 (excluding SSBNs), 95 of which are nuclear-powered. They are tasked not only with the disruption of shipping in the North Atlantic, but also with hunting down the US carriers before they could project their striking power into the seas adjacent to the Soviet Union.

Support for Submarines
The building of a large Soviet blue water surface fleet for ASW operations began in the early sixties as an attempt to counter the Polaris submarines of the US Navy which posed a new threat to the homeland. Lack of success in detecting the SSBNs, together with

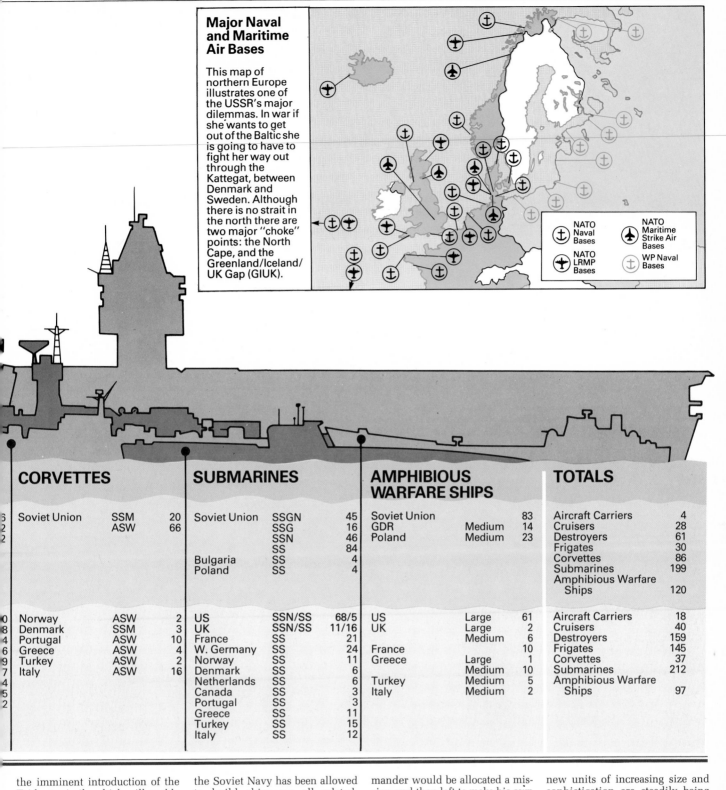

Major Naval and Maritime Air Bases

This map of northern Europe illustrates one of the USSR's major dilemmas. In war if she wants to get out of the Baltic she is going to have to fight her way out through the Kattegat, between Denmark and Sweden. Although there is no strait in the north there are two major "choke" points: the North Cape, and the Greenland/Iceland/UK Gap (GIUK).

Legend:
- NATO Naval Bases
- NATO LRMP Bases
- NATO Maritime Strike Air Bases
- WP Naval Bases

CORVETTES

Soviet Union	SSM	20
	ASW	66
Norway	ASW	2
Denmark	SSM	3
Portugal	ASW	10
Greece	ASW	4
Turkey	ASW	2
Italy	ASW	16

SUBMARINES

Soviet Union	SSGN	45
	SSG	16
	SSN	46
	SS	84
Bulgaria	SS	4
Poland	SS	4
US	SSN/SS	68/5
UK	SSN/SS	11/16
France	SS	21
W. Germany	SS	24
Norway	SS	11
Denmark	SS	6
Netherlands	SS	6
Canada	SS	3
Portugal	SS	3
Greece	SS	11
Turkey	SS	15
Italy	SS	12

AMPHIBIOUS WARFARE SHIPS

Soviet Union		83
GDR	Medium	14
Poland	Medium	23
US	Large	61
UK	Large	2
	Medium	6
France		10
Greece	Large	1
	Medium	10
Turkey	Medium	5
Italy	Medium	2

TOTALS

Aircraft Carriers	4
Cruisers	28
Destroyers	61
Frigates	30
Corvettes	86
Submarines	199
Amphibious Warfare Ships	120
Aircraft Carriers	18
Cruisers	40
Destroyers	159
Frigates	145
Corvettes	37
Submarines	212
Amphibious Warfare Ships	97

the imminent introduction of the Trident missile which will enable US submarines to maintain patrols at even greater distances from the Soviet Union, appear to have led to the abandonment of this aim in favour of support of the Soviet Navy's own submarines. Apart from defending the perimeters of the SSBN havens, this support also involves contesting the Greenland/Iceland/UK (GIUK) gap to enable torpedo- and missile-armed submarines to break out into the North Atlantic.

The total absence of Soviet sea-based air power until the late seventies can be directly attributed to an essentially defensive maritime strategy resulting from the dominance of the Army in military thinking. The missions for which the Soviet Navy has been allowed to build ships are all related, directly or indirectly, to the defence of Soviet territory, and this applies not only to the large numbers of short-range craft built to protect coastal waters, but also to the larger surface and amphibious units, and even to the submarine arm. Soviet philosophy envisages the close cooperation of its land-based naval aviation forces in securing domination over its own sea-space. The surface units are therefore tied to land in a way that the carrier task forces and amphibious fleets of the US Navy are not.

Command Structures

The different command structure which results is also significant. The US carrier task force commander would be allocated a mission and then left to make his own assessment of how best to execute it, taking full account of local conditions; his Soviet counterpart, however, would in all probability be sitting in a bunker somewhere on the Kola Peninsula co-ordinating a number of different units – aircraft, submarines, cruisers – to enable them to make saturation missile attacks on their opponent. The US carrier commander would want to concentrate his forces for mutual support and protection. The Soviet commander, on the other hand, would want to keep his forces well spread so that the carrier could not concentrate its strike aircraft against them.

The pattern of Soviet naval operations is always shifting and new units of increasing size and sophistication are steadily being added to the fleet. Yet in 1981 the "battle-cruiser" Kirov bears no more resemblance to any NATO vessel than did the Kynda class rocket cruiser in 1964. Nor should we expect ships designed with such different roles in mind to look like those in service with the NATO navies. This makes any comparison between the two sides an even more complex task than it would otherwise be. Ultimately, however, it does not matter how many submarines the Soviet Navy has or how many carriers NATO has. It is what these forces are intended to achieve, and whether they would be capable of fulfilling their required missions that really counts.

Aircraft Carriers and Naval Aviation

▲ Sikorsky H-3 anti-submarine helicopter "hot-fuelling" at sea.

▲ USS *Enterprise,* nuclear powered carrier (89,600 tons).

▲ USS *John F. Kennedy,* conventionally powered carrier (82,000 tons).

▲ USS *Dwight D. Eisenhower,* nuclear powered carrier (91,400 tons).

▲ Operations room on a USN aircraft carrier.

NATO's naval strike capability is centred on the twelve big US Navy carriers. Following the termination of US military operations in SE Asia in the early 1970s a pattern was established whereby two carriers from the Atlantic Fleet were forward deployed to the 6th Fleet in the Mediterranean and two carriers from the Pacific Fleet forward deployed to the 7th Fleet in the Western Pacific. *Midway* is in fact home-ported on Yokosuka, Japan, while the other ships rotate on six-month deployments. Recent developments in the Middle East have disrupted this pattern, and one of the 6th Fleet carriers is at present deployed instead to the Indian Ocean, together with a second carrier from the 7th Fleet.

The strain on resources imposed by this new commitment has resulted in a call to expand the carrier force from 12 to 15.

NATO "Swing Strategy"

In the event of a conflict between NATO and the Warsaw Pact the 2nd Fleet carriers would make up the core of the all-important Striking Fleet Atlantic. Two or three carriers would be available at relatively short notice, while the remaining two would probably be undergoing refit or maintenance. These forces would be further strengthened by the transfer of perhaps two CVs from the 3rd Fleet on the West Coast as part of the so-called "swing strategy". This, however, could take a matter of weeks, depending on the state of

readiness of the ships, because they are too wide to pass through the Panama Canal.

Likely missions for the 2nd Fleet carriers include cover for amphibious operations on the northern flank of NATO, the elimination of any Soviet surface units which might sortie to oppose the landings, strikes against Soviet military targets in the Kola Peninsula, support of surface forces maintaining the ASW barrier in the GIUK gap, and distant cover for military convoys crossing the North Atlantic.

The 6th Fleet carriers would attempt to eliminate the Soviet Mediterranean Squadron, and might find themselves supporting amphibious landings on the southern flank.

The possibility of an offensive campaign in the N.W. Pacific against the Soviet fleet based on Vladivostok would depend very much on how many carriers were available after the transfers to the Atlantic Fleet. But a task force including two carriers cruising just outside the ring formed by the Japanese Islands would certainly give the Soviet Pacific Fleet commander cause for concern.

Carrier Aircraft

The offensive power of the US carrier lies in its three attack squadrons. Two of these are 12-plane squadrons equipped with the lightweight A-7 Corsair; the third is a 10-plane squadron of all-weather A-6 Intruders, supported by a detachment of four A-6 tanker

▲ Grumman F-14 Tomcat launching AIM-54A Phoenix long-range air-to-air missile.

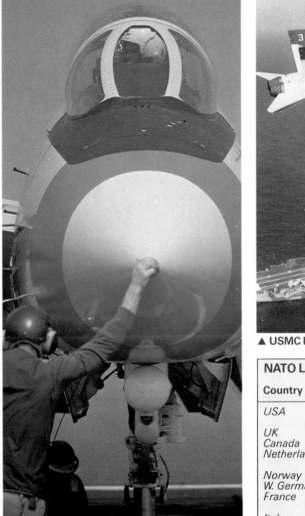

▲ Readying a Tomcat on *Forrestal*.

▲ USMC F-18 Hornet overflies *Nimitz*.

NATO Long Range Maritime Patrol Aircraft			
Country	Squadrons	Aircraft	Type
USA	24	216	P-3C Orion
	13 reserve		P-3A/B Orion
UK	4	38	Nimrod
Canada	4	18	CP140 Aurora
Netherlands	1	13	P-3 Orion
	1	7	Atlantic
Norway	1	7	P-3 Orion
W. Germany	1	14	Atlantic
France	4	28	Atlantic
	1	11	P-2H Neptune
Italy	2	18	Atlantic

aircraft. Both the A-7 and the A-6 could be expected to make strikes up to 500nm (926km) from their parent ship. They might be accompanied on some missions by EA-6 electronic counter-measures (ECM) aircraft, whose mission is to jam enemy radar transmissions to reduce the effectiveness of their missile defences.

In the absence of assistance from other sources, enemy surface forces would be detected by one of the four E-2 Hawkeye early warning aircraft, which are fitted with a very capable search radar inside a revolving radome.

The Hawkeye would also provide warning of air attack, to counter which the CV carries two 12-plane squadrons of fighters. Some of the older US carriers still operate the F-4 Phantom as their interceptor. The newer ships, however, are equipped with the much more capable F-14 Tomcat. Fitted with a relatively jam-proof radar capable of handling up to 24 targets, the Tomcat can launch six Phoenix missiles simultaneously in a fire-and-forget mode with a good chance of success against aircraft 60 to 100nm (111 to 185km) away. An important addition to the carrier air wings during the seventies has been a squadron of 10 S-3 Viking ASW aircraft, which give the CV a long-range capability against Soviet submarines. Able to undertake lengthy patrols, these aircraft could be expected to respond quickly to data from passive area detection systems such as SOSUS – NATO's system of under-water hydrophones which rings the North Atlantic and forms a vital part of the GIUK ASW barrier – and the new towed array systems now becoming available. The Viking would then attempt to localise the position of the submarine using sonobuoys and its own sophisticated data processing equipment, and attack with homing torpedoes or depth bombs.

At closer ranges a defensive ASW patrol would be mounted by SH-3 Sea King helicopters, of which a squadron of six is carried.

Soviet Counter-Measures
Clearly the US carriers would be a prime target for the Soviet Navy in the event of hostilities and, in the absence of any sea-based air of their own, the Soviets have de-veloped a variety of measures to deal with the threat they pose.

A large force of naval land-based bombers armed with stand-off missiles has been built up in each of the four fleet areas. The new long-range Backfire is now being deployed in significant numbers. The carriers would be located by an Ocean Surveillance System combining intelligence satellites and long-range reconnaissance aircraft.

In the Mediterranean the US 6th Fleet carriers are subjected to continual close shadowing by specially modified Soviet destroyers armed with four surface-to-surface missiles (SSMs) with a 20 miles (32km) range. In a crisis these ships would be ideally placed for a preemptive strike.

▲ A-7 Corsair II attack bombers.

▲ USS *Nimitz* (CVN 68). Aircraft include Phantom, Corsair II, Hawkeye and Intruder.

▲ Operations room on USS *Nimitz*.

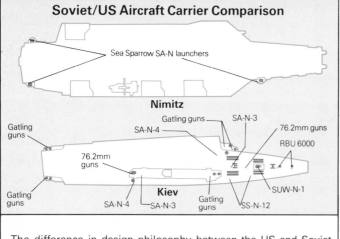

Soviet/US Aircraft Carrier Comparison

Sea Sparrow SA-N launchers

Nimitz

Gatling guns

SA-N-4

Gatling guns

SA-N-3

76.2mm guns

RBU 6000

76.2mm guns

Kiev

Gatling guns

SUW-N-1

Gatling guns

SA-N-4

SA-N-3

Gatling guns

SS-N-12

The difference in design philosophy between the US and Soviet navies is clearly shown in these two plan views. USS *Nimitz* is an aircraft carrier with the most basic ship's armament (3 Basic Point Defence Missile Systems). The Soviet *Kiev* (below) is, however, a heavily armed warship in its own right with 4 SA-N-3 launchers, 8 SS-N-12 SSM launchers, 1 SUW-N anti-submarine launcher, 2 SA-N-4, and numerous lighter weapons.

▲ E-2 Hawkeye early warning and surveillance aircraft.

Finally, the Soviet Navy has built up a fleet of about 60 cruise-missile submarines, 45 of which are nuclear-powered. The older submarines have a long-range missile which requires mid-course guidance and has to be fired from the surface, but the 15 Charlie class submarines, nearly all of which serve with the Northern Fleet, have a shorter range missile which can be fired while submerged and gives little warning time.

Tomcat Plus Phoenix

In the event of attack from land-based bombers the carrier would rely heavily on its Hawkeye early warning aircraft to enable the Tomcat fighters to intercept before the bombers could launch their missiles. The Hawkeye would be

posted some 50 to 100 miles (80 to 160km) out from the carrier in the direction from which attacks might be expected, with the combat air patrol close by. With their long-range Phoenix AAMs the Tomcats would hope to engage the attacking aircraft at around 150 to 200nm (278 to 371km) from the carrier, beyond the range of the Kingfish missile carried by the Backfire. The Soviets are reportedly developing a Mach 3.5 ASM with a range of 500nm (926km) to enable the Backfire to stand off well outside the air defence perimeter of the carrier. The Phoenix missile, however, also has a good capability against the missiles themselves.

Any aircraft breaking through the fighter screen would be en-

gaged by the area defence missile systems of the escorting cruisers and destroyers. Defence against the missiles themselves, however, would be a matter for the point-defence missile and gun systems of the target ship, plus the all-important electronic counter-measures. This is an area which has not received the priority it deserves in the US Navy, and only now are systems with the requisite performance becoming available.

Carriers a Prime Target

One thing is absolutely clear: from the moment hostilities commenced the Soviet Navy would do everything in its power to sink or disable the US carriers wherever they might be. They would not wait for the carriers to come to

them. The initial threat would therefore seem to come from shadowing submarines and, in the Mediterranean, from shadowing surface units, both armed with short-range cruise missiles which would strike suddenly and with little warning.

It is difficult to predict the outcome of such an attack, as it would be dependent on variables such as the number of missiles launched and the relative effect of electronic countermeasures. Even a hit from an SSM could not guarantee to disable a ship the size of the US carriers, and here again the damage caused would depend on where the missile struck, whether there were planes or fuel trucks nearby, and other factors.

After the first few hours of con-

▲ AV-8B version of the very successful Harrier has now been ordered for USMC, giving many improvements over earlier models.

▲ McDonnell Douglas F-18 Hornet prototype on carrier trials.

▲ S-3A Vikings on ASW patrol from USS *Saratoga*.

▲ USS *John F. Kennedy* (CV-67) with a variety of aircraft types embarked, including F-14.

US Navy Carriers

(Year commissioned in brackets)

Atlantic: 2nd/6th Fleets
CVN	Eisenhower	(1977)
	Nimitz	(1975)
CV	John F. Kennedy	(1968)
	America	(1965)
	Independence	(1959)
	Saratoga	(1956)
	Forrestal	(1955)

Pacific: 3rd/7th Fleets
CVN	Enterprise	(1961)
CV	Constellation	(1961)
	Kitty Hawk	(1961)
	Ranger	(1957)
	Midway	(1945)

flict the threat to the carrier would subside, and she could reasonably hope to locate and kill SSGNs attempting to close on her, especially if the latter were moving at the high speeds that would make them that much more audible to passive area detection systems.

Multiple Threats

The greatest threat would undoubtedly materialise if the Atlantic Striking Fleet were to attempt to break into the Norwegian Sea, as it almost certainly would in the event of NATO marines being sent to Norway. Prolonged operations in this hostile area could result in serious attrition of the carrier's aircraft, making a minimum of two and preferably three carrier task forces necessary

to accomplish the task. Moreover, the environment would grow more hostile the closer the carriers operated to Norway itself. The Soviet Navy could be guaranteed to throw everything into the battle if the Kola Peninsula were threatened.

The task forces would no longer encounter handfuls of maritime bombers, but massed air strikes which would be all the more frequent because of the proximity of the Soviet bases. Torpedo- and missile-armed submarines would be placed across the line of advance of the carriers, and would be less likely to be detected because they could be patrolling quietly at low speed. And Kresta class "rocket cruisers" supported by smaller missile-armed craft

would round the North Cape awaiting the right moment to strike.

Early Warning for NATO

The carriers could expect early warning of air strikes from the NADGE radar system and from patrolling AWACS aircraft. Fighters from Norwegian airfields could hope to down some of the bombers before they even reached the defence perimeters of the carriers. Massed attacks from several quarters remain the greatest threat, however, and the outcome of such a battle would depend on the ability of the Soviets to coordinate their attacks and the ability of the NATO forces to prevent them achieving this aim.

In addition to the carrier attack

squadrons there are in Europe a number of land-based aircraft assigned to maritime strike duties. The North Sea area is covered by a squadron of RAF Buccaneers based in East Anglia and there are two 30-plane squadrons of German Starfighters – soon to be replaced by the much more capable Tornado – in the northern province of Jutland. The latter are now equipped with the powerful Kormoran anti-shipping missile. They are equally well placed to cover the Baltic approaches, where they would play a key role in the event of an amphibious assault by forces of the Warsaw Pact.

On the Northern Flank the Norwegians, too, maintain a squadron of Starfighters for maritime strike, based at Bodo.

Aircraft Carriers and Naval Aviation

▲ French carrier *Foch* (R-99) is limited to rotary-wing aircraft.

▲ *Clemenceau* (R-98) operates fixed-wing aircraft, unlike *Foch*.

▲ British carrier HMS *Invincible* (19,500 tons).

▲ Dassault Super Etendard strike fighter aboard carrier *Clemenceau*.

▲ Italy's *Andria Doria* has 4 helicopters.

ASW Patrol

Most of the NATO air squadrons assigned to maritime duties are, however, engaged in long-range ASW patrol. The US Navy has no less than 24 squadrons of P-3 Orions, with a further 13 in reserve. Of the first-line squadrons 13 are based on the United States east coast, with regular deployments to Sigonella, Sicily, and to Keflavik, Iceland. The west coast squadrons deploy to Japan and Hawaii.

Norway and the Netherlands also operate Orions, and Canada is now taking delivery of a P-3 built to its own specifications, the Aurora.

The United Kingdom operates four squadrons of Nimrods, three of which are based in Scotland while the other covers the Southwest Approaches. Other NATO countries operate the French Breguet Atlantic.

These aircraft are equipped with a variety of acoustic and non-acoustic sensors, including search radars, low-light TV, infra-red detectors and magnetic anomaly detectors. The Nimrods and Orions also carry the latest processing systems to analyse the data from their sonobuoys and thereby enable them to make a quick kill. Armament normally comprises depth charges and homing torpedoes, but all could carry anti-ship missiles to use against surface targets.

There can be no doubt that NATO LRMP aircraft, working in conjunction with area detection systems such as SOSUS would stand a good chance of effectively reducing the threat from Soviet submarines in the North Atlantic. Their dependence on SOSUS for their initial "contacts" does, however, ensure that the SOSUS terminals themselves will be a target for attack in the event of hostilities, and after the initial stages of conflict this source of information might dry up.

ASW Carriers

Following the scrapping of HMS *Ark Royal* the Royal Navy no longer operates carriers with a maritime strike capability. The new Invincible class carriers, of which the first was completed in 1980 with a further two building, are designed to operate nine Sea King ASW helicopters and five Harrier jump-jets, although this figure would probably be exceeded in wartime. The Harrier was a late addition to *Invincible*'s designed complement of aircraft, and has a reasonable short-range strike capability — especially now that payload has been increased by the introduction of ski-jump take-off — but very limited performance as an interceptor. The former commando carrier *Hermes* will probably remain in service with a similar air complement until the third ship commissions.

The mission for which *Invincible* was primarily designed was ASW patrol in the GIUK gap, a role for which she is admirably equipped. She has a large multi-code sonar comparable to those on the

▲ Flight-deck of an RAF Nimrod ASW aircraft.

▲ Lockheed P-3B Orion maritime reconnaissance and anti-submarine aircraft.

▲ BAe Sea Harrier V/STOL fighter of the British Fleet Air Arm in the hover.

▲ Breguet Atlantique anti-submarine aircraft of the French Aeronavale.

latest US Navy ships, and excellent data processing and ASW control facilities incorporated into a spacious operations room from which the ship's main weapons can also be fought.

Although a high-value target, the Invincibles would not expect the same attention from the Soviet bombers as the American carriers, nor would they expect to operate in such a hostile environment. They therefore rely on their Seadart area defence missile system – and in all probability other such systems on accompanying destroyers – to protect them from air attack. The Harrier would be expected to deal only with shadowing reconnaissance planes.

The position of the Invincibles astride the GIUK gap is probably only tenable as long as there are American carriers around to keep Soviet missile-armed surface units at bay.

Mediterranean Allies

In the Mediterranean the Italian Navy is building the carrier *Giuseppe Garibaldi* to perform a similar ASW role to *Invincible*. They also have the older *Vittorio Veneto*, a carrier-cruiser hybrid which has a medium-range area defence missile system and other weapons forward, and a flight deck aft with a hangar for nine AB 212 ASW helicopters. Although useful, this ship cannot compare with *Invincible* in view of the short range of the helicopters carried, the dated sonar, and inferior data processing facilities.

The French, who in the late 1950s decided to quit NATO's command structure, have pursued a naval policy dictated by national rather than NATO demands. They continue to operate their own strike carriers, *Foch* and *Clemenceau*, although these are much smaller than the American vessels. The size factor has made it impossible for them to operate large modern fighters and attack aircraft. Normally they carry one fighter squadron of 10 obsolescent Crusaders, whose main limitation lies in their lack of modern avionics, two squadrons of home-built Super Etendard strike aircraft, which have a nuclear and conventional weapons capability, and a number of ageing Breguet Alizé ASW aircraft supplemented by ASW helicopters.

At present only *Clemenceau* operates as a strike carrier while *Foch* operates helicopters. The withdrawal of one of the American 6th Fleet carriers from the Mediterranean has made the French carriers more important to NATO.

The Nuclear Factor

Aircraft carriers are particularly vulnerable to the effects of nuclear weapons. It is impossible to close them down if they are to continue to operate aircraft, and aircraft parked on the flight deck would suffer blast damage even if the weapon exploded some miles away. It must therefore be concluded that the effectiveness of the NATO carriers would be significantly reduced if a conflict escalated into a nuclear exchange.

Aircraft Carriers and Naval Aviation

Soviet Naval Aviation

Type	Aircraft	Number operational	Operational radius	Fleet deployment
Bombers	Tu-26 Backfire*	50+	2,000nm (3,706km)	NF/PF
	Tu-16 Badger	250	1,250nm (2,316km)	NF/PF (mainly)
	Tu-22 Blinder	50	500nm (926km)	BF/BS
Reconnaissance	Tu-95 Bear	45	4,000nm (7,412km)	NF/PF
	Tu-16 Badger	70	2,000nm (3,706km)	NF/PF (mainly)
Long Range	Tu-142 Bear	15	3,000nm (5,559km)	NF/PF (?)
Maritime	Il-38 May	60	1,500nm (2,779km)	NF/PF
Patrol (LRMP)	M-12 Mail	75	500nm (926km)	All 4 fleets

*Also known as Tu-22M

▲ Ilyushin Il-38 (May) dropping a sonobuoy.

▲ Basic ASW version of Kamov Ka-25 (Hormone-A).

▲ Tupolev Tu-16 (Badger-F) fitted with underwing electronic pods.

▲ Aerial view of Moskva shows flightdeck aft and heavy armament forward.

▲ Armament and radar on *Moskva*.

AT present the entire strike capability of Soviet naval aviation is encompassed within the land-based bombers of the Naval Air Force (AV-MF).

The standard naval bomber is the Tu-16 Badger, of which about 250 remain in service, mainly with the Northern and Pacific Fleets, supported by a further 80 tanker conversions. It is now being superseded by the Tu-26 Backfire, which has brought a new dimension to Soviet naval aviation. Its greatly increased combat radius – almost double that of the Badger – enables it to cover much of the Norwegian Sea, posing a new long-range threat to the NATO carriers.

The Badgers and Backfires are armed with Kipper, Kelt or Kingfish stand-off anti-ship missiles which have estimated ranges of 100–150nm, and are probably guided to their target by a combination of auto-pilot and active radar or passive IR homing.

Before an attack could be launched the Soviet bomber forces would need detailed and accurate information regarding the position and composition of the opposing forces. This information would be provided by some 70 Badger reconnaissance aircraft, many of which are fitted for ECM and electronic support measures (ESM), plus about 45 long-range Tu-95 Bears, which can reach far into the North Atlantic. The latter also provide mid-course guidance for the long-range surface-to-surface missiles in service with the Soviet Navy.

Most of the long-range reconnaissance aircraft service in the North and the Pacific, while in the Baltic and the Black Sea reconnaissance, and probably strike as well, is performed by the shorter-range Tu-22 Blinder.

Satellite Reconnaissance

Although satellites are clearly playing an ever-increasing part in tracing the movements of NATO forces, it is difficult to assess the quality of the intelligence thus gathered. Photographic reconnaissance is probably well developed, but the Soviets could not hope to rely on this in the all-important northern theatre, where there is usually plenty of cloud cover to conceal NATO forces. Active radar could detect a group of ships

without necessarily revealing its composition, while passive electronic intelligence satellites could assess the composition of a force by monitoring its radar transmissions but would be vulnerable to deception measures. It is therefore likely that the Soviet Navy still depends heavily on aircraft reconnaissance. This is a potential weakness in view of the notorious vulnerability of lumbering recce bombers to supersonic interceptors.

A more serious weakness is one common to all land-based aircraft tasked with maritime missions, namely a significant reduction in effectiveness as the distance from base to target increases. This problem would be particularly acute in the northern theatre. A long-range attack would involve a

126

▲ Ka-25 ASW helicopter with chin and tail radars and nose-mounted "Homeguide" yagi antennas.

▲ Tupolev Tu-22M (Backfire) bomber of the Soviet Naval Air Force.

▲ Moskva-class cruiser in the Mediterranean; 18 Ka-25s are carried.

longer transit time – and therefore a reduction in the number of sorties – and greater incidence of engine failure or action damage. It would also give early warning of impending attack to the defending forces, enabling a NATO carrier, for instance, to take evasive action and to intercept the bombers with large numbers of fighters. Furthermore the extended communication links between the bombers and their bases would be susceptible to jamming, especially if Norway were to remain in NATO hands. One would therefore expect the Soviets to hold back their land-based bombers until the NATO carrier task forces were well advanced in the direction of Norway before launching a series of massed air strikes, which they

would hope to coordinate with attacks from submarines and surface units.

ASW Aircraft

In the 1960s the only ASW aircraft serving with the Naval Air Force was the M-12 Mail amphibian, of which about 75 are still in service, mainly in the Northern and Black Sea Fleet areas. The M-12 was superseded in the early seventies by a conversion of a military transport plane, the Il-38 May.

Although clearly inspired by the US P-3 Orion, the May does not appear to be equipped with the wide range of detection devices available to Western ASW aircraft, and the weapons capacity is relatively small, with no external stores pylons.

Recently a new ASW version of the Bear bomber has appeared. It has a greater range than the May, but it is difficult to see how it can operate effectively without an area detection system comparable to NATO's SOSUS – a possibility which geography, rather than technology, has denied.

Inferior Electronics

The greatest weakness of the Soviet ASW aircraft, however, lies in their inferior data processing capabilities. Basically, this means that given the same data return from sonobuoys the Soviet aircraft are less likely to be able to distinguish the noises emitted by a submarine from the surrounding clutter than are their Western counterparts.

Moskva Helicopter Carrier

Until the late 1960s ASW in the Soviet Navy was predominantly the concern of coastal forces. In 1967, however, the helicopter carrier *Moskva* made her appearance, and her sister *Leningrad* followed her into service shortly after. They are hybrid vessels, with the armament of a cruiser forward and a flight deck and hangar for ASW helicopters aft, and are in conception not unlike the Italian *Vittorio Veneto*. They are, however, much larger and more heavily armed than the latter.

The "cruiser" weapons comprise a pair of area defence missile systems, and a launcher for ASW missiles, plus a variety of smaller guns and rocket-launchers. About 15 Kamov Ka-25 Hormone ASW

▲ Kiev class aircraft carrier with 4 Ka-25 and 1 Yak-36 (Forger-A) on deck.

▲ Yak-36 (Forger-A) coming in to land on *Kiev*. These first-generation VTOL aircraft are not proving very effective.

helicopters can be accommodated in the hangar aft. The Moskva-class carriers have a large low-frequency hull sonar, and there is a variable depth sonar (VDS) set into the stern.

The time of building, their novel configuration, and their deployment in the area of the Black Sea Fleet, point to a primary mission involving the hunting of US Navy Polaris submarines operating in the Eastern Mediterranean from their base at Rota, Spain.

In the early days of Polaris, when the missiles had a range of only 1,500nm (2,780km), the Eastern Mediterranean provided some of the best launch points against targets in the Soviet Union. With the advent of the 2,500nm (4,632km) A-3 missile, the Eastern

Mediterranean diminished in importance. The base at Rota has now closed, and the introduction of the Trident missile will almost certainly mean the end of SSBN deployments in the Mediterranean by the US Navy. While there is no evidence that the Moskvas have managed to detect an SSBN during their twelve years of service, there can be little doubt that the significant growth of Soviet ASW capabilities in the Mediterranean has led the US Navy to move its missile submarines to safer waters.

Of course, there are still numerous NATO submarines, including US Navy SSNs, in the Mediterranean. The Moskvas are now, however, in the position of hunting submarines whose main mission is to hunt them!

In the event of hostilities, whichever Moskva carrier found itself on the Mediterranean station would be in a difficult position. Against the aerial might of the US 6th Fleet – to which might be added the two French carriers – she would have only her own surface-to-surface missiles, and those of any accompanying units, to protect herself.

Kiev-class Carriers

When the Moskvas were designed there may well have been a good prospect of the availability of friendly airfields in the Middle East from which an air umbrella could be provided in the Eastern Mediterranean, but there was no such prospect in the Norwegian Sea or the Pacific, which would be

the operating areas of the Moskvas' successor, *Kiev*. The Soviets obviously therefore hoped to take advantage of the latest developments in VTOL to provide the new carriers with their own shipborne fighters. While broadly retaining the hybrid carrier/cruiser configuration of *Moskva*, the Soviets have added a squadron of 10 to 12 Yak-36 Forger attack aircraft to the 18 or so ASW helicopters they carry.

The Forger does not appear to have fulfilled its designed purpose. It is a fragile aircraft, with inadequate performance and range to make it an effective interceptor, and an attack capability limited by its low payload, which cannot be improved – as has the Harrier's – by fitting a ski-jump ramp, because

▲ Yak-36s on the deck of *Minsk*.

▲ Kiev-class carry a heavy armament.

▲ *Minsk;* rust indicates a long time at sea.

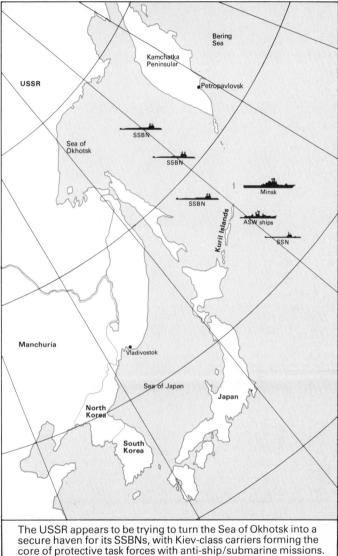

The USSR appears to be trying to turn the Sea of Okhotsk into a secure haven for its SSBNs, with Kiev-class carriers forming the core of protective task forces with anti-ship/submarine missions.

the Forger is incapable of a rolling take-off. While it would be a useful aircraft for reconnaissance and ground support operations, and for strikes on small surface units without their own air cover, it would be incapable of defending its parent ship against the attack squadrons of a US carrier and totally ineffectual in the attack role if pitted against F-14 Tomcats.

The main offensive armament of *Kiev* in fact resides in her massive SS-N-12 surface-to-surface missiles, of which she carries eight in paired launchers on the forecastle with a further 16 reloads between decks. The SS-N-12 has an estimated range of about 250nm (463km), and is fitted with a large warhead with great destructive capability. It would, however,

need mid-course guidance, either from one of *Kiev*'s own specially-fitted Hormone B helicopters, or from the Tu-95 Bear. Moreover, even the long range of the SS-N-12 puts it well inside the combat radius of the US carrier attack squadrons. It is therefore unlikely that a Kiev-class vessel would be pitted against a US Navy carrier unless it were close enough to its home base to enjoy protection from adequate air cover.

Kiev/Minsk Deployment

Since the value of ASW operations against SSBNs appears to have declined in the Soviet estimation, the most likely deployments of *Kiev* (Northern Fleet) and *Minsk* (Pacific Fleet) in the event of hostilities is in defence of the Soviet SSBN bas-

tions. If, however, a more favourable operating environment were to be created in the Norwegian Sea by the Warsaw Pact occupation of Norway, the elimination by whatever means of the threat from US carriers, and the suppression of NATO air bases in Iceland and Scotland, one would expect *Kiev*, accompanied by *Kirov* and other missile cruisers, to attack the NATO surface forces defending the ASW barrier in the GIUK gap, and to sit astride the gap itself, hunting the NATO submarines on patrol there, and employing her Forgers to drive away any Orions or Nimrods flying over the area. This would give Soviet submarines the free passage into the North Atlantic which is so crucial to their effectiveness.

New Aircraft Carrier

It has been recently reported that a new nuclear-powered through-deck carrier, apparently scheduled for completion in 1985, will undoubtedly enable the Soviet Navy to deploy to forward positions more quickly, since reports suggest it will be fitted with catapults which would enable high performance fighters to be carried. What is not yet clear, however, is whether the new carrier will operate specialised attack squadrons like the US Navy carriers, or whether its main role will be to provide fighter cover for ASW and anti-ship units in the GIUK gap. The MiG-27 Flogger which has been linked with the new carrier would provide a secondary attack capability.

SSGN Submarines

▲ Damaged Echo II SSGN limping home to the USSR for repairs.

▲ Echo II class SSGN; 5800 tons; 29 built.

▲ With the Charlie class Soviet designers have at last tried to overcome the problem of underwater noise.

THE Soviet cruise-missile submarines were initially conceived as an answer to the threat from NATO carrier task forces.

Although some experimental conversions of Whiskey class boats were undertaken during the 1950s the first major classes to be designed for the purpose were the nuclear-powered Echo class boats and their diesel-electric companion, the Julietts.

The Echo class is a large first-generation nuclear boat adapted from the November class SSN. The first five units carried six long-range SS-N-3 missiles (since removed) but were soon superseded by the even larger Echo II design (with eight missiles), of which there are 29 in service.

Of their conventional counterpart, the Julietts, only 16 units were built out of large numbers planned. They were basically an adaptation of the Foxtrot SS, with a high hull casing in which four missiles could be accommodated.

The SS-N-3 is fired from elevating launchers stowed flush with the hull casing, with prominent indentations behind the launchers to deflect the blast.

Deployment

Most – if not all – of the Juliett class serve with the Northern Fleet, while the Echo class is divided evenly between the Northern and Pacific Fleets. This distribution is interesting in that the older and, on the face of it, less powerful Julietts serve almost exclusively with the

most important of the Russian fleets. The reason for this may be that the greater endurance of the Echo is regarded as essential to anti-carrier operations in the Pacific. This in turn suggests that the Julietts in the Northern Fleet would deploy closer to their home bases. Certainly their relatively quiet diesel-electric propulsion system would be better employed if the submarines were to patrol in the line of advance of NATO carrier task forces than if they were required to hunt the carriers down – a task for which they have inadequate speed. The Julietts are also frequently deployed to the Mediterranean, where their small size gives them an advantage over the Echo class boats.

The major weakness of both sub-

marines lies in the nature of the missile they carry. Not only does it have to be fired from the surface, inviting all sorts of trouble from ASW aircraft, but it also requires target data and mid-course guidance from an external source (eg, aircraft) if it is to attain its maximum range with any hope of success. If the target is indeed a carrier, it is highly unlikely that the latter will allow Bear recce bombers to cruise around for any length of time supplying this sort of data to the submarine or its missile. Only in a very confused tactical situation would such a manoeuvre be possible.

Although the older Soviet cruise-missile submarines have been somewhat overtaken by advances in technology they

▲ 29 of these nuclear-powered Echo II boats are in service.

▲ Juliett class conventionally-powered cruise-missile submarine.

▲ A Juliett; the hull is very noisy.

Warsaw Pact SSGN/SSG Submarines

Class	No.*	Missiles
1st Generation		
Echo II SSGN	29	8 SS-N-3
Juliett SSG	16	4 SS-N-3
2nd Generation		
Charlie I SSGN	11	8 SS-N-7
Charlie II SSGN	4	8 SS-N-7
Papa SSGN (exp)	1	10 SS-N-7?

*No. in Service

remain useful against surface targets other than carriers in open ocean operations and also have a significant capability against land targets such as the Norwegian coastline. The SS-N-3 packs a powerful punch and could possibly be armed with an alternative nuclear warhead.

Charlie Class

The other SSGN in the Soviet armoury is the Charlie class, of which the majority serve with the Northern Fleet, with one or two units in the Pacific. The later boats have a lengthened bow section, suggesting that they are also fitted to fire the SS-N-15 anti-submarine missile.

The Charlie, which first appeared in 1968, is a second-generation nuclear submarine which is a significant improvement in every respect on the earlier Echo class. It is smaller, quieter and faster than the earlier boats. Most important, however, is the SS-N-7 missile, of which it carries eight in vertical launch-tubes set into the bow casing and covered by hatches. The SS-N-7 is a short-range (25nm, 46km) missile which can be fired while the submarine is submerged. It needs no relay aircraft and can be fired on the basis of target information from the submarine's own sensors. The only weakness in the system lies in the problems that the missile – and probably the submarine itself – might have in identifying the carrier from amidst its escorts, particularly in the face of determined ECM.

Defence Against SSGNs

It would, however, be easier for a NATO task force to defend against the submarine itself than against the missile, which might descend on it suddenly from an unexpected quarter. An important NATO countermeasure would be to have SSNs clear a path in the line of advance of the task force. Soviet SSGNs directed to intercept from other positions would have to move at high speed, and would thereby become vulnerable to detection by passive sonar or hydrophone arrays. The carrier could then direct its S-3 Viking ASW aircraft to the spot to kill the submarine or at least force it to abandon its mission. This should be relatively easy with the older Echo-class boats in view of their extremely noisy propulsion system and unsatisfactory hull-form. Even the newer Charlie-class boats have free-flood holes in their casing, and their propulsion system is noisier than that of their NATO counterparts.

It would also be difficult for the Soviet Navy to "surge" SSGNs through the GIUK barrier to attack American carriers closer to their bases without support from surface units and other submarines. The greatest threat to the carriers, even from the Soviet SSGNs, remains in the Norwegian Sea, where the proximity of their home bases (and all the support that this implies) and extensive reconnaissance by land-based aircraft would enable the SSGNs to concentrate their strength.

SSN Submarines

▲ Victor class submarine on patrol in the South China Sea.

▲ Victor class nuclear attack submarine; 18 built.

▲ November-class SSN in distress in the Atlantic. These were the first Soviet nuclear-powered submarines.

Warsaw Pact SSN Strength

1st Generation
13 November
 5 Echo I (converted SSGN)

2nd Generation
16 Victor I
 6 Victor II
 2 Victor III
 3 Yankee (converted SSBN)
 4 Alfa

▲ Echo I class. Originally cruise-missile launchers, they are now fleet submarines.

ALL Soviet nuclear-powered submarines are based in the Arctic or Pacific. None operates in the land-locked Baltic or Black Sea, partly because these large boats are little suited to such constricted waters, but also because the long range conferred on them by nuclear propulsion would to a large extent be negated should they become trapped in these inland seas.

The 13 November class submarines were the first nuclear boats built for the Soviet Navy. They were built in a hurry, their design being based on intelligence sources rather than lengthy research. They are much longer than contemporary American SSNs, their hull casing is lined with free-flood holes, and they have an ex-

tremely noisy propulsion system which nevertheless drives them at a maximum submerged speed of only 25 knots. Following the abandonment of their original strategic mission, for which they were to be armed with a nuclear-tipped torpedo, the Novembers were given an anti-carrier role, using conventional torpedoes. Their value in even this role is now questionable, given the capability of modern sonars and the introduction of the S-3 Viking into the NATO carrier air wings.

The other major class of SSNs in service is the Victor class. The first Victor appeared in 1968, and it has continued in production, albeit with some modifications, into the 1980s – a sure indication that the Soviet Navy is pleased with its per-

formance. It is a second-generation submarine with improved hull-form, greater diving depth, and a much quieter propulsion system producing a speed of around 30 knots underwater. Later versions of the Victor are thought to be armed with the SS-N-15 anti-submarine missile.

With the Charlie class SSGNs in full production by the end of the 1960s the Russians were unable to build the number of SSNs they would have liked, and the five oldest SSGNs of the Echo I class were modified to boost SSN numbers. Since the Echo design was derived from the November it must suffer similar limitations as an SSN.

A more recent conversion has been that of three Yankee class

SSBNs, which have had their missiles removed to conform to the terms of the SALT agreement.

Deployment Missions
Of the two Soviet fleets operating SSNs, the Northern Fleet has been allocated nearly all the modern Victors, together with about half the Novembers. The Pacific Fleet is therefore left with the remaining Novembers, the five Echo Is and a few Victors. This mirrors the way the US Navy deploys its own SSNs, although it must be remembered that the latter are more numerous because of the Soviet Navy's division of its own attack boats into SSNs and SSGNs. This means that Soviet torpedo-armed submarines might be attacking in concert with missile-armed boats, particularly

The Soviet View of the GIUK ASW Barrier

In the event of conflict, Soviet submarines (probably Victor SSNs and Charlie SSGNs) could be expected to attempt to thrust out into the North Atlantic and North Sea through the Greenland–Iceland–United Kingdom (GIUK) gap, one of the most heavily protected NATO waterways which has an elaborate system of anti-submarine defences, including surface, sub-surface and air systems. The map shows how the Soviets themselves see the barrier confronting their submarines. It is anticipated that NATO could seal off whole sections of the gap with Captor mines which release a homing torpedo if a submarine passes close to them.

▲ November class nuclear attack submarine; 13 were built.

▲ Yankee class SSBN; some are being converted to SSN.

against a convoy or task force, the function of the SSGN being to create a more favourable environment for the SSNs by firing its missiles at the escorts, disabling some and creating the sort of confusion on which torpedo-armed submarines thrive.

The arming of the Victor II with the SS-N-15 makes it clear that these submarines have an important ASW role. Their ability to perform this mission effectively would, however, depend on where and how they were employed. In trying to break through the GIUK barrier themselves or assisting other submarines to do so the Victors would have the disadvantage of operating against NATO submarines which would be moving slowly to minimise self-noise and optimise their own sonar performance. The Victors would probably be approaching at high speed to evade surface patrols, and are in any case noisier boats with less capable sensors than their NATO counterparts.

Where the Victors would be very effective would be in the Norwegian Sea, where they could lie in wait themselves for advancing carrier task forces or for NATO SSNs endeavouring to break into the SSBN sanctuaries.

Alfa Class

Outside the general line of Soviet SSN development are the Alfa-class submarines. These are very small for nuclear boats, indicating an advanced reactor design, and the use of titanium in the construction of the hull is thought to give them a diving depth of over 1,968ft (600m). They are credited with the astonishing submerged speed of 40 knots, which even given their small size would be a remarkable technical achievement. Problems with leaks in the hull casing appear, however, to have caused long delays in putting the submarine into production and the original unit has been broken up.

The Alfa was almost certainly conceived as a design with a specialised anti-SSBN mission, although it is difficult to see how it would locate its target, particularly in the open ocean. It is rather surprising that, in an era when high speed has lost much of its tactical value due to the development of stand-off weapons and advances in ASW sensors, the Soviets should have chosen to concentrate valuable R&D resources into a design which appears to rely on "brute force" rather than sophistication or deception to break through the NATO ASW barriers.

The combination of high speed and great diving depth, however, would certainly make the Alfa difficult to hit, even if detected. US Navy concern about this new development is evidenced by experiments with a new deep-diving homing torpedo. High speed manoeuvres by the submarine would make it difficult for long-range anti-submarine rockets with inertial guidance, such as ASROC, to deposit their homing torpedoes close enough to the target to be effective.

▲ USS *Los Angeles* (SSN 688); 39 are planned at the moment.

▲ USS *Drum* (SSN 677) Sturgeon class attack submarine.

▲ Swiftsure class of the British Royal Navy; 6 will be built.

▲ Sturgeon class SSN; 37 built.

▲ USS *Los Angeles* at speed on the surface. US aims to have 90 SSNs by mid-1980s.

AT present the only NATO navies which operate nuclear-powered attack submarines are the US Navy and the Royal Navy, although the French Navy has a class of small SSNs under construction and plans to operate a squadron of nuclear boats both in the Atlantic and the Mediterranean.

The first American nuclear boat was completed as nearly as 1954, giving the US Navy an estimated five-year lead over the Russians. Although the Soviet Navy has now overtaken the US Navy in terms of the number of nuclear-powered submarines in service, few of their SSNs and SSGNs possess the advanced features common to all American submarines since the early 1960s.

The earliest SSNs still in first-line service with the US Navy are the five Skipjacks. These are small, handy submarines capable of speeds of well over 30 knots. They lack the advanced sonar systems of the later ships, however, and are conventionally armed with six bow torpedo tubes.

The Permit and Sturgeon classes which followed were larger boats, which enabled them to carry a more advanced sonar outfit and to fire SUBROC, a nuclear-tipped anti-submarine missile with a range of 25 to 30nm (46 to 56km). As there was no increase in the size of the nuclear reactor, however, speed declined to about 28 knots.

The current type under construction is the massive Los Angeles class, which show a 50 per cent increase in displacement over earlier SSNs. In addition to the installation of more advanced sensors and fire control equipment (now being retro-fitted in the Permit and Sturgeon classes), the Los Angeles class has regained the 5 knots speed which has been lost since the Skipjacks.

Missions and Technical Priorities

Unlike their Soviet counterparts, US Navy SSNs would not be operating as part of a combined force subject to centralised command, because operating procedures in the Soviet surface navy make it unlikely that there would be a group of ships comparable to a NATO task force against which they could be concentrated. US SSNs are therefore designed for three basic roles: the ASW hunter-killer role, which they would perform in areas such as the GIUK gap; the independent forward area role, in which they would probe the enemy's defences; and the protection of task forces and convoys.

The key to success in operations against other submarines is quietness, which enables the hunter to evade detection, allied to a powerful sensor outfit with which to detect an opponent at the earliest possible moment. For the Soviet Navy these two qualities are "nice to have"; for the US Navy they are essential.

Whereas submarines of other countries have their torpedo tubes in the bow, US Navy submarines since the Permit class have had

▲ USS *Skipjack:* 6 of this class were built; 1 was lost in 1968.

▲ Permit class SSN; 1 of this class was also lost in 1968.

▲ USS *Los Angeles* (SSN 688) name-ship of her class

▲ USS *Gudgeon* (SS 567). 6 Tang class boats were built in the late 1940s; 4 remain.

NATO's SSN Strength		
US Navy	**Atlantic/**	**Pacific**
5 Skipjack	1	3
13 Permit	5	8
37 Sturgeon	26	11
1 Narwhal	1	
1 Lipscomb	1	
11 Los Angeles	8	3
UK Royal Navy		
1 Dreadnought	1	
5 Valiant	5	
6 Swiftsure	6	
	54	25

their tubes amidships, freeing the bow for a large active sonar with passive hydrophones along the outside of the hull. This is not only the most favourable position for detection but keeps the sensors away from the propulsion plant.

Quieter Operators
Nuclear propulsion is a relatively noisy way of propelling a submarine, particularly at the high speeds which constitute its main advantage over diesel-electric plant, but successive classes have shown improvements in this respect, and in the Los Angeles class particular attention has been paid to quiet operation, the large hull making it easier to "cushion" the machinery.

The increase in speed in the Los Angeles class reflects an increasing tactical requirement for the defence of fast carrier task forces against hostile SSGNs. Even the Los Angeles class would be at a disadvantage if proceeding at speed towards a patrol-line of enemy submarines lying in wait. "Sprint and listen" tactics would therefore seem appropriate, and this would require very high speeds on the "spring" leg to enable the SSNs to keep well in front of their charges.

The qualities necessary for defensive measures against enemy submarines are, of course, also well suited to attack in enemy-held seas. The Soviets are well aware of this, and have duly created ASW barriers to protect their SSBNs. Moreover, all American SSNs except the Skipjacks will be fitted with Harpoon in the near future, giving them a new capability against surface units. Harpoon, unlike the cruise missiles carried by the Soviet SSGNs, has the advantage of being launched from torpedo tubes, and therefore requires no special launching apparatus.

The bulk of the modern SSNs of the US Navy are based in the Atlantic, where they would play a major part in the defence of the sea-lanes.

Britain's SSNs
The other SSNs in the NATO alliance are those of the Royal Navy. The earliest of these, *Dreadnought,* has an American Skipjack propulsion plant, but the later Valiant and Swiftsure classes are of completely British design.

The British boats have generally followed the pattern of development of their US Navy counterparts. The Valiant class correspond roughly with the Permit and the Swiftsure class with the Sturgeon. Frequent deployments take place in company with surface units, and the designation Fleet Submarine makes it clear that the Royal Navy sees the role of its own SSNs in the same light as the US Navy. The new Trafalgar class will, like the US Navy's Los Angeles, have higher speed.

The layout of the British boats is more conventional, with all tubes in the bow, and there is no equivalent to the SUBROC missile, but will soon have Harpoon.

SS Submarines

▲ A somewhat tattered looking Foxtrot class patrol submarine passes a Kashin class destroyer.

▲ One of the five Tango class diesel patrol submarines built in the early 1970s.

▲ Well over 80 of the very successful Foxtrot class have been built, many of them for export.

FOR many years the numbers of operational Soviet submarines have been boosted by large numbers of conventional boats, which have always outnumbered their nuclear counterparts. With the Whiskey and Zulu class submarines built during the 1950s now being paid off this is no longer the case. There is in fact almost an equivalence between nuclear- and diesel-powered attack boats in the Soviet Navy as it stands in the early 1980s.

In any consideration of the influence conventional submarines could have in a given conflict distance must be taken into account. Frequent comparisons have been made between the number of submarines operational in the Soviet Navy and the smaller numbers Hitler had at his disposal at the height of the Battle of the Atlantic. Such comparisons fail to take into account the fact that the German submarines were operating from Norway and from the West Coast of France, less than 1,000 miles (1,609km) away from the Atlantic shipping routes. Soviet submarines operating from the Kola Peninsula, however, would have to travel more than double that distance, and besides would have to pass through the NATO ASW barrier in the GIUK gap. It is therefore questionable whether the medium submarines built in such large numbers during the 1950s could have sustained a campaign against Atlantic shipping. Transit alone would take up over half their estimated 7,000nm

(12,970km) range, while in terms of days they could spend a maximum of 15 on station out of a total of 45. These figures would, moreover, apply only to the more northerly of the accepted Atlantic shipping routes.

Only the 2,000 ton (2,032 tonnes) submarines of the Zulu class and their successors the Foxtrot and Tango classes could be usefully employed on such missions, and even these suffer the standard disadvantages of diesel-electric submarines, namely the slow transit times essential to conserve fuel in long-range operations, and the vulnerability of the submarine when surfaced or snorting to patrolling ASW aircraft, especially once it approaches the GIUK gap. Their NATO counter-

parts, the Dutch and British boats, would have a transit of less than 5000 miles (804km) to their own patrol stations if operating from Scotland, and would be operating entirely within NATO air space.

Moreover the relatively small numbers of large Soviet submarines built and the way they are deployed do not suggest that the Soviets intend to use them in a conventional anti-shipping role. The Tango, which has succeeded the standard Foxtrot design, is being built at a rate of only two units per year, and both these types are spread evenly between the four Soviet fleets, two of which would have no access to the open seas in the event of a conflict.

Of the medium submarines only a few obsolescent Whiskey class

▲ Romeo class; 12 were built, based on the earlier Whiskeys.

▲ Another Foxtrot showing the bow sonars particularly clearly.

▲ Foxtrot class diesel/electric submarine on patrol.

and the 12 Romeos remain, and all will probably soon pay off.

Defensive Role?

The only possible conclusion is, therefore, that even the large ocean-going submarines now have the defence of the waters surrounding the Soviet Union as their primary mission.

In the Northern Fleet this defensive role would clearly take in the Norwegian Sea, where Foxtrots would patrol given sectors as part of an overall line of defence and join with other WP forces in co-ordinated attacks on NATO shipping.

In the Pacific they would have a similar role, holding a line around the SSBN sanctuaries and attempting to break up any attempted blockade of the Tsushima Straits by US Navy forces.

Those units assigned to the Black Sea Fleet already make an important contribution to the Mediterranean Squadron. Several of the more recent Tango class operate here, and these boats are thought to carry the SS-N-15 A/S missile in their extended bow section in addition to the usual torpedo tubes. This would greatly increase their effectiveness against the big SSNs of the US Navy belonging to the 6th Fleet, particularly if used in conjunction with surface units in the combined ASW operations favoured by the Soviet Navy. Any NATO submarine which gave away its presence by firing torpedoes at the accompanying cruiser or destroyer could find itself promptly dispatched by a submarine-launched missile, which could be fired from a considerable distance.

The Baltic is probably the area least suited to the deployment of such large submarines, not only because of its relatively shallow and constricted waters, but because there is a distinct lack of suitable targets. It is not, therefore, impossible that we shall see a new small/medium submarine emerge in the near future for Baltic or Black Sea operations.

Minelaying

All Soviet submarines, nuclear and diesel-electric, are capable of mine-laying operations, and can carry between 30 and 60 mines in place of their torpedoes. The Fox-trots could be employed in this role as far afield as the North Sea without such a mission involving the dangerous transit through the GIUK gap. Certainly their large mine capacity would be their one great advantage in the Baltic.

The Soviet Navy, unlike the US Navy, receives little support from its allies in submarine operations. Only a handful of obsolescent Whiskey and Romeo class boats have been transferred, and these serve with the Polish and Bulgarian Navies.

The Polish Navy has four elderly Whiskey class boats transferred from the Soviet Navy and the Bulgarians have two Whiskeys and two Romeos. All will soon need replacement, probably by second-hand Soviet boats.

SS Submarines

▲ Dutch Dolfijn class boats have three pressure hulls.

▲ Daphne class patrol submarine of the French Navy.

▲ U-18, a Type 206 submarine of Federal German Navy.

▲ Toti class inshore patrol submarine of Italian Navy.

IT IS somewhat surprising, in the context of the "horror stories" one reads about Soviet submarine numbers, to discover that NATO countries themselves possess a total of no less than 136 conventionally-powered submarines. All but five of these are in service with the European allies and Canada, the remaining US Navy boats having been "relegated" to service in the Pacific.

Submarine construction among the NATO countries, however, reflects widely divergent needs, and divides quite neatly into three separate categories: the large ocean-going submarine favoured by the countries which see their NATO role in terms of operations in the North Atlantic; the small coastal submarine built for those countries who are concerned with defending their own coastline, or who would have to fight in shallow or constricted waters; and the medium submarine in service with the Mediterranean NATO countries. The overall total can therefore be broken down into more meaningful figures of 59 ocean-going boats (1,300 tons, 1,321 tonnes or over), 25 medium submarines (750 to 1,300 tons, 762 to 1,321 tonnes) and 52 coastal submarines.

NATO's Successful Ocean-Going Subs

Foremost among the ocean-going submarines are the Oberon and Sealion classes operated by the Royal Navy and Canada. These are large boats with good endurance and very capable sensors. They are also very quiet, and have achieved some remarkable successes in NATO exercises. They are designated "patrol" submarines by the Royal Navy, which suggests that they too would be employed in the GIUK gap. Their near-silent operation when cruising on electric motors would make them very difficult to detect. They would be supported in this role by the Dutch boats, which operate frequently with the Royal Navy's submarine squadrons. The two Zwaardvis-class boats have an excellent reputation, and a new improved class is under construction. The four older Dolphin class boats have all been updated, and also make a useful contribution to NATO strength.

Coastal Subs

The coastal submarines are nearly all of German design and manufacture. W. Germany herself has 24 submarines of the 205/206 classes in service. These are small boats of 370 to 450 tons (376 to 457 tonnes) but they carry a heavy armament of torpedoes for their size. They are deployed in two submarine squadrons in the Baltic, where they would help guard the Danish straits and would be particularly useful in the likely event of an amphibious assault on Germany's Baltic coastline. Their small size and manoeuvrability, together with their eight bow tubes, would enable them to get among the opposing forces and get off their torpedoes quickly and to great effect. They are also fitted for

▲ British O-class submarine.

▲ U-4, a Type 205 submarine of the Federal German Navy; 18 were built for service in the Baltic.

NATO's SS Submarine Strength

Class	No.	Displace-ment
US Navy (all Pacific)		
Barbel	3	2,150t
Darter	1	1,720t
Tang	1	2,050t
UK Royal Navy		
Oberon	16	2,030t
Sealion	3	2,030t
Royal Canadian Navy		
Ojibwa	3	2,030t
Dutch Navy		
Zwaardvis	2	2,300t
Dolfijn	4	1,500t
W. German/Navy		
Type 206	18	450t
Type 205	6	370t
Danish Navy		
Narvhalen	2	370t
Delfinen	4	600t
Norwegian Navy		
Type 207	15	400t
French Navy		
Narval (At)	6	1,630t
Agosta (Med)	4	1,450t
Daphne (Med)	9	870t
Arethuse (Med)	4	540t
Portuguese Navy		
Daphne	3	
Italian Navy		
Sauro	4	1,460t
Toti	4	520t
ex-US Navy	4	2,100t
Greek Navy		
Type 209	8	1,100t
ex-US Navy	3	2,000t
Turkish Navy		
Type 209	5	1,000t
ex-US Navy	10	2,000t

▲ The Royal Navy has 16 of the successful O and P class.

▲French Daphne: efficient conventional hunter/killer.

mining – a very important consideration in the waters where they would be operating.

Denmark also operates two modified Type 205 submarines, together with four older boats of Danish design which are now approaching the end of their useful lives.

The other NATO country to operate small submarines is Norway, which has 15 modified Type 205s, all built in W. Germany. Although Norway contributes to wider-ranging forces such as the Standing Force Atlantic, her Navy is basically geared to defence of her own coastline. These submarines would therefore operate in a similar role to the German boats in the Baltic. Similarity of requirements between the Federal Ger-

man and other navies has led to the adoption of a new joint design for a 750 ton (762 tonnes) submarine, and it is likely that the Danes will also participate.

The French Navy's Submarine Force

The French Navy operates in both the Atlantic and the Mediterranean, and therefore has a wide variety of submarines in service. The six ocean-going Narval class operate in the Atlantic, and will probably be replaced by the new class of SSNs. The most modern French submarines, however, serve in the Mediterranean, where the four Agosta and seven of the nine Daphne class are based. The Agosta class are large modern boats with good endurance and

high underwater speed. They have been designed for very quiet operation and can discharge their torpedoes down to their full diving depth. The Daphne class is smaller and, although accident-prone – two have been lost in Mediterranean waters – is regarded as a successful design. The even smaller Arethuse class will probably be disposed of in the near future.

Mediterranean Countries

The Italian Sauro class is similar in size and performance to the French Agosta, while the Toti class is a very small design similar to the French Arethuse. The Italians also operate four older ex-American boats of the Guppy and Tang classes.

Greece and Turkey also operate a number of these big ex-US Navy submarines. Although all 12 boats were modernised prior to being handed over in the early 1970s, they must be regarded as of limited military value in view of their age. Their length makes them unsuited to operations in the Mediterranean, which has traditionally favoured the smaller submarine.

Much more suited to Mediterranean operations are the 13 German-built Type 209 submarines now in service with these two countries. Apart from possessing the right dimensions, the Type 209 has excellent endurance, high underwater speed, and modern sensors and fire control, and further units are under construction in Turkey.

Major Surface Vessels

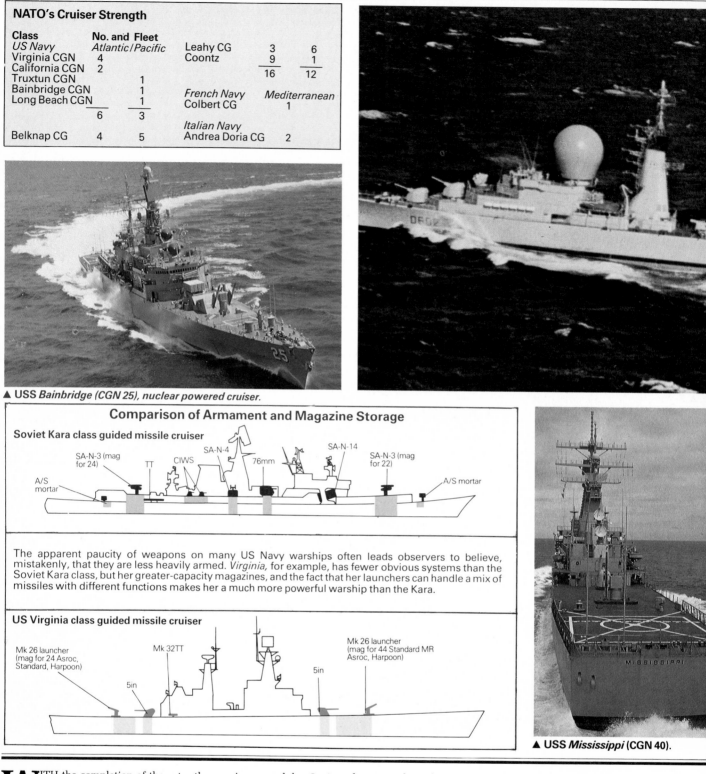

NATO's Cruiser Strength

Class	No. and Fleet			
US Navy	*Atlantic* / *Pacific*	Leahy CG	3	6
Virginia CGN	4	Coontz	9	1
California CGN	2		16	12
Truxtun CGN	1			
Bainbridge CGN	1	*French Navy*	*Mediterranean*	
Long Beach CGN	1	Colbert CG	1	
	6 3			
		Italian Navy		
Belknap CG	4 5	Andrea Doria CG	2	

▲ USS *Bainbridge* (CGN 25), nuclear powered cruiser.

Comparison of Armament and Magazine Storage

Soviet Kara class guided missile cruiser

A/S mortar · SA-N-3 (mag for 24) · TT · CIWS · SA-N-4 · 76mm · SA-N-14 · SA-N-3 (mag for 22) · A/S mortar

The apparent paucity of weapons on many US Navy warships often leads observers to believe, mistakenly, that they are less heavily armed. *Virginia,* for example, has fewer obvious systems than the Soviet Kara class, but her greater-capacity magazines, and the fact that her launchers can handle a mix of missiles with different functions makes her a much more powerful warship than the Kara.

US Virginia class guided missile cruiser

Mk 26 launcher (mag for 24 Asroc, Standard, Harpoon) · 5in · Mk 32TT · 5in · Mk 26 launcher (mag for 44 Standard MR Asroc, Harpoon)

▲ USS *Mississippi* (CGN 40).

WITH the completion of the big carriers of the Forrestal class in the late 1950s the US Navy embarked on a series of missile-armed AAW escorts to accompany them. At first classified as "frigates", all except the Coontz class have since been redesignated cruisers. Their AAW capability centred around the Terrier area defence missile, while for ASW they were fitted with the new anti-submarine missile ASROC. The Coontz class, the first of the series, had a twin Terrier launcher aft, while the middle group, the Leahy class, were "double-enders", with a second launcher forward replacing the 5in gun on the earlier ships. The Belknap class reverted to a single Terrier launcher but, in recognition of the growing threat

to the carriers posed by Soviet SSNs and SSGNs, showed a marked increase in ASW capabilities. In addition to the large multi-mode SQS-26 sonar they were the first US Navy ships to operate a manned helicopter.

These three classes, each of nine or ten ships, still form the backbone of the US Navy AAW escorts. In peacetime two ships of this type are included in the composition of every carrier task force. All but one of the Coontz class, presumably because of their lower endurance, serve in the Atlantic, while the bulk of the longer-range Leahy class operate with the Pacific Fleet. The Belknaps are divided evenly between the two.

The construction of the Nuclear-powered carrier *Enterprise* in the

late 1950s brought with it the need to provide escorts with a similar propulsion system, the argument being that there was little point in providing at great expense a carrier of virtually unlimited range with the ability to deploy at sustained high speed if its escorts did not enjoy the same advantages. A large nuclear-powered cruiser, the *Long Beach,* was already under construction, but the two units completed during the 1960s, *Bainbridge* and *Truxtun,* were of more modest dimensions, and apart from their propulsion system are near-sisters of the *Leahy* and *Belknap* respectively.

The practice of building nuclear-powered escorts to accompany nuclear-powered carriers has continued, with the new California

and Virginia classes being built as escorts for the new Nimitz class CVNs in the Atlantic.

Keeping Abreast of the Threat

The capability of the CGs and CGNs against Soviet land-based bombers is crucial to the survival of the US Navy's carriers, and no expense has been spared in constantly updating the electronics of the older ships to enable them to track more targets and to make more rapid decisions as to which attackers pose the greatest threat. Computerised data links ensure the maximum of cooperation within the task force, and the original Terrier missile has now been replaced by the Standard ER, extending the effective range of

▲ *Suffren* (6,090 tons), an excellent French design.

▲ SPS-48 radar antenna on a Leahy class cruiser.

▲ USS *Halsey* (CG23), one of 9 Leahy class missile cruisers.

▲ Leahy class firing Terrier SAM from aft launcher.

engagement from 20 to 35nm (37 to 65km).

The increasing ability of Soviet forces to launch massed attacks, threatening to saturate the task force defences with large numbers of anti-ship missiles, has exposed potential inadequacies in the conventional rotating radars, which are limited in the number of targets they can handle simultaneously.

Pros and Cons of the New US Cruiser: The CG-47

The US Navy is therefore building a new cruiser, the CG 47, derived from the Spruance class destroyer and fitted with the advanced Aegis system. The latter is centred around four fixed planar radars with electronic scanning, capable of handling a virtually unlimited number of targets. It should be particularly effective against anti-ship missiles, and incorporates a new area defence missile with a range of over 60nm (111km). The major advantage of the SM-2 over all previous installations lies in its need for target illumination only in the terminal phases, enabling far more targets to be engaged simultaneously than would be possible with conventional systems.

Some critics of the CG-47 are concerned about the wisdom of placing such a high-value system as Aegis in a hull with rather limited endurance – less, in fact, than the Leahy and Belknap classes – and feel that the Aegis ships should have had nuclear propulsion.

It is, nevertheless, questionable how far uniform nuclear-powered task forces would be viable in wartime. While the advantages of such a group in the wide expanses of the Pacific are self-evident, these advantages are less obvious in the North Atlantic, where the much greater threat from Soviet submarines would appear to demand more ASW protection than a pair of specialised AAW cruisers could provide. It would therefore seem likely that in the event of hostilities conventionally-powered ASW destroyers would have to accompany even the CVNs.

France and Italy

Apart from the US Navy, only France and Italy among the NATO allies continue to operate cruisers. The French *Colbert* is one of a trio of AAW escorts – the other two are the Suffren-class destroyers – tasked with the protection of the French attack carriers, and therefore performs a similar role to the American ships. She was rebuilt in the early 1970s with Masurca area-defence missiles and an up-dated AA gun battery. Her extensive radar and communications outfit enables her to control aircraft operations and serve as flagship of a task force.

The two Italian ships, *Andrea Doria* and *Caio Duilio*, are ASW cruisers like their successor *Vittorio Veneto*. They have an American Terrier system forward and a large hangar for four small ASW helicopters aft. They will be replaced soon by the new ASW carrier *Giuseppe Garibaldi*.

Major Surface Vessels

▲ Three Soviet warships in the Mediterranean. From left to right: Kara class cruiser, Kashin class destroyer, Kynda class cruiser.

▲ Kynda class cruiser; note the SS-N-3 launcher abaft funnel.

▲ The new battlecruiser *Kirov* with its huge helicopter pad.

IT IS customary for reference books to place Soviet ships of cruiser size in the American CG classification. None of the Soviet vessels is, however, designed to provide area defence for other ships – indeed, the Kievs and Moskvas are provided with their own area defence capabilities, and could therefore be termed "self-escorting". Although most of the Soviet cruisers have double-ended SAM systems, these are intended for self-defence, and are a direct result of the lack of Soviet seaborne aircraft.

The tactical organisation of the Soviet Navy owes nothing to that developed by the NATO allies as a result of their experience in World War II, but has its origins in the Soviet belief that the next war would be a nuclear one. Task forces, which are based on a strict division of labour (aircraft on carriers/area defence in cruisers/ ASW in destroyers) would be vulnerable to nuclear attack. Each and every Soviet cruiser is therefore designed for independent operations and carries its own AAW systems. The importance of the latter, and of the formidable range of ECM equipment fitted to Soviet cruisers, has increased with the current concept of forward deployment.

Independent operations also provide further justification for the centralised command system favoured by the Soviets. Whereas the ships which make up a task force are within signalling distance of one another, inde-pendently operating Soviet units, even if engaged in the same task (eg, anti-ship missile attack on a NATO surface force), would have to be strictly coordinated by a land-based commander, who would be the only man with a full picture of the tactical situation.

Rocket Cruisers

The Soviet Navy divides its major surface ships into two categories; one with an anti-ship role, the other for ASW. The Rocket Cruisers (RKr), which grew out of the concept of area defence, were intended to guard the outer perimeter of Soviet seaspace against carrier task forces. The four Kyndas are armed with two massive quadruple launchers for the SS-N-3 missile (also fitted in the early SSGNs), and carry a further eight reloads. Although they have a SAM launcher forward, they rely very much on land-based aircraft for their own defence and for targeting data and mid-course guidance for their missiles. In the following Kresta class the number of SSM launchers was halved, and reloads abandoned altogether because of handling difficulties, but in compensation they carry their own missile-targeting helicopter and have SAM launchers fore and aft.

RKRs operate with each of the Soviet Fleets in contact with NATO carriers. The Northern Fleet has three Krestas, the Pacific Fleet one Kresta and two Kyndas, and the remaining two Kyndas serve in the Black Sea and Mediterranean.

▲ The heavily armed Kara class. (See also the diagram on page 140.)

▲ *Kirov* sports a mass of effective weapons.

▲ *Kresta II* guided missile cruiser has powerful ASW and AAW armament.

Large ASW Ships

The other cruiser category is the Large ASW Ship (BPK), which replaced the RKr in the shipyards in the late 1960s when NATO's Polaris submarines began to take precedence over the carrier threat. The first BPKs were in fact a conversion of the Kresta-class RKR designated Kresta II. The basic changes comprise replacement of the anti-ship missiles by two quadruple launchers for ASW missiles, the substitution of a Hormone ASW helicopter for the missile-targeting version, and a more powerful sonar. A more advanced SAM system was also fitted.

At least seven of the Kresta II class serve with the Northern Fleet, and probably two in the Pacific. The main operating area of this class is therefore the Norwegian Sea, where the ships would guard the SSBN havens, undertake ASW operations in open waters wherever it might be thought profitable, and hopefully be able to deploy forward as far as the GIUK gap to give assistance to Soviet attack submarines.

More Air Defence

The other major BPK is the *Kara*, which appeared shortly after the *Kresta II* and has continued in parallel production. The major differences lie in the greater number of air defence systems and propulsion by gas turbines, which may result in reduced range. As the bulk of the class serves with the Black Sea Fleet – two went to the Pacific with *Minsk* in 1979 – it

seems likely that the design changes reflect the greater threat from the air in the Mediterranean threatre.

Although the Hormone helicopter carried by the Soviet BPKs compares well enough with Western models the small number of ASW missiles carried compared with NATO ASW vessels is a weakness. It is also not clear whether Soviet sonar capabilities are good enough to exploit the range advantage of the SS-N-14 over Western types.

Nuclear-powered Kirov

The most recent addition to the Soviet surface fleet is the nuclear-powered cruiser *Kirov*. At about twice the displacement of the US Navy CGNs she is a formidable

ship, armed with a great variety of weapon systems including 20 vertically-launched SSMs, large numbers of vertically-launched SAMs, plus ASW missiles and helicopters. She is clearly designed to operate in a hostile air environment such as the GIUK gap, employing her multiple SAMs against attacking aircraft, her SSMs against NATO surface units, and her ASW helicopters and missiles against patrolling submarines. *Kirov* must therefore be seen as the logical conclusion of Soviet cruiser philosophy, namely the incorporation of the power of a task force into a single unit. Whether such a high-value ship would be risked in the GIUK gap if American strike carriers remained intact is another matter.

Destroyers and Frigates

▲ Kanin class destroyer; 8 were converted from Krupny class.

▲ Kashin class, with 3in guns and SA-N-1 launchers.

▲ Kashin class were first major warships to rely on gas-turbines.

▲ Krivak I destroyer, 3,900 tons, a very successful class.

THE older Soviet destroyers of the Kotlin and Skory classes, few of which remain in service, are given the traditional Soviet destroyer classification, EM. Newer vessels, however, are designated in similar fashion (RKr and BPK) to the cruisers, indicating similar roles.

The 14 Kashin class destroyers and the eight Kanins are designated BPK, the same classification applied to the Kresta II and Kara classes. Neither class of destroyer was specifically designed for ASW, however. The Kashins were probably intended to accompany the Kynda class Rocket Cruiser, providing additional AAW and ASW protection. They are fitted with a SAM system fore and aft, two twin AA mountings, and four

anti-submarine mortars. There is a small bow sonar but no helicopter or stand-off A/S missiles.

The Kanin is a conversion of the Krupny-class Rocket Ship which preceded the Kynda. The bulky Scrubber SSMs were removed and replaced by a single SAM launcher and three A/S mortars, and a bow sonar was fitted, giving the Kanin similar capabilities to the Kashin. Nine Kotlin-class destroyers underwent a similar conversion.

General Purpose Destroyers

Although they have the same BPK classification as the larger ASW cruisers, the Kashins and Kanins must be regarded as "second-rate" counterparts of the former. Their obsolescent SAM systems and

lower endurance mean that they could not operate in such a hostile environment as the cruisers. Nor are they particularly well-equipped for ASW with their short-range mortars and dated sonars. They therefore tend to be used rather as general-purpose destroyers, undertaking a variety of duties.

The Kanin, which has proved a relatively successful conversion, serves with the Northern and Baltic Fleets, while most of the Kashins serve with the Black Sea and Pacific Fleets. The Kotlin SAM conversion serves with all four fleets, and one ship has been transferred to the Polish Navy – the only major surface combatant in service with the allies of the Soviet Union.

In the early 1970s five Kashins

and three older Kildin-class destroyers underwent a conversion which gave them four SS-N-2 surface-to-surface missiles. They are now classified as Large Rocket Ships (BRK). This conversion appears to have been motivated by a desire to equip some Soviet destroyers for specific shadowing duties with NATO carrier task forces. Their high speed enables them to manoeuvre in and out of task force formations, and in the event of hostilities they would fire off their missiles in the direction of the carrier and run for safety. The Kashins are particularly well-suited to this mission because their gas-turbine propulsion system would enable them to accelerate quickly away. The tactic of exposing a lesser unit in the hope of dis-

▲ Grisha class corvette, 1,000 tons. There are several variants of this class in service.

▲ Petya I class frigate, 1,150 tons. Over 50 are in service and building continues. There are at least 3 versions in service.

▲ Stern view of a Petya class frigate in the Baltic.

abling a high-value unit such as a carrier is a simple and effective one. It is, moreover, almost certain that American carriers within the reach of Soviet naval forces would be at sea in a time of crisis.

As one would expect, all the converted Kildins and most of the Kashins serve with the Black Sea Fleet, and can frequently be seen in company with carriers of the US 6th Fleet. The other ships serve with the Northern and Baltic Fleets, where they would presumably perform the same shadowing mission in the event of NATO manoeuvres in the Norwegian Sea at a sensitive time.

Krivak-class destroyers which followed the Kashins were originally given the same BPK classification. Recently, however, they were re-designated SKR – Patrol Ship. This caused some surprise in the West, as the Krivaks are far more capable ASW ships than any of the other Soviet destroyers. They have a quadruple launcher forward for anti-submarine missiles and a large bow sonar, in addition to the mortars carried by the Kashin and Kanin. On the other hand they have no area defence missile system and would therefore be more at risk in the open oceans, where they could be attacked by aircraft armed with stand-off missiles which outranged their own defences. The small number of A/S missiles carried and their relatively low endurance may also be factors in their "relegation" to the SKR category.

The primary mission of the Krivaks is almost certainly that of holding the outer ring of Soviet ASW defences. Multi-ship sub-hunting operations, probably in conjunction with ASW patrol aircraft and helicopters from accompanying cruisers, would enable them to exploit the long range of the SS-N-14 stand-off missile.

Krivaks serve with all four Soviet fleets. In the Baltic they have replaced larger surface units, freeing the cruisers for service with the Northern Fleet, and they would almost certainly play a major part in escorting any amphibious assault mounted against West Germany or Denmark.

The numerous Petya- and Mirka-class corvettes are also rated SKRs. These are much less capable ships than the Krivaks, designed to hold the inner barrier in the Soviet defence zones and to undertake general escort duties in the waters close to the Soviet Union. Short on endurance and sea-keeping ability, they are armed only with mortars and homing torpedoes plus a pair of 76mm mountings for use against aircraft or FPBs. They would rely on numbers, rather than sophistication, to perform their mission. Surprisingly none serves with the Warsaw Pact allies.

Until recently the only ships in the escort category serving with the latter navies were a few obsolescent Rigas. The last two years, however, have seen the emergence of a new Soviet export design, the Koni class, and two of this type now serve with East Germany.

Escort Vessels

▲ One of the symbols of NATO's solidarity and determination to resist is Standing Naval Force Atlantic (STANAVFORLANT).

NATO's Escort Strength

Anti-aircraft warfare	Anti-submarine warfare		
United States		**Belgium**	
23 C.F. Adams	30 Spruance	None	4 Wielingen
4 Decatur	8 Forrest Sherman		
7 Oliver Hazard Perry	46 Knox	**Netherlands**	
6 Brooke	10 Garcia	2 Tromp	4 Standard
	2 Bronstein		6 Van Speijk
			6 Friesland
Canada		**Norway**	
None	4 Iroquois	None	5 Oslo
	8 Annapolis/St. Laurent		2 Sleipner
	7 Mackenzie/Restigouche		
		West Germany	
		3 Lutjens	4 Hamburg
United Kingdom			6 Koln
1 Bristol	3 Broadsword		
5 County	26 Leander	**Portugal**	
7 Sheffield	8 Amazon	None	4 Joao Belo
	6 Rothesay		3 Al. Pereira
			10 Joao Coutinho
		Italy	
France		2 Audace	4 Lupo
2 Suffren	5 C-65/F-67/C-70	2 Impetuoso	2 Alpino
4 Bouvet	7 T47/T53/T56		4 Bergamini
	10 A-69	**Turkey**	
	9 Commandant Riviere	None	2 Berk

STANAVFORLANT: Ships are from (l to r): Norway, West Germany, Denmark, United Kingdom, Netherlands, Canada and the USA. ▲

THERE can be little disagreement about the overriding need for quality and sophistication in a carrier task force intended to take the war to the enemy and operate on his doorstep. Where there has been considerable disagreement, however, is on the best way to keep open the sea-lanes which link the United States and Canada to Europe and which link all the western nations to the raw materials essential to their industries.

Nobody questions the superiority of NATO over the Warsaw Pact in the numbers of destroyers and frigates in service with the respective alliances. As we have seen, however, the Soviet Union needs only enough escorts to guard her own coastal waters and the SSBN bastions. The problem for NATO is of an entirely different order. Few people in NATO believe that there are enough escorts to fulfil all missions, and many argue that the necessary increase in numbers can only be obtained by building cheaper, less sophisticated ships.

The North Atlantic

The size of the problem in the North Atlantic alone is a daunting one. It is estimated that in the first month of an emergency NATO would need 500 ship-loads to move initial reinforcements across the Channel and double that number from North America. After the first month a steady 500 ship-loads would be needed to move supplies and stores across the North Atlantic every month.

In the first month escorts would probably also be needed for the two US Marine Crops PhibRons pledged to the immediate reinforcement of Europe, plus two or three carrier task forces and perhaps two ASW hunting groups centred on the British carriers. Other destroyers and frigates would be needed to patrol the GIUK gap and to keep clear the approaches to the European ports.

It would, however, be wrong to assume that the problems of the North Atlantic in the 1980s, and consequently the solutions to those problems, are the same as they were in 1942.

The major threat would indeed be submarines. They would not all, however, be armed with torpedoes.

Some would carry cruise missiles with a range of up to 180nm, far beyond the likely detection ranges of the most capable sonar. Almost all would be nuclear-powered, so that even torpedo-armed submarines could only be successfully engaged by ships equipped with a sophisticated sonar allied to stand-off weapons or a helicopter.

Moreover, a merchant convoy would no longer be moving at 10 to 12 knots, but at double that speed, making it unlikely that an escort left to pursue a submarine contact would be able to catch up again.

The number of submarines the Soviets could sustain in the North Atlantic is also debatable. There are 30 to 35 SSNs and about 30 SSGNs available to the Soviet Northern Fleet. At least a third of

▲ USS *Spruance,* first of vital new destroyer class.

▲ Tartar SAM firing from USS *Sampson* (Adams class).

▲ USS *Charles F. Adams* in typical Atlantic weather.

▲ 5in gun and ASROC launcher on USS *Elliott* foredeck.

the latter and some of the SSNs would probably be specifically tasked with anti-carrier operations. Not all of the submarines would be immediately available. They, no less than the NATO escorts, would have to be stretched to cover all the various NATO movements we have discussed, and could only be reinforced by submarines from the Norwegian Sea or the far-off Kola Peninsula via the GIUK gap. Given these factors, the Soviet Navy might well decide to concentrate its strength against the carrier and amphibious task forces, which pose a more immediate threat to Soviet military supremacy in Europe.

It is, therefore, by no means self-evident that NATO needs vast numbers of escorts, or that the

escort itself is the only effective counter to the submarine threat. The value of LRMP aircraft and SSNs allied to passive area detection systems such as SOSUS or the new towed arrays should not be underestimated, especially in the initial stages when NATO could reasonably hope to locate many of the Soviet submarines already in the North Atlantic; nor should we underestimate the ability of the ASW forces in the GIUK gap to prevent at least some of the Soviet submarines from reinforcing those already present. Only area detection and ASW barriers can, moreover, solve the problem of the SSGN with long-range cruise missiles. The trend in escorts therefore seems likely to move towards the operation of towed

arrays and ASW helicopters, which are the only shipborne systems capable of being carried by an escort with the requisite speed and range to cover the area of threat. Good communications and data links will also be essential, and this is probably the one area in which the multi-national NATO escort force is at present deficient.

Different Countries, Different Styles, Different Jobs

The US Navy operates two classes of escort. One is designed to operate with carrier task forces and therefore has good all-round qualities, including the high speed necessary for fleet work; the other is intended for more run-of-the-mill tasks such as escorting

convoys or amphibious units, and therefore economises on its propulsion system, which produces a steady 25 knots on a single shaft. The first type is called a destroyer, and the second a frigate. Each category is divided into a lesser number of AAW ships with the Tartar area defence missile, and a larger number fitted almost exclusively for ASW, with a large LF bow sonar, ASROC and one or two helicopters. The principal destroyer in the AAW category is the *Charles F. Adams*, which is now approaching the age at which extensive modernisation is needed. The ASW destroyer is the new *Spruance*, in which everything has been subordinated to the need for the quiet, effective anti-submarine vessel. Apart from the

Escort Vessels

▲ The Dutch make a major contribution to NATO; this is *Tromp*.

▲ Ships of Naval On-call Force Mediterranean.

▲ USS *Perry*, lead ship of a major class of escorts.

▲ HMS *Broadsword*, lead ship of effective Type 22 class.

ability to operate two helicopters, the *Spruance* carries 24 missiles in her ASROC reload magazine – an interesting comparison with the eight missiles of the Soviet ASW cruisers.

The *Knox* class typifies the American frigate philosophy of putting a first-class ASW outfit into a second-class hull, while the latest escort, the *Oliver H. Perry*, sacrifices a first-rate sonar and ASROC for a Tartar missile system and an extra helicopter, the idea being that the *Perry* will serve as a helicopter platform for ships with a more capable sonar such as the *Knox*.

Both the latter classes have been, or are being, produced in large numbers, but they are shared between the Atlantic and the Pacific,

and frequently have to be employed as task force escorts. Much of the responsibility for the protection of shipping in the North Atlantic falls, therefore, on Canada, the United Kingdom and the Netherlands.

Canada operates 12 large destroyers built around a Sea King – the only escorts in the world to operate an ASW helicopter of this size and capability. The latest destroyers of the Iroquois class carry two, and for this reason alone must be regarded as formidable adversaries for any submarine.

The United Kingdom is by far the largest operator of escorts of all the European allies, and was the first NATO country to adopt the shipborne ASW helicopter on a wide scale. The Anglo-French

Lynx which is carried by nearly all first-line British escorts is smaller than the American Seasprite and much smaller than the Sea King, but it is fast and manoeuvrable, and has been purchased for the French, Netherlands and Federal German Navies.

British AAW/ASW
British escorts, like those of the US Navy, can be divided into those with area defence missile systems, and ships specialising in ASW. Unlike American escorts, however, both types operate at fleet speed, with the AAW units being designated "destroyers" and the ASW ships "frigates". The main area defence weapon is Seadart, a very effective missile which equips the one-off *Bristol* and the

new Sheffield class. *Bristol* is specially fitted to serve as a flagship, while the smaller Sheffields would be used for more general escort work, particularly in support of the new ASW carriers.

The latest ASW ships are the Broadsword class, which combine a large multi-mode sonar similar to the latest American models with two Lynx helicopters. They are specifically designed to patrol the GIUK gap, and besides their ASW weapons are fitted with Exocet missiles for defence against Soviet surface units and the short-range Seawolf missile for defence against aircraft and missiles. The ten most recent ships of the Leander class are being refitted to similar standards, while earlier units have all received a half-life modernisa-

▲ HMS *Birmingham,* part of the Royal Navy's major contribution to NATO's fleet.

▲ Sea Wolf missiles on RN Type 22 class have anti-air and anti-missile capability.

tion in which they have been fitted either with Exocet and the Lynx, or with the Ikara A/S missile.

North European Escorts

The Royal Netherlands Navy plans to operate three ASW groups, each of well-equipped modern ships, in the East Atlantic area. Two of these will comprise an AAW destroyer of the Tromp class and six of the new Standard class frigates (each of which operates two Lynx) and will operate in the North Atlantic. The other group will comprise an AAW version of the Standard plus the six Leander class frigates, which are being extensively modernised, and will operate in the Channel and the North Sea. This group would be supported by the German destroyers, the new Belgian frigates,

and the Norwegian Oslo class, soon to be joined by the German Standard class vessels now under construction. Nearly all are fitted with SSMs, and most with short-range missile systems such as NATO Sea Sparrow. To these ships would fall the responsibility for keeping open the approaches to the ports of Norway and Northern Europe. Moreover each of the four countries concerned, together with the UK, Canada and the United States, contributes an escort to the Standing Force Atlantic, which spends much of its time operating in these waters.

French Escort Ships

The French Navy, like the US Navy, operates a high/low mix of ships. Escorts such as the A69,

however, are second-class ships not only in terms of speed but also in terms of weapons and sensors. They are designed to fit in with national defence policy rather than NATO strategy, and would be of limited use in a NATO/Warsaw Pact conflict. The first-class escorts, on the other hand, are excellent ships. In addition to the T47/T53/T56 series, which although elderly have all undergone AAW or ASW modernisations, there are two modern AAW destroyers of the Suffren class serving in the Mediterranean, where their role would be to protect the attack carriers, and the C65/F67/C70 classes which are specifically designed for ASW operations in the Atlantic. All the modern ASW units except *Aconit* carry two Lynx helicopters,

and the first two types have the Malafon anti-submarine missile.

Escorts on NATO's Southern Flank

Apart from the French ships serving in the Mediterranean, Italy, Greece and Turkey all operate destroyers and frigates. The Greek and Turkish destroyers are all ageing ex-American vessels, but the Italians have two excellent modern destroyers of the Audace class, and four of the smaller Lupo-class frigates, which carry a heavy battery of anti-ship missiles in addition to an ASW helicopter. A new improved Lupo, the *Maestrale,* is under construction for Italy, while Greece is soon to acquire modern Standard frigates from the Netherlands.

Amphibious Warfare Forces

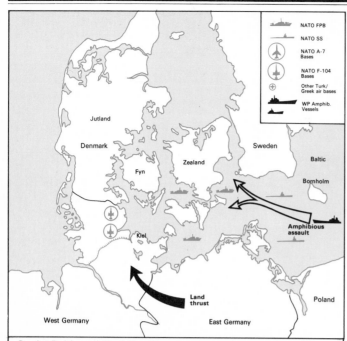

Soviet Baltic and Black Sea Fleets' access to the oceans would depend on early seizure of the respective straits. The maps show how an amphibious assault in either area would be combined with a thrust by WP land forces striking from E. Germany or Bulgaria. NATO naval forces charged with defence against amphibious assault would be missile-armed fast patrol boats and small submarines.

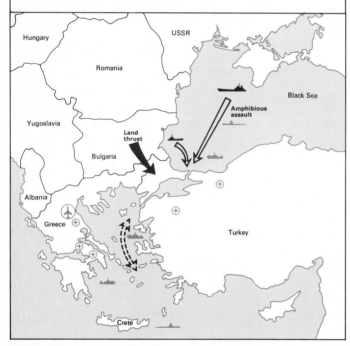

▲ East Germany has 12 of these Frösch class LSTs.

▲ Polish OT-62 APCs landing from a Polnocny class LST.

IN all the aspects of naval warfare mentioned hitherto the over-riding factor has been the great disadvantage suffered by the Soviet Navy in terms of its geographical position.

The only way this situation could be dramatically altered would be for the Soviet Union to change its maritime geography, and this would be possible only if countries which at present block Soviet access to the open seas were occupied. The occupation of Denmark and S.W. Norway, for example, would uncork the bottle which contains the Baltic Fleet, would renew the link between the ASW cruisers of the Northern Fleet and the Leningrad shipyards, and would enable Soviet submarines to operate from Norway, thus halving the distance which at present separates them from the North Atlantic. The occupation of Norway would also allow the Soviet Naval Air Force to dominate the Norwegian and North Seas. NATO sea traffic between the United Kingdom and the ports of Northern Europe would no longer be a viable proposition and would probably be restricted to the English Channel. Indeed the vital strategic position of the UK as the major resupply base for NATO ground and air forces in Europe would be seriously undermined.

The other straits crucial to the effective operation of the Soviet Navy in the event of conflict are the Turkish Straits. The occupation of the area surrounding the Bosphorus and Dardanelles would give free passage to the Black Sea Fleet, and forward basing of the Naval Air Force would go some way to providing the air umbrella necessary for the survival of the Soviet Mediterranean Squadron. It is, however, possible that the Soviet Defence Staff might regard any excursion in the direction of Turkey as a dangerous diversion of resources from the main front in the West.

Amphibious Forces

Both the Danish and the Turkish straits fall within the traditional ambit of Soviet amphibious operations, and the bulk of the amphibious units themselves serve with the Baltic and Black Sea Fleets. Since Soviet naval construction is generally wedded to specific tasks rather than to abstract concepts of seapower most of their landing ships are short-lift vessels designed for these constricted waters. No attempt has been made to establish a blue-water amphibious capability on the pattern of the US Marine Corps. Only the new Ivan Rogov and the Alligator class ships are regularly deployed out of area, and both types appear to be designed for single-ship operations in support of Soviet foreign policy rather than for integration into an amphibious assault fleet. Significantly many serve with the Pacific Fleet, with deployments to the Indian Ocean and the East Coast of Africa. In terms of size only Ivan Rogov herself can match any of the 60 major amphibious units of the US Marine Corps, and

▲ Aist class hovercraft of the Soviet Naval Infantry.

Warsaw Pact Amphibious Forces		
Type	No.	Class
Soviet Union		
LPD	1	Ivan Rogov
LST	14	Alligator
	13	Ropucha
	55	Polnocny
East Germany		
LST	15	Frosch
Poland		
LST	23	Polnocny

▲ Soviet Marines have grown dramatically in both numbers and capability in the past 20 years.

▲ Helicopter platforms have recently been added to Polnocny class LSTs.

▲ Soviet amphibious ship, *Ivan Rogov*.

there are no indications that series production of this type is planned.

A new element in NATO's amphibious forces is the American Rapid Deployment Force, formed from elements of all three services to provide a rapid intervention capability. The RDF is based on the principle of forward deployment of equipment in heavy-lift RO-RO ships, the troops being flown directly from the USA.

The backbone of the Soviet amphibious fleet is formed by the Polnocny and Ropucha classes, backed up in the Baltic by a strong force of Polish Polnocny class ships plus a dozen of the East German Frösch class. All are conventional landing ships with a single tank deck and a bow ramp for beaching, although the larger

Ropucha has significantly greater accommodation for troops. In major amphibious exercises their numbers have been supplemented by the addition of mercantile roll-on roll-off (Ro-Ro) ships.

Role of Naval Infantry

Because there are no LPDs or LSDs capable of carrying their own landing craft the basic equipment of the Naval Infantry comprises amphibious tanks and APCs. These are old and of limited military value, and serve to illustrate the extent to which the Naval Infantry, far from being capable of independent operations, depends on the Soviet Army both for its equipment and its raison d'être. Not only is it smaller numerically than the US Marine Corps – 20,000 men

divided between the four fleet areas compared with the USMC's 190,000 – but it has no specialised equipment of its own and no integral air support. Soviet amphibious operations envisage an assault, probably accompanied by army parachute landings, on enemy-held coastline ahead of the main army thrust, threatening the flank of the enemy forces.

A number of major Warsaw Pact amphibious exercises have taken place in the Baltic in recent years and these have been getting larger and closer to Denmark. The success of amphibious operations on this front might be crucial to the success of the Warsaw Pact ground forces. Significantly the last ten years have seen a shift away from LST construction in the Soviet

Navy in favour of large numbers of air cushion vehicles of the Aist, Lebed and Gus classes, which would be particularly well suited to operations at the western end of the Baltic.

The only effective NATO counter to these tactics is the continued presence of large numbers of missile-armed FPBs and maritime strike aircraft based on Denmark and Northern Germany, and the use of minefields to block a major assault by amphibious displacement vessels. The ability of the NATO ground forces to contain the expected initial thrust by the Warsaw Pact armies is therefore essential to prevent the position of the defending forces from being seriously undermined.

▲ US Marines storming ashore from a landing-craft during a NATO exercise in the Mediterranean.

▲ Logistic ships are essential to the projection of power.

▲ Boeing CH-46s on ship-to-shore delivery missions.

▲ Iwo Jima class assault ship with crowded flight deck.

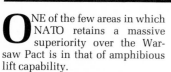

▲ LVTP-7 amphibious assault vehicles of the USMC.

ONE of the few areas in which NATO retains a massive superiority over the Warsaw Pact is in that of amphibious lift capability.

There are two sides to this particular coin, however. The positive side is the ability of NATO – and the US Navy in particular – to transfer powerful specialised assault forces and all their heavy equipment over great distances to virtually any point on the globe. The negative side is the necessity for NATO to have such a capability, given the problem of already having an inferiority in the numbers of troops in place in the European theatre, and political and geographical weaknesses on the exposed Northern and Southern Flanks.

US Marine Corps

The US Marine Corps is not only the most powerful of the allied marine forces, but it is now the only one capable of operating independently of other elements such as regular air force units or merchant shipping.

There are currently three active Marine divisions, each supported by a Marine Air Wing (MAW). The fixed-wing element of the latter is made up of a Fighter Attack Wing comprising three to five squadrons of F-4 Phantoms, an Attack Wing with three to seven squadrons of A-4 Skyhawk light attack planes, A-6 Intruder all-weather strike aircraft or AV-8A Harriers, and recce and ECM squadrons. Although intended to provide support to Marine operations

ashore from existing or improvised air strips, all of these aircraft can operate from US Navy carriers.

The greater part of the 3rd Marine Division is at present based in Okinawa, with most of its accompanying MAW (the 1st) shared between that island and the Japanese mainland.

The 1st Marine Division and 3rd MAW are based in California, but are committed to NATO in the event of a conflict.

The only Marine division committed to Europe and in the right place – at least in terms of its shipping – is the 2nd Division, together with its 2nd Air Wing, which in compensation is much larger than the other two.

The amphibious lift for the Marine divisions comprises some

60 modern amphibious units specialising in a variety of tasks and designed to complement each other. Just under a third of them are LSTs, which land the tanks and vehicles they carry directly on to beach via a bow ramp. The 27 LSDs and LPDs specialise in "horizontal" assault, and carry vehicles, marines, and landing craft of various sizes to ferry them ashore. The seven LPHs are for "vertical" assault, and carry up to two dozen helicopters to land their marines behind enemy lines. They carry much larger numbers of troops than other classes, but only light vehicles and no large landing craft.

The most recent addition to this amphibious fleet is the five-ship Tarawa class (LKA), in which the capabilities of the LPH, LPD and

NATO's Amphibious Forces

Type	No.	Class	Troops	Landing Craft	Helicopters
US Marine Corps					
LCC	2	Blue Ridge	(Command Ships)		
LHA	5	Tarawa	1,900	4 LCU / 2 LCM	25-30
LPH	7	Iwo Jima	2,100		20-25
LPD	12	Austin	900	1 LCU / 4 LCM	6
	2	Raleigh			
LSD	5	Anchorage	350	3 LCU	
	8	Thomaston			
LST	20	Newport	350		
UK Royal Navy					
LPD	2	Fearless	700	4 LCM	
LST	6	Sir Lancelot	500		
France					
LSD	2	Ouragan	350	2 LCU	
LPH		Jeanne d'Arc	700		8
LST	2	Champlain	180		
	5	Argens	300		
Greece					
LSD		Nafkratoussa		3 LCU	
LST	10	ex-US Navy	150-350		
Turkey					
LST	4	ex-US Navy	150-350		
	1	Cakabey	100?		

▲ USS *Juneau* can carry a battalion group with tanks.

▲ There are five of these Tarawa-class amphibious assault ships which confer an unrivalled capability on the US maritime forces.

LSD are all rolled into one type.

Assigned to the LKAs, LPHs and LPDs are helicopters from the squadrons of the three Marine Air Wings. Each wing has two Heavy and two Medium Helicopter Squadrons for troop-lift, an Attack Squadron for fire support, and a Light Helicopter Squadron for general-purpose work. The standard heavy helicopter is the CH-53 Sea Stallion, which can carry 37 fully-equipped marines, while the medium helicopter is the CH-46 Sea Knight, which can carry 17 to 25 troops. All of the helicopters in service with the US Marines are specialist designs, illustrating the importance and prestige of the Corps itself within the US military set-up.

The amphibious units are divided up into eight squadrons distributed evenly between the Atlantic and Pacific Fleets. The standard five-ship PhibRon comprises an LPH, an LPD, an LSD, and two LSTs, although the advent of the Tarawas has brought about an alternative composition consisting typically of an LKA, and LPD and an LST. The PhibRon carries a reinforced Marine battalion (Marine Amphibious Unit). The Marine Corps intends this to be a quick-reaction force, the composition of which depends on the mission it has been assigned. Generally an MAU comprises between 1,600 and 2,500 marines with tanks, APCs, artillery and smaller weapons, supported by 20 to 25 helicopters.

Two PhibRons are forward deployed in the Western Pacific, and one in the Mediterranean. The ships are therefore designed for long-term troop accommodation.

Atlantic vs Pacific

Even this massive force of ships is limited in its carrying capacity. If all 60 ships were operational – and 15 per cent are normally in refit – they could lift slightly more than one reinforced Marine Division plus its supporting air and ground units (designated a Marine Assault Force). Even so only the assault echelon could be carried, leaving follow-on echelons to make their transit in mercantile vessels. As only half the amphibious shipping would already be in the Atlantic and ten of the ships based on the West Coast would be in the Western Pacific it would take a considerable time to assemble anything like this number.

It is therefore accepted that a major assault could take place either in the Atlantic or the Pacific, but not in both simultaneously. A major assault force would, moreover, require time to assemble, involving a choice between "a little soon" and "a lot later", and an accurate assessment of what might happen to the land situation in the coming weeks.

In the event of a conflict between NATO and the Warsaw Pact, Northern Europe could therefore rely on only two PhibRons with about 5,000 men being immediately available, and these would have to be brought safely across the North Atlantic in the face of deter-

Amphibious Warfare Forces

▲ USS *Guadalcanal* with CH-46/CH-53 helicopters embarked.

▲ US Navy Amphibious Assault Landing Craft on trials.

▲ USMC M60 coming ashore from a utility landing craft.

▲ Trucks disembark from Newport class tank landing ship.

mined opposition from above and below the water. The third active PhibRon serving in the Atlantic Fleet would in all probability remain in the Mediterranean to counter any attempt by the Warsaw Pact to seize the Dardanelles.

There must, however, be a question mark against the ability of the US Marine Corps to integrate successfully into the NATO command structure in Europe and even against the value of the traditional amphibious assault within the Northern Theatre itself. The organisation and equipment of the US Marines is still primarily geared to long-range assault operations in the Pacific, with the Army hanging on to their shirt-tails. In the event of a determined drive through Northern Germany and

into Denmark by forces of the Warsaw Pact, however, the comparatively lightly equipped Marines might find themselves fighting alongside regular army units already in place, with their Air Wing bolstering the air squadrons of AFCENT.

The only task for which the amphibious forces seem ideally equipped would be an assault on Northern Norway, and by the time the Marines arrived in Europe such as assault might well be aimed at cutting the communication and supply lines of Soviet forces already driving towards the south. This would be a hazardous venture if the air-fields of Northern Norway were in Soviet hands. Moreover, the US Marine Corps has been a late convert to the special needs of

warfare in the Arctic, and until recently has been poorly trained and equipped for this particular style of operation. Only now are steps being taken to remedy this.

Initially, therefore, the NATO response to any threat on the Northern Flank would have to come from Europe itself, and the amphibious forces available would be strictly limited.

The Europeans

The United Kingdom operates two Assault Ships (comparable to the US Navy LPD) and six smaller Logistics Ships, which have a roll-on, roll-off tank deck plus accommodation for troops. The British 3rd Commando Brigade is an elite force comprising three battalion-sized Commandos plus light artil-

lery and support regiments. 45 Commando is specially equipped and trained for Arctic warfare, exercising in Norway every year, while 42 Commando has limited arctic training and equipment. The Royal Marines have close associations with the Royal Netherlands Marine Corps, whose 1st Amphibious Combat Group is assigned to AFNORTH. Attached to this group is an independent company which serves alongside the British 45 Commando, and has identical equipment.

The Netherlands forces are totally dependent on their allies for amphibious lift, and the latter capability has declined dramatically in recent years. Britain's Royal Navy formerly operated two carriers as vertical assault ships, but

▲ USMC LVTP-7 can travel at 8.4mph (13.5km/h) in water.

▲ LVTC-7 command/communications version has extra radios.

▲ British AV-8A Harrier hovers over USS *Tarawa*. USMC has now confirmed its order for 300+ AV-8B Harriers.

in 1977 these were redesignated ASW carriers, and exchanged their Wessex troop carrying helicopters for ASW Sea Kings. They could still be easily adapted for use as commando carriers, and the Royal Marines retain two squadrons of helicopters which have recently been strengthened by the addition of the new Sea King Mk IV. Increasingly, however, the defence of Norway depends on the seven infantry battalions of the multinational ACE Mobile Force, which would be positioned by airlift. The stance of the European Marines has shifted from amphibious assault to rapid deployment, preferably before the outbreak of hostilities, with much of the heavy equipment and supplies following on in mercantile Ro-Ro ships. They

would then await the arrival of the 1st Battalion of the Canadian Brigade, which is assigned to Norway and trained for Arctic warfare but dependent on transatlantic shipping, and later reinforcement by the US Marine Corps.

NATO's Flanks

Successful defence of the Northern Flank is more than possible against the small defensive Soviet ground formations at present stationed in the Kola Peninsula. The proximity of Northern Norway to the major Soviet naval bases and airfields would, however, make it difficult to defend should the Russians switch other army formations to this front.

The Southern Flank of Europe is also a key area as regards amphib-

ious operations, as the Soviet Union shares a border with Turkey and Bulgaria with Greece. The Russians themselves have large short-range amphibious forces in the Black and Caspian Seas, suggesting that they might attempt to secure the exit of their naval forces to the Mediterranean by an assault on the Dardanelles.

To counter such moves NATO not only has the US Marine Corps PhibRon serving with the 6th Fleet, but also the numerous ex-American LSTs of the Greek and Turkish Navies. The French Navy also has a significant amphibious force, comprising the two *Ouragan* class assault ships, seven smaller logistics ships, and the *Jeanne d'Arc*, which can serve as a vertical assault ship or an ASW carrier. The

French ships would, however, probably be scattered around the globe at the outbreak of a conflict.

The NATO amphibious forces in the Mediterranean are a rather motley collection of ships and men, and their effectiveness would be severely undermined by the non-participation of the French Navy in previous exercises, and the past political antagonisms between Turkey and Greece.

A new element is NATO's amphibious forces is the American Rapid Deployment Force, formed from elements of all three services to provide a rapid intervention capability. The RDF is based on the principle of forward deployment of equipment in heavy-life RO-RO ships, the troops being flown directly from the USA.

Naval Armaments

▲ SS-N-2 has been used in three wars and is now rather old.

▲ Rare photo of (possibly) SA-N-4 launch.

▲ Hoisting SS-N-2 aboard Komar missile boat.

▲ SS-N-2 being launched from an Osa class patrol boat.

▲ SA-N-1 launcher on foredeck of a Soviet destroyer.

A MAJOR problem in assessing the quality of Soviet naval hardware is the little of it has seen service in a maritime environment. Of the mis-siles only the Styx has been widely exported (and used) and then prob-ably only in its earliest form. We should therefore treat all the per-formance figures given here and in other Western reference books as estima-tions that must be considered with a degree of caution.

The factor which is of greatest assistance in this respect is that much of the naval hardware is derived from weapons which first entered service with the ground forces, allowing at least some parallels in performance to be established. On the one hand this means that the Soviets benefit from

lower development costs and greater standardisation of equip-ment and spares; on the other it frequently results in equipment which is less than ideally suited to a maritime environment or to being accommodated in the cram-ped, space- and weight-critical confines of a ship.

Larger, Fewer Missiles

Soviet missiles and radars there-fore tend to be bulkier and heavier than their Western counterparts, and the awkward shape of the anti-ship and ASW missiles in particu-lar has made it impossible to carry them in below-decks magazines on any but the largest Soviet vessels. This has resulted in topweight problems in some classes (notably the *Kyndas*) and reduced comple-

ments of mis-siles compared with NATO ships.

The three standard Soviet anti-ship missiles are the SS-N-2, the SS-N-3, and the SS-N-9. The SS-N-2 Styx was designed for small fast attack craft but has also been fitted in an updated version to modified destroyers of the *Kashin* and *Kildin* classes. It has an effective range of between 10 and 20nm (18.5 and 37km), and therefore requires no external form of guidance. Earlier versions of the missile were easily decoyed by skilful use of ECM in the 1973 Middle East War, but it is thought that later versions may employ a modified homing system.

The SS-N-3 Shaddock is a long-range (150 to 200nm, 278 to 370km) missile designed for cruiser-sized

vessels and submarines. Unlike Styx it depends on the provision of an external relay to guide the missile to its target and requires a bulky tracker radar on the parent ship to follow it through the initial part of its cruise phase. A more recent version of the SS-N-3, de-signated SS-N-12, has appeared on *Kiev*, and is credited with even greater range than its predecessor.

Intermediate between the Styx and the Shaddock is the SS-N-9, which has a range of over 60nm (111km). Like Styx it is generally fitted in smaller ships, but like Shaddock it requires an external relay and an on-board tracking radar.

All three of these anti-ship missiles have an aeroplane con-figuration, with boosters mounted

▲ RBU-4500A six-barrel anti-submarine rocket launchers are installed on many Soviet warships. Range is 4.5km.

▲ SA-N-1 being launched from a Kashin destroyer.

▲ SS-N-3 tubes with (above bridge) Peel Group radar for SA-N-1.

beneath the fuselage. This enables them to pack a much greater "punch" than NATO anti-ship missiles, which all have a narrow cylindrical body, and also allows more room for sensors. The larger missiles are thought to have folding wings and are carried in cylindrical launchers topsides. Elaborate reloading arrangements exist in the *Kynda* and *Kiev*, but only in a ship the size of the latter is such an operation practicable. Significantly the new *Kirov* carries all twenty of her missiles (designated SS-N-19) in fixed vertical launchers inside the hull with no reloads.

Also of aeroplane configuration is the SS-N-14 ASW missile, which carries a homing torpedo in similar fashion to the French Malafon and the British/Australian Ikara. It is

credited with greater range than any NATO ASW missile, but as the ranges of the latter are linked to the likely range of sonar contacts it is difficult to see how this advantage could be fully exploited by the Soviet Navy. Generally the SS-N-14 is side-mounted to free the ends of the ship for AAW weapons, and only in *Kirov* is there any reload system. Like the Western Ikara and malafon, it is command-guided.

Moskva and *Kiev* are fitted instead with a twin-arm launcher for the FRAS-1 missile, which is thought to carry a nuclear warhead. Like the American ASROC it is a simple ballistic rocket, and can therefore be accommodated in much larger numbers in a below decks magazine beneath the launcher.

Cruise Missiles

Apart from the large SS-N-3 two other cruise missiles are carried by Soviet submarines. The SS-N-7 Siren is a horizon-range missile designed for anti-carrier operations and is fired from vertical launchers in the bow casing of the Charlie class submarines. The SS-N-15 is a nuclear-tipped missile for use against other submarines and is carried by the *Victor* and *Tango*. Like the American SUBROC it is fired from a torpedo tube and has a range of over 15nm (28km). Both missiles rely on the submarine's own sensors for target data.

For defence against aircraft the Soviet Navy, like the ground forces, relies on a variety of missiles and guns, with the emphasis on defence-in-depth rather than

over-reliance on a single high-technology system. Large numbers of launchers and gun mountings are preferred to large magazine capacities, and each individual launcher and mounting is provided with its own fire control system, enabling a massive barrage of fire to be put up over a short period of time and allowing enough redundancy to compensate for mechanical breakdowns or action damage. There is, however, less capability for sustained operations in a hostile environment than in equivalent NATO ships.

Until recently the two standard medium-range surface-to-air missiles were the SA-N-1 Goa and the SA-N-3 Goblet. The former is derived from the land-based SA-3

▲ Loading a torpedo on an East German fast patrol boat.

▲ FRAS-1 A/S (left) and SS-N-14 missiles on *Moskva*.

▲ SA-N-1 Goa on foredeck of a Kashin-Mod destroyer.

▲ SA-N-1 Goa missiles on launcher on Soviet warship.

and must therefore be regarded as obsolescent. Unlike the NATO navies, however, the Soviet Navy rarely updates its weapons or electronics. The half-life refit which brings many NATO ships up to the same standard as the latest construction is unknown among the countries of the Warsaw Pact. A twenty-year-old Soviet vessel generally carries twenty-year-old weapons, and this factor must be taken into consideration when assessing the relative effectiveness of the NATO and Warsaw Pact navies.

Goblet Faster
Although little is known about the SA-N-3 it must clearly be regarded as a major improvement on its predecessor. It is thought to

have a range of around 18.6 miles (30km) compared to the 9.3 miles (15km) of Goa, and is much faster in flight. Both missiles are launched from a twin-arm launcher, beneath which is a magazine containing some 22 missiles (those in *Kiev* may contain more). Two launchers are generally fitted, although some early ships have only one. The Goa launcher is stabilised, indicating initial problems with missile acquisition from a rolling ship, but these problems appear to have been resolved with the advent of Goblet. All Soviet SAMs use command guidance, which is less accurate at longer ranges than the semi-active homing method adopted by all NATO navies for their area defence systems.

For short-range defence against low-flying aircraft many Soviet warships, large and small, are fitted with the SA-N-4. This probably has a range of around 4.3 miles (7km) and is fired from a twin-arm "pop-up" launcher normally concealed inside a cylindrical "bin". The bin also contains the magazine, making the system particularly well suited to modular installation. The principle of a "pop-up" launcher seems to derive from the need for maximum missile readiness in severe weather conditions. Reloading, however, must be relatively slow, putting the SA-N-4 at a disadvantage compared with the sextuple and octuple point-defence missile systems of the West.

Advanced SAM
The latest Soviet SAM is the SA-N-6, a vertically-launched missile which has just appeared on the new *Kirov*. Little is known about the performance or configuration of this missile, but reports credit it with exceptionally high speed in flight. Even with a conventional fire control system this would enable more targets to be engaged in rapid succession. Vertical launch also has the advantage of instant missile readiness, with none of the technical hitches associated with loading mechanisms. It does, on the other hand, involve violent manoeuvres by the missile in the initial acquisition phase and is therefore best suited to use against high-flying targets.

Soviet naval guns are generally

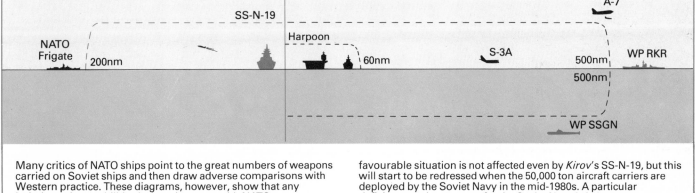

▲ Hai class corvette of East German Navy firing RBU-1800 250mm anti-submarine rockets.

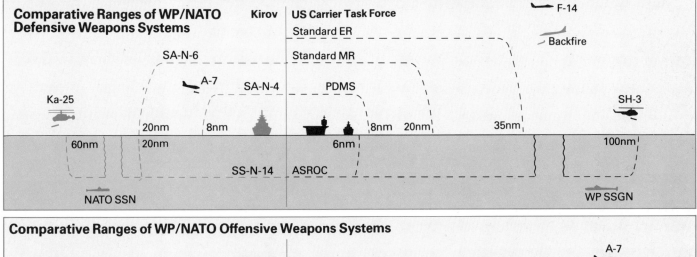

Comparative Ranges of WP/NATO Defensive Weapons Systems

Kirov — US Carrier Task Force — F-14

Standard ER

SA-N-6 — Standard MR — Backfire

Ka-25 — A-7 — SA-N-4 — PDMS — SH-3

20nm — 8nm — 8nm — 20nm — 35nm

60nm — 20nm — 6nm — 100nm

SS-N-14 — ASROC

NATO SSN — WP SSGN

Comparative Ranges of WP/NATO Offensive Weapons Systems

SS-N-19 — A-7

NATO Frigate — Harpoon — S-3A — WP RKR

200nm — 60nm — 500nm

500nm

WP SSGN

Many critics of NATO ships point to the great numbers of weapons carried on Soviet ships and then draw adverse comparisons with Western practice. These diagrams, however, show that any imbalance in capabilities is the other way, with NATO weapons having a longer range and greater terminal effects. Such a favourable situation is not affected even by *Kirov*'s SS-N-19, but this will start to be redressed when the 50,000 ton aircraft carriers are deployed by the Soviet Navy in the mid-1980s. A particular deficiency at the moment for the Soviet Navy is in long-range reconnaissance, there being no equivalent to the S-3A.

---

derived from weapons in service with the ground forces. It can therefore safely be assumed that they combine robustness and reliability with unspectacular performance.

Small-calibre Guns
Until recently the three main calibres in use were the 76mm, housed in a twin stabilised mounting, the 57mm, either in the older open quadruple mount or in a twin fully-enclosed automatic mount, and the 30mm, either in a twin mounting or a sextuple "gatling" type mounting for anti-missile defence. Only the older cruisers and destroyers built in the 1950s had major calibre weapons (152mm and 130mm respectively) for use against other ships.

Recently, however, there has been a shift away from twin AA guns in favour of single dual-purpose weapons. This has resulted in the new single 100mm which has been fitted in place of the twin 76mm mounts in the latest *Krivaks* and also in *Kirov*, and the new single 76mm which is being fitted to many of the new corvettes and hydrofoils.

ASW Mortars Indicate "Defence in Depth"
In addition to stand-off ASW missiles, the Soviet Navy continues to fit even its larger ships with multi-barrelled anti-submarine mortars, of which the six-barrelled RBU 1000 and the twelve-barrelled RBU 6000 are the standard models. NATO navies are

steadily discarding short-range ASW weapons, and their retention by the Soviet Navy is yet another illustration of the "defence-in-depth" philosophy. On the larger anti-submarine ships they provide some compensation for the small numbers of A/S missiles carried, while smaller units armed with these mortars would act in concert to lay down a massive barrage around a suspected submarine contact, thereby compensating for the weapon's lack of accuracy. These aging mortars must, however, be something of a maintenance nightmare, especially in view of the preferred positioning of them close to the bow.

The standard torpedoes in service with Soviet surface ships are the 533mm anti-ship torpedo

and the 400mm anti-submarine homing torpedo. The former is mounted in triple, quadruple or quintuple banks on all major surface units and may also have an anti-submarine capability. The 400mm is fitted in quadruple or single mounts on small ASW ships, and many submarines built in the early 1960s also have stern tubes from which it can be fired. Although very little is known about the latest 533mm submarine torpedoes, but there is good reason to expect that they will be on a par with the latest developments in the West.

Some of the more recent light craft and amphibious units are fitted with a launcher for SA-N-5 Grail heat-seeking missiles, adapted from the land-based SA-7.

▲ British Sea Dart missile has both surface-to-air and surface-to-surface capability.

▲ Many USN ships are now equipped with the ASROC (RUR-5A) anti-submarine rocket system.

▲ SM-2 Standard SAM of USN.

THERE are two things that you can do with superior technology: one is to put more performance into the same weapon without increasing its size; the other is to put the same performance into a smaller weapon. Western missiles tend to be smaller than Soviet missiles of similar size and capabilities, bearing out the generally held belief that Soviet technology, in spite of massive investment in research and development, still lags behind that of the West.

Missile size is a particularly important consideration for ships, which are space- and weight-critical, since it affects magazine capacity. The average capacity of a Western SAM magazine is 40 missiles, compared with an esti-

mated 22 for Soviet warships. A cruiser of the Leahy class, with two SAM launchers, therefore carries nearly twice as many missiles as a Soviet Kresta II.

Uneven Technology

This is not to say that technological attainments are uniform in the West. National and political considerations have resulted in expensive separate developments, particularly in the area of the large surface-to-air and anti-submarine missile. Thus the French Masurca, which has a range of 24.8 miles (40km), is longer than the American Standard ER, which has a range of 37.7 miles (60.6km), while the even more recent British Seadart, which is powered by a. ramjet and is therefore capable of

ranges in excess of 49.6 miles (79.8km), is little more than half the length of the other two missiles. Similarly the French Malafon ASW missile, which is almost identical in conception and operation to the Australian Ikara in service with Britain's Royal Navy, is more than twice the size yet has a range of only 7nm (12.9km) compared with an estimated 12nm (22.2km) for Ikara. Because of this the French Suffren can carry only 13 missiles compared with an estimated 32 for the Royal Navy's Bristol, which is of similar size and has the same carrier escort role.

A further factor which must be taken into account when comparing US Navy practice in particular with that of the Soviet Navy is the American predilection for

large mixed magazines with two or even three different types of missile sharing the same launch system. This has frequently led to ill-informed criticism of US Navy ships because they appear to be less heavily armed than their Soviet counterparts. The Virginia CGN, for example, has only two twin missile launchers and two single 5in (127mm) guns compared with four twin SAM launchers, two quadruple ASW missile launchers, two twin 3in (76mm) guns, plus a variety of smaller weapons for the Soviet Kara. The Mk 26 launcher on the Virginia, however, can handle not only the Standard MR surface-to-air missile, but also the ASROC anti-submarine missile and the Harpoon anti-ship missile. Allied

▲ Australian Ikara anti-submarine weapon in service with RN.

▲ Sub Harpoon missile breaking the surface during RN trials.

▲ Malafon Mq 2 ASW missile which arms several French vessels.

▲ Knox class DE launching Harpoon SSM.

to the greater capacity of her missile magazines this factor makes *Virginia* a much more powerful ship than the *Kara*.

Similarities Useful

The multi-missile handling capability of US Navy ships has been made possible by the deliberate development of missiles of similar dimension for different purposes. Standard, ASROC and Harpoon are all around 15ft (4.6m) in length and 12in (0.3m) in diameter and can therefore easily be accommodated and handled in the same magazine ring or the same box launcher. Harpoon, unlike the French Exocet, the Italian Otomat and the Soviet anti-ship missiles, does not need to be "bolted" on in separate containers,

with the attendant top-weight problems, but can be installed in ships already fitted with launchers for SAM or ASW missiles. Air defence ships with the Mk 13 launcher can therefore be easily modified to fire Harpoon, as can ASW ships such as the *Knox* which have only an ASROC launcher. This practice also enables ships to carry a different "mix" of missiles for different missions – an important consideration when a destroyer might find itself operating in the Norwegian Sea or in the open expanses of the Atlantic.

Other NATO countries which do not possess the enormous resources of the United States have not attempted to copy this multi-missile handling capability. Only

the French have produced missiles of their own manufacture for all three tasks, and these have followed separate lines of development which have necessitated specialised launch systems.

Bolt-on Missiles

Both the British and the French ASW missiles are reloadable, and therefore need only a single launcher compared with the multiple launchers favoured by the Soviet Navy for its SS-N-14. All the anti-ship missiles in service with the navies of Western Europe, however, are bolted on in single box launchers or multiple canisters. Four is the usual number for Exocet, which is operational with the navies of France, the UK, Belgium, Greece and West Germany,

but Harpoon, which has been adopted by the Netherlands, Denmark and Turkey, comes in a smaller canister which can be mounted in two blocks of four.

Since NATO strategy envisages the delivery of anti-ship missile attacks at long range by carrier-based aircraft no ship-based weapon comparable to the Soviet SS-N-3 has been developed. Exocet and the small Norwegian Penguin missile have been designated for actions limited by the radar horizon of the parent-ship, while Harpoon would need external targeting data to be fully effective at its longer range of 60nm (111km). Helicopters, which are carried by most NATO surface warships, would assist in providing such data, and could also

Naval Armaments

▲ Close-in Weapons System (CIWS) kills incoming target.

▲ French destroyer *Suffren* (D-602) fires a Masurca SAM.

▲ The heart of US Navy's CIWS is 3,000 rds/min. Vulcan/Phalanx.

▲ Sea Sparrow SAM and Basic Point Defense Missile System.

observe the success or failure of an attack. The Royal Navy is also fitting a small anti-ship missile to its own helicopters for use against FPBs. Against larger Soviet ships, however, helicopters would be vulnerable to SAMs.

Smaller, Less Powerful Missiles

NATO anti-ship missiles have the advantage of presenting a small cross-section to enemy search radars, but pack a much smaller punch than their Soviet counterparts. A single hit would in all probability fail to disable a ship the size of a Soviet cruiser given the Soviet practice of fitting two launchers for each weapon system together with independent fire control systems. (In contrast the

US Navy *Belknap* would lose not only its entire AAW capability but much of its ASW capability if its single Mk 10 launcher were hit or damaged). NATO SSMs, which use blast fragmentation warheads, therefore rely on crippling the electronics of an enemy ship.

The other disadvantage suffered by NATO SSMs is the lack of an overwater area detection and targeting system such as the Soviet Ocean Surveillance System. Surface units operating away from the carrier task forces would rely more heavily on their own detection and targeting resources (eg, helicopters) than their Soviet counterparts, which would be directed to their own firing positions from a centralised command post.

Anti-Missile Defence

In terms of countering Soviet anti-ship missiles NATO does, however, possess a number of advantages. Unlike NATO SSMs the Soviet variety is virtually a pilotless aircraft. The long stand-off ranges of the anti-ship missiles carried by Soviet bombers may have taken the aircraft themselves out of range of most NATO area defence systems, but the size of the actual missiles means that even the larger Western SAMs must have a good chance of shooting them down. What the Soviets have tried to achieve with these long stand-off ranges is a low attrition rate of the parent aircraft against fighter combat patrols, enabling the maximum number of missiles to be launched. Saturation of the de-

fences, rather than the actual performance of the missiles themselves, therefore constitutes the main threat.

NATO's answer to this has been the adoption of a "layered" missile defence system on the Soviet pattern, with long-range SAMs like Standard, Seadart and Masurca backed up by point defence missile systems such as NATO Sea Sparrow, the British Seawolf and the French Crotale, with small rapid-firing guns like the US Navy's Phalanx as the last-ditch weapon. Chaff systems are also being fitted to almost all NATO warships to confuse the missile homing system.

Warships of West European navies tend to have either an area defence system or a point defence

162

▲ The British Sea Wolf missile system is extremely effective against both aircraft and anti-ship missiles.

▲ Deck launch of a US Navy lightweight Mark 46 torpedo.

▲ Mark 48 Mod 1 torpedo aboard the USS *Pargo* (SSN-650).

▲ Subroc breaks the surface at a typical angle. The mission profile of this system remains unique.

system. Operations in open ocean areas would therefore be generally performed by a group of complementary ships offering mutual protection. The need for an AAW unit able to deal virtually single-handed with saturation attacks in hostile areas such as the Norwegian Sea has resulted in the new Aegis cruiser. All Soviet and other NATO AAW ships are limited in the number of targets they can engage by the number of tracker/illuminator radars available – generally either two or four – but the Aegis ship can put any number of missiles into the air on pre-determined intercept courses and switch its four illuminators rapidly between targets in order to light up the terminal phase of the missile.

Anti-submarine Missiles
The three ASW missiles in service with NATO were developed during the 1950s and early 1960s. The American ASROC is a simple ballistic rocket with a range of 1 to 6nm (1.85 to 11km). Malafon and Ikara, on the other hand, are command-guided and can therefore adjust in flight to the latest sonar data available. Plans to develop a longer-range ASROC to complement the newer sonars were dropped in favour of the manned helicopter, and the French and British now appear to have abandoned the concept of the ASW missile for the same reason. There is, however, as yet no such thing as an all-weather helicopter – at least on destroyer-sized ships – and the anti-submarine missile therefore

continues to retain its value under severe weather conditions.

Guns and Torpedoes
There is little uniformity within NATO regarding gun requirements. The Americans and Italians retain the 5in (127mm) as their major calibre, but the American weapon is designed for simplicity and reliability while the Italian model is designed for high performance. The Royal Navy, with its 4.5in (114mm) Mk 8, has opted like the US Navy for a reliable, accurate weapon of otherwise moderate performance. The French and Germans continue to use the 4in (100mm) as their main calibre. The only gun to have attained widespread use is the OTO-Melara 3in (76mm), which has been adopted

for many FPBs and frigates to complement a main surface armament of SSMs.

Torpedo development has followed the pattern of many other weapons, with sophisticated homing heads and wire guidance generally taking over from high speed performance. The most widely-used ship- and helicopter-launched anti-submarine homing torpedo continues to be the American Mk 46, which has received numerous up-dates in its electronics. Anti-ship torpedoes in surface warships have been largely abandoned, but among those fired by submarines the American Mk 48 and British Tigerfish must be singled out as being the most outstanding examples of their type.

Mines and Mine Countermeasures

WP Mine Warfare Forces			
Type	**No.**	**Class**	**Hull**
USSR			
Ocean	65	T-43	Steel
M/S	49	Yurka	Steel
	30	Natya	Steel
Coastal	15	Sasha	Steel
M/S	72	Vanya	Wood
	3	Zhenya	GRP
	30	Sonya	Wood/GRP sheathing
	30	Yevgenya	GRP
Mine-layers	3	Alesha	
East Germany			
Coastal M/S	50	Kondor	
Poland			
Ocean	12	T-43	
M/S	12	Krogulec	
Bulgaria			
Ocean M/S	2	T-43	
Coastal M/S	4	Vanya	

▲ E. German and Polish sailors training on mines.

▲ Soviet Natya class ocean minesweeper making its way down the English Channel. Some 30 of these ships are now in service.

THE MINE has traditionally been a favoured weapon of the Soviet Navy because of its cheapness, simplicity and suitability for mass production. The Soviet Union probably has the world's largest stock of mines, and the transfer of advanced mine technology first from the United States and then from Germany during the 1940s has resulted in extensive use of acoustic, electrical and magnetic firing devices in both bottom and moored mines. There are also indications that the Soviets are developing tethered, electrical homing mine-torpedoes and wire-controlled mines.

Mine warfare strategy can be divided into "defensive" minelaying to protect one's own sea area from incursions by enemy forces,

and "offensive" minelaying to disrupt the enemy's sea lines of communication. There is ample evidence to suggest that the Russians are past masters of the former and well aware of the possibilities of the latter. Hardly any specialist minelayers are employed, but large numbers of the smaller Soviet surface units, including most of the minesweepers, are fitted with rails for this purpose.

Defence of Ports

Standard "defensive" mine-laying operations would involve defence of Soviet naval and commercial ports, especially against incursion by submarines, the protection of the flanks of Warsaw Pact ground forces against amphibious land-

ings, and support of their own landing operations. The new wire-controlled mines would be particularly useful in the first two roles, as they would be activated only in the event of enemy attack, leaving Soviet forces to manoeuvre freely under normal circumstances.

Of far greater concern to NATO countries, which would themselves be deploying defensive minefields for similar purposes, is the "offensive" use of mines by the Soviet Navy. Water depths in the sea area adjacent to N.W. Europe are generally 200ft (60m) or less. The entire North Sea, the English Channel and the Atlantic approaches to the United Kingdom and France lie above shallow continental shelf, and maritime traffic is restricted to narrow

channels in many places because of the numerous shoals and banks. It is therefore an area ideally suited to offensive mining. It is also a key area for NATO shipping, which must be able to move freely in and out of the ports of the UK and Northern Europe if the allies are to supply and reinforce their ground forces in conflict.

Submarine Mines

Offensive minelaying in this area could not, of course, be carried out by surface forces. The mines would have to be delivered by submarine or by aircraft. The NATO air defence forces, backed up by early warning radars, would hope to intercept minelaying aircraft before they could discharge their mission. The minelaying sub-

▲Soviet subs can carry up to 50 mines.

▲Soviet T-43 ocean minesweeper. Some 70 were built; about 30 remain.

▲ East German mine warfare training.

▲Sonya class coastal minesweepers are being built at about 4 per year.

▲ Soviet Navy Mi-14 (Haze) helicopter has an MCM as well as ASW role.

marine, however, would be more difficult to detect, and if undetected would lay its mines unseen.

All Soviet submarines are fitted for minelaying, and are thought to be able to replace each torpedo they carry by two mines, giving each boat a capacity of 30 to 50. Nuclear submarines would be best suited to this task, as it would involve operating where NATO ASW defences would be strongest, but SSNs would be so much in demand for open-water operations in the North Atlantic that it is unlikely that more than one or two could be spared for minelaying operations. The task would therefore probably fall to the diesel-electric Foxtrot class, which would be far more vulnerable to detection when operating close to

the surface in the North Sea.

The development of a homing mine-torpedo is a clear indication that the Soviet Navy would attempt to mine the approaches to vital naval bases such as the SSBN base on the Clyde, and this particular threat has compelled NATO countries in Europe to invest in sophisticated and expensive MCM craft to counter such operations.

Mine Countermeasures

Soviet MCM development, unlike that of NATO, has been steady and continuous, with no long periods of neglect nor any dramatic breakthrough. The Soviet Navy still operates large numbers of ocean minesweepers, the major classes being the aging T-43 and

the more recent Natya and Yurka classes. Unlike Western minesweepers they have hulls of steel or non-magnetic alloy, which are made necessary by their ancillary tasks of minelaying and ASW patrol. The coastal minesweepers generally have wooden hulls, although GRP sheathing and mouldings are more in evidence among the latest types. Many of the minesweepers operated by the Warsaw Pact allies are of Soviet origin, although the Poles and East Germans have designed and built their own ships (the ocean-going Krogulecs and the Kondor coastal minesweepers, respectively).

For minesweeping operations traditional methods are employed: the streamed-wire approach with cutting devices for moored mines,

cables or other streamed devices to produce a magnetic signature, and towed acoustic noisemakers.

Vulnerable to Mining?

No true minehunter in the sense of the word exists, although a streamed TV apparatus has been observed on a few of the latest ships. Mi-8 Hip helicopters flying from the ASW cruiser Leningrad were used in the Suez Canal clearance operation, but neither these nor the Soviet MCM vessels employed were particularly effective. This suggests that the Warsaw Pact countries themselves might be very vulnerable to offensive mining of their own harbours, especially in the Baltic, where the small West German submarines would be operating.

Mines and Mine Countermeasures

PAP 104 Minehunting System

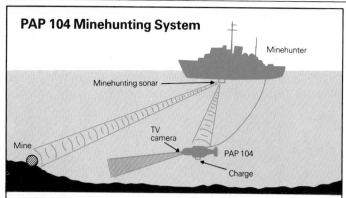

The French PAP-104 system. Following detection by sonar the submersible is guided to the mine using remote control from the mine-hunter. A demolition charge is then placed beside the mine and detonated. A TV camera is in the nose of the submersible.

▲ HMS *Nurton* (M-1166) a British Ton-class minehunter.

▲ HMS *Abdiel* was built in the late 1960s as an exercise minelayer for use in training RN minesweepers/hunters.

MINES HAVE traditionally been deployed by countries which are less dependent on maritime traffic. NATO interest in mine warfare since World War II has therefore been generally concerned with countering mines rather than laying them.

All except a handful of the minesweepers in service with the NATO allies are wooden hulled boats built to British or American designs during the 1950s. They therefore constitute practically the only example of standardisation on a large scale among the NATO navies.

The efficacy of traditional mine-sweeping tehniques has declined, however, due to the use of delay systems and ship count clocks in some of the more modern mines.

The shallowness of the European continental shelf, moreover, favours ground mines, which are at present more difficult to locate and to sweep than are the tethered variety.

Following experiments with minehunting sonars in the early 1960s a number of sweepers were converted to "minehunters", and this process is still continuing.

PAP Minehunter

The French Circé class of the early 1970s broke new ground in being fitted with two "selfpropelled fish" (PAP), which were subsequently adopted by a number of other NATO countries for use on their own minehunters. The PAP is an unmanned, retrievable vehicle equipped with a TV camera. Once

the mine has been located and classified by the ship's sonar the PAP is lowered to the spot and deposits a charge which is then detonated, with the ship being at a safe distance.

An alternative system of mine destruction is the German Troika system, in which a trio of small unmanned vessels fitted with a variety of sweep gear is controlled by a mother-ship.

The US Navy operates large RH-53 Sea Stallion helicopters for minesweeping. Helicopters have the advantage of being invulnerable to underwater blast and can therefore sweep most types of mine quickly and effectively. Their weakness lies in their low endurance, which makes them unsuited to the anti-mine patrols

for which the latest surface-vessel minehunters have been designed.

A new generation of mine-hunters is now in production to incorporate the advances of the last 25 years. Belgium, France and the Netherlands have embarked on a joint programme which should produce 40 new minehunters of the so-called Tripartite design, and Italy has ordered four of a similar type. Even more sophisticated are the British Hunt class, of which probably a dozen will be built.

All the new minehunters will have a hull of moulded GRP, giving them a low magnetic signature without the maintenance problems involved in wooden construction.

The sophistication of these vessels is such that there is no

▲ Mark 6 anchored mine about to be laid on USN exercise.

▲ RH-53D Airborne Mine Countermeasures (AMCM) helicopter.

▲ Minesweepers of NATO Standing Force Channel.

▲ RH-53D towing a "sled" to clear magnetic-influence mines in shallow waters.

NATO's Mine Warfare Forces

Minelayers

	Large	Coastal
Denmark	4	3
Norway		3
Greece		2
Turkey	1	6

Minehunters/Minesweepers

	Ocean	Coastal	Ocean	Coastal
Belgium	7	2		4
Denmark				7
Netherlands		4		14
FRG		12		28
Norway				10
Portugal				4
UK		17		16
USA			3	
France	10	5		16
Italy		4	4	26
Greece				14
Turkey				23

question of one-for-one replacement of the MCM ships built in the 1950s. They will therefore rely heavily on high technology to compensate for their lack of numbers. The British Hunt class are designed to keep an area under constant surveillance, using helicopters for resupply. A computer memory bank allied to their detection equipment enables them to detect any "foreign object" in the areas they are patrolling. Nevertheless, lack of numbers makes it questionable that more than the key naval harbours of Western Europe could be adequately safeguarded in the face of a determined Soviet campaign to mine NATO ports, and while detection of mines has become easier, clearing them is still a very slow job indeed. The most effective counter to "offensive" mining is to sink the submarine or down the aircraft before it can release its load. Air search radars and fighters, sonars and ASW ships are therefore equaly important in the battle against the mine.

Protecting NATO's Flanks

Defensive minelaying has for long featured in NATO plans for closing off the exits from the Baltic and Black Sea. Denmark, Greece and Turkey all operate specialist minelayers, while West Germany has submarines, minesweepers and FPBs capable of laying mines. Norway has mines already laid and declared in her territorial waters, and also operates specialist minelayers.

All these countries would use minefields in combination with fast attack craft, making it difficult for the enemy to penetrate them or to sweep them.

The US CAPTOR

In recent years the US Navy too has become aware of the possibilities offered by mining. As part of the anti-submarine barrier across the GIUK gap it has developed CAPTOR, which can be laid down to a depth of 1,967ft (600m) and comprises a Mk 46 homing torpedo inside a tube which is released when a submarine passes by. The deployment of large numbers of these weapons in the gap would effectively reduce the areas which NATO ASW forces would have to patrol.

Two other mines have been developed for offensive operations. The first, Quickstrike, is a modified 1,000lb (453kg) bomb for use in shallow water, its great virtue being the ease with which it can be laid by aircraft. The second, PRAM, is a tethered mine which is propelled upwards towards its target when it senses a ship passing. This mine would be moored in deeper water, out to the edge of a continental shelf.

If in the event of conflict the Western Alliance were to lose the northern battle for Denmark and Norway an aggressive NATO mining campaign in the North Sea using weapons such as these could be quickly expected to negate quickly most of the advantages gained by the Soviet Navy.

Light Forces

▲ Osa class missile-armed fast patrol boat with SS-N-2.

▲ Osa class missile patrol boats in a Baltic port.

▲ There are 14 of these Hai class patrol vessels in service with the East German Navy. All would serve in the Baltic in war.

THE TRADITIONAL emphasis in the Soviet Union on coastal defence – a philosophy that grew out of a position of maritime inferiority and the need to secure the flanks of the army – has made the Soviet Navy the world's largest operator of light attack and patrol craft.

The light forces can be divided into three distinct categories: missile attack craft, torpedo attack craft, and patrol craft. Within these broad categories there may be differences in displacement, relating to the range at which the ship is intended to operate from its base, and differences in hullform, propulsion and armament which relate to the latter consideration, to advances in technology, or to changes in weapon philosophy.

Most units serve in the Baltic and Black Sea, where their numbers are boosted by vessels with a similar role belonging to the Warsaw Pact allies. Few serve with the Northern Fleet. They are therefore deployed in almost identical fashion to the amphibious and mine warfare forces, and their missions are closely linked to the activities of both these other elements. Together with the mine warfare forces they would be responsible for protecting sea lines of communication, for coastal patrol and ASW defence of the approaches to ports, and for defence against amphibious landings by NATO forces on the flanks of the Warsaw Pact armies. For offensive missions fast attack units would operate in conjunc-

tion with Warsaw Pact amphibious forces, fending off any attempt by NATO surface units to interfere with the landings, while the larger patrol craft would give ASW protection. Offensive operations against enemy surface units and NATO sea lines of communication would be undertaken only with heavy air support unless under the cover of night.

Soviet FPBs

Soviet tactical doctrine envisages combined operations by missile- and torpedo-armed fast patrol boats. The basic missile boat remains the Osa class, of which about 120 are operational with the Soviet Navy. The SS-N-2 Styx missile carried by these boats proved relatively unsuccessful

against other FPBs in the 1973 Middle East War, but is still being fitted in a modified version to newer missile boats, suggesting that improvements may have been made in the homing system and in its resistance to countermeasures.

The Shershen torpedo boat dates from the same period as the Osa, and is fitted instead with four 533mm anti-ship torpedoes. In an attack on an enemy convoy or amphibious force the Osas would fire off their missiles at the escorts leaving the Shershens to finish off the escorts and attack their charges. Both types are fitted with only short-range AA guns and would be vulnerable both to air attack and to NATO FPBs, which have more sophisticated missiles and heavier guns. They therefore

▲ P-6 class fast patrol boats armed with torpedoes.

▲ Shershen class torpedo boats of the East German Navy.

▲ Soviet Osa I patrol boat launches an SS-N-2 Styx missile; 4 are carried.

Warsaw Pact Light Forces		
Soviet Missile Craft		
No.	Class	Weapons
2	Tarantul	4 SS-N-2
18	Nanuchka	6 SS-N-9
3	Sarancha (H)	4 SS-N-9
7	Matka (H)	2 SS-N-2
120	Osa	4 SS-N-2
Soviet Torpedo Craft		
No.	Class	Weapons
30	Turya (H)	4 TT
40	Shershen	4 TT
Soviet ASW Craft		
No.	Class	Weapons
38	Grisha	2 MBU/TT
64	Poti	2 MBU/TT
70	Stenka	TT

Warsaw Pact Allies	FPBs missile/torpedo		ASW Craft
GDR	12	50	14
Poland	13	10	13
Bulgaria	4	6	9
Romania	5	52	30

rely very much on speed and manoeuvrability for their own protection. Both the Shershens and Osas are now being superseded by hydrofoils, which are even faster.

The Sarancha-class hydrofoil is fitted with the 60nm (111km) range SS-N-9 missile, but the more recent Matka class has reverted to the Styx. This may be due in part to doubts about the effectiveness of the larger missile against NATO FPBs, allied to problems with mid-course guidance. It may, however, also be a result of Soviet concern about the weakness of the artillery of their older FPBs compared with that of the new German and Danish boats, since the Matka has been fitted with a new single 3in (76mm) mounting in compensation for her smaller complement of

missiles. Further evidence can be seen in the Turya, the hydrofoil replacement for the Shershen, which has a large twin 2.2in (57mm) mounting aft.

Larger Missile Boats

In addition to the small FPBs there are the large missile boats of the Nanuchka and Tarantul classes. The former has six of the longer-range SS-N-9 missiles, and can be regarded as the successor to the older rocket ships of the Krupny and Kildin classes. Too slow to operate with the FPBs, but better able to defend themselves against aircraft, the Nanuchkas appear to be designed to counter incursions into Soviet sea-space by enemy surface units, and have in addition seen considerable service

in the Mediterranean. They pack a big punch for a small craft but are unsuited to rough-water operations. The new Tarantul is faster, and reversion to the Styx missile allied to the fitting of a 3in (76mm) mounting suggests that these ships may be used as leaders for the smaller FPBs.

Patrol Craft

The Soviet Navy operates two types of patrol craft. The Poti and its successor the Grisha are large boats with a main armament of anti-submarine mortars and torpedoes. They would be responsible for patrolling the approaches to Soviet ports and could also undertake escort duties. The Stenka, on the other hand, is a fast patrol craft which would use

its high speed to close on suspected submarine contacts in the vicinity of Soviet harbours. It is armed with homing torpedoes and DCTs.

The most recent patrol craft, the Pauk class, employs the same hull and layout as the Tarantul class missile boats, but is armed with a single 76mm gun, homing torpedoes and two A/S rocket launchers, and appears to be a replacement for the aging Poti.

The Warsaw Pact allies all operate a system of coastal defence identical to that of the Soviet Navy. Many of the boats themselves, especially the missile boats, are of Soviet origin. Poland and East Germany use their own torpedo boats and small patrol craft; Romania uses Chinese designs.

Light Forces

▲ USS *Pegasus* hydrofoil, with 8 Harpoon SSMs and 3inch gun.

▲ Italy's Sparviero guided missile hydrofoil with Otomats.

▲ Bundesmarine Type 143 with Seal 21inch torpedo tubes.

▲ Penguin SSM launch from Norwegian Storm class missile boat, P 967 *Skud*.

▲ *Pegasus* at speed in Pacific.

WHILE THE structure of the light forces of the Warsaw Pact remains essentially that which developed in World War II – only the missile boats are a new development – the structure of the NATO light forces has only evolved in its present form over the past decade.

One of the major differences lies in the almost total absence of small ASW patrol craft in NATO navies. Turkey, which has a long Black Sea coastline to patrol, operates large numbers of small gun-armed craft, but the patrol craft operated by other NATO navies are almost exclusively for fishery protection and patrol of their Economic Zones. Many are converted minesweepers, or trawler-based designs such as the British Island

class. Generally they are armed with a small gun, but the emphasis is on seaworthiness and endurance rather than military qualities. In the event of hostilities only the five frigate-sized Danish vessels of the Hvidbjornen class, which have a small sonar and a helicopter, would be capable of escort duties, and even these have a maximum speed of only 18knots.

In coastal areas, the role of the World War II subchaser has largely been taken over by helicopters, especially the Sea King, which is fitted with a dunking sonar and its own data processing equipment.

NATO FPBs

NATO's light attack forces have also taken a different line of development to their Warsaw Pact

counterparts. Countries which at the end of World War II operated large numbers of MTBs, such as the United Kingdom, no longer have any in service (in this particular case because the enemy is no longer on the other side of the English Channel). For the NATO allies which share a border with countries of the Warsaw Pact, however, fast attack boats have become a greater necessity than ever before because of their quick reaction-time, and because of the advantages conferred on them by their small size and manoeuvrability in what are generally constricted and shallow waters. The need for a high degree of operational readiness can best be illustrated by pointing out that the distance between the Warne-

münde Naval Base in the GDR and Neustadt Naval Base in West Germany is about 30 miles (48km).

In the 1960s, therefore, West Germany, Denmark and Norway all continued to build torpedo-armed attack craft. The German *Jaguar*, the Norwegian *Nasty* and the Danish *Soloven* were all traditional designs, with four 21in (533mm) torpedoes, a pair of 1½in (40mm) AA guns, and very high speed. Many remain in service, but others have since been replaced by more modern units.

It took a single success by a Soviet Styx missile in the 1967 Middle East War to change this pattern of development, and since that time all NATO FPB designs have had a main armament of anti-ship missiles.

NATO's Fast Attack Craft					
No.	Class	Weapons			
Denmark			*Italy*		
3	Niels Juel	8 Harpoon	3	Sparviero (H)	2 Teseo
10	Willemoes	8 Harpoon	4	Freccia	2 TT
6	Soloven	4 TT			
			Norway		
France			7	Hauk	6 Penguin/4 TT
4	Trident	6 SS-12	6	Snogg	4 Penguin/4 TT
			20	Storm	6 Penguin
			12	Nasty	4 TT
West Germany					
10	Type 143	4 Exocet/2 TT	*Turkey*		
20	Type 148	4 Exocet	4	Dogan	8 Harpoon
10	Zöbel	2 TT	17	Jaguar/Nasty	4 TT
			USA		
Greece			1	Pegasus (H)	8 Harpoon
10	Combattante	4 Exocet/2 TT			
12	Jaguar/Nasty	4 TT	(H) *denotes Hydrofoil*		

▲ German Type 143. Main armament is 4 Exocet SSMs and 2 3inch guns.

▲ *Skarv*, a Norwegian Nasty class patrol boat; it can be used as torpedo boat or gunboat.

The Norwegian Hauk and Storm classes are armed with their own Penguin missile, a short-range infra-red homer with a variable trajectory. The German *Type 148* and *143* and the new Greek boats have the French Exocet, which is a horizon-range sea-skimmer. And the Danish *Willemoes* and Turkish *Dogan* have the American Harpoon, which has much longer range with a climb-and-dive final phase.

The Danish Willemoes class can replace some of their missiles with torpedoes. Many of the Norwegian boats, which carry a relatively light gun armament, have forward-firing torpedoes in addition to their missiles, while the latest German and Greek boats have two stern tubes for wire-guided torpedoes.

All the latest boats except the small Norwegian *Hauk* mount an OTO Melara 3in (76mm) gun in addition to smaller AA weapons, and this gives them an important advantage over all but the latest Soviet MPBs. They also have a superior electronic counter-measures capability, which should enable them to evade many of the missiles fired at them in combat.

Operating Procedures

Differences in operating procedures obviously reflect the different tactical needs imposed by geography. The Norwegian boats are smaller and would be scattered among the islands and inlets of Northern Norway. The Danish and German boats, on the other hand, have to operate within a much more constricted area and would probably be facing a much greater concentration of enemy surface units. They would therefore tend to operate in larger groups and would need better coordination in order to achieve maximum effectiveness. The Danish solution to this problem has been to build larger missile corvettes of the Niels Juel class armed with similar offensive weapons to the Willemoes class but with a superior radar and communications outfit, to serve as command and control ships for the FPBs. The Germans, on the other hand, have opted to put more sophisticated command and data links into the FPBs themselves using AEG Telefunken as main contractors for the Type 143 boats.

With adequate air support there can be little doubt as to the effectiveness of the new NATO fast attack squadrons. Operating at high speed between friendly minefields, or concealed among the Danish islands or Norwegian inlets, they should be able to preclude any penetration of the Baltic Straits by enemy surface units, and to disrupt any amphibious landings attempted by the Warsaw Pact. The new Greek and Turkish boats in the Aegean would also make it very difficult for ships of the Soviet Mediterranean Squadron to return to their bases in the Black Sea. Easy successes by the forces of the Warsaw Pact in these areas could be achieved only with massive air superiority. (See maps in Amphibious Warfare Forces – Warsaw Pact, page 150.)

The Balance of
AERIAL FORCES

OUTNUMBERED in front-line strength by a potential adversary who can afford apparently limitless aircraft-building programmes, NATO seems at first to be sight seriously deficient in air strength. More detailed assessment shows that the balance, although shifting in favour of the Warsaw Pact, is more even then mere numbers would suggest. NATO is currently re-equipping with aircraft such as the McDonnell Douglas F-15 Eagle and F-18A Hornet, General Dynamics F-16 Fighting Falcon and Panavia Tornado, while many East European air forces are still operating such veteran types as the MiG-19 Farmer, Su-7 Fitter or even the MiG-17 Fresco in the first years of the 1980s.

Frontal Aviation, the air arm of the Soviet Union which would come into direct conflict with the West during any conventional war on the Central Front, was massively re-equipped during the 1970s but still has no aircraft which can match the performance of the latest Western types.

Airfields Imbalance
There are currently about 170 military airfields in East Germany, Poland and Czechoslovakia, 30 of which are partly or wholly used by Soviet units of Frontal Aviation. Several hundred grass strips are also available, although their usefulness for protracted operations is questionable due to the lack of maintenance and support facilities and the soil erosion which could

be caused by protracted operations. NATO has around 69 main operating bases.

Both sides have put much effort into hardening programmes intended to protect aircraft and facilities from air attack. The Soviet programme began in 1966, and has even been extended to bases of the PVO-Strany, home-defence force in the Soviet Union. Shelters have been built for aircraft, along with underground facilities for maintenance and even for aircraft storage.

NATO and Warsaw Pact air bases are protected by gun and missile systems and attacks against such heavily defended targets would be costly in terms of aircraft and aircrew in the opening phases of a conventional conflict,

but on the NATO side there may not be enough systems or reload rounds to mount a sustained defence. The NATO defenders could eventually be overwhelmed by repeated attacks and would probably run out of ammunition in a prolonged conflict.

Although the post-1973 energy crisis has hit NATO training, aircrew still enjoy better training than their Warsaw Pact counterparts. There is probably little to choose between the standard of basic aircrew training on both sides, but marked differences at more advanced levels. Western training aims to produce an all-round pilot who can then be selected for further training in low- or high-performance aircraft, but Pact training is more specialised

172

The 1970s saw the Soviet Air Force transformed from a fair-weather defensive force with limited offensive capability into a powerful all-weather air arm able to conduct a highly sophisticated offensive. All Warsaw Pact air forces are receiving advanced Soviet aircraft to replace older equipment, while a further generation of aircraft and missiles is expected to enter Soviet service in the mid-1980s. Despite the slowly dwindling size of the NATO air forces, their superior equipment and training maintain the tactical balance between East and West, but the concern of NATO commanders is that by the end of the 1980s the Warsaw Pact may well have attained superiority.

towards the role to which the trainee will ultimately be assigned. It is possible for a Soviet pilot to spend his entire operational career flying one type of aircraft.

More emphasis is also given in the West to intensive combat-orientated training, aggressiveness and initiative being stressed, compared with Soviet-style obedience to orders.

Combat Experience

Western observers have, for several years, taken some comfort from the fact that the USAF and US Navy had large numbers of Vietnam veterans who not only possessed direct combat experience but could be relied on to pass the fruits of this to younger aircrew. Tactical exercises such as the Nellis Air Force Base Red Flag operations are preserving and honing this knowledge (and they involve non-US NATO pilots, too) but the steady turnover of US military personnel – partly a result of relatively low salaries – has seen many of these seasoned aircrew replaced by newly-trained men.

As a result of experience in Vietnam, the USAF and US Navy both established dissimilar air combat training schemes to give fighter pilots the skill required to help them survive the critical first few combat missions. The F-5E-equipped 527th Tactical Fighter Training "Aggressor" squadron based in the UK and similar USAF and USN F-5E units in the USA give pilots the experience of flying against opponents who use aircraft and tactics very different to their own. There are no known equivalent units in Frontal Aviation or any other Warsaw Pact air arm.

NATO pilots train also more thoroughly than their Warsaw Pact counterparts, flying some 20 hours per month, a level which Pact aircrew may achieve only during the summer months. A Frontal Aviation pilot may fly only on every second or third day, a total of no more than five hours per month for much of the year. Western aircrew are generally posted to specialised training units before joining their operational squadrons, but up to a third of each Soviet Frontal Aviation regiment is devoted to training.

In the past, Soviet training of aircrew has been somewhat conservative, allowing the pilot little initiative in combat. The one-pass "hit and run" tactics used by the North Vietnamese Air Force against US aircraft seem to have been typical of Soviet tactical thinking, the emphasis being on rigid pre-planned tactics rather than traditional dogfighting.

For every hour which a combat aircraft spends in the air, many man-hours must be spent by ground crews in preparing it for action. For some aircraft this back-up can amount to more than 100 man-hours per flying hour.

A Warsaw Pact aircraft is supported by fewer personnel than its Western equivalent. According to a recent report prepared by the Brookings Institution of Washington DC, the US Air Forces in

The Balance of Aerial Forces

The Air War Over the Central Front: The First Thirty Days

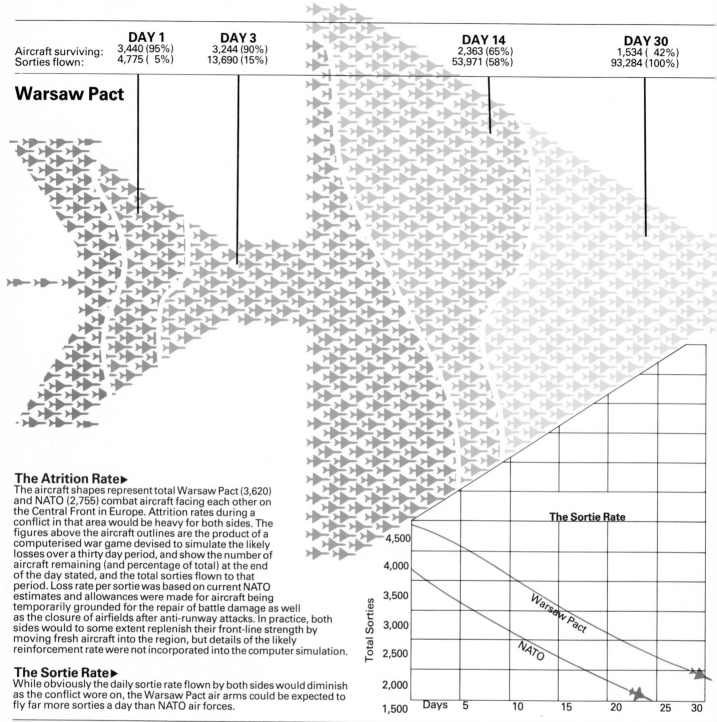

	DAY 1	DAY 3	DAY 14	DAY 30
Aircraft surviving:	3,440 (95%)	3,244 (90%)	2,363 (65%)	1,534 (42%)
Sorties flown:	4,775 (5%)	13,690 (15%)	53,971 (58%)	93,284 (100%)

Warsaw Pact

The Atrition Rate▶
The aircraft shapes represent total Warsaw Pact (3,620) and NATO (2,755) combat aircraft facing each other on the Central Front in Europe. Attrition rates during a conflict in that area would be heavy for both sides. The figures above the aircraft outlines are the product of a computerised war game devised to simulate the likely losses over a thirty day period, and show the number of aircraft remaining (and percentage of total) at the end of the day stated, and the total sorties flown to that period. Loss rate per sortie was based on current NATO estimates and allowances were made for aircraft being temporarily grounded for the repair of battle damage as well as the closure of airfields after anti-runway attacks. In practice, both sides would to some extent replenish their front-line strength by moving fresh aircraft into the region, but details of the likely reinforcement rate were not incorporated into the computer simulation.

The Sortie Rate▶
While obviously the daily sortie rate flown by both sides would diminish as the conflict wore on, the Warsaw Pact air arms could be expected to fly far more sorties a day than NATO air forces.

Europe have more than 100 people per combat aircraft, while the Soviet 16th Air Army based in East Germany has only around 70. This simple statistic does not take into account the simpler design of Warsaw pact equipment, which may need less maintenance, or the numbers of personnel in some Western air forces whose time is largely devoted to maintaining the higher standard of living which their personnel expect.

Most Soviet aircraft have a high availability rate, probably a reflection of their relatively simple design. Even the MiG-21 is reported to have a rate of up to 80 per cent (although this figure probably refers to the basic MiG-21F rather than the later all-weather versions). For the more complex aircraft such as the Flogger series, the rate may have fallen to around 70 per cent.

Liberal Safety Factors
Soviet designers apply liberal safety factors to components in order to keep maintainability high, they are reported to make more extensive use of forgings than their Western counterparts, while some of the construction techniques used differ distinctly from Western practice. Spot-welding techniques used to mount engine stator vanes to the engine casing would not meet US military specifications, for example, but produce a weight saving of almost 10 per cent.

Combat effectiveness also is reduced by the centralised maintenance system used, aircraft being returned to central depots for all major work. During the early 1970s this time-consuming procedure resulted in Warsaw Pact aircraft spending 80 per cent more time out of service than equivalent NATO types. Rather than introduce modifications gradually, the Soviet Air Force prefers to hold them for introduction into a later model. Aircraft can be reworked to later build standards, but this task would not normally be done at operational bases.

In the past, NATO planning has assumed that Warsaw Pact superiority in numbers could be overcome by the West's higher standard of pilot training and more effective aircraft. This doctrine is already being questioned as a result of the introduction in large quantities of better aircraft such as the MiG-23/27 Flogger and Su-24 Fencer as well as what may be the start of the more liberal Pact command and control techniques mentioned earlier. Indeed, it is arguable whether such an approach by NATO was ever really feasible.

Despite the claims made for advanced technology as a "force multiplier", numbers do count. The US Air Force learned much about the art of air combat during the latter 1970s AIMVAL/ACEVAL (Air Intercept Missile Evaluation/ Air Combat Evaluation) trials. Confronted by the smaller F-5E Tiger II, larger and more expensive aircraft such as the F-4 Phantom, F-14 Tomcat and F-15 Eagle did not do as well in mock combat as

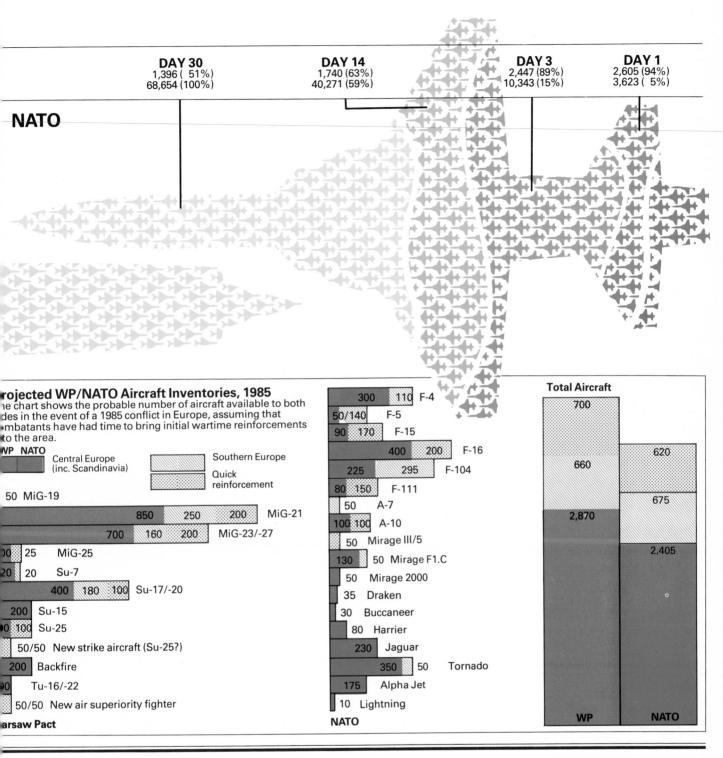

DAY 30
1,396 (51%)
68,654 (100%)

DAY 14
1,740 (63%)
40,271 (59%)

DAY 3
2,447 (89%)
10,343 (15%)

DAY 1
2,605 (94%)
3,623 (5%)

NATO

Projected WP/NATO Aircraft Inventories, 1985

The chart shows the probable number of aircraft available to both sides in the event of a 1985 conflict in Europe, assuming that combatants have had time to bring initial wartime reinforcements to the area.

Legend (WP NATO): Central Europe (inc. Scandinavia) · Southern Europe · Quick reinforcement

Warsaw Pact

Aircraft	Values
MiG-19	50
MiG-21	850 / 250 / 200
MiG-23/-27	700 / 160 / 200
MiG-25	25
Su-7	20
Su-17/-20	400 / 180 / 100
Su-15	200
Su-25	100
New strike aircraft (Su-25?)	50/50
Backfire	200
Tu-16/-22	
New air superiority fighter	50/50

NATO

Aircraft	Values
F-4	300 / 110
F-5	50/140
F-15	90 / 170
F-16	400 / 200
F-104	225 / 295
F-111	80 / 150
A-7	50
A-10	100 / 100
Mirage III/5	50
Mirage F1.C	130 / 50
Mirage 2000	50
Draken	35
Buccaneer	30
Harrier	80
Jaguar	230
Tornado	350 / 50
Alpha Jet	175
Lightning	10

Total Aircraft

	WP	NATO
	700	620
	660	675
	2,870	2,405

USAF had expected they could.

Confusion in the heat of action seems to play a greater part in deciding the outcome of an air-to-air engagement than does the technology of the participating aircraft. AIMVAL/ACEVAL suggested that most of the kills in future air combat are likely to be made at visual range. When three or more smaller aircraft take on a single opponent, the latter may well be able to pick off some of the attackers at long range using medium range missiles such as the AIM-7 Sparrow or even the long-range AIM-54 Phoenix, but once the engagement enters the visual-range phase, the aircrew of the single aircraft must attempt to keep continuous track of their remaining opponents during the manoeuvres which follow.

For the pilot of a single-seat aircraft, this task may be more difficult since he lacks the advantage of a second pair of eyes in the back cockpit to help with this task.

Multi-targeting Problems

Even when the odds are evenly matched, AIMVAL/ACEVAL suggested, Western advanced technology may not make the difference in combat which is often claimed. At no time during four-against-four engagements in ACEVAL did any aircraft manage to target a missile against all four "enemy" aircraft.

No accurate guide to the likely level of losses which both sides would experience in a Central Front conventional conflict has ever been published in unclassified form. NATO currently assumes that it can hold its loss rate down to between two and three per cent per sortie.

US experience in Vietnam has perhaps made the US Air Force and US Navy optimistic as to the likely attrition rate they would face.

Initial USAF and British reinforcements would serve to bring West European air power up to full wartime strength, but most if not all of the aircraft arriving after the outbreak of hostilities would be replacements for attrition losses. With some 60 squadrons – a total of more than 1,000 aircraft – due to arrive, how well these could be integrated with existing units is questionable. In a high-intensity conflict, incoming units are likely to be assigned to whatever country and air base could house them rather than to the locations defined by pre-prepared war plans.

In general, the NATO air forces are outnumbered by about 1.5 to 1. In the direct line of a Warsaw Pact thrust, they could face odds of as high as 4 to 1. Only the higher standard of training and better aircraft with which the West is equipped offer a chance of dealing with such superiority, but excessive faith cannot be placed in such "force multipliers". At a time when the Warsaw Pact air arms grow steadily stronger with more and better equipment, NATO cannot afford to run the risk of letting high defence costs nibble away at its front line strength.

Tactical Attack Aircraft

▲ Jugoslav/Romanian Orao which has been developed with help from Western Europe, notably UK, Italy and France.

▲ Poland was one of the first Warsaw Pact allies to operate the Su-20 Fitter.

Tactical Aircraft (Warsaw Pact)						
Aircraft	Hard-points	Max. payload pounds (kg)	Cannon	Radar	Weapon-aiming system	Radar-warning receiver
MiG-27	7	10,000 (4,500)	1×23mm	terrain avoidance	laser ranger EO system in port wing	Sirena III
SU-17/20	8	10,000 (4,500)	2×30mm	SRD-5 High Fix— terrain avoidance on Fitter D.	laser ranger on Fitter D	Sirena III
SU-24	?	10,000? (4,500?)	?	terrain avoidance (or following?)	radar + laser ranger?	Sirena III?

THE SOVIET Union is likely to commit around 1,000 aircraft to the initial wave of any conventional attack on NATO's Central Front. These would be backed up by bombers of Long-Range Aviation and aircraft from the satellite air arms. These first attacks could be expected to last for about six hours.

The attackers' first task would be to carve routes for the subsequent waves of strike aircraft through the NATO defences. Su-24, Su-17 and MiG-27 fighter-bombers would attack missile sites and radar stations with AS-9 passive-homing anti-radar missiles, electro-optical guided missiles and bombs, as well as conventional iron bombs. All these aircraft are equipped with terrain-avoidance radar, and pro-

bably terrain-following radar in the case of the Su-24 Fencer.

Range and payload performance of NATO aircraft are generally better than those of the Warsaw Pact. Estimates of the maximum payload of the Su-24 vary from 9,930 to 17,640lb (4,500 to 8,000kg), far short of 30,870lb (14,000kg) carried by its admittedly larger counterpart, the General Dynamics F-111. Maximum payload of the MiG-27 Flogger – at 9,930lb (4500kg) – compares poorly with that of the F-4 Phantom (15,876lb, 7,200kg), F-16 Fighting Falcon or A-7E Corsair II (14,994lb, 6,800kg).

These strike formations would be escorted by MiG-21 and MiG-23 fighters which would attempt to keep NATO air-defence fighters at

bay while the attackers did their job. ECM support would be given by stand-off An-12 and Tu-16 jamming aircraft.

If, or when, this was accomplished, further waves of aircraft would strike at NATO's airfields, command and control installations, fuel and weapon storage sites (particularly those for nuclear weapons), and the nuclear-armed Pershing missile wings of the West German Luftwaffe and Lance-equipped missile units of the NATO armies.

NATO bases for Pershing II and Ground-Launched Cruise Missiles might well also be targeted "just in case" although, given any degree of warning of impending attack, the missile launchers would have been moved to alternative loca-

tions which would require extensive and time-consuming reconnaissance efforts before they could be located.

More Distant Targets
While these essentially short-to-medium-range operations were underway, the Tu-16, Tu-22 and Backfire bombers of Long Range Aviation would be tackling similar targets in the UK, France and other distant areas. The bombers would be supported by stand-off jamming aircraft and MiG-23 escorts for at least part of the way, while some targets might be attacked using Su-24 fighter-bombers.

At the end of the first day, both sides could be expected to lose up to 15 per cent of their aircraft. For the rest of the conflict, Frontal

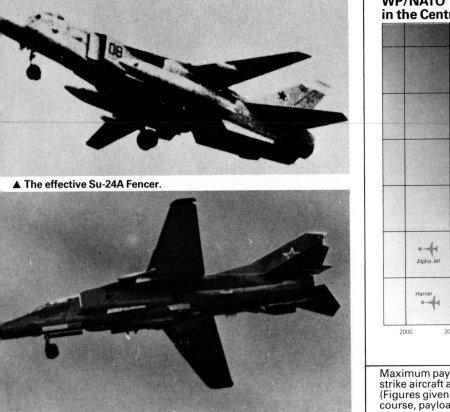

▲ The effective Su-24A Fencer.

▲ MiG-27 the ground-attack version of Flogger.

WP/NATO Tactical Attack Aircraft in the Central Region

Maximum payload and maximum tactical radius of the latest NATO strike aircraft are better than those of the current Soviet types. (Figures given are for lo-lo-lo, except where asterisked; and, of course, payloads and ranges are not possible simultaneously.)

▲ Rocket attack by the ageing Su-7 Fitter.

▲ Polish low-level fighter-bombers on patrol.

▲ Swing-wing Soviet Su-17 Fitter C.

Aviation sorties would be largely directed towards direct support of the ground operations. Even if air superiority were not won in the first day, it is doubtful if attacks on this scale would be repeated in view of the high casualties likely to have been incurred, and the disruptive effect of NATO counter-air operations. Repeat attacks would obviously be made against many of the targets hit on day one, but, as the conflict continued, Frontal Aviation would probably concentrate much of its attention on trying to maintain operations over the battlefield and disrupt any NATO counter-offensive.

No Close Air Support
It is unlikely that the sort of close-support operations which

Western ground forces take for granted would be available to support the advancing Warsaw Pact forces. The NATO ratio of ground combat units to aircraft is much higher than that of the Pact, while Soviet tactical doctrine does not make use of forward air controllers. In the West, the notion that a forward-based officer of relatively junior rank may request air strikes has long been accepted but, in the Warsaw Pact, requests for close air support must filter their way through several levels of a formal command structure. If granted, the request would result in a set-piece air operation involving a squadron of 10 or 12 aircraft or even a three-squadron air regiment – probably arriving too late to be useful.

American reports have suggested that a Soviet equivalent of the A-10 is about to enter service, designations such as "T-58" and "RAM-L" having appeared in print. A new strike aircraft is undoubtedly under development, but some intelligence sources doubt whether this is an A-10 style close-support aircraft.

Reconnaissance sorties would be flown by MiG-25 Foxbat B (photographic) and Foxbat D (radar) and MiG-21R Fishbed H (photographic) aircraft. The Yak-26 Mandrake has long been phased out, while the Yak-27 Mangrove lacks the performance required to survive in the face of modern air defence. Coverage at longer ranges would be provided by satellite, perhaps backed up by

dedicated versions of the Su-24 and Backfire.

The steady replacement of older aircraft with new types has now resulted in some 80 per cent of the front-line strength of Frontal Aviation having been replaced during the 1970s. These new-generation aircraft have some three times the payload-carrying capacity of the aircraft they have replaced and have completely changed the appearance of Frontal Aviation. From having been a fair-weather force capable of operating mainly over the battlefield, it has become an all-weather air arm capable of conducting long-range tactical air strikes. When the current rigid tactics are replaced by more flexible operating methods it will become even more effective.

▲ USAF F-111D demonstrates usefulness of camouflage at low level.

▲ US A-7 with Norwegian F-5A.

▲ Italian F-104.

▲ USAF F-4 Phantoms.

Tactical Aircraft (NATO)

Aircraft	Hard-points	Max. payload pounds (kg)	Cannon	Radar	Weapon-aiming system	Radar-warning receiver
A-7H Corsair II	8	20,000 (9,000)	1×20mm	APQ-126	(radar)	ALR-45 and -70
A-10A	11	16.000 (7,250)	1×30mm GAU-8/A	none	Pave Penny laser seeker	ALR-46 (V)
Alpha Jet	5	4,960 (2,250)	none	none	KM808 HUD plus Lear Siegler LSI 6000E gyro platform	none?
Buccaneer	4	12,000 (5,500)	none	Airpass III	(radar)	ARI 18228
Harrier	7	5,000+(2,270+)	none	none	Laser Ranger & Marked Target Seeker + FE451	ARI 18223
Jaguar	5	10,500 (4,700)	2×ADEN (UK a/c)	none	(UK) Laser Ranger & Marked Target Seeker + NAVWASS	ARI 18223
			2×DEFA (Fr. a/c)		(Fr.) Weapon-aiming computer plus CSF laser ranger	CFTH
Mirage IIIE	5	8,800 (4,000)	2×DEFA	Cyrano II	(radar)	?
Tornado IDS	7	16,000+ (7,250+)	2×27mm Mauser	Texas Instruments multi-mode	Radar plus Ferranti laser ranger/seeker	made by Elettronica

DURING an initial Warsaw Pact thrust, NATO air forces would have to attempt to slow up the advance until reinforcements could reach the front in an attempt to hold or drive back the attackers. In support of the land operations, NATO air forces would fly close-support missions, carry out strikes against second and third echelon Warsaw Pact forces moving up to the front, and attempt to pin Pact aircraft to their bases by means of anti-airfield strikes.

USAF operating methods are to some degree coloured by the experience of the Vietnam conflict. The service remains firmly wedded to the concept of fighting for and winning air supremacy over the battlefield and deep into hostile airspace. Within this doctrine, enemy air defences would be supressed by a mixture of offensive operations by "Wild Weasel" anti-radar aircraft, strikes against air bases and missile sites and the use of advanced counter-measures.

The initial mauling which Israeli aircraft received at the hands of Egyptian and Syrian SA-6 Gainful missile batteries and ZSU-23-4 Shilka guns initially did little to bring the USAF literally down to earth. Mid-1970s publicity films for the Fairchild A-10 showed the aircraft diving on targets in a way which only the virtual absence of enemy air defences would permit in reality. It is now accepted that the A-10 would spend its combat life at low level "down among the weeds", but the weather in West Germany is among the worst in Europe and it remains to be seen just how well the average A-10 pilot could navigate to his target and carry out an attack under poor conditions, given the austere avionics on his aircraft.

Drain on Resources

Even if this suppression of the defences worked, it would doubt-less be a severe drain on USAF aircraft and resources in wartime. By opting to take on the Warsaw Pact in an area where the latter enjoys considerable superiority in numbers, the USAF could end up diverting too large a portion of its resources to the battle for air superiority, at the expense of its other roles.

Most West European air forces are committed to the concept of fast low-level air strikes as a means of avoiding the hostile missiles and fighters. Defence suppression would take too long, they consider, and in any case would be too expensive a tactic in money and aircraft for smaller air arms.

Conceived as a dedicated close-support aircraft during the Vietnam War, the Fairchild A-10A Thunderbolt II is now deployed in Western Europe where it would face anti-aircraft defences far more effective than anything in Southeast Asia.

One result of its ancestry is the virtual absence of the sophisticated avionics found in most other strike aircraft. Lacking terrain-avoidance radar, the A-10A must

▲ French Air Force Mirage IIIE armed with AS.37 Martel anti-radar missile.

▲ The A-10 Thunderbolt II could spend most of its time at low level, but over WP tanks.

be flown very low, high manoeuvrability being used to make the most of terrain masking to tax the traversing ability of hostile anti-aircraft systems.

USAF aircrew are under no illusion that the large-scale use of armour and system redundancy aboard their mount makes them totally resistant to anti-aircraft fire. A light anti-aircraft missile in the class of Rapier or the Soviet SA-8 Gecko would write off any tactical aircraft if it scored a direct hit, while a good burst of cannon fire from an ZSU-23-4 Shilka self-propelled anti-aircraft gun could slice the wing clean off an A-10A or any other aircraft.

As a result of initial operating experience, the USAF has decided to fit the A-10A with a Litton

inertial navigation system and, at a later date, the Martin Marietta LANTIRN forward-looking infra-red/laser pod for all-weather and night attack use.

Once the RAF retires its Vulcan medium bombers, the UK-based USAF F-111 fighter-bombers will be longest-range deep penetration tactical aircraft available to NATO. The aircraft based in the UK are a mixture of F-111E and F-111F models. The early F-111A aircraft are being rebuilt as EF-111A electronic-warfare platforms while the F-111D serves only in the USA. Operational availability of the E and F models is generally comparable with that of any other complex weapon system, but the F-111D has acquired a reputation of being unreliable. It is reported

that in 1980 some 60 per cent of the F-111F fleet were available for use at any one time, while F-111D rate was only about 35 per cent.

Like the later F-16, the F-104 Starfighter was originally conceived as a lightweight fighter able to defeat high-performance Soviet types.

Mediterranean Air Powers

Most production F-104 aircraft were F-104G fighter-bombers, and the type provided the combat "teeth" of the Belgian, Canadian, Danish, West German, Netherlands and Norwegian air arms during the 1960s and 1970s. Now being replaced by F-16 and Tornado, the F-104 plays a less important role on the central front, but will continue to serve in the

Mediterranean area with the air forces of Italy, Greece and Turkey.

The West German decision to deploy the Alpha Jet as a replacement for the Fiat G.91 was one of the most surprising defence decisions of the 1970s. The Soviet 16th Air Army and the East German LSK on the other side of the border have no intention of using trainers as front-line combat aircraft, so the degree to which the Luftwaffe decision was based on political and economic considerations must remain a matter for speculation.

Alpha Jet is similar in size and weight to the Swedish B3LA project of the late 1970s but lacks both the engine thrust and advanced avionics and guided weapons originally planned for the Swedish

179

▲ Interestingly, Luftwaffe Alpha Jets could well be used for close-support missions on the Central Front.

▲ RAF Jaguar leaves its hardened shelter in Germany.

▲ Laser-nose Harrier GR.3 demonstrates its VTOL performance.

aircraft. One of the tasks it may handle is that of a "Hind-killer" – a method of coping with the threat posed by the Mi-24 helicopter, particularly the latest Hind E variant.

The only land-based air arm to be convinced of the usefulness of V/Stol operation, the RAF is determined not only to keep operating Harrier, but also to deploy a V/Stol successor. Current avionics are low-cost, limiting the aircraft in poor weather but the type is effective in providing close-support from the crudest of base locations.

Advanced Harriers
Production of Harrier and its Sea Harrier naval variant is expected to run until the end of 1984 on the

strength of existing orders, but British Aerospace is already proposing the "Big-Wing" Mk.5 version to meet the RAF requirement for a follow-on V/Stol fighter. This would have a new wing of 247.5sq ft (23sq m) area instead of the current 200.2sq ft (18.6sq m) and a fuselage broadly based on that of Sea Harrier. Unlike the US AV-8B project, the Harrier Mk.5 is optimised for manoeuvrability rather than for range/payload performance, since the RAF expects that future tactical fighters will have to be capable of taking on the latest patterns of Warsaw Pact fighters in air combat. The service also gave consideration to using the AV-8B fighter as a potential Harrier follow-on and a decision to adopt this aircraft was made as

this volume was in preparation.

First conceived as a dual purpose strike aircraft/advanced trainer, the Sepecat Jaguar now serves with the French Air Force and Royal Air Force as a strike aircraft. Both nations have equipped the aircraft with low-cost avionics, limiting the ability to find and hit targets in poor weather, but the RAF aircraft are better equipped than their French counterparts. British Jaguar S aircraft are fitted with digital inertial navigation/attack systems while the French Jaguar A relies on an analogue Doppler system. RAF examples are also fitted with a Ferranti laser ranger and marked-target seeker which eases the task of providing accurate delivery of ordnance in the close-support role.

Britain and France will both need to start replacing their Jaguar fleets before the end of the 1980s with an aircraft capable of fighting its way through to the target and back past the next generation of Warsaw Pact fighters. German requirements for an F-4 replacement call for a more advanced aircraft than either the British or French have in mind, resulting in the failure of the European Combat Aircraft (ECA) projected in 1980. Similar versions of the ECA proposal were under discussion in 1981 but off-the-shelf purchases seem the most likely eventual solution. Plans for Big-Wing derivatives of Jaguar have been dropped, leaving the F-18 and Mirage 2000 and 4000 as the most likely candidates for the biggest

▲ Tornado is being eagerly deployed by three NATO allies.

▲ Dassault-Breguet's private-venture Super Mirage 4000.

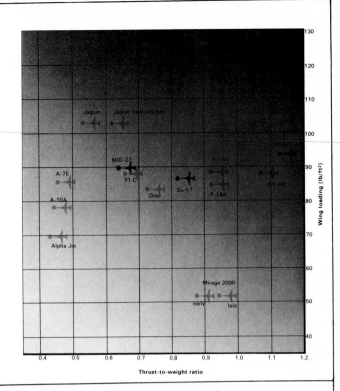

WP/NATO Strike Aircraft Compared

High thrust-to-weight ratio gives strike aircraft the ability to accelerate rapidly if "bounced" by fighters, while higher values of wing loading give a smoother ride at low level.

▲ RAF 12 Sqn Buccaneer S.2A. Some will be kept in service even once Tornado is deployed.

series of aircraft orders since Western Europe adopted the F-16.

Effective Buccaneer

With its analogue avionics, first generation turbofan engines and "coke-bottle" lines, the Buccaneer seems almost an anachronsim beside types such as the F-111, particularly when it is realised that it was ordered by the Royal Air Force as a replacement for the planned F-111K force. In practice, its relative simplicity has made it both affordable in significant numbers and free from the troubles which have dogged more complex designs. It lacks the ability to find and hit small and mobile targets, but has generally proved an effective successor to the Canberra.

So trouble-free had RAF experience with the BAe Buccaneer been, despite the type's demanding low-level role, that it came as a surprise when fatique finally reared its head in 1980 after the crash of an aircraft during Red Flag exercise. The basic cause of the problem seems to have been the greater level of stress imposed on the airframe by low-level flight over land – the type was originally developed and deployed as a naval strike aircraft. Some aircraft were grounded, repairs being considered uneconomical, but the majority will stay in service until replaced by Tornado.

No aircraft in service with NATO or the Warsaw Pact offers the same capabilities as the Panavia Tornado in so small a package. The only design to approach this level

of performance is the proposed Strike Eagle two-seat F-15 derivative. Conceived as a strike aircraft to enter service in the mid 1970s, Tornado did not enter service with training units until 1980.

During trials Tornado has clocked up indicated air speeds of 800 knots, the equivalent of 920 mph (1,480km/h). Indicated air speed is a good measure of the actual level of aerodynamic stress being applied to an airframe; most current NATO types are limited to between 700 and 750 knots (802–862mph, 1,295–1,387km/h). First low-level tests with retarded bombs suggest that weapon-delivery accuracy will be high. Radar-aimed and manually aimed 1,000lb (453kg) bombs landed on target or within a few yards, while

toss-bombing runs with weapon release taking place three miles or more (about 5km) from the target saw seven out of the nine bombs released landing within 9.8 yards (9m) of the target.

The latest generation of NATO tactical aircraft are superior in quality to those in service with the Warsaw Pact. More importantly, they are likely to be superior to whatever new tactical fighters the Soviet Union will deploy in the mid-1980s.

This edge must not only be maintained but if possible increased in the future to counter the gradual but steady improvement of Warsaw Pact military strength. If the equipment and tactics are not adequate, there will be no chance to put things right and try again.

▲ Despite the limited performance of its Spin Scan radar, the MiG-21 has been used at night.

MiG-23S Flogger B (note belly-mounted GSh-23 twin 23mm cannon). ▼

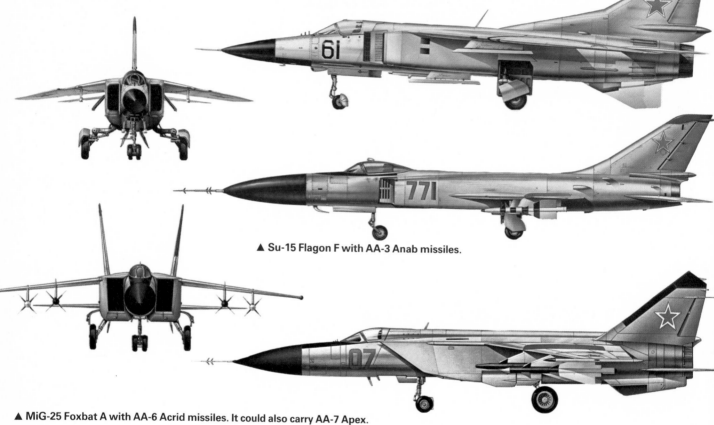

▲ Su-15 Flagon F with AA-3 Anab missiles.

▲ MiG-25 Foxbat A with AA-6 Acrid missiles. It could also carry AA-7 Apex.

ALTHOUGH no longer the most numerous Soviet Air Force fighter, the MiG-21 Fishbed is still in widespread service, particularly with the air arms of Eastern Europe. Most agile of the current generation of Soviet fighters, it is still the interceptor most likely to be met by NATO strike and close-support aircraft.

During its operational career with the Soviet Air Force, the MiG-21 has been developed through a range of designs from the earliest day-only fighters to the current multi-role versions. First version to enter widespread service was the MiG-21F Fishbed C which carried only a single 30mm NR-30 cannon and two AA-2 Atoll heat-seeking missiles. This was re-placed in the early 1960s by the all-weather MiG-21PF and PFM (Fishbed F), which carried Spin Scan fire-control radar in the in-take centrebody. Later-series PFMs carry the twin-barrel GSh-23 can-non in place of the older NR-30.

The MiG-21PFMA (Fishbed J) saw the introduction of two addi-tional wing pylons, making this the first of the family to have a use-ful ground-attack capability. The wing structure was also improved. A more powerful engine was in-stalled, making this the first variant to have supersonic (Mach 1.08) dash performance at low level.

Latest stage in the upgrading process was the MiG-21bis (Fish-bed N). This retains the Jay Bird radar, but uses the latest Tumanski R-25 engine with an extra 13 per cent of afterburning thrust. This may not be sufficient to take the aircraft into the F-16 performance class, but does give a thrust-to-weight ratio of greater than 1:1 with half the internal fuel re-maining and two AA-2 missiles carried.

Step-by-step Problems

Among potential disadvantages of the process of continuous development is that the flying characteristics of the aircraft can be affected by the growth in weight and addition of equipment. The original MiG-21F day-fighter seems to have been well-liked by pilots, but the later and heavier MiG-21MF seems to have suffered centre-of-gravity problems.

Maximum internal tankage was 572 (2,600 litres), but the rearward movement of the aircraft centre-of-gravity as fuel was burned off eventually reached the point where the fighter could not be prevented from pitching nose-up at low airspeeds.

Other reported problems include a tendency for the engine to flame out if pod-mounted un-guided rockets are fired, and a gyro gunsight which topples at 2.75g, making it virtually useless in a dogfight. The latter problem was not cured until the deployment of the third-generation MiG-21bis variant. Forward visibility is re-stricted during landing, said to be another common failing in Soviet fighters.

The MiG-23 Flogger is broadly comparable in aerodynamic and systems performance to the F-4

▲ Soviet Air Force MiG-23S Flogger interceptors.

▲ Most MiG-21s carry a pair of heat-seeking missiles.

▲ Third-generation MiG-21s carry the Jay Bird radar.

▲ MiG-23s at altitude.

Fighters (Warsaw Pact)

Aircraft	Cannon	Missiles	Hardpoints	Fire-control radar	Radar-warning receiver	Electro-optical system
MiG-21MF	1 × twin 23mm	AA-2 Atoll	5	Jay Bird	Sirena III	none
MiG-23	1 × twin 23mm	AA-2 Atoll AA-8 Aphid AA-7 Apex	5	High Lark	Sirena III	IR system reported
MiG-25	optional gunpack	AA-6 Acrid	4	Fox Fire	Sirena III	?
"Super-Foxbat"	twin?	AA-9	4?	new type	Sirena III?	?
Su-15	1 × 23mm	AA-6 Acrid	4	RP11 Skip Spin	Sirena III	?

Phantom. Like the US fighter, it was not designed as an air-superiority fighter and so would be at a disadvantage in a dogfight with aircraft such as the Mirage 2000, F-15 or F-16. It is possible that the MiG-23 was originally developed not as an interceptor but as a strike aircraft for Frontal Aviation and was only adopted as an interceptor with the gradual shift away from all-out nuclear warfare to theories of flexible response and the need to be able to fight a prolonged conventional campaign.

The High Lark radar fitted to the MiG-23S (Flogger B) has only a nominal look-down capability, but the radar fitted to the latest Flogger G version of the aircraft is much improved, giving a significant low-altitude interception capability. There seem to have been difficulties with the wing-sweep mechanism, which has reportedly jammed in the fully-swept position. Aircrew converting to the Flogger have compared its handling characteristics unfavourably with those of the MiG-21.

Flagon and Fishpot

The main Soviet interceptor for home defence is the twin-engined Su-15 Flagon, but the earlier single-engined Su-11 Fishpot remains in service in diminishing numbers. Although many analysts believe the powerplant of Flagon to be the Lyulka AL-21 turbojet or even the newer Tumanski R-29 turbofan, the more than ten tonnes of thrust of these powerplants give the aircraft a suspiciously high thrust-to-weight ratio. A more likely engine is the Tumanski R-13 turbojet used in second-generation MiG-21s. The latest Flagon E and F have additional cannon, a revised wing incorporating a cranked leading-edge and better low-altitude manoeuvrability.

The MiG-25 Foxbat interceptor can best be described as a well-conceived response to a misguided operational requirement. Foxbat remains in production, but current deliveries are being made only to Third World client states seeking the ultimate supersonic status symbol.

An aircraft referred to in American reports as "Super Foxbat" is expected to enter service in the near future. It will have a new radar with look-down capability and will be armed with the new AA-9 missile. Most sources believe it will carry a two-man crew.

Although the designation "MiG-29" has been widely circulated as that of a Soviet fighter in the class of the F-16, there is still no firm evidence that such an aircraft exists. At least two new fighter types are known to be on trial at test establishments and may have been accepted for service. One, thought to be a product of the Mikoyan bureau, is similar in size and configuration to the McDonnell Douglas F-18 while a larger aircraft, perhaps from the Sukhoi bureau, is virtually a Soviet F-14. Both are likely to enter service by 1985.

Fighter Aircraft

▲ Relatively simple yet effective – the Mirage F1.C

▲ F-16A (left) and F-16B, seen from TF-104G front seat.

▲ Some RAF Phantoms, still potent, will remain in service until the late 1980s.

▲ French Mirage 2000.

I N AIR-to-air combat NATO would hope to avoid dog-fighting with MiG-21s and MiG-23s but would try to pick off as many of the attackers as possible at long range using weapons such as AIM-7 Sparrow and Sky Flash. So long as the Pact relied on the heat-seeking AA-2 Atoll missile, such tactics were viable, since the Soviet missile could only be used to make attacks from astern of the target. With the deployment of Soviet "all-aspect" air-to-air missiles, the result of such engagements is often a one-for-one stand-off in which the Western aircraft might well destroy its victim but is itself destroyed by the latter's missile.

In order to break out of this impasse, NATO needs a medium-range "fire-and-forget" missile which will allow the launch aircraft to break off after launch, thus avoiding coming under attack itself. Such a weapon is already in the early stages of development under the joint USAF/US Navy AMRAAM (Advanced Medium-Range Air-To-Air Missile) programme, and is due to enter service late in 1985.

Europe's Fighters

At first sight, the Dassault-Breguet Mirage F1.C seems an uninspired design, lacking the new techno-logy which puts the latest US fighters in a class of their own. Although far short of the standard of the Mirage 2000, when teamed with the Super 530 missile it has given the French Air Force an

interceptor capable of bridging the gap between the Mirage III and the latest delta offering. Thrust-to-weight ratio may be modest and the wing loading higher than ideal, but the basic aircraft is not much different in this respect to the MiG-23 Flogger. Within NATO only France and Greece operate the type, the chances of a massive NATO order having been frustra-ted by the success of the F-16.

Much more impressive is the newer Mirage 2000. Designed basically as an interceptor, the Mirage 2000 has a better perform-ance, particularly at low altitude, than the Mirage III or F.1C. Prob-lems with the air-interception radar have delayed service de-liveries of what is for the moment Western Europe's answer to the

F-16 and of course to whatever the Warsaw Pact forces will field as a MiG-21 replacement. A thrust-to-weight ratio of better than unity at combat weight coupled to a wing loading as low as that of any of its high-performance contemporaries makes this an aircraft which, in the hands of a good pilot, should be able to cope with fighters such as the MiG-21bis.

Tornado ADV

The latest interceptor developed by the European NATO nations is the Tornado Air Defence Variant (ADV). Developed by Panavia from the basic Interdiction/Strike Tor-nado to meet a Royal Air Force requirement, the aircraft is being built by all three project partners. Tornado ADV – to be known as the

▲ F-15 Eagle: probably the world's hottest fighter.

Fighters (NATO)

Aircraft	Cannon	Missiles	Hardpoints	Fire-control radar	Radar-warning receiver	Electro-optical system
F-104S	1×20mm	Sidewinder Sparrow Aspide	9	R21G/H	EL-70	none
F-4E	1×20mm	Sidewinder Sparrow	9	ABQ-120	several types possible	Tiseo (some)
F-14	1×20mm	Sidewinder Sparrow Phoenix	6	AWG-9	ALR-45 or -46	TCS (some)
F-15	1×20mm	Sidewinder Sparrow	5	APG-63	ALR-56,	AAR-38 IR warning receiver
F-16	1×20mm	Sidewinder	7	APG-66	ALR-69	None
F-18A	1×20mm	Sidewinder Sparrow	9	APG-65	ALR-67	None
Mirage F1.C	2×30mm	Magic Super 530	7	Cyrano IV	BK	None
Mirage 2000	2×30mm	Magic Super 530	9	RDI	new system	?
Tornado F.2	1×27mm	Sidewinder Sky Flash	8	"Fox Hunter"	Marconi Avionics	Visual Augmentation System (VAS)

Tornado F.2 in RAF service – is intended as an interceptor for the identification and destruction of intruders into UK airspace. It was not developed as an agile "dog-fighter", but intensive studies have confirmed that it will be able to hold its own in air combat against the MiG-23 Flogger. When it enters service in the mid-1980s, it will replace the Royal Air Force's surviving Lightning force, then the F-4 Phantoms.

Main armament is a quartet of Sky Flash missiles carried semi-recessed beneath the fuselage in the type of mounting first popularised with the F-4 Phantom. These are backed up by an internal cannon and AIM-9L Sidewinder missiles carried on the sides of the underwing pylons.

In order to make room for the Sky Flash missiles, the fuselage was stretched by 53in (1.34m). This provided two useful bonuses. The modified fuselage can carry an estimated 1,400lb (640kg) of extra fuel, while the increase in length, coupled with the effect of a more pointed nose radome, has increased the fineness ratio, thus decreasing supersonic drag.

Wing sweep is varied automatically according to aircraft speed and angle of attack. There are three normal positions – fully forward, 45 degrees and fully swept. The fly-by-wire flight-control system includes a spin-prevention system.

Production of the McDonnell Douglas F-4 Phantom ended in 1978, despite the company's

tentative plans for a new F-4T air-superiority version. Aerodynamically, the Phantom was hardly the perfect fighter, with less than optimum handling characteristics when heavily loaded at low level. As a fighting machine, however, it turned out to be the right aircraft at the right time, bearing the brunt of the air-to-air combat during the Vietnam War, providing the Israeli Air Force with a fighter to more than match the MiGs and Sukhois it met in the 1973 Yom Kippur War, and serving with five of the NATO air forces.

Modernising Phantoms to 1980s Standards

During its long production run the aircraft was fitted with a wide range of air-interception radars.

Most aircraft now carry the Westinghouse AWG-10 or APQ-120. Unlike the more modern sets on the F-15 and F-16, these have only a limited look-down capability. The F-4E was the first NATO fighter to carry a long-range electro-optical viewing system to help the aircrew identify targets at beyond visual range.

Several operators are reworking their aircraft to keep them effective through the 1980s. Lear-Siegler reworked USAFE F-4s to add the AN/ARN-101 digital navigation and attack system, while the US Navy and Marine Corps are re building their F-4J fleets to the F-4S standard to maintain the effectiveness of their aircraft until F-18A strength builds up. These aircraft will be fitted with

▲ Turkey and Italy both use the F-104S interceptor, the only variant of the type to carry Sparrow missiles.

▲ Like the earlier F-104G, the F-16 Fighting Falcon is being licence-built in Western Europe.

manoeuvring slats and the improved AWG-10A radar. Luftwaffe RF-4E Phantoms are being reworked to give them a secondary air-to-ground role.

Since entering operational service in 1974, the McDonnell Douglas F-15 Eagle has remained the highest-performance fighter in the world. The MiG-25 may have recaptured the world record for climb-to-height, but remains essentially a manned missile with minimal manoeuvring capability.

Despite this level of performance, or perhaps due to it, the F-15 has suffered a range of minor teething troubles. Shortage of technicians with F-15 experience, and low reliability of the built-in test equipment and some items of ground-based test equipment,

have affected operational readiness. There have been development problems with the Pratt & Whitney F100 turbofan, partly a reflection of the engine's high performance. At one time, only some 35 to 40 per cent of the available F-15 fleet were usable at any one time, but this has now risen to around 80 per cent.

US Lead in Avionics

Production of the F-15 will continue through the early 1980s, the USAF now having a total of 765 on order, having added 36 more in the Fiscal Year 1982 budget to keep the force up to strength for three years longer than originally planned. Few other aircraft so convincingly demonstate the American lead in aircraft avionics, particularly in

the fields of airborne radar and signal processing. At a time when the Soviet Union is just bringing into service its first airborne radars with a genuine look-down capability, the pilot of the latest F-15C/D variant is receiving an improved version of the Hughes APG-63 radar. Doppler beam sharpening techniques made possible by the addition of a programmable digital signal processor give a much higher resolution in air-to-ground mapping mode, and provide a "raid assessment" mode capable of discriminating between individual targets in a tight formation at long range. Track-while-scan performance and improved electronic counter-countermeasure performance are promised for the future.

In its present form, the General Dynamics F-16 Fighting Falcon has only a limited all-weather capability, causing the USAF to reconsider the build standard of its planned second batch. Greater payload/range performance, more internal avionics space and an improved radar are all considered desirable by the USAF. One of the type's weaknesses as initially deployed is the lack of a radar-guided air-to-air missile. The aircraft currently carries only the heat-seeking AIM-9L Sidewinder. Sparrow and Sky Flash test rounds have been fired from a YF-16 prototype, and trials have determined the optimum location for such relatively large weapons which will produce the lowest drag. In practice, any future armament-

▲ USAF F-4 "intercepts" Soviet Tu-16 Badger.

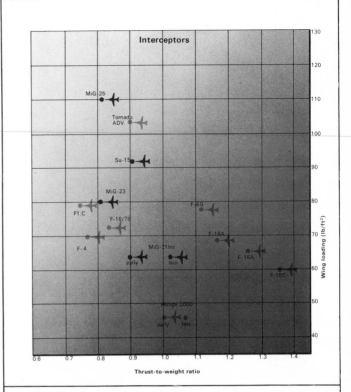

Interceptors

Thrust-to-weight ratio (x-axis: 0.6 0.7 0.8 0.9 1.0 1.1 1.2 1.3 1.4)

Wing loading (lb/ft²) (y-axis: 40 50 60 70 80 90 100 110 120 130)

MiG-25
Tornado ADV
Su-15
MiG-23
F1.C
F-16/75
F-5G
F-4
MiG-21bis
F-18A
early   late
F-15A
F-15C
Mirage 2000
early   late

WP/NATO Interceptors Compared

The best fighters for air-to-air combat are those with a high thrust-to-weight ratio and low wing loading. At the present time NATO types are generally better than those of the Warsaw Pact.

▲ The RAF will be strengthened with Tornado interceptors.

▲ The new F/A-18 may be deployed from land bases.

upgrading programme is more likely to rely on the AMRAAM missile which will pack Sparrow performance into a missile not much heavier than Sidewinder.

Although developed as a carrier-based aircraft, the McDonnell Douglas F-18A Hornet has already been sold as a land-based aircraft to Canada and has been offered to several other NATO nations. The aircraft is already acquiring a reputation of being easy to fly.

Minor development problems with the aircraft have received much publicity, particularly in the US technical press, but fixes are already in hand. The aircraft already exceeds US Navy speed requirements, having attained Mach 1.9 rather than the specified Mach 1.7.

It is claimed that, starting from low speeds, the F-18A can out-accelerate the F-4, F-14 and F-15 until higher speeds are reached. This suggests that the aircraft will be an excellent dogfighter – a role in which good low-speed acceleration is a must.

Back in the early 1950s, USAF pilots flying F-86 Sabres were able to maintain a kill ratio of 10:1 or better against the MiG-15. By the late 1960s, the trend had swung the other way, with the North Vietnamese Air Force winning a 1.15:1 kill ratio against the USAF. Such figures do not automatically indicate that the F-4 Phantom was less effective than the MiG-21, since the US Navy was able to maintain an edge over the NVnAF throughout the same conflict, partly by

means of better training methods such as the "Top Gun" training scheme. In Vietnam, the US air arms never found themselves faced by large numbers of opposing fighters but had to cope with small numbers of MiGs using "hit-and-run" tactics. In a Central Front conflict, NATO pilots are likely to be faced with large numbers of opponents, so Phantoms might well score a better kill ratio over the MiG-21.

NATO's Technological Lead

With the current generation of fighters, the West has been able to maintain or even increase its technological supremacy over the Soviet bloc. The F-15 Eagle has many more performance advantages over the MiG-23 Flogger than

the F-4 has over the MiG-21. Given the level of training resulting from dissimilar air combat exercises pilot skills may well match the aircraft performance.

NATO is a defensive alliance, so an attacker would be able to make his own choice of battleground, deploying his forces so as to achieve the heavy numerical advantage which Soviet tacticians favour. In order to break even, NATO fighter pilots would have to win an exchange ratio of 4:1 or better. Even the best aircraft and pilots are powerless if ammunition is not available to cope with this intensity of operations, and it is disturbing to note that stocks of late-model Sparrow and Sidewinder missiles are well below the NATO planned requirements.

Transports and Tankers

▲ The An-12 Cub is the Soviet equivalent of the C-130 Hercules.

▲ An-72 Coaler Stol transport.

▲ Tu-16 demonstrates the Soviet "wing-tip-to-wingtip" refuelling system.

▲ An-12 Cub.

▲ Soviet paratroops prepare for a jump.

▲ An-22 Cock.

MILITARY Transport Aviation, the Soviet Air Force equivalent to the US Military Airlift Command has some 1,700 aircraft – sufficient tactical transport strength to airlift an airborne division complete with all equipment and sufficient supplies for three days over distances of up to almost 1,120 miles (1,802km).

On at least three occasions, Soviet airlifts have tipped the balance of power in Third-World conflicts. The best-known case is probably the supply of weapons and ammunition to Egypt and Syria during the 1973 Yom Kippur War. According to US sources, a fleet of around 220 An-12 and An-22 transports delivered 15,000 tons of materiel.

Soviet transport aircraft are generally of simple but robust construction, always sacrificing something in performance to reduce the requirements for maintenance. The largest types such as the Il-76 and An-22 carry extra personnel whose task is basic maintenance, allowing the aircraft to operate away from its home base for several months.

Rough Airstrip Operations

Some types eschew such features as pressurisation which would be standard on Western aircraft, but all have large and rugged undercarriages, often with more wheels than a Western designer would use. As a result, these aircraft can operate into and out of the roughest of airstrips.

The same basic type is usually supplied both to the air force and to Aeroflot, the state-run airline. This reduces the number of types which the industry must produce, and provides Long-Range Aviation with both a source of reserve aircraft and crews and a "cover" for military operations.

Most of the current Soviet bloc military transports are products of the Antonov design bureau. The most numerous is the An-12 Cub, a four-engined aircraft similar in concept but inferior in performance to the US C-130 Hercules. Maximum payload is around 44,100lb (20,000kg) but the cargo compartment is unpressurised, limiting the cruising altitude and thus the effective range if passengers are carried. Like most Soviet military transports it is supplied both to the air force and to Aeroflot, the state-run airline. This reduces the number of types which the industry must produce, and provides Long-Range Aviation with both a source of reserve aircraft and crews and a "cover" for military operations.

Most of the current Soviet bloc military transports are products of the Antonov design bureau. The most numerous is the An-12 Cub, a four-engined aircraft similar in concept but inferior in performance to the US C-130 Hercules. Maximum payload is around 44,100lb (20,000kg) but the cargo compartment is unpressurised, limiting the cruising altitude and thus the effective range if passengers are carried. Like most Soviet military transports it is fitted with tail armament – two 23mm cannon. The Gamma rearward-facing radar mounted just above the gunner's position at the base of the tail fin provides tail warning, while the chin-mounted Toad Stool radar is used for navigation.

The only Warsaw Pact members to operate the An-12 are Poland (45) and the Soviet Union (approx. 600), but the smaller An-24/26 Coke/Curl series is in service with Bulgaria, Czechoslovakia, East Germany, Hungary, Poland and the Soviet Union. The An-24 Coke is the military version of the civilian An-24 airliner, while the An-26 Curl is a specialised military derivative with a tail ramp. Both are powered by the Ivchenko AI-24 turboprop, but the latter is fitted

▲ The world's third largest aircraft, the An-22 dwarfs the jet-powered Tu-124.

▲ The Il-76 Candid is used by the Soviet Air Force and (often militarily) Aeroflot.

with the uprated -24T version. "Hot and high" performance of the An-24 series has been widely criticised by users. The eventual Soviet solution to this problem was perhaps the ultimate triumph of brute force over the law of gravity, and probably the most drastic up-engining to which any airliner has been subjected. In place of the two 2,820hp Ivchenkos, the An-32 mounts two of the same bureau's 5,180hp AI-20M engines. Ground clearance for the larger propeller is provided by mounting the engine in over-wing pods rather than under-wing as on the An-24/26.

At least some of the An-24/26 fleet is being replaced by the twin-turbofan An-72 Coaler which first flew in 1977. The first jet-powered aircraft from the Antonov bureau,

it bears a superficial resemblance to the Boeing YC-14 transport. It is powered by two high bypass-ratio Lotarev D-36 turbofans which blow air back over the wings and trailing edge double-slotted flaps to give increased lift, while the wing is also fitted with triple-slotted flaps on the outboard sections and full-span leading edge slats.

Soviet designers traditionally prefer to use simple wings with a minimum of complex slots or flaps, but in the case of the An-72 the move towards complexity has paid off. The aircraft can lift payloads of up to 16,537lb (7,500kg) out of 3,934ft (1,200m) runways. As is normal with Soviet military transports, the cargo hold has a built-in hoist.

Deliveries of the giant An-22 Cock transport have ended but the aircraft has already made its mark on world affairs by flying Soviet weaponry to Third-World client states. It is still the only Soviet transport capable of air-lifting main battle tanks.

New Transport
At least one Soviet design bureau is known to be working on a heavy transport in the class of the C-5 Galaxy. US sources have quoted the designation "An-40" but this has never been confirmed.

More than 100 Il-76T Candid transports have now entered service with the Soviet Air Force, replacing some of the An-12s. This aircraft is the Soviet equivalent to the USAF C-14 Starlifter. The

massive 20-wheel undercarriage and built-in cargo-handling equipment allow it to operate from the most primitive airstrips, taking part in operations such as the 1977 airlift of Soviet weaponry to Ethiopia. The cargo hold is pressurised and can carry loads of up to 88,200lb (40,000kg).

Standard in-flight refuelling tanker of the Soviet Air Force is the Tu-16 Badger. There is still no evidence that the Soviet Union is developing a tanker version of the Il-86 wide-body airliner. At present only the long-range bombers and maritime patrol aircraft use airborne refuelling, but the technique could greatly expand the range of the Su-24 Fencer should this aircraft be fitted with a refuelling receptacle.

Transports and Tankers

▲ USAF's C-5A Galaxy is likely to remain in service until the end of the century.

WP/NATO Transport Aircraft

Aircraft	Maximum range nm (km)	Maximum payload pounds (kg)	Take-off run ft (m)	Landing run ft (m)	Undercarriage Nose	Main
C-5A Galaxy	3,100 (5.740)[1]	245,000 (111,000)	8,000 (2,400)	2,950 (900)	Quadruple	4 × 6
C-130H Hercules	2,100 (3,890)[1]	43,500 (19,700)	4,700 (1,400)	1,750 (530)	Twin	2 × 2
C-141B Starlifter	2,780 (5,150)[1]	74,200 (33,650)	5,000 (1,500)	1,900 (580)	Twin	2 × 4
G.222	2,670 (4,950)[2]	19,840 (9,000)	2,170 (660)	1,790(545)	Twin	2 × 2
Transall C.160	2,750 (5,100)[3]	35,300 (16,000)	2,950 (900)	2,300 (700)	Twin	2 × 2
DHC-5D Buffalo	1,770 (3,280)[4]	18,000 (8,150)	950 (290)	550 (170)	Twin	2 × 2
AN-12 Cub	1,832 (3,395)	44,100 (20,000)	2,790 (850)	2,820 (860)	Twin	2 × 4
AN-22 Cock	5,900 (10,932)	176,350 (79,886)	3,300 (1,005)		Twin	2 × 6
AN-26 Curl	1,200 (2,223)	12,100 (5,481)	2,600 (792)	2,400 (731)	Twin	2 × 2
An-32 Cline	1,200 (2,200)[2]	13,200 (6,000)	1,650 (550)	?	Twin	2 × 2
An-72 Coaler	1,730 (3,200)[2]	16,500 (7,500)	1,550 (470)	?	Twin	2 × 2
Il-76T Candid	3,500 (6,500)	88,000 (40,000)	2,800 (850)	1,500 (460)	Quadruple	4 × 4

1. At maximum payload.　2. With maximum fuel.　3. With airborne refuelling.　4. With no payload.

TRANSPORTS and tankers may not make the headlines but they are an essential component of NATO air strength, allowing men and material to be moved quickly to where they are most required. Sea transportation still plays a major role in US planning but only the use of long-range transport aircraft can provide the flexibility necessary to respond to the unexpected.

America's strategic airlift capability was developed by the demands of the Vietnam War. Up till that time, the US Army made relatively little use of long-range airlifting and the USAF lacked the ability to handle the likely wartime requirements. The concept received its first real test in 1973 when over a period of one month

22,000 tons of weaponry and ammunition were flown from the United States to Israel by less than 600 aircraft sorties. By the time that this airlift was fully underway, fighting was focussed on the Sinai Front. C-5 Galaxy transports were able to deliver equipment directly to airfields in Sinai where Israeli troops were waiting to take it straight into combat. Modern military formations are profligate consumers of suppliers. A Lockheed report drawn up in the 1970s indicated that to move four US Army divisions, plus existing bases in the USA and West Germany to bases in Iran involved transporting a total of around 150,000 personnel and almost 400,000 tons of cargo.

Most of the huge USAF transport

fleeet is permanently based in the continental USA, less than 50 C-130s normally being assigned to overseas locations such as Western Europe and the Western Pacific.

Transports at Risk

The use of airlift strength to support movements into a distant theatre of war depends on nations whose territory must be overflown en route giving clearance to the flights, including landing rights for any refuelling which may be necessary. At the other end, local air superiority is essential since heavily laden transports would be an easy target for even the simplest fighters. The growing number of Backfire bombers in Soviet Air Force strength also raises the possibility that modified versions

of this aircraft could be used to attack NATO transports en route for Europe in wartime. Such a move would force the NATO allies to divert fighters and tankers to the task of escorting the transports.

Several nations are currently rebuilding all or part of their existing transport fleets, or even reopening production lines. The process of stretching transport aircraft represents an attempt to make the best use of its performance. Many military loads are bulky, but relatively low in density. As a result, the aircraft cargo compartment can often be completely filled while take-off weight remains well below its maximum limit. Stretching the cargo compartment thus allows more cargo to be carried without exceeding

▲ A C-5A can carry up to 270 personnel.

▲ Like the WP, NATO plans using airliners for trooping.

▲ Luftwaffe C-130D Transall operating from roads.

▲ Take-off of a French C-160F.

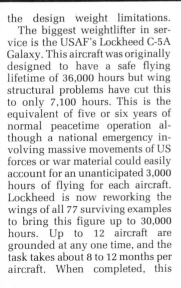

▲ C-130 in low-level delivery of a Sheridan light tank.

▲ C-130s line up for take-off at Dyess AFB, Texas.

the design weight limitations.

The biggest weightlifter in service is the USAF's Lockheed C-5A Galaxy. This aircraft was originally designed to have a safe flying lifetime of 36,000 hours but wing structural problems have cut this to only 7,100 hours. This is the equivalent of five or six years of normal peacetime operation although a national emergency involving massive movements of US forces or war material could easily account for an unanticipated 3,000 hours of flying for each aircraft. Lockheed is now reworking the wings of all 77 surviving examples to bring this figure up to 30,000 hours. Up to 12 aircraft are grounded at any one time, and the task takes about 8 to 12 months per aircraft. When completed, this programme should allow the C-5A to remain in service at least until the end of the century. Given new avionics and engines, the C-5A could continue to serve into the first decade after that.

The USAF would like to procure an additional 50 transport aircraft, but the chances of this being funded are minimal. The service has expressed a requirement for a new CX transport to supplement the C-5A fleet. Like the Lockheed aircraft, it would be designed for long-range missions, but would have only a secondary tactical role, perhaps with reduced payload.

Civil Airline Fleets

Although American civil airlines own more than 350 wide-body transport aircraft, only some 50 of these are convertible passenger/freight models or all-cargo versions. By the mid-1980s a further 100 wide-bodies are likely to enter service. These aircraft, particularly those equipped to carry freight, could be a valuable supplement to NATO's airlift capability. Under the USAF's Civil Reserve Air Fleet (CRAF) scheme, airlines could be recompensed for the additional purchase and running costs of convertible passenger/cargo aircraft. Initial airline reaction has been cool, but the USAF would like to see 30 aircraft involved in the CRAF programme by the mid-1980s. The European NATO allies also intend to make some of their civil airliner fleets available for use in any emergency reinforcement of Western Europe.

The C-130 Hercules has virtually become the standard NATO medium-range transport, being in service with Belgium (12), Canada (28), Denmark (3), Greece (12), Italy (12), Norway (6), the UK (61) and the USA (more than 1,000). Despite its age, this 25-year-old design is still being produced at a rate of three per month, and is likely to remain in production through the 1980s. Britain has decided to "stretch" the fuselage of half of its C-130 fleet by adding two new sections which increase its length by 14.7ft (4.5m). This modification increases the capability of the C-130 fleet by the equivalent of eight more aircraft.

Lockheed now offers all-new Hercules with this modification under the designation C-130H-30.

Transports and Tankers

▲ C-141A Starlifter unloading M113-series tracked vehicle.

▲ Veteran KC-135 tanker will remain in service for decades.

▲ Victor, RAF's standard tanker, refuels Jaguars.

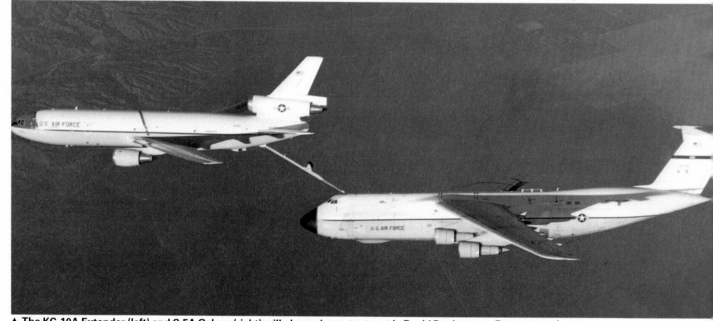

▲ The KC-10A Extender (left) and C-5A Galaxy (right) will play an important part in Rapid Deployment Force operations.

The modification allows 40 per cent more palletised cargo to be carried.

Although the use of paratroops could only be contemplated against an unsophisticated enemy, or against an opponent whose anti-aircraft defences have been considerably blunted to the point where the likely aircraft losses would be acceptable, Britain has decided to re-introduce a limited parachute-assault capability. The C-130 fleet will be equipped with navigation aids to help with station-keeping in a tight formation and the aircrew will be trained for this role. The goal of the project is to give the RAF the capability to drop a battalion group within 15 minutes.

Like the C-5A and C-130, the Lockheed C-141A Starlifter is currently the subject of a reworking programme. All 285 USAF examples are being stretched by 24.26ft (7.4m) and given air-refuelling capability. By mid-1982, the entire fleet will have been converted to this C-141B standard, giving the USAF a capacity increase equivalent to 90 additional aircraft. Use of air-refuelling will extend the range, making the USAF less dependent on overseas governments during large-scale air movements of men or materiel in pursuit of US national interests.

NATO's Tankers

The standard USAF tanker since the late 1950s has been the Boeing KC-135. Rather than attempt to replace these aircraft, the USAF hopes to keep them operational into the next century by a process of structural rebuilding and replacement of the present noisy and fuel-inefficient Pratt & Whitney turbojets on the earliest models with GE/Snecma CFM56 turbofans. An improved fuel dispensing system capable of reducing refuelling time by 25 per cent will also be fitted. France also operates 11 of the 12 KC-135s originally purchased to support the Mirage IV bomber force, while Canada has two tanker-capable CC-137s – military versions of the basic Boeing 707 airliner – which are used to support the CF-5 fighter fleet. In an emergency, two squadrons of CF-5s would be moved to Norway.

To supplement the KC-135s the USAF plans to operate up to 20 KC-10A Extender tanker/cargo variants of the DC-10 airliner. Delivery of the first KC-10s was originally scheduled for the autumn of 1980 but this slipped to early 1981 due to minor problems with the flight refuelling system. The digitally controlled "flying boom" can operate over a greater range of flight conditions than earlier systems, and can deliver more than 1,232 gallons (5,600 litres) of fuel per minute. Once operational, the Extender fleet would be able to deliver to Western Europe in only three days enough cargo to support more than 200 F-15 Eagles.

The availability of a large tanker fleet and fighters equipped for airborne refuelling gives the West an important tactical edge over the

192

▲ C-141 StarLifter drops US paratroops.

▲ Canadian DHC-5D (C-8B) can operate from dirt strips.

▲ Italy is the only NATO nation to operate the G222. Here, paratroops leave in a stick.

Soviet Union if military support must be given to a distant ally. USAF and RAF fighters can be flown directly to where they are required, assuming that any necessary overflying rights can be obtained. The Soviet Union must negotiate landing and refuelling rights somewhere en route, or send the aircraft by sea or air as cargo.

Airlift and RDF
The United States, and to a lesser degree Britain and France, maintain military interests in areas outside of the official NATO boundaries. Britain and France maintain a minimal ability to transport forces over long distances, but the US Rapid Deployment Force set up in 1980 is intended to give the US an ability to intervene in the

Middle East, Africa or Asia with anything from a small unit of Rangers to several Army and Marine divisions supported by air and naval forces.

Airlift strength is critical to RDF operations, since the initial light components of a Rapid Deployment Task Force would be flown into the area to establish an immediate US involvement. In countries where the internal communications are poor, RDF units may rely on aircraft for tactical movements of personnel and supplies.

European Stop-gap Measures
In addition to the C-130 fleet mentioned earlier, the Royal Air Force operates limited numbers of several other transports, most

important of which are eleven VC10s. Most of the fleet of BAe 748 Andovers have now been disposed of, a few remaining as short-range and VIP transports.

The current British tanker is the Victor K.2, but the 24 aircraft of this type which currently serve are being supplemented by nine VC10 K2 tanker derivatives of the now-retired VC10 airliner. The RAF has purchased the last surviving civil VC10s for cannibalisation as a source of spares.

A tanker fleet of this size will help the service maintain long-range patrols of Tornado F.2 (ADV) interceptors and Nimrod Mk.3 AEW early-warning aircraft, both critical to the task of monitoring air and surface movements through the eastern section of the strate-

gically important Greenland-Iceland-UK gap.

France and West Germany have re-opened the Transall production line to meet a French requirement for an additional 25 aircraft of improved standard. These C.160F aircraft will have air-refuelling capability and additional fuel tanks in the wing centre section. Transall currently serves with only two NATO nations, France (48) and West Germany (89).

Similar in configuration to the Anglo-French aircraft is the Aeritalia G.222, a lighter design which has been sold within NATO only to the Italian Air Force (205 aircraft). Sales of the Fokker F.27 Troopship within NATO have likewise been confined to the nation of origin, with only 10 examples in service.

Aircraft Armaments

WP/NATO Aircraft Gun Capabilities												
Aircraft	Weapon (and ammo weight)	Rounds per second										
		10	20	30	40	50	60	70	80	90	100	110
A-10A	GAU-8A (0.37kg)											
F-14, F-15 F-16, F-18	M61 (0.35kg)											
Jaguar, Mirage	Aden/DEFA (0.25kg)											
MiG-21bis	GSh-23 (0.2kg)											
MiG-27	23mm Gatling (0.2kg)											
Su-7/Su-17 Su-20	NR-30 (0.4kg)											

Aircraft cannon effectiveness is related to the number of rounds fired per second and the projectile mass. In this drawing, the size of the projectiles is proportional to their mass.

▲ Almost obsolete AA-1s on MiG-1

▲ Warsaw Pact "Iron" bombs.

▲ AA-5 Ash is carried only by the Tu-28P Fiddler interceptor.

THE weapons which arm Warsaw Pact aircraft are in many cases inferior to those in service with NATO. This technological gap is reflected even in such relatively simple hardware as aircraft cannon. After World War II, Soviet designers continued to produce slow-firing aircraft cannon of conventional pattern, ignoring the rotary-breech principle devised by Mauser and the US use of multi-barrel Gatling guns.

Like many Western air forces, the Soviet Air Force may have questioned the continuing usefulness of cannon for air-to-air combat with the arrival of guided missiles. Early MiG-21 Fishbed A fighters were equipped with two NR-30s, but the production Fishbed C version carried only one cannon.

When a new Soviet fighter cannon finally appeared, its configuration came as a surprise to the West. Service introduction of the MiG-21 Fishbed J saw the first use of the twin-barrelled 23mm GSh-23, a weapon thought to result from collaboration between Nudelmann and Kalashnikov, the veteran designer of small arms. The GSh-23 is an unusually compact weapon with short barrels, but it is reported to be effective in combat. Rate of fire is around 3,000 rounds per minute, about halfway between that of a single-barrelled cannon and that of Gatling-type weapons.

Since Czarist Russia was a user of the original Gatling gun – duly re-named the Gorloff Gun after the officer who was responsible for its adoption and local production – it

was hardly surprising that a Gatling-type weapon finally appeared on the MiG-27 Flogger D. This weapon retains the 23mm calibre of the GSh-23, although a 30mm Gatling is reported to have been developed for a new ground-attack aircraft. The Soviet Union has already deployed 30mm Gatlings; weapons of this calibre (and not 23mm as commonly assumed) are used for point defence of Soviet warships.

Missile Designs

In the development of air-to-air missiles, Soviet designers were more bold, although the earliest designs fielded were of limited effectiveness. First Soviet air-to-air guided missile to see operational service was the AA-1 Alkali, a

200lb (90kg) missile which was used by MiG-17, MiG-19 and Su-9 all-weather interceptors. This obsolete weapon used beam-riding guidance, a system not adopted for operational air-to-air use in the West. Maximum range was around 5 miles (8km). Alkali may have given the Warsaw Pact air arms valuable experience in the field of air-to-air missiles, but aircrew must have been glad to retire it once better weapons appeared.

Similar in appearance to the US AIM-9 Sidewinder, the AA-2 Atoll is the most widely used Soviet air-to-air missile. Two Soviet designations have been reported – K13A and SBO6. Like the US missile on which its design may have been broadly based, Atoll uses passive infra-red guidance, although a

▲ AA-3 Anab (on Su-15) was widely deployed on Soviet interceptors.

▲ Radar-guided AA-5 Ash missiles.

▲ Performance of the AA-6 Acrid (here on MiG-25s) is lower than its size might suggest.

Warsaw Pact Air-launched Missiles

Designation	Role	Guidance	Range nm (km)	Warhead lb (kg)
AA-2 Atoll	air-to-air	IR	2.7 – 3.8 (5 – 7)	13 (6) HE
AA-3 Anab	air-to-air	IR or SAR	8.5+ (16+)	HE
AA-5 Ash	air-to-air	IR or SAR	16 (30)	HE
AA-6 Acrid	air-to-air	IR or SAR	IR: c. 27 (50) SAR: c. 12 (22)	HE
AA-7 Apex	air-to-air	IR or SAR	IR: c.8 (15) SAR: c.18 (33)	90 (40) HE
AA-8 Aphid	air-to-air		IR: c.3.5 (7) SAR: c.8 (15)	13 (6) HE
AA-9 ?	air-to-air	SAR?		?
AS-4 Kitchen*	air-to-surface	inertial?	up to 170 (320)	nuclear
AS-5 Kelt*	air-to-surface	active radar		
AS-6 Kingfish	air-to-surface	inertial + radar seeker?	120 (220	200 kT nuclear
AS-7 Kerry	air-to-surface	radio command	5 (10)	HE
AS-9 ?	air-to-surface	passive radar seeker	c.50 (90)	HE

*Unlike other missiles quoted here, Kitchen and Kelt are liquid-propellant rockets; all others are (or are believed to be) solid-propellant rockets.
IR = passive infra-red; SAR = semi-active radar

semi-active radar-homing version has been reported. An improved AA-2-2 version has been fielded in an attempt to overcome some of the deficiencies. By the mid-1980s a further-improved version with an all-aspect seeker head is expected to enter service.

Most other Soviet air-to-air missiles were developed to arm interceptors rather than air-superiority fighters. All second-generation types apart from Atoll are very much larger and heavier than the equivalent weapons in NATO service, giving Soviet interceptors the appearance of being armed with more lethal weaponry than their Western counterparts. In practice, these large missiles have a lower accuracy than would be considered acceptable in weapons

such as Sparrow. Their size is dictated partly by the size of warhead carried in order to make up for the deficiencies of the guidance systems.

The AA-3 Anab and AA-3-2 Advanced Anab are the standard air-to-air missile armament for a wide range of Soviet interceptors such as the Su-11 Fishpot and early-model Su-15 Flagon. This missile is available in radar or infra-red guided versions and operates in conjunction with the Skip Spin air-interception radar. This trio of second-generation weapons was completed by the even larger AA-5 Ash which arms only the Tu-28P Fiddler.

Three missiles make up the third generation of air-to-air guided weapons. Replacement for the

AA-2 is the infra-red guided AA-8 Aphid, which may be a derivative of the earlier weapon. Intended to serve as a "dogfight" missile, it is carried by the MiG-23 Flogger and may be fitted to late-model MiG-21 Fishbed fighters. Standard weapon for the MiG-23S is now the AA-7 Apex, a Sparrow-class missile optimised for medium and low-altitude use. Like most Soviet air-to-air missiles, it is available in radar or infra-red guided versions.

High-altitude Missile

No photographs of Apex have been published, while the only photograph of the Aphid seen in print is of very poor quality. Better data is available of the third member of this group, the AA-6 Acrid. Carried by late-model Su-15 Flagon inter-

ceptors and by the MiG-25 Foxbat, Acrid is probably optimised for high-altitude use. Its performance seems low for a weapon of this size, maximum range being only 72 to 80 miles (45 to 50km) for the radar version and 32 to 40 miles (20 to 25km) for the infra-red version – extremely modest when compared to that of the much lighter AIM-54 Phoenix.

All of these weapons seem to be a great improvement over their predecessors, being smaller, lighter and presumably more accurate than earlier types. Broadly comparable with the last generation of NATO missiles, they will play a major role through the 1980s. Development of their replacements is already well in hand, with several known to be on flight test.

195

Aircraft Armaments

▲ Three NR-30 cannon arm a Bulgarian MiG-19.

▲ The NR-30 in action on a Soviet Su-7 Fitter.

▲ Ground crew train by arming an Il-28.

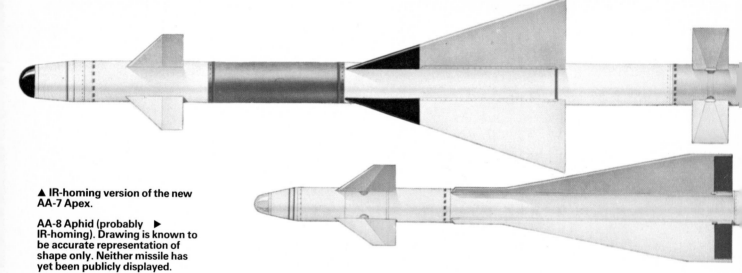

▲ IR-homing version of the new AA-7 Apex.

AA-8 Aphid (probably ▶ IR-homing). Drawing is known to be accurate representation of shape only. Neither missile has yet been publicly displayed.

The first fourth-generation weapon to begin trials was the AA-9, shortly to enter service with the "Super Foxbat". This has carried out a successful series of "snapdown" missile attacks against drone targets and will give the Soviet Union a significant shootdown capability for the first time.

During trials at Vladimirovka in the Soviet Union, a "Super Foxbat" was observed to engage drone targets flying below 1,000ft while remaining at a cruising altitude of 20,000ft. On one occasion the drone was flying at less than 200ft. Maximum range of the AA-9 is dependent on launch altitude. At height, it can cope with targets up to 28 miles (45km) away during head-on attacks, but this progressively falls to 25 miles

(40km) at medium altitudes and 14 miles (22.5km) at low altitude. Tail-chase engagements cut the range performance even more, maximum engagement range being anything from 3 to 6 miles (4.8 to 9.6km).

These performance variations in no way reflect on the quality in design. Similar limitations will be familiar to the users of any air-to-air missile, but details are normally classified. In the case of the AA-9, the performance figures were published via the magazine *Aviation Week and Space Technology*.

By 1984, two further air-to-air missiles may have entered the Soviet inventory. Like the AA-9, the AA-XP-1 has a good snapdown performance and can be used in attacks from any direction

out to a range of 21 miles (33.8km) at high altitude, and 12 miles (19.3km) at low altitude. The AA-XP-2 offers even more range – up to 43 miles (69.2km) at high altitude, 24 miles (38.6km) at low. No predicted in-service date is available for the final fourth-generation weapon. This is understood to be an infra-red homing "dogfight" weapon in the class of Magic and the AIM-9L.

Air-to-ground Missiles

Soviet (air-to-ground) missiles have until recently been relatively large weapons primarily for anti-ship use. No equivalent to the US Bullpup or French AS.20/30 series was deployed in the 1950s or 1960s, despite the relative simplicity of such weapons. The

earliest Soviet air-to-ground missiles such as the AS-1 Kennel, AS-2 Kipper, AS-3 Kangaroo all used turbojet powerplants and were virtually pilotless aircraft. Kennel and Kangaroo may even have been derivatives of the MiG-15 and Su-7 respectively. Kipper was similar in appearance to the now-retired USAF Hound Dog missile. All may have been intended primarily for anti-ship use.

The AS-5 Kelt armed the Tu-16 Badger G, while the AS-4 Kitchen served on the Tu-22 Blinder B. Both were large weapons powered by liquid-propellant rocket motors. Although similar in configuration to the AS-4, the AS-6 Kingfish is a new design with a much higher accuracy than any of the earlier members of the "AS-"

▲ Sukhoi interceptor fires a practice missile.

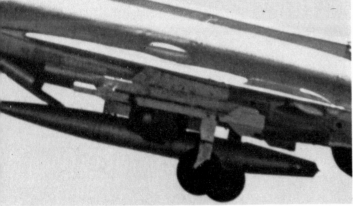

▲ The AA-2 Atoll has been widely exported.

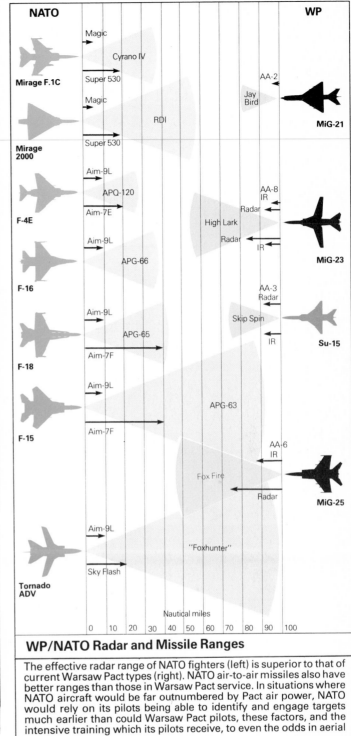

NATO										WP

Mirage F.1C — Magic →, Cyrano IV, Super 530

Mirage 2000 — Magic, RDI, Super 530

F-4E — Aim-9L →, APQ-120, Aim-7E

F-16 — Aim-9L →, APG-66

F-18 — Aim-9L →, APG-65, Aim-7F

F-15 — Aim-9L →, APG-63, Aim-7F

Tornado ADV — Aim-9L →, "Foxhunter", Sky Flash

MiG-21 — AA-2, Jay Bird

MiG-23 — AA-8 IR, Radar, High Lark, Radar, IR

Su-15 — AA-3 Radar, Skip Spin, IR

MiG-25 — AA-6 IR, Fox Fire, Radar

Nautical miles

0 10 20 30 40 50 60 70 80 90 100

WP/NATO Radar and Missile Ranges

The effective radar range of NATO fighters (left) is superior to that of current Warsaw Pact types (right). NATO air-to-air missiles also have better ranges than those in Warsaw Pact service. In situations where NATO aircraft would be far outnumbered by Pact air power, NATO would rely on its pilots being able to identify and engage targets much earlier than could Warsaw Pact pilots, these factors, and the intensive training which its pilots receive, to even the odds in aerial combat.

series. Probably designed to arm the Backfire, AS-6 seems to have suffered from development problems. When the big swing-wing bomber entered service, it carried the older AS-4. Now AS-6 is carried by Backfire and at least one version of the Tu-16 Badger.

First missile for battlefield use seems to have been the command-guided AS-7 Kerry, a weapon broadly in the class of the Anglo-French Martel. This serves as interim armament on the Su-24 Fencer. Early reports of electro-optical "smart" weapons have mentioned the designations AS-8 and AS-10 for a Hellfire-class missile to arm helicopter gunships but these may be early references to the laser-guided AT-6 Spiral tube-launched weapon which now arms

the Mil Mi-24 Hind D helicopter. More recent reports suggest that the AS-10 is a Maverick-class missile carried by the MiG-27, Su-17 and Su-24. Reported to be some 10 feet (3m) length and powered by a solid-propellant rocket motor, it has a cruising speed of Mach 0.8 and a range of six miles (9.6km). A long-range weapon combining inertial and electro-optical guidance is reported to be under development but its existence has never been confirmed.

A wide range of free-falling bombs are available, newer models being fielded to replace earlier types. High-explosive weapons in the FAB series range from 220 to 2,200lb (100 to 1,000kg) in weight, while a new series of ordnance for the delivery of incendiary and

chemical munitions has entered service to replace earlier weapons. First deliveries of fuel/air explosive munitions took place in the mid-1970s. A wide range of cluster bombs has been deployed, including the PTAB and RPK series. Anti-runway "concrete dibbers" are available in two sizes – 550 to 1,100lb (250 and 500kg).

"Smart" Bombs

No specific details of "smart" bombs are available, although the Su-17 Fitter, Su-24 Fencer and MiG-27 Flogger are all equipped to carry four or more, while the use of tandem store pylons may have allowed six or more to be carried. Guidance is probably by means of a semi-active laser seeker.

Soviet tactical nuclear weapons

have a higher yield that their NATO equivalents. According to *Jane's Weapon Systems*, a 2,200lb (1,000kg) weapon with a yield of around 350 kT is being replaced by a 1,540lb (700kg) weapon of 250 kT yield.

Given the wide range of ordnance listed above, the Soviet pilot is unlikely to find himself facing a task for which there is not a weapon available. The performance of his equipment may often be inferior to that used by NATO, but the hardware is likely to be available in sufficient quantity to permit lavish use. Being fully standardised throughout the Warsaw Pact, weaponry at any one base is likely to be suitable for re-arming visiting aircraft (except, of course, more advanced types in Soviet service).

Aircraft Armaments

▲ Most AIM-7 Sparrow rounds are used to arm the F-4, but the missile is also carried by types such as the F-14, F-15 and F-16.

▲ French Beluga sub-munitions dispenser on Alpha Jet.

▲ Earlier Sidewinders can be rebuilt to AIM-9J standard.

▲ The A-10's GAU-8/A 30mm gun intended for anti-tank use.

▲ Super 530 offers good snap-up/snap-down performance.

THE variety of aircraft-mounted weaponry available to NATO is far in advance of that used by the Warsaw Pact. US commentators often speak of the need to get "more bang per buck" out of the US defence budget, but NATO can already claim to get "more bang per pound (or kg)" than its potential opponents. One inevitable price it rhas paid in so doing is that of questionable reliability in the case of some advanced weaponry.

The standard US aircraft cannon is the 20mm General Electric M61 Gatling gun. Capable of firing at rates of up to 6,600 rounds/minute, this weapon has led to the development of a range of Gatling guns from 5.56mm calibre up to 30mm which have armed US fixed-

wing aircraft and helicopters. European designers have been more conservative, relying on the single-barrel rotating breech concept pioneered during World War II by Mauser. This principle has been used to produce the 30mm ADEN (UK) and DEFA (France) cannon as well as the 27mm Mauser cannon developed for use on Tornado.

Air-to-air Missiles

In the field of air-to-air missiles, NATO fields a wide range of weapons, many of which have been combat-tested.

Attempts to replace the veteran AIM-9 Sidewinder have failed, new versions keeping this weapon effective while its intended replacements fall by the wayside.

The two most important current versions are the AIM-9L and AIM-9J, an improved and rebuilt version of the earlier AIM-9B and -9E.

The J version has a higher-impulse motor and improved infra-red seeker and servos. These changes have resulted in better manoeuvrability and improved performance against modern afterburning aircraft. The L was a more drastic re-design, with double-delta canard control surfaces, an advanced homing head of high sensitivity incorporating a self-contained closed-cycle coolant system and an improved blast-fragmentation war-head with a laser fuse.

The L standard is being further improved to produce the AIM-9M which has a better performance in

the face of countermeasures or the potential distraction of hot background terrain. The USAF took delivery of the first AIM-9P versions at the beginning of the decade. This has a rocket motor which produces less smoke than earlier patterns.

The only real rival to the latest Sidewinder versions is the Matra R.550 Magic dogfight missile. Capable of being fired from ranges as short as 984ft (300 metres), Magic can carry out successful interceptions when released from aircraft pulling up to 6 g.

During the Vietnam conflict, the AIM-7E Sparrow acquired an unenviable reputation for unreliability. Study of combat reports shows the degree to which pilots relied on closing to short range and

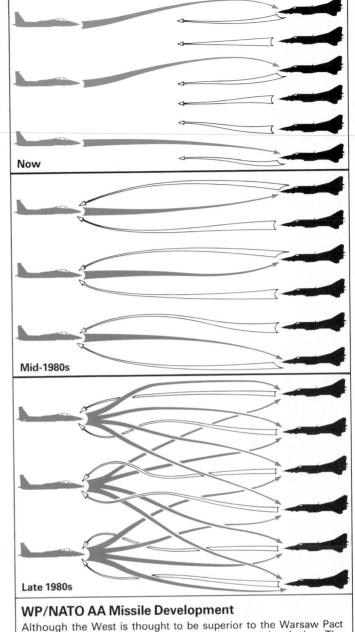

Now

Mid-1980s

Late 1980s

WP/NATO AA Missile Development

Although the West is thought to be superior to the Warsaw Pact nations in missile technology, that gap is seen to be closing. The diagrams show that (top) at present NATO's aircraft, though outnumbered, could use long range missiles to pick off their out-ranged Warsaw Pact rivals, reducing the odds before close-range combat begins. But once the Pact is similarly equipped with long-range missiles (centre), NATO aircraft, still out-numbered, would be brought under superior firepower. When NATO fighters become armed with such "fire-and-forget" missiles as AMRAAM (bottom) the odds could be evened up again.

▲ Experimental SRAAM heat-seeking "dogfight" missile.

▲ The F-16 is armed with AIM-9L Sidewinders.

using the heat-seeking AIM-9 Sidewinder or even gunfire. Part of the problem seems to have been inadaquate maintenance and handling procedures.

Newer AIM-7F is an all-aspect weapon with a maximum effective range of 28 to 34 miles (45 to 55km). Minor problems were reported when it first entered service, such as accidental disconnection of the motor firing cable and a tendency for the safe/arm system to return to the "safe" position, but these have now been overcome. The greatest weakness is probably the continued use of conical-scanning in the seeker head, since this technique is known to be vulnerable to electronic countermeasures (ECM).

Raytheon has now completed development of the further-improved AIM-7M missile, which incorporates a monopulse seeker, digital signal processor, new auto-pilot and new proximity fuse. This is expected to have a better resistance to electronic counter-measures and performance against low-level targets.

European Developments

Faced with the need to develop a new medium range missile during the 1970s, both Italy and the UK adopted Sparrow as the starting point for new designs. The British Aerospace Sky Flash is based on the AIM-7E but has a strengthened airframe low-drag wing profile and an all-British guidance and control system incorporating a monopulse seeker. Selenia's Aspide has an

improved motor and guidance system, complete with a mono-pulse seeker. Sky Flash entered Royal Air Force service in the late 1970s, but Aspide first saw service in the surface-to-air role and only started air-to-air trials in the early 1980s.

Once again, France developed an indigenous weapon, the Matra Super 530. This semi-active radar homing missile can carry out "snap-up" and "snap-down" attacks against targets flying 22,953ft (7,000m) above or below the launch aircraft. Shoot-down ability should be greatly improved when the missile enters service on the Mirage 2000.

If NATO is to continue to rely on stand-off beyond-visual-range tactics, then new missiles are re-quired. The obvious limitation of Sparrow-class weapons for future combat against Soviet fighters armed with all-aspect air-to-air missiles may have sped Britain's decision early in 1981 to abandon the planned Sky Flash Mk 2.

The prime candidate to replace Sparrow and Sky Flash is the US AMRAAM. The weapon is intend-ed to have full fire-and-forget performance, and will combine strap-down inertial mid-course guidance with an active radar seeker for terminal guidance. A high-impulse solid-propellant rocket motor will reduce flight time and the whole weapon will be smaller than Sparrow. AMRAAM is due to enter operation service late in 1985 and could be adopted as a NATO standard weapon.

▲ AIM-54 Phoenix has a range of more than 100 miles (160km).

▲ AJ. 168 Martel passive-homing anti-radar missile.

▲ AGM-65A Maverick demonstrates its accuracy.

▲ Sky Flash AAM is based on the US AIM-7E Sparrow.

▲ F-14A with pairs of AIM-54A, AIM-7F and AIM-9G.

▲ AIM-54A Phoenix operates in conjunction with AWG-9 radar.

According to an intergovernmental Memorandum of Understanding, Britain and West Germany are to develop an Advanced Short-Range Air-to-Air Missile (ASRAAM) to enter service in the late 1980s or early 1990s. This again would be adopted as a NATO standard weapon, with the US building rounds under licence for its own use.

Unmatched Phoenix
No other missile can match the impressive range of the Hughes AIM-54 Phoenix. This US Navy weapon can cope with targets more than 124 miles (200km) away from the launch aircraft. Originally developed for the F-111B fighter project of the mid-1960s, the basic AIM-54A version arms US Navy

F-14 Tomcat fighters. At the same time as the latter's AWG-9 radar is being updated by the addition of a digital programmable signal processor, Hughes is developing the improved AIM-54C Phoenix which will have a digital autopilot and signal processor, plus a new proximity fuse and solid-state transmitter/receiver.

The US industry has developed several "smart" air-to-ground missiles, but the rest of NATO has been slow to adopt these as replacements for earlier weapons such as the Bullpup. Almost 100 Hughes AGM-65 Maverick rounds have been fired in combat with a success rate of over 80 per cent. The A and B versions use TV guidance, while the D version uses an imaging-infra-red seeker system more

suited to conditions in Europe. Development of the semi-active laser guided C version has led to the improved E version due to be adopted by the US Marine Corps.

Guided flight tests of the Aerospatiale AS.30L laser-guided missile have been successful and the company has prepared the weapon – which operates in conjunction with the ATLIS II laser designator pod – for production to arm French Air Force Jaguars. France is also developing the ASMP nuclear-armed air-to-ground missile for tactical attack. This ramjet-powered weapon is due to enter service in the mid-1980s.

The Vietnam War saw the combat debut of electro-optically guided "smart" bombs. First-

generation weapons included the Hughes-Martin Marietta AGM-62 Walleye and Texas Instruments Paveway series. Currently under development is the GBU-15 which exists in two versions – the Rockwell Cruciform-Wing weapon for use against point targets and the longer-range Hughes Planar-Wing variant for use against area-defence systems and other high-value targets.

Two problems to which NATO is paying particular attention are methods of attacking armoured formations and airfields. In order to reduce the numerical strength of a hostile armoured column, a weapon capable of taking out several vehicles during a single pass is required. According to the US Department of Defense, an air-

▲ France plans to deploy the Matra laser-guided bomb.

▲ A direct hit from an AGM-84A Harpoon missile (launched here from an A-7) would cripple all but the largest of warships.

▲ The French Durandal rocket-propelled anti-runway weapons.

NATO Air-launched Missiles

Designation	Role	Guidance	Range nm (km)	Warhead lb (kg)
R.550 Magic	air-to-air	IR	10+ (18+)	27.5 (12.5) HE
AIM-54 Phoenix	air-to-air	SAR + active radar terminal homing	108+ (200+)	132 (60) HE
AIM-9 Sidewinder	air-to-air	IR	5 – 10 (10 – 18)	HE
Sky Flash	air-to-air	SAR	up to 25 (50)	66 (30) HE
AIM-7 Sparrow	air-to-air	SAR	-7E: up to 25 (50)	66 (30) HE
			-7F: up to 50 (100)	88 (40) HE
Super 530	air-to-air	SAR	18 (35)	HE
AS.30	air-to-surface	command (30L: semi-active laser)	6 (12)	506 (230) HE
AGM-85A HARM	air-to-surface	passive radar	10 (18.5)	HE
AS-37 Martel	air-to-surface	passive radar seeker	16 (30)	330 (150) HE
AJ-168 Martel	air-to-surface	passive radar seeker	16 (30)	330 (150) HE
AGM-65 Maverick	air-to-surface	-65A & B TV homing -65D semi-active laser homing -65E imaging infra-red	12 (22.5)	130 (59) hollow-charge HE or 300 (135) HE
AGM-45 Shrike	air-to-surface	passive radar seeker	8.5 (16)	146 (66) HE
AGM-78 Standard ARM	air-to-surface	passive radar seeker	13 (25)	HE
AGM-62 Walleye*	air-to-surface	TV plus command	?	Walleye I; 850 (385) Walleye II; c.2000 (900)

*Unlike the other missiles quoted, Walleye is unpowered.

craft armed with cluster bombs – the current NATO solution – can expect to knock out only 0.5 tanks per sortie. The use of high-accuracy weapons such as Maverick or the GAU-8/A cannon on the A-10 may account for between one and three AFVs per sortie, but this is still an expensive method of dealing with the armoured threat.

The Wide Area Anti-Armour Munitions (WAAM) programme is intended to produce weapons capable of killing six to ten AFVs per sortie. Three approaches are under consideration – the Anti-Armour Cluster Munitions (ACM), the Extended Range Anti-Tank Mine (ERAM) and the Wasp mini-missile.

Britain's planned anti-armour weapon was the Hunting Engineering VJ291 guided cluster bomb, intended for attacking targets on either side of the launch aircraft's flight path from ranges of 13,116 to 26,232ft (4,000 to 8,000m). VJ291 would have armed RAF Tornado, Jaguar and Harrier but was cancelled due to delays and trials shortcomings. Germany has developed the MW-1 sideways-firing sub-munitions dispenser.

Heavy Air Defences

Attacks against airfields are made hazardous by the heavy concentrations of anti-aircraft weaponry which normally protect such high-value targets. Britain and the USA funded the Hunting Engineering JP233 sub-munition dispenser which will scatter "concrete-dibber" bomblets to break up runway surfaces and other bomblets intended to delay repair operations. Although Britain intends to deploy JP233 in the mid-1980s, USAF is openly sceptical of the survival chances of any aircraft assigned the task of overflying a Warsaw Pact runway in the late 1980s, so it was hardly surprising that the service withdrew from the JP233 project in 1981. Like JP233, the Matra Durandal runway-penetration bomb relies on the launch aircraft overflying the target. Along with the smaller Thomson-Brandt BAP bomb, it has been tested by USAF, who may be looking for an interim anti-runway weapon. Britain remains committed to the JP233.

Britain, West Germany and the USA are currently studying manoeuvrable sub-munitions dispensers which would allow stand-off attacks to be mounted against runways, but this work is at an early stage. The US Navy has pulled out of the planned Medium-Range Air-to-Surface Missile (MSARM) project, a planned air-to-ground variant of the Tomahawk cruise missile which the US Air Force intended to use as a long-range anti-airfield weapon.

To back up the weapons listed above, the NATO allies are armed with a wide range of conventional bombs and unguided rockets. These are supplemented by a range of free-falling nuclear weapons including the B3 (US), Green Parrot (UK) and AN-52 bombs.

Glossary of Terms

A

AA
Anti-aircraft.

AA-
NATO designations for Soviet air-to-air missiles (eg, AA-2).

AAA
Anti-aircraft artillery.

AAM
Air-to-air missile.

AAW
Anti-aircraft warfare.

ABM
Anti-ballistic missile. A missile capable of destroying hostile ballistic missiles or their payloads before they impact on their target.

ABM Treaty
Effective from 3 October 1972, the ABM treaty limits the deployment of ABM systems to two sites in each of the USA and USSR. One site is the national capital and the other an ICBM field. No more than 100 launchers and 100 missiles are allowed at each site. There are also limits on associated radars. (See also SALT.)

Accidental war
War which occurs without deliberate design.

ACE
Allied Command Europe (NATO).

ACLANT
Allied Command Atlantic (NATO).

Active
Emitting its own electromagnetic signals, eg, in a missile. (See also *Passive.*)

Active defence
Use of armed forces to protect friendly assets.

ACV
Air cushion vehicle, also known as hovercraft.

AEW
Airborne early warning.

AFCENT
Allied Forces Central Europe (NATO).

AFB
Air force base (US).

AFNORTH
Allied Forces Northern Europe (NATO).

AFV
Armoured fighting vehicle (tanks, armoured cars, etc).

Aggregate
A term used in SALT (qv) referring to the overall total of ICBM launchers, SLBM launchers, heavy bombers and ASBM (qv).

AGS-
Automatichesky Granatomat Stanovky: automatic grenade launcher (eg, AGS-17). (USSR).

ALBM
Air launched ballistic missile.

ALCM
Air launched cruise missile.

AP
Armour piercing.

APC
Armoured personnel carrier.

APDS
Armour piercing discarding sabot, a high velocity sub-calibre anti-tank round.

APFSDS
Armour piercing, fin stabilised, discarding sabot. An APDS (qv) round but with fin stabilisation.

AS-
NATO designations for Soviet air-to-surface missiles (eg, AS-7).

ASAT
Anti-satellite interceptor.

ASBM
Air-to-surface ballistic missile. A ballistic missile launched from an aircraft against a target on the Earth's surface.

ASM
Air-to-surface missile.

Assured destruction
Ability to inflict unacceptable damage on an aggressor or combination of aggressors, even following a surprise first strike.

ASU-
Aviadesantnya Samakhodnaia Ustanovka: airborne self-propelled carriage (eg, ASU-85). (USSR).

ASW
Anti-submarine warfare. All measures designed to reduce or nullify the effectiveness of hostile submarines.

AT-
NATO designations for Soviet anti-tank missiles (eg, AT-2).

ATGW
Anti-tank guided weapon.

AV-MF
Aviatsiya Voenno-morskovo Flota: naval air forces (USSR).

AWACS
Airborne Warning and Control System. An aircraft mounted radar system designed to detect and track enemy bombers/cruise missiles, and then direct defensive actions.

B

Backfire
Soviet bomber variously designated as either Tupolev Tu-26 or Tu-22M. (NATO designation).

BAOR
British Army of the Rhine.

Ballistic missile
A rocket powered projectile which is propelled into space and then follows a ballistic trajectory, governed mainly by gravity

and aerodynamic drag.

BB
Battleship (US).

BMD
Bronevaya Maschina Desantnaya: airborne combat vehicle (USSR).

BMEWS
Ballistic Missile Early Warning System. US electronic surveillance system designed to detect attacks by hostile ballistic missiles.

BMP
Bronevaya Maschina Piekhota: armoured vehicle, infantry (USSR).

BPK
Bolshoy Protivolodochny Korabl: large anti-submarine ship (USSR).

BRDM-
Bronevaya Rasvedyvateinaya Dosornaya Maschina: armoured reconnaissance machine (eg, BRDM-2). (USSR).

BRK
Bolshoy Raketny Korabl: large rocket ship (USSR).

BTR-
Bronentransportr: armoured personnel carrier (eg, BTR-60). (USSR).

Bundeswehr
The armed forces of the Federal Republic of Germany. They are divided into: Bundesmarine: Navy; Bundesheer: Army; Luftwaffe: Air Force.

Bus
See "Post-Boost Vehicle".

BW
Bacteriological warfare.

C

CBR
See NBC.

CD
Civil Defence. Passive measures to minimise the effects of enemy action on all aspects of civil life, and to restore utilities and facilities following an attack.

CEP
Circular Error Probable. A measure of the accuracy of missiles, the CEP is the radius of a circle in which half the shots are statistically likely to fall. (Usually expressed in nautical miles.)

CG
Cruiser, Guided-Weapon armed (US).

CGN
Cruiser, Guided-Weapon armed, Nuclear powered (US).

CIWS
Close-In Weapon System (US).

Cold Launch
"Pop-up" technique which ejects ballistic missiles from

silos or launch tubes using motors other than those in the missile itself.

Command, Control and Communications (C³)
Equipment, personnel and procedures used to acquire, process, and disseminate data needed by decision-makers to plan and control operations.

CONUS
Continental United States (US).

Conventional
A form of conflict in which nuclear weapons are not used.

Counterforce
Attacks directed against enemy weapons and military forces, especially nuclear weapons.

Counter-military potential (CMP)
A static measure of ability to damage hard targets, such as missile silos; influenced by accuracy and yield. Delivery accuracy is measured in terms of CEP; hence the ability to destroy hard targets is also expressed as a probability. CMP is stated mathematically as:

$$CMP = \frac{(Yield)^n}{(CEP)^2}$$

Where Y > 200KT n = 2/3
Where Y > 200KT n = 4/5

Countervalue
Attacks directed against enemy industry or society (eg, cities, factories, industrial complexes).

Cruise missile
A missile that flies for long distances supported by lift from wings or body. Power is provided by an air-breathing engine.

CV
Attack aircraft carrier, conventionally powered (US).

CVN
Attack aircraft carrier, nuclear powered (US).

CW
Chemical Warfare.

D

DD
Destroyer (gun armed) (US).

DDG
Guided missile destroyer (US).

Detente
Lessening of tensions in international relations. May be achieved formally or informally.

Deterrence
Steps designed to prevent opponents from armed action or to inhibit escalation if combat should start.

DEW
Distant Early Warning (line). A chain of early warning stations intended to detect manned bombers approaching CONUS (US).

Division Equivalent
Separate brigades, regiments and supporting arms whose overall capability equates to that of a division, except, perhaps, in staying power.

DoD
Department of Defense in USA (also known as the Pentagon). (US).

E

ECCM
Electronic counter-counter measures. A form of electronic warfare designed to overcome enemy use of ECM (qv) and thus continue to make effective use of the electromagnetic spectrum.

ECM
Electronic counter measures. A form of electronic warfare designed totally or partially to prevent effective use by the enemy of part of the electro-magnetic spectrum.

Effective megatons (EMT)
A static measure of damage potential against "soft" targets, eg, above-ground HQs, or cities. The effect at a specific distance from ground zero (GZ) is proportional to the cube-root of the yield, while the area affected is proportional to the square of the distance. From this it can be deduced that:
$EMT = Y^{2/3}$ (but where $Y > 1MT$; $EMT = Y^{1/2}$).

ELINT
Electronic intelligence. Intelligence derived from enemy electronic transmissions other than tele-communications (ie, radar). (See also SIGINT.)

EMP
Electro-magnetic pulse. A sharp pulse of radio-frequency electromagnetic radiation produced by a nuclear explosion. It can cause extensive damage to unprotected electrical and electronic equipment over large areas.

ER
Enhanced radiation. (Also known as the "neutron bomb".) A nuclear weapon which is designed to release about 80 per cent of its yield in high energy neutrons, which results in a weapon more deadly to people than to military equipment or structures.

ESM

Electronic support measures.

Esminyets
Fleet torpedo ship (USSR). Equivalent to "destroyer" in Western navies.

F

FA
Frontovaya Aviatsiya: frontal aviation, ie, tactical air forces (USSR).

FEBA
Forward edge of the battle area (NATO).

First-strike
The first offensive move in a conflict. As applied to general nuclear war it implies the ability to eliminate effective retaliation by the enemy, ie, a "second-strike" (qv).

FF
Frigate (US).

Flakpanzer
German designation for armoured self-propelled anti-aircraft weapon.

Flexible response
Strategy based on the capability to act effectively across the entire spectrum of war, at the time, place, and manner of the user's choosing.

FLIR
Forward looking infra-red.

FLTSATCOM
Fleet Satellite Communications system (US).

FOBS
Fractional Orbit Bombardment System. Warhead delivery by a partial satellite orbit enabling an approach to be made from any direction.

FPB
Fast patrol boat.

Fratricide
Fratricide occurs when multiple attacks on one target, or nearly simultaneous attacks on area targets, lead to one weapon's explosion destroying or diverting others. The arrival of two warheads on a target can be arranged so that they reinforce each other, thus raising probability of damage (see P_D) while minimising fratricide.

FROG
Free Rocket Over Ground. NATO acronym used to classify Soviet free-flight artillery rockets; FROG-1, FROG-2, etc.

G

GDR
German Democratic Republic (Deutsche Demokratische Republik,

East Germany).

General war
Armed conflict between the major powers in which the national survival of at least one is at stake. Usually taken to refer to a major conflict between the USSR and the USA.

GIUK
Greenland-Iceland–UK gap. The major choke points restricting Soviet Navy access to the Central and Southern Atlantic (NATO).

GLCM
Ground Launched Cruise Missile.

GRP
Glass-reinforced plastic (as for hull of some mine counter-measures vessels, for instance).

GSFG
Group of Soviet Forces in Germany. Soviet designation for their forces located in the German Democratic Republic in peacetime.

GZ
Ground zero. The point on the earth's surface upon, above or below which a nuclear explosion takes place. (All effects are calculated at distances from "GZ".)

H

Hardness
The ability of a target to resist explosions, usually nuclear, and their effects of overpressure, heat, radiation, EMP, and ground shock. Normally expressed in pounds-per-square-inch (psi) of overpressure (qv).

HE
High explosive.

HEAT
High explosive anti-tank, also known as "hollow-charge" or "shaped charge" (qv). An anti-tank round in common use in both NATO and WP armies.

HF
High Frequency: 3-30 MHz.

HESH
High explosive squash head, known as HEP (high explosive-plastic) in US Army.

I

ICBM
Intercontinental ballistic missile. Land-based missile with range in excess of 3,000nm (5,600km).

IOC
Initial operational capability. Date when a weapon system can be considered capable of being

used by troops even though not fully developed and troops not fully trained (US).

IR
Infra-red.

IRBM
Intermediate range ballistic missile. Land-based missile with range of 1,500nm (2,780km) to 3,000nm (5,600km).

K

Kreyser
Cruiser (USSR).

KT
Kiloton. Explosive yield equivalent in effect to 1,000 tons of TNT. (See "TNT Equivalent".)

L

Launch-on-warning.
Retaliation triggered on perception of incoming enemy ballistic missiles, to prevent attrition of own missile forces. In practice efforts would be made to carry out some form of assessment, but any serious delay would transform situation into one of "launch-under-attack" (qv).

Launch-under-attack.
Retaliation in which ballistic missiles are launched while the silos are actually under attack. (This implies a later executive decision than for "launch-on-warning" (qv).)

Launch weight
Total weight of a fully loaded missile at the time of launch; ie, boosters, post-boost vehicle plus payload.

LAW
Light Anti-Tank Weapon.

LF
Low Frequency: 30–300 kHz.

LHA
Amphibious Assault Ship (US).

Limited war
A conflict in which the participants exercise some form of voluntary restraint to prevent an escalation of the conflict or a widening of its geographical extent.

LKA
Amphibious Cargo Ship (US).

LMG
Light machine-gun.

LPD
Landing Platform Dock (US).

LPH
Amphibious Assault Ship (Helicopter) (US).

LRMP
Long-range maritime patrol.

LRRP
Long-range reconnaissance patrol.

LST

Glossary of Terms

Landing Ship, Tank (US).

LVTC
Landing Vehicle, Tracked, Command (US).

LVTP
Landing Vehicle, Tracked, Personnel (US).

M

MAD
1. Magnetic Anomaly Detector. ASW equipment designed to detect disturbances in normal magnetic fields of force.
2. Mutually Assured Destruction. The ability of the two super powers to inflict unacceptable damage upon each other at any time in the course of a nuclear war, even following a surprise first strike.

MaRV
Manoeuvrable Re-entry Vehicles. Multiple re-entry vehicles which have on-board systems for locating the target and for steering the warhead onto that target. This is potentially capable of an accuracy of tens of yards.

MAW
Marine Air Wing (US).

MBT
Main battle tank. Principal armoured vehicle of an army. Although not defined officially it can be taken to mean one over 30 tons in weight.

MCM
Mine counter-measures (NATO).

MICV
Mechanised infantry combat vehicle. An APC (qv) armed with a gun turret and with ports from which the infantry can fire their weapons while on the move. Sometimes designated ICV – infantry combat vehicle.

MIRV
Multiple Independently Targetable Re-entry Vehicles. Multiple re-entry vehicles on a ballistic missile which can each be targeted upon a separate and arbitrarily located target (in practice several hundreds of miles apart).

MOD
Ministry of Defence (UK).

Mod
Modified. Used in NATO designations of Soviet equipment to signify a major modification to a basic equipment (eg, SS-18 Mod3 is the third major variant of the SS-18 missile).

MRBM
Medium range ballistic missile. Land-based missile with range of 600nm (1,100km) to 1,500nm (2,780km).

MRV
Multiple Re-entry Vehicles. The re-entry vehicle/s of a ballistic missile with multiple warheads where the missile does not have the capability of independently targeting the warheads. MRVs are similar in concept to the pellets in a shot-gun cartridge.

MSBS
Mer-Sol Ballistique Strategique. French designation for their M-20 ICBM. (Note that such a range brings it within the US definition of an IRBM.)

MT
Megaton. Explosive yield equivalent in effect to 1,000,000 tons of TNT. (See "TNT Equivalent".)

MX
US designation for their next generation ICBM. (Literally: "Missile Experimental".)

N

NADGE
NATO Air Defense Ground Environment. A chain of radar stations and related command and control elements.

NATO
North Atlantic Treaty Organisation. Currently comprises: Belgium, Canada, Denmark, France, Federal Republic of Germany, Greece, Iceland, Luxembourg, Netherlands, Norway, Portugal, Turkey, UK and USA.

Nautical Mile
One minute of great circle of the earth, standardised at 6,080ft (1,853m) but actually varying with latitude from 6,046ft to 6,108ft (1,842-1,861m).

NBC
Nuclear biological and chemical (warfare). Sometimes known as CBR: chemical biological and radiological.

NCA
National Command Authority. The top national security decision-makers in a country. In the USA this comprises the President and the Secretary of Defense and their duly authorised deputies.

Nuclear weapon
Bomb, artillery shell, missile warhead, or other deliverable ordnance (as opposed to an experimental device) which explodes as a result of energy released by reactions from the fission, fusion, or both of atomic nuclei. The term excludes delivery means whenever such equipment is separable from the explosive projectile.

Nuclear yield
The energy released by the detonation of a nuclear weapon, measured in equivalent thousands of tons (Kilotons = KT) or millions of tons (Megatons = MT) of TNT. (See "TNT equivalent"; "yield".)

Neutron bomb
See ER (enhanced radiation).

NORAD
North American Air Defense Command. A combined US and Canadian HQ responsible for surveillance and defence of North America against attack by either aircraft or ballistic missiles (US).

O

OTH-B
Over-the-Horizon Backscatter Radar. This transmits signals that extend beyond the line-of-sight along the ground. Range is of the order of 1,800 miles (2,896km).

Overpressure
The transient pressure exceeding the ambient pressure, manifested in the shock-wave from a nuclear explosion. Usually expressed in pounds-per-square-inch (psi).

P

Passive
Not itself emitting. Usually used when describing detection devices which do not use electromagnetic emissions to operate. They cannot be detected in the way that "active" devices can. (See also "active".)

Passive defence
Measures, other than active ones, to deter or minimise the effects of enemy actions. These include Civil Defence, cover, concealment, dispersion, camouflage, shelters, etc.

Payload
Weapon and/or cargo capacity of an aircraft or missile.

Penaid
Penetration aid. A device to confuse, decoy or dilute enemy defences in order to assist the delivery of a missile warhead to its target (US).

Post-boost vehicle.
That part of a missile payload carrying the re-entry vehicles, guidance package, fuel and thrust devices so that RVs can be dispensed sequentially towards their targets. Sometimes known as a "bus".

PRC
People's Republic of China.

Probabilty of damage
An expression of the probability of damaging silos is expressed mathematically as:
$$P_D = 1\text{-}0.5\ \text{Exp}\left(\frac{\text{Total CMP}}{\text{silo hardness}}\right)$$

Protivo Lodochny Kreyser
Anti-submarine cruiser (USSR).

PT-
Plavuchii tank: amphibious tank (eg, PT-76). (USSR).

PVO-Strany
Protivo Vozdushnoi Oborony-Strany: national Air Defence Forces (USSR).

R

RAF
Royal Air Force (UK).

Raketny Kreyser
Rocket cruiser (USSR).

RDF
Rapid Deployment Force (US).

Recce
Reconnaissance.

Re-entry
Ballistic missile payloads have to ascend into space and then plunge back into the atmosphere at hypersonic speed, without burning up through friction or kinetic heating.

RN
Royal Navy (UK).

Ro-Ro
Roll-on/Roll-off, a ferry with doors in both bow and stern.

RPG-
Reaktivniy Protivotankovyi Granatomat: rocket anti-tank grenade launcher (eg, RPG-7). (USSR).

RV
Re-entry vehicle. Protective vehicle designed to ensure that a missile payload survives re-entry (qv) intact.

S

SA-
Surface-to-air. NATO designation for Soviet surface-to-air land-based missiles (eg, SA-2).

Sabot
Attachment, usually arranged to come apart in sections, to guide a projectile along the bore of a gun barrel (see APDS).

SAC
Strategic Air Command (of

the USAF).

SACEUR
Supreme Allied Commander Europe. NATO appointment invariably held by a 5-star American general (NATO).

SACLANT
Supreme Allied Commander Atlantic. NATO commander (invariably a 4-star admiral of the USN) with his HQ in Norfolk, Va.

SACLOS
Semi-Automatic Command to Line-of-Sight. System for guiding missiles to their targets.

SAGW
Surface-to-Air guided weapon.

SALT-I
Strategic Arms Limitation Treaty-I. Signed in Moscow 26 May 1972, came into force on 3 October 1972.

SALT-II
Signed in Vienna 18 June 1979, but not yet ratified by the USA.

SAM
Surface-to-air missile.

SA-N-
NATO designations for Soviet shipborne surface-to-air missiles (eg, SA-N-2).

SAS
Special Air Service. Unit of the British Army with a variety of covert roles.

SAU-
Sanochodnaya Artilleriskiy Ustenovka: self-propelled artillery carriage (eg, SAU-122). (USSR).

Second strike
A strategic concept in which the victim of a nuclear first-strike (qv) retains sufficient retaliatory capability to inflict unacceptable damage on the aggressor.

Semi-active homing
Homing on radiation reflected or scattered off the target, but originally transmitted by an illuminator not flying with the missile.

Shaped charge
Warhead whose forward face has the form of a deep re-entrant cone, usually lined with copper. Upon exploding this directs a jet of gas and vaporised metal forward at such a speed that it can melt thick armour (Monro effect). (See also "HEAT".)

SIGINT
Signals intelligence. Intelligence derived from enemy telecommunications (see also ELINT).

SIOP
Single Integrated Operational Plan. US national contingency plan for strategic retaliation in the event of a Soviet first-strike.

SLBM
Submarine-launched ballistic missile.

SLCM
Submarine-launched cruise missile.

"Smart"
Device possessing precision guidance. Normally used to describe ASMs with terminal guidance to differentiate them from "iron" or gravity bombs.

Sonar
Acronym for *Sound Navigation And Ranging*, an acoustic system for locating submarines under water.

Sonobuoy
A small sonar device dropped by aircraft into the sea. The device floats for several hours and transmits information to the aircraft above. It then sinks automatically to prevent retrieval by a hostile agency.

SOSUS
Sound Surveillance System. A passive, long-range system comprising a chain of hydrophones on the seabed to detect Soviet submarines (US).

SS
Sub-surface. Naval designation for conventionally powered attack or patrol submarine.

SS-
Surface-to-surface. NATO designation system for Soviet surface-to-surface missiles (eg, SS-12, SS-20).

SSBN
Sub-Surface, Ballistic, Nuclear; ie, ballistic missile submarine (US).

SSBS
Sol-Sol Ballistique Strategique. Surface-to-surface ballistic missile. French designation for their S-2 and S-3 missiles. (Note that their range actually brings them within the US definition of an IRBM.)

SSKP
Single-shot kill probability. The chance of one warhead destroying an enemy missile or missile silo with one round. Expressed either as a decimal (0.8) or as a percentage (80%).

SSM
Surface-to-surface missile.

SSN
Attack submarine, nuclear powered (US). Fleet submarine, nuclear powered (UK).

SS-N-
NATO designations for Soviet naval surface-to-surface missiles (eg, SS-N-8, etc).

Soft
Not hardened (qv), ie, unprotected target.

SSG
Sub-Surface, Guided Missile; ie, guided-missile armed, conventionally powered submarine.

SSGN
As above, but nuclear powered.

STANAVFORLANT
Standing Naval Force Atlantic (NATO).

Stealth
"Stealth" technology is used to render aircraft or satellites "invisible" to visual, radar, or infra-red detection.

Storozhevoy Korabl
Escort ship (USSR).

T

Throw-weight
The aggregate payload of a ballistic missile. In SALT-II terms throw-weight is defined as the sum of: the RV or RVs; any PBV or similar device; any ABM penaids, including their release devices.

Time-sensitive target
A counterforce target which is vulnerable only if it can be hit before it takes off (aircraft), is launched (missiles) or re-deploys (mobile missiles, ground troops).

TNT equivalent
A measure of the energy released in the detonation of a nuclear weapon, expressed in terms of the mass of TNT (abbreviation of Trinitrotoluene) which would release the same amount of energy when exploded. The basis of TNT equivalence is that the explosion of 1 ton of TNT is assumed to release 10^9 calories of energy.

Triad
The US concept of three interacting nuclear weapons systems with a common mission but separate characteristics. Currently this comprises manned bombers, ICBMs and SLBMs.

U

UHF
Ultra-High Frequency: 300MHz-3GHz.

UKWMO
United Kingdom Warning and Monitoring Organisation.

USA
Apart from United States of America, United States Army.

USAF
United States Air Force.

USAFE
USAF forces in Europe.

USMC
United States Marine Corps.

USN
United States Navy.

V

VDS
Variable depth sonar. A device trailed from a surface ship for detecting and tracking submarines. (See also "sonar".)

VHF
Very High Frequency: 30—300 MHz

VLF
Very Low Frequency: 3—30 KHz.

V-TA
Voenno-transportnaya Aviatsiya: air transport force (USSR).

VVS
Voenno Vozdushniy Sily: military aviation forces (ie, Soviet air force). (USSR).

W

WP
Warsaw Pact. Signed in Warsaw 14 May 1955. Members: Bulgaria, Czechoslovakia, German Democratic Republic, Hungary, Poland, Romania, USSR.

Y

Yield
Explosive power, especially of a nuclear weapon, expressed in KT or MT (qqv).

Z

ZSU-
Zenitnaia Samokhodnaia Ustanovka: self-propelled anti-aircraft carriage (eg, ZSU-23-4). (USSR).

Index

207

Index

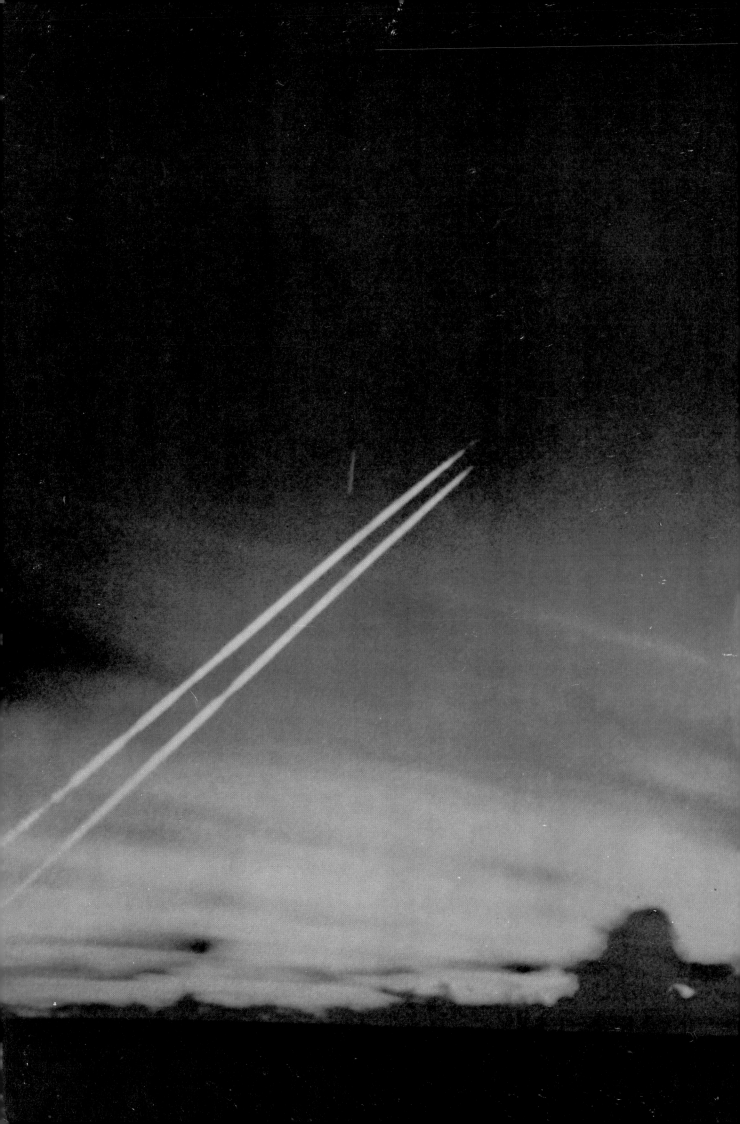